CRITICAL ISSUES IN CURRICULUM
John Willinsky, EDITOR

Gender In/forms Curriculum

FROM ENRICHMENT TO TRANSFORMATION

Jane Gaskell
John Willinsky

EDITORS

The Ontario Institute
for Studies in Education

Teachers College
Columbia University

Published by Teachers College Press, 1234 Amsterdam Avenue, New York, NY 10027

Copyright page continues on p. xiv

Library of Congress Cataloging-in-Publication Data

Gender in/forms curriculum: from enrichment to transformation / edited by Jane Gaskell and John Willinsky.
     p. cm.—(Critical issues in curriculum).
    Includes bibliographical references and index.
    ISBN 0-8077-3402-0 (cloth : acid-free paper).—ISBN 0-8077-3401-2 (paper : acid-free paper)
    1. Sexism in education. 2. Curriculum planning. 3. Educational equalization. 4. Feminism and education.   I. Gaskell, Jane S. (Jane Stobo) II. Willinsky, John, 1950–   . III. Title: Gender informs curriculum. IV. Title: Gender in Curriculum. V. Title: Gender forms curriculum. VI. Series.
LC212.8.G46   1995
370.19'345—dc20   94-37267

Canadian Cataloguing in Publication Data

Gender in/forms curriculum: from enrichment to transformation
(Critical issues in curriculum)
Includes bibliographical references and index.
ISBN 0-7744-0419-1
1. Sexism in education. 2. Curriculum planning.
3. Educational equalization. 4. Feminism and
education. I. Gaskell, Jane S. (Jane Stobo)
II. Willinsky, John. 1950– . III. Series.
LC212.8.G45 1995   370.19'345   C95-930244-1

ISBN 0-8077-3401-2 (paper)
ISBN 0-8077-3402-0 (cloth)

Printed on acid-free paper
Manufactured in the United States of America

02 01 00 99 98 97 96 95   8 7 6 5 4 3 2 1

Contents

Preface

The authors contributing to this book represent a diverse set of perspectives on the significance of recent developments in research on gender and on what it means for the school curriculum. The introduction to the book describes in some detail what happened as we gathered the authors together to write and discuss their work and what we learned from the process about the collective experience of curriculum reconceptualization and reform. "Introduction Revisited: Better a Maroon Than a Mammy," contributed by Annette Henry, one of the participants in this project, supplements the Introduction. As the introduction and its supplement are occupied with the crucial issues of deliberation, dissent, and reflection, this preface will simply provide an overview of each of the chapters in the book, pointing to the particular focus of each, orienting the reader to what is included, and giving a first overview of the arguments of each author. Each chapter is designed to stand on its own, addressing a common subject area of the school curriculum, from art education to technology studies. Less readily apparent from the titles of the chapters are the diverse ways in which the authors have handled the scholarship on gender, the different ways they have approached the question of an informed curriculum. The chapters are arranged alphabetically by author, a technique that avoids the complicated politics of imposing a conceptual scheme to organize the various school subjects that are discussed or the approaches that are taken to the study of gender and curriculum. In highlighting the contributions of each of the chapters here, we pay special attention to how the basic question of gender and curriculum is addressed. Our aim is to encourage readers to cross discipline boundaries in a comparison of strategies for taking up the larger question of how gender in/forms curriculum. We have much to learn from our differences.

In Chapter 1, "So We've Got a Chip on Our Shoulder! Sexing the Texts of 'Educational Technology,'" Mary Bryson and Suzanne de Castell engage the contested construction of gender amid increasing emphasis on the role of technology in education. Their analysis resists the typical notion that the participation rates and attitudes of female students are the issue in the face of a benign technology. Instead, they suggest that what is made to seem to be a "programming" problem with female students needs to be focused instead on the machines and their exponents. Bryson and de Castell find a gap in the literature on the educational use of computer technology, as this work tends to overlook "the ways in which differences are produced through social relations and institutional practices." Although they do give examples out of their own recent teaching experience, the aim of this chapter, as they clearly state, is not to identify a new best approach to the use of computers and other technology in the classroom. Instead, they seek to bring forward radical interventions, through such devices as cyborg manifestoes and protopolitical technologies, which recast the relationship between women and technology, taking them as signs that things could be otherwise.

Georgia Collins pursues the book's original theme of enrichment and gender in the context of art education. She points out the degree to which school subjects are already set within an economy of gender that discounts art as an area of enrichment for the curriculum. Chapter 2, "Art Education as a Negative Example of Gender-Enriching Curriculum," argues the importance of recognizing that this gendered curriculum precedes feminist interests in reforming the way subjects are taught and studied. Through this historical analysis of the development of art in the curriculum, we can begin to appreciate how existing categories tend to marginalize realms of experience and gendered states. The enrichment theme, in the case of art, becomes itself a critique of the processes of curriculum reform and rationale. Collins does not hesitate to recommend that art educators move beyond an obsession with rationales, which appears as its own form of defensiveness. After describing how discipline-based art education would "defeminize" art to raise its curricular status, she concludes by suggesting that the achievement of gender equity in education will require challenging the masculine values that have played a dominant role in determining the purpose and function of America's public schools.

Jane Gaskell takes up the ways in which schools are most directly involved in preparing young women for employment in "Making It Work: Gender and Vocational Education" (Chapter 3). In an assessment that links the realms of school and work, she provides a reading of the gendered implications of business education and other vocational programs in terms of gender differentiated job demands. Gaskell explores the ways in which women are being trained for work in these courses—to which they are expected to bring the subtle skills in caregiving that are taken for granted as women's work even as they are discounted as contributions to the workplace. Her interviews with a range of business education teachers dramatize the need for a far more informed curriculum around issues of how women's work is undervalued and misconstrued and how it needs to be rethought as a source of greater equity in the workplace. It becomes clear through this chapter that what is taken as *work* and *skill*, especially within the context of gender, points to a need for education and development of progressive vocational programs.

Chapter 4, "Reading and the Female Moral Imagination: 'Words Mean More Than What Is Set Down on Paper'" by Francis Kazemek, presents the basis for an ethics of engagement in reading programs and language arts classes. He draws on a number of the works dealing with women's ways of caring and knowing, as well as readings of *King Lear* and Maya Angelou's autobiography, to construct his vision of the reader's moral imagination. As much as it derives from the response and situation of women, Kazemek stresses that this moral sensibility does not need to be regarded as gender-specific. It comes of reading lessons that foster a commitment to "care, concern, and a multiperspectival view of life." Using instances from the challenging and rewarding literature available for young readers, he sets out the basis for an individualized program in reading that asks students to respond to the books they read in imaginative and collaborative ways. It is a program concerned with immersion in the experience of narrative, but one that is also concerned with the positioning of both texts and readers within the ideological landscape of these often troubled times.

Ursula Kelly's "'The Feminist Trespass': Gender, Literature, and Curriculum" (Chapter 5) pursues the dynamics of the English class as a forum for challenging the curricular acts of cultural imperialism by drawing on poststructural and feminist developments in literary theory. She argues for an understanding of how the teaching of literature, as an institution, has been constructed around masculine identities. Within the critical framework she develops in this chapter, the traditional and exclusionary literary canon falls before the call for a far wider range of literature. Students are invited by Kelly to respond out of their own experience, finding in it the basis for a critical reading that redresses the gendered inequities that have long marked the English class. She discusses the study of literature in its tendency to position students within a given set of gendered identities that have the force of something larger than fiction. This relationship between identity and writing, she recommends, should itself become part of the subject of English literature classes, as she concludes her chapter with a series of intimations toward "a curriculum and a pedagogy for and of difference."

In Chapter 6, "Tone Deaf/Symphonies Singing: Sketches for a Musicale," Roberta Lamb renders a critique of music education in multiple parts. By way of an improvised "fiction theory," she explores the forms of representation, the nonlinear patterns of recurring motifs that are otherwise missing from a field that she finds tone deaf to "the symphonic chorus murmuring beneath the surface." This piece, with its tribute to the unsung, its powerful pastiche of poetry and criticism, brings out true stories in master-apprentice models of music education. Amid parts long practiced and played, it offers hopeful moments of children working the music of their daily lives through their own productions and compositions. It asks students of music to think about composing as women, to hear with the female ear, instead of, as it has long been, the other, masculine way. The chapter comes with its own commentary on how the author has played it. It is a chapter that not only advocates but also demonstrates the process of recomposing the texts of gender and curriculum.

Arlene McLaren and Jim Gaskell, in "Now You See It, Now You Don't: Gender as an Issue in School Science" (Chapter 7), use the experience of girls enrolled in senior secondary physics classes to make suggestions for the transformation of science teaching. They place their analysis within the larger dilemma of how to make gender explicit in a school system that claims to be gender blind, and often sees gender blindness as equivalent to gender equity. The girls they interview have persevered in a subject where girls are markedly underrepresented, and they point both to the continued male dominance of science classes and to the difficulties of bringing about change. While recognizing that every classroom will be different, McLaren and Gaskell suggest making gender a part of the official science curriculum so that questions can be raised publicly and attacked collectively.

Jane Roland Martin takes the organization of curriculum subjects itself as the focus of her analysis in Chapter 8, "The Radical Future of Gender Enrichment." School subjects, she points out, "were never just 'out there' in the world." The human processes involved in deciding which things will serve as the basis for a school subject, which things will count as part of a liberal education, are deeply gendered. Physics, but not parenting; political science, but not education. Educational goals and subjects reflect the priority given to *productive* processes in society, to those areas of activity that have been dominated by men. This priority reflects the scorn men have for women and their work in the home, and can only be addressed by a concerted attack on misogyny in all its guises. The hidden curriculum of antidomesticity must be replaced through many small acts of courage.

In Chapter 9, "Family Studies: Transforming Curriculum, Transforming Families," Linda Peterat reviews the way feminists in the area of

family studies curriculum have understood and responded to gender equity. Family studies was included in the curriculum due to the efforts of
the women's movement in the nineteenth century. But by the 1970s it was
seen by many as an oppressive force, reinforcing women's identification
with the domestic. Efforts to enroll boys have succeeded to some extent,
but the content of the curriculum and forms of pedagogy have emerged
as more critical and intractable issues. The marginal status of the subject
and its identification with women, Peterat states, offer unique possibilities for transformation. "Probably no school subject has the potential to
be more effective in changing gender outlooks, understandings and practices of students."

Jane Bernard-Powers's "Out of the Cameos and Into the Conversation: Gender, Social Studies, and Curriculum Transformation" (Chapter
10) examines the belated recognition of women in the development of the
subject area of social studies teaching. She questions a tradition of
gender-blindness in the study of history, as the sins of the parent disciplines in the university are visited on the education of the young in social
studies. Using specific instances from around the United States, Powers
points out how the valiant efforts to redress this long-standing imbalance
in curriculum programs and textbooks are only now beginning to be developed as the necessary resources for achieving a greater degree of gender equity in social studies. Her review of the research on these changes,
however, brings to the fore the sometimes superficial efforts in improving
women's role in the classroom materials. Her focus is on the field's responsibility for improving the situation of the social studies curriculum, and
she finds some very promising responses from a series of relevant professional organizations. The chapter combines an interest in the materials
that support pedagogical practices with concern over the development of
resources that bring the study of women into the realm of the integrated
social studies program.

Kathleen Rockhill and Patricia Tomic, in Chapter 11, "Situating ESL
Between Speech and Silence," explore the area of English as a second
language, starting with the striking observation that learning the language is a process of empowerment, yet it is simultaneously a process of
colonization. Women particularly suffer from not knowing the dominant
language, but in the process of learning it, they are defined as "other," as
culturally and linguistically inferior. The contradiction cannot be erased
in a racist society. The authors argue for an approach they call "situated
ESL," wherein the dominance of Whiteness is replaced by the possibility
of transcultural identities, and the process of learning about dominance,
linguistic and otherwise, is as important as the skill of learning English
words and grammar. This chapter faces head on the difficulties of joining

discourses of race with those of (hetero)sexism, and notes the power of language always to situate us in our social context.

In "Gender and the Physical Education Curriculum: The Dynamics of Difference" (Chapter 12), Patricia Vertinsky gives broad coverage of physical education and health-related subject areas. She covers the considerable literature on the inequitable treatment of women in physical education programs that range from basic differences in the level of investment based on sex to the exaggeration of physical differences as a means of perpetuating a masculinist ideology of sport. Her comparison of the trade-offs of coeducation and segregated physical education classes reveals that there are not going to be any simple solutions to the gender equity issue. More promising than these structural efforts are developments, she argues, in gender-sensitive programming aimed at fitness and well-being, at an "active living" philosophy rather than the production of elite athletes. Vertinsky deals with the specifics of recent work in the psychological development of the young with special attention paid to gender and minority differences. While these are sometimes treated far too glibly in school programs, she still sees strong possibilities of building far more of a "caring community," beginning with the experience and education of teachers.

John Willinsky takes on the "essential" process of writing itself in Chapter 13, "Learning to Write: Gender, Genre, Play, and Fiction." The differences between the styles and language of men and women who write have too long been the focus of scholarship on gender and writing. Instead, Willinsky argues, teachers and students should explore the way writing has shaped our understanding of maleness and femaleness, and how the processes of writing are organized within structures of difference based on gender. Who has written and who has been written? Using Nadine Gordimer's reflections on writing responsibly within her divided country, he explores a curriculum that would play against the confinements of traditional genres.

In the book's final chapter, Sue Willis takes on a number of dimensions in "Mathematics: From Constructing Privilege to Deconstructing Myths" (Chapter 14) by confronting the loss of an initial confidence in working with numbers especially among female students. While situating her work within a variety of approaches to gender and mathematics education, she is able to draw from her own research the prevailing prejudices over who mathematics is for, as well as to describe a program that she directed in its reconstruction of what it means to be good at mathematics in ways that increase the subject area's relevance to the "real world." Her approach is both to advance the cogency of the curriculum and to turn its attention to issues of social import in the lives of the students.

The chapters are various, then, in audience, theory, language, and subject. Placing them together serves to highlight the diversity, while at the same time it invites the reader to link them, and places them within a single conversation. This conversation is addressed to our increased, if always imperfect, ability to formulate, think about, and create gender equality in the schools.

ACKNOWLEDGMENTS

We would like to thank The Social Services and Humanistic Research Council, the B.C. Ministry of Education and The University of British Columbia for their support of this project. We would also like to express our appreciation to Brian Ellerbeck, Pam Johnston, Connie Chou, Olivia de La Cruz, Lance Kraus, and Neil Stillman for their assistance in seeing this manuscript into print.

The Politics of the Project

JANE GASKELL AND JOHN WILLINSKY

This book is not easily introduced. The coming together of its chapters is marked by both the optimism of the project and the decided differences and continual rethinking that emerged in its process. Although editors typically pave over the inevitable conflicts in collective projects when it comes to writing the introduction, this s(m)oothing over will not do with *Gender In/forms Curriculum*. Those of us whose work is gathered in this book believe that there is much to be learned from reflecting on what might otherwise go unsaid about this instance of the workings of feminist theory and feminist practice in the academy and school. So, as editors, we tell something of how this book came to be, illuminating along the way current dilemmas in feminist and educational practice, dilemmas that arose in the gathering of contributors that produced this neatly packaged form, dilemmas that can be read through this text. How is it that books are made as acts of center and margin, knowledge and power? What of the curriculum that engendered this book? As we turn to examine the curriculum of the schools, we also need to examine the knowledge, practices, and politics of which we ourselves are part.

The two of us, as initiators and editors of this project, would be the first to admit that at times we were at a loss for ways to bring the contributors together in the collaborative spirit we had imagined. And at times we were convinced that it was not possible, desirable, or our responsibility to do so. But here we are, the ones reporting on what went on, if only after sharing this version with other contributors for comment and critique. Although we have tried to write an introduction that remains open to the differences that were felt among contributors as well as by the two of us, readers are still forewarned. Textual appropriation of the other is an inevitable consequence of such writing. To introduce this book, then, is to set before you our view of the project's original intentions, the discussion that led up to the gathering together of contributing authors and teachers, and the drama of that meeting, itself an instance in the politics of implementation. The reader is invited to (re)write the text.

The whole thing began simply enough. On coming to the University of British Columbia to direct the Centre for the Study of Curriculum and Instruction, John Willinsky wanted to spark new dialogues about curriculum in the Faculty of Education, especially around important issues that he felt had yet to have a public hearing. He had just taken on the editorship of the series, Critical Issues in Curriculum, at Teachers College Press, and he thought to begin his tenure as director and editor with a project on gender. He had worked with teachers to develop curriculum materials that brought a feminist perspective to English teaching. John approached Jane Gaskell to work with him on the project, as someone who had written far more extensively than he had on gender issues. She agreed, glad to see the Curriculum Centre taking on the issue, anxious to involve the faculty and teachers in the province in discussion of feminist practice.

More generally, our involvement in the project was motivated by the frustration we had felt in putting gender on the agenda of the schools and universities, especially within the mixed moral economy of the early 1990s. Official support for gender equity and status of women committees coexisted with a growing backlash that dismissed feminism as a form of political correctness. The sense that women had now made it because some had taken administrative positions and more were taking science and math courses coexisted with a continuing silence about the gendered nature of knowledge and the growing harassment of girls and women in classrooms, staff rooms, and hallways. We wanted to find a way to support teachers who faced resistance to feminist ideas in education and teachers who were just beginning to become interested in the educational issues at stake. It was clear to us that the curriculum inevitably took up the topic of gender, and it was equally apparent that the curriculum needed to do it better. We envisioned drawing on advances from a variety of feminist theories and research projects to critique existing practice and propose changes to the curriculum that would be persuasive to those in schools and in faculties of education, or at least help in the arguments that feminist teachers were having with their colleagues and administrators.

We began with two assumptions about how to get gender on the school curriculum agenda. One was to use a school-subject focus and the other was to strike an upbeat tone. Both of these assumptions later became the center of tough questions and substantial critiques; both of them pose a special challenge to any project that hopes to open a part of the world afresh. First, to further focus the project for teachers we decided to use the specific subject areas typically taught in the schools as a starting point. The secondary teachers we knew thought about their teaching as subject-specific, and the faculty in our university organized much of their methods instruction for teachers by subject area. Identification with the subject arises not only from the practical question of what to teach in art—or whatever—class, but as a point of professional discussion, organization, and reading among both teachers and education scholars. We wanted to bring into the context of the school curriculum feminist approaches to art, literary theory, history, science, and so on across the disciplines; we wanted to share with teachers insights from the research on gender and reasoning, self-esteem, reading, mathematics, computers. To our knowledge there was not yet a volume that specifically addressed the full range of subjects taught at the middle and high school levels. We imagined that a volume that spoke to teachers from each of their subject areas might find its way into the staff room as it was shared and discussed across department lines. We wanted to create a collection that brought together for each subject area a critical survey of the scholarship on gender, that considered the implications and applications of feminist principles in an effort to imagine new forms of education, that reimagined how knowledge was to be produced, shared, built upon.

Second, and clearly related to the first point, we felt challenged as educators to present this new body of knowledge and experience as effectively as possible. The focus of our early talk together about the project had been about how to improve the reception of such a book, how to interest more teachers in taking up issues of gender in the curriculum. We saw ourselves as writing in the territory between the two work-sites of school and university—of gathering together the relevant materials, research, and teaching experiences, and setting them out in a helpful manner for those working in the other educational setting. The goal for us was both to create a space for this issue in the midst of a packed curriculum and to find a language that would be heard among the many demands made on the life of the teacher; it was to assist those who had begun to give the question some thought in exploring what feminist educators had developed in other settings and forums. We thought that it would be best to use a decidedly upbeat approach for the project as a means of drawing a greater number of teachers to consider the place of gender in their teaching. We saw setting a positive and constructive tone as one way of being strategic and audience-sensitive. We sought the contribution that could come of critique, the lessons that could follow from the research. The plan was to begin with a language that already had currency in educational circles, that would carry our concerns at least past the first level of resistance. We agreed to frame the work that had been done on gender and education as a potential point of enrichment for the school curriculum. Our initial theme for the project was expressed in our title, "Gender Enriches Curriculum."

Based on the focus we had selected, we sought contributors to the project by working from a list of school-subject areas that went from art to technology studies. We tried to represent a variety of feminist points of view, but worked primarily on covering the subject areas, asking our colleagues and graduate students for names and looking in conference programs from subject specialist groups in our efforts to find individuals who had been writing interesting things about each area. We tried to include a number of younger people and we wanted about half the contributors to be Canadian, because we knew, admired, and wanted to encourage Canadian feminist scholars, and also appreciated the exigencies of national funding policies. Our invitation to potential contributors stressed the reach and tone that we first imagined for the project:

> We are planning a comprehensive collection that looks at what might be termed the integration of women's studies across the curriculum. This would include describing its contribution to specific subject areas, from art to zoology, as well as its positive influence on our general thinking about curriculum and instruction issues. As we imagine it, the book is about how an awareness of gender can enrich the school curriculum, add to the relevance of course content, alter ways of working with students, and open up new areas of study and methods of inquiry.

Our proposal was accepted by 20 scholars. Some of the participants were well known in the broad area of curriculum; some were known primarily within an area such as science, art, or reading. Some had published a great deal; some had not. Some were known in Canada; some were known across several continents. A few were men; most were women. All except one was White, an imbalance of which we were only too uncomfortably aware.

Inviting contributors from different subject areas seemed a point of promising growth and exchange for the project, but we were also concerned that it might undermine the coherence of the book. Working from different bodies of knowledge and points of reference, the contributors might well write chapters that stood isolated from each other, that missed opportunities to connect and build. In an effort to take advantage of the intellectual diversity of the contributors with a common interest in curriculum and to improve the coherence and intratextuality of the book, we decided to bring the contributors together in a small-scale public conference to discuss their chapters with each other and other interested educators. The contributors would then have an opportunity to revise their work in light of this conversation. We were awarded a grant from Canada's Social Sciences and Humanities Research Council to fund the conference. A grant supporting gender equity projects from British Columbia's Ministry of Education covered the costs of release time and travel for 10 teachers to attend the conference from across the province.

As the papers began to arrive in advance of the conference, so did the critique of our original proposal. Our title, "Gender Enriches Curriculum," worked as a lightning rod, drawing flashes of insight and outrage, traces of which still crackle through this collection. *Enrich?* Or was it smash, transform, reinvent? If we were looking for a way through the front door of the school, to join in the line of special subjects that enriched the curriculum, from critical thinking skills to computer technologies, the title, many pointed out, thoroughly sold the work on gender short. The proposal was too meliorist, we were told; and it was not based on enough consultation with those who had been asked to be a part of the work. The word *enrich* conjured up the "add women and stir" approach to curriculum in the minds of many of the contributors. To enrich is to add on, to accept the existing structures as the basis for making something better. It is to marginalize. Feminism involves a critique, not just of content, but of the underlying structures of power and knowledge. To enrich is to suggest a nonconfrontational model, where sugar is slipped into the coffee with no fuss, no muss, and no objections. Change in schools, on the other hand, involves struggle and pain, plucking up one's courage, and weathering the fight. To enrich is also an extra, a frill, a matter of taste. White flour will do, though it is better if it is enriched. A misogynist curriculum, on the other hand, will not do. To enrich it might mean confirming it, making it more palatable when it should be thrown out in favour of a completely new approach. All in all, the word *enrich* suggested a benign view of the existing curriculum and of the processes of change in school. Its overtones of wealth and the food industry made for some pointed writing in the papers, which became the one best reason for maintaining a trace of it in the title of the book. Some still object to its use at all, for as Roberta Lamb has put it, "We are involved in struggles and complexities that are not addressed in the E-word." Suzanne de Castell suggested that we consider whether "Gender In/forms Curriculum" might not make a better title for the project.

Some of those who were invited to write for the book were thinking about its theme and organization as the first expression of what was being said about gender and curriculum. They saw centralized and expedient decision making. Instead of simply being grateful for the opportunity to participate, as in traditional academic projects, they were asking to have a hand in shaping the project, in giving it a direction that was more responsible and responsive. Their support came in the form of difficult questions. How had we decided on the theme, on the chapter headings, on the authors? Who had we consulted, why, and at what point? The points raised were well taken, and we looked up from our mailings, grant applications, and room bookings, to reflect on whether this was indeed just another example of two relatively senior academics exercising their power, almost out of habit, to define the agenda so as to provide selected others with a vehicle that might nonetheless drive their own careers only slightly forward. It became another point for reflection on the relation of practice and product, of how the work does matter, as process and substance.

There were also contributors who, for one reason or another, dropped out of the project leaving gaps that we decided to live with, until our contributor on antiracist curriculum wrote, "I must admit, albeit reluctantly, that given my present workload, I cannot meet the deadline for paper submission for your conference." Her withdrawal posed a more serious problem for what we thought the book needed. We had realized women of color get called on to serve on committees, write chapters in books, give presentations at conferences, and take part in panels—at an alarming rate. How do we go on asking for this representation without overtaxing them; how do we ask women of color to handle the racism question when it is so clearly a White issue? The question of racism has recently been front and center in debates about feminist theory and practice. Kathleen Rockhill approached the question of color and representation through her ongoing collaboration with Patti Tomic from Chile, a woman of color, even going so far as to find additional funding for her because our budget was fully committed. We were not the only ones who were thinking about how to work with this issue. One contributor noted, "At this moment in the field of women's studies and elsewhere, intense struggles are being waged to find methods and theoretical frameworks adequate to the task of understanding the intersections of gender with race and class. It would seem imperative that this book and conference grapple with these issues head on."

While we figured that a number of the papers would take up the issue of race as part of the question of difference that included gender, we felt it important to commission a chapter that pursued developments in a curriculum of difference specifically in its antiracist form. When we did call on another woman of color for a chapter on the intersection of feminism and antiracist education, she, too, asked all the right questions. Why was she being asked so late? Why were there only two people of color contributing to the project? Shouldn't antiracist education be incorporated throughout the various subject areas and chapters? After sharing with her our thinking, and even though there was not enough time for her to prepare a draft chapter for the conference as the others were doing, she agreed to participate.

At the same time, we were struggling with the role of the teacher, as the apparent subject of this work, at the conference and in the book. We were committed to making this book useful in schools, and wanted to involve teachers directly in the reading and discussion of the chapters, holding out the possibility to them of writing about their response to the work and their experience with gender in the classroom. The 10 teachers whom we had specifically invited were divided between those who had been active in promoting feminist ideas in their schools and those who had simply expressed an interest in learning more about the topic. Collaboration around practice in schools was ultimately what this was all about. Yet we were aware of the difficulties that repeatedly plagued meetings of "the community" and "academics" in the women's movement, or "practitioners" and "theorists" in educational settings. Discussions often grind to a halt amid an air of mutual suspicion; language seems a matter of intimidation and exclusion. A couple of contributors pointed out that they had not been fully informed prior to the meeting about the participation of the teachers, which disrupted for them the sense of the project's purpose. What did it mean, to begin as we were with a group of academics bringing prepared chapters to teachers? How could we locate within this structure the fair basis of exchange? It means something considerably different to ask for a chapter from a faculty member than from a school teacher, for whom writing is quite outside the terms of their job. As editors, we kept bumping up against the themes of center and margin, of difference and other, and wondering how to bring these inevitable differences productively into the work, instead of treating them as distractions on the way to the imagined goal.

As the conference approached, there was a good deal of discussion among a number of us on how to organize the actual event. The structure shifted, from working groups to theme panels, in search of the perfectly equitable, the most effective, format. However, we were soon faced with a far more pressing issue on fair treatment and representation around issues of gender in educational settings. About 2 weeks before the conference, it became clear that the unions representing the clerical, technical, trades, and service workers on our university campus were preparing to go on strike. One of the major issues was pay equity. The predominantly female clerical union was being offered a lower percentage increase than the predominantly male faculty. The low salary of single mothers in the unions was suddenly being openly contrasted with the high salary of the male president. We were clearly going to respect the picket lines that were set up a few days before the scheduled beginning of the conference. The conference was canceled, 4 days before it was to begin, leaving us in a quandary about our obligations to our sponsors, contributors, participants, and the project as a whole.

We consulted with contributors and teachers, and with one exception and some strong reservations, they were agreed that, with the conference canceled, we should still take this opportunity to meet off campus to discuss the project. We had obligations to our sponsors and to the project. Little would be gained by our not meeting, and the importance of the issues was, if anything, more pressing. On the day that people started to arrive from across the continent and Australia, with arrangements made on the run, we left instructions on Jane's answering machine about where to meet, as we organized copies of late papers, ordered in food, picked up wine and juice, rounded up coffee urns, and generally looked forward to meeting people. Here was a chance, in the spontaneity and anarchy of the makeshift, to work informally on the project; to share the concerns, dilemmas, and frustrations that were felt in writing the chapters; and to make the book, as a whole, work.

That evening, 28 of us gathered in John's house to decide how we might navigate this hastily contrived "nonconference." Expressed in the introductions each participant made to the group were some of the tensions that had emerged intermittently over the preceding 3 months. A White teacher asked what one woman meant when she described herself as "Black," and the volatile politics of self-naming entered the room. Someone else asked what was meant by the use of the word *debate*, and this opened up the question of how we might talk, and what the uses of opposition and struggle were. The varying usage of language opened a gulf of difference and distance that threatened to swallow our best intentions for the work in the 2 days ahead. We could hear, even at that point, a difference in language that was becoming a point of offense, a point that seemed to echo again and again, *you don't understand what I mean, what these words, what this issue, really mean to me or to those on behalf of whom I am speaking*. Domestic space, as the women's movement has continually pointed out, is not free of conflict. Neither was this housebound meeting. Yet this was surely the very space in which to talk across the differences; this was the divided house in which we had chosen to work.

Over the next 2 days, the assembly broke into groups and met as a whole. The talk was about the schools and the chapters, the project and its prospects. The moments of tension that arose brought to mind for some the consciousness-raising tensions of years gone by, as we searched desperately for ways of hearing and articulating deeply felt ideas about what was going on with this project, what was going on in the room among us. We had not foreseen the level of anger and hurt, both our own and others', within what we imagined was a common project. Underlying what was described later as our "living room brawl" was the question of power, of who is privileged and who is silenced. Some spoke out about their anger, their disappointment, over those who were absent, silenced in our work and our talk. They challenged in that crowded room the silencing of what had been repeatedly taken for granted about sexuality, race, social class, of what could be meant by gender, feminism, color. The silences were declared to be presumptuous, threatening, hostile. If feminist scholarship had long been a marginal voice in the academy, asserting its claim for power and authority with increasing pointedness, it had formed new centers within those margins that now had to be named, challenged, upset. Who finally spoke for whom? Who could speak with whom?

The strike of the university's support staff and tradespeople was also present in the house. John's partner was coming and going to serve her time on the picket line. Calls from the union to set up the picket line duty schedule interrupted discussions of critical theory. Flyers explaining the union's demands littered the front hall. Someone proposed that we join the picketers. But we did not bring in a speaker from the union, meet on the picket line, or use the occasion to mobilize support for the strike from across North America. Still, we were uncomfortably enmeshed in a concrete and bitter struggle over women's wages and the undervalued contribution women, as "support" staff, make to the education that professors ostensibly provide to students.

If our meetings as a whole in the overcrowded living room were marked by faltering starts at discussion, punctuated both by dramatic statements and cathartic humor, the smaller groupings succeeded in forming consolidated pockets of exchange and collegiality. Divided we stood, or at least worked, together well. Those who met in the dining room focused on discussing one or another of their draft chapters, taking critical looks at the handling of the specific issues raised in the papers. Those who met on the back porch, after having provided the most trenchant critique of the project, discussed the critical and poststructural possibilities of pedagogy and the limits of experiences such as this one. In the living room, with the majority of the teachers, the discussion involved the expression of concerns with the introduction of new programs and other innovations as a lesson for work on gender and curriculum. The common ground proved to be, not surprisingly, the kitchen, where we bumped into each other over jokes about who had kindly made the coffee and what they might possibly have used to have made it taste like it did.

As the day progressed, and we met as a whole again, the "back porch group" (the label proudly espoused, playing again on center and margin, inside and out, bringing to that sunny deck outside the house haunting images of master/mistress and slave) pressed on with questions focusing on racism, heterosexism, and postmodern critiques. The issues had been marginalized in our original proposal, and were not present in a number of the chapters prepared for the book. The exchanges were angry at times, but the points being made about the inadequacy of representations of race and sexual orientation were sharp and clear. Silence on such issues protects power at the center. Feminists know only too well how silence about gender reproduces gender inequality. And feminist theory, in trying to talk about women and men, has marginalized and silenced discussion of race, class, and sexual preference, for they break up the category "woman," they risk the sounding of race, class, gay and lesbian discourses that speak for a larger language of difference. It was becoming apparent, as Mary Bryson noted, that being any gender is a drag.

In that crowded room, there were twists to this theme of silence and voice, margin and center. To break the silence and speak on the margins is to open oneself to ridicule. It is not safe, in most settings. It is not safe if there are inequities of power and knowledge. And there are such inequities in most places. In John's house, some people were editors; some were audience; some were full professors, some untenured; some taught in universities, some in schools. As editors, we had originally conceived the book as situating gender in the curriculum as part of this sense of critique, of being on the margins and wanting to be heard by "the schools," who tend to see feminism and critical scholarship of any kind as beside the point. But the contradictions are right there. The book can only be accomplished because feminism is not as marginal as it once was. Some would claim (a claim we think misrepresents the issues thoroughly) that feminism is the new orthodoxy, tenured and empowered. Yet we had overlooked and set aside many differences in raising the money for this meeting, deciding on the participants, and planning the book. We were part of that straight and privileged realm, with predictably comfortable homes, seemingly complete with spouse and children in evidence to love us. We had to be reminded that such a domestic setting points directly to our privilege, even as it points for others to the violence that home and family can represent. There is no neutral ground, no safe or tidy house. The difficult, heartfelt, and articulate statements that were made during those meetings on behalf of the unspoken and silenced, amid the apparent warmth of familiar surroundings, made the *personal* and *private* central to everyone's experience of the discussion. The refrain of some participants—about powerlessness—was, "I am not fully informed," as the editors had too often decided things without much explanation. Liberal pluralism suggests that everyone can speak on an equal footing, and that the result will be a judicious weighing of all versions. But the footing is not equal.

The teachers spoke about the power of the official curriculum, of innovations from on high, pointing to shrink-wrapped materials sent out to the schools to improve their teaching. Most of these texts stayed, it was added, in their wrapping. To bring teachers in the secondary schools together with teachers in the universities must involve talking across difference in a way that doesn't privilege academic knowledge, in a way that acknowledges that languages arise in communities of practice and are learned and habitual ways of knowing. When the discussion was directed to a number of the teachers, as themselves women of color, some made it clear that they did not think of themselves or their work in those terms, however much it might be making a difference to their lives. So it was that this project had presumed to bring feminist concerns through *our* writing to *them*. How could the contributors to this book unwrap the issues and work through differences in language practices as well as differences in work settings and contextual understanding? We are all educators facing a number of the same challenges in our work. Yet teachers live under different conditions from university professors, with, as one pointed out, a strong sense of "less time, few resources, too many kids." They live in patriarchal institutions where you get dismissed with a laugh for raising feminist ideas, if you dare. They spoke of seeking academic work to verify and legitimate their concerns, hence the utility of the book and the conference. But who verifies whom? The professor appears before an audience of teachers seeking affirmation of her work's contribution to the field.

So who is at the center, who at the margin? Who is colonized? Who has power? Whatever the language for expressing privilege, the concepts shift and dissolve as they appear in different contexts. When we met as a whole, the back porch group came to dominate the agenda. They forcefully described the hostility that they felt, the silences that they heard. They articulated the high cost of doing this form of critical work in their own lives. They also embodied the physical closeness and exclusivity of their marginal status by meeting together, supporting each other verbally, and meeting after the conference in a different house. They spoke from the margins, invoking the weight of moral and scholarly authority on their side, disrupting the imagined collectivity of "woman," as well as "teacher," as singular categories of a common experience. Those who had not raised the issues of sexual preference and race in their papers, in something of a reversal of fortunes, felt silenced, isolated, dismissed. We quickly reached an impasse and did not know where to begin to build again, where to start to take a risk, that is, to speak. To speak if one is privileged is to oppress, on the one hand, and to produce resistance and opposition, and to get criticized, on the other. To listen without speaking appears to do little to disrupt the distance and power. As Audré Lorde points out, "It is not difference which immobilizes us, but silence. And there are so many silences to be broken" (1984, p. 17). That those who broke the silence in the room, bringing *difference* to the fore, were lesbian and women of color scholars, added to the intersection of the personal and political, even as it brought to the fore divisions and boundaries in understanding. There were a number of fumbled attempts to cross the gap that opened in that room, to create a bridge for talking about difference and silence, in the book and in schools. We discussed what it would mean to bring issues of race and sexuality more forcefully to the chapters of the book: would it be genuine, we asked ourselves, or genuflection. In the heat of critical exchanges over what was required, over what constituted an adequate response, we saw the discussion gradually narrow until it culminated during the final few moments of the meeting in a sarcastic debate about how to write bibliographical references in a feminist fashion.

As humorously academic as that may sound now, the process often felt awful. One participant made it clear at the conference that she had been up most of the night in tears. As another participant put it later, "I must admit frankly that I was dispirited by our meeting. I thought it was to be a time for collaborative exchange, helpful suggestions, and scholarly community building. Instead, I found it to be a time of tension and spiritual and psychological bullying." Some destruction went on—of relationships and possibilities, of what might have been there. As editors, we did not listen to criticism without resisting, without wanting to say, "Hey, this is the way this project has been put together, if you want a different project, you organize it." As writers, we reflected on the gaps in our papers, on the differences that each of us brought to this project, that we would now attend to differently, that we would continue to hold to after reflecting on them. It was a powerful instance of the new paths that were being cut through the academy by poststructuralist, deconstructive discourses concerned with revitalizing conceptions of democracy within the language of difference. In a similar vein, perhaps, the reviewers for Teachers College Press pointed to the need to avoid "the White middle-class bias of the feminist theory" and the need for more "well-known figures in American scholarship." It was another reminder of the status of this project as attending to, but still at many points removed from, the new centers of radical academic authority in its contributors and its audience.

If those centers have been openly taken up by some of the contributors in this book, they have been equally resisted by others, or as Frank Kazemek put it after the conference: "I wrote my chapter for teachers and those who prepare them, that is, professors in preservice programs and those who do in service work. I work with these people daily and I *know* them. The abstract, theoretical and all encompassing critiques that the reviewers want may be appropriate for academics but they will not affect the way teachers approach instruction." The reviewers who found the original formulation of the project lacking "a sufficiently well developed focus on the politics of curriculum," will at least find, beginning with this introduction, a variety of answers about how change occurs and where the focus for that change is. But each of us knows in a different way those for whom we write and with whom we work.

The resulting book, still marked then by differences and silences, by learning and reflection, is a better book for the difficult process of its realization. We do learn from conflict, if only slowly. In this reframing, power is central to how the issues are taken up. Power cannot be ignored in pedagogy, in classrooms where the teacher, if not at the front of the room any longer, is still expected to decide on what is to be covered and how it is to be displayed and evaluated. Power cannot be ignored in political struggles to create coalitions for institutional change. We have to learn to work constructively across differences in power, as well as differences in experience. To demand that power be equally shared before a dialogue can take place is to demand a utopian world; it means that we cannot hope for dialogue to take place.

And power circulates. It is not the fixed property of a person or a location, even given the huge and obscene disparities of wealth in the world, but is maintained in relationship to others. The margin and the center shift, certainly in the competitive and combative world of academic discourse. We garner resources so that our voices will be heard, and in the process produce a center that must, in turn, be challenged by yet others who are marginal. Speaking from the margins represents its own bid for moral authority and power. The proletariat knows better; the subaltern must speak. The epistemological privilege of the oppressed must be recognized. The context shifts as we work through our relations with our loved ones, friends, schools, universities, communities, and colleagues. In one moment; out the next. Secure, then frightened.

Is a supportive and safe environment, one where there is trust and kindness and a shared sense of the project, a necessary condition for learning? To be optimistic and open and warm is a sign of privilege, so we were told. To be angry and oppositional, expecting the worst, is a product of exclusion, and one that turns back on itself. We all have our moments of optimism and opposition. Feminism must live with contradiction, no longer seeking the clean, pure, correct analysis of which forms of criticism are legitimate or of how gender informs curriculum. Our answers are provisional, if strongly held, and will continue to develop, informed by the encouragement and opposition we face in working with these issues in our own teaching and writing.

Where does this leave us with the politics of a curriculum in/formed by gender in the schools? This book proposes a variety of perspectives to rethinking the curriculum, to coming at many of the school subject areas from a new angle, but it also offers a lesson drawn from the very process of working and working together on this question. It remains with each of us to work in our classrooms and texts to find the educational strength and value in this process of redefining difference. It is our job to see that a book such as this, no less than any proposal for change in ourselves and institutions, arises in what seems a moment of possibility. In this case, we worked together on its realization through sharing, struggle, and anger, that now, recollected in some modicum of tranquillity, can be useful for educators of many persuasions, we hope, educators who are working across differences with respect, attention, and a willingness to learn. Readers should bring some sense of this charged thinking-in-action with them as they read their way into this book, and also as they come to appreciate the issue of gender and curriculum as contested at every turn, but as the worthwhile focus of our teaching and learning.

REFERENCE

Lorde, Audré. (1984). *Sister outsider.* New York: Crossing Press.

~
INTRODUCTION REVISITED
~

Better a Maroon Than a Mammy

ANNETTE HENRY

And if a house be divided against itself, that house cannot stand
—*The Bible,* Mark 3:25

Behold, your house is left unto you desolate!
—Matthew 23:28

I have spent many months and moments ruminating over the possibilities and limitations of the "Gender In/forms Curriculum" project. I ambivalently accepted an invitation to participate in the book project a few weeks before the conference/working symposium was to begin. I was unaware at that time that the project had been in process for at least a year or that the woman of color whose presence I was replacing withdrew from the project because she could not meet the deadline for paper submission for the conference. Yet, I was encouraged to attend without a paper, which I was to write and submit at a later date. Of course, I realized that it was important that the conference have the correct color coordination. I was disempowered from the beginning. The outcome of this "divided house" left me so depleted and broken that I decided not to contribute a chapter on race and curriculum but to move on with my life.

A haunting desire to believe that people can work together across political, cultural, and ideological differences was the original impetus for my agreeing to participate in the project. This has been my hope in the turbulent historical moment in which we are living. Educational and academic conferences and projects are bespeckled with the presence of

---

Maroons were runaway slaves, part of organized movements in the Caribbean and other parts of the Americas, who resisted the plantation and postplantation order.

people of color. Yet unless disruptive moments occur, unless participants are obliged in some way to interrogate how oppression and power circulate in our everyday thoughts and actions, and how each of us is embroiled in processes that contribute to the oppressions of others as well as ourselves, it might seem as if oppressions are being eradicated in our society. Some theorists argue that this is a historical moment in which the disempowered might more easily speak and find our voices. But how is the subjectification to come about? Not without much conflict and confrontation. "Gender In/forms Curriculum" proved to be the third in a trilogy of conferences, including ones held by the National Women's Studies Association and Ontario Institute for Studies in Education, that I have recently attended in which Black women have been systematically disempowered. Such events do not just happen ("hap" implies luck, circumstance). They are part of larger social processes. They reflect Eurocentric ideological thinking. They represent the systematic manipulation and exploitation of Black women's labor in the North American capitalist political economy.

And so, almost a year after the initial communication with the editors of this book, I realize that I must speak. To remain silent about this process assigns me, yet again, to the status of object, someone whom others define, someone about whom others speak and theorize. To remain silent, I become, yet again, someone's data collection. I must speak from my own perspective as a Black woman.

In the introduction to this book, a White conference participant laments that instead of a process of "collaborative exchange, helpful suggestions, scholarly community building," she experienced a "time of tension, and spiritual and psychological bullying." I can only agree. I found it could be a savage environment. I am that Black woman whose self-identity as "Black" was questioned by a Canadian White woman who corrected me that Black was "passé, in the States" amid a silent gaze of onlookers, sitting, ironically, in the coziness of a circle. At that moment, I was reminded that I was in the "master's" house, put in my place, told I could not speak. Gratefully, I found solace "out back" on the porch with other women who experienced marginalization in their daily lives and in conversations in other rooms of this house. Those who felt bullied need to think about how psychologically draining it is to raise issues of power, oppression, and self-representation as marginalized people. It would be far less stressful for me to acquiesce, to remain silent, to be seen as the complacent, happy "house slave." But I cannot sleep at night without saying those things during the day that I feel it necessary to say. Raising important issues is not an act of psychological bullying but rather an act of love and desire.

In the introduction, the editors depicted the kitchen as "the common ground . . . where we bumped into each other over jokes about who made the coffee." However, I found it a place of awkward smiles, a place to flee from the living room of confrontation. The kitchen conversations represent, for me, the frequent "politeness" of racism (albeit a contradiction in terms). What is important about this process is that we did move beyond discussions of how good the coffee tasted and how wonderful the weather is in British Columbia. I do recognize that each of us starts from and lives within a different place in this process of learning called life. With humility, I remind myself that these awkward smiles in the kitchen might, in reality, be testimonials of pain that I shall never know or understand.

At the conference questions were raised about how White people understand the nomenclature "women of color." When I asked how many women of color were attending the conference, I was told that I would be the only one. Yet upon my arrival I met three or four women of color! Indeed, I was the only Black person. I implored the women of East-Asian descent to speak as women of color, because I had not heard any of them name themselves as such or speak about their subjective experience during this conference. (It was meant as an invitation not as an obligation.) Only one woman responded. She replied that race/culture were not issues in her life. Such a response raised many questions for me. What was she saying? Was she telling me to behave—"don't rock the boat"? Did she feel that it was unsafe or inappropriate to express herself at that moment with that particular audience? Did her understanding of how the world works exclude an analysis of racism? Did she, a school teacher, feel intimidated by the (false) dichotomy theorist/practitioner, university teacher/elementary school teacher? What dynamics and possible meanings emerge when a woman of color negates the subjective experience of racism to another woman of color amid ashen stares?

All of us in that divided house shared the experience of being a teacher. I want to focus on this commonality as I conclude by emphasizing the significance of an antiracist teaching practice. I want to deflect from individuals at the conference. Indeed, the issues I am raising go beyond the conference. Thus, to illustrate my point, I shall digress to another time and place in which I was a teaching assistant in a teacher education program in Ontario.

In one course, for the last lecture of the semester, the professor had assigned the students to read Enid Lee's *Letters to Marcia: A Teacher's Guide to Anti-Racist Education* (1989). He introduced the book by asking for students' "impressions." A White woman stood up in the large room with over 100 students and said that she liked the entire book except the letter involving the guidance counselor. After being alerted to his racism, Enid Lee portrays the counselor as sulking for the rest of the day. He had denied a Black boy the opportunity of going to another school on the basis of the boy's race. "I feel sorry for that guidance counselor. He went around all day 'sulking,'" the student whined. "What about that guidance counselor's self-esteem?" At that point, I interjected that I found that particular letter to be significant because it showed that, when dealing with issues of racism, not everyone can come away, at the end of the day, feeling fine. Soon afterwards, another student stood up and recounted a story from her practicum experience. She spoke about a little Black girl in Grade 4 who was constantly alienated by her White peers. "I think it's racism," she exclaimed. The professor retorted, "Maybe it's not racism, maybe she's just a nasty Black person. There are nasty Black people you know." I attempted to argue that this alienation was working along the dimension of race. Another student passionately cut me off, arguing that this exclusion might not be racism, but might be due to the child's personality. Interestingly, after class she revealed to me in private that she was "not White."

The professor in this teacher education course had no pedagogy for challenging racism. Instead, he asked for "impressions." Without a pedagogy to help students understand their own agency in the promulgation of White racist oppression, we perpetuate dominant ideological thinking. Thus, in a preservice teacher education class, sadly, anti-Black racism was never problematized. A White woman ends up coddling the "wounded" White male guidance counselor; the instructor and a student help to sustain Western cultural representations of Black people as "nasty" people whose inherent characteristics (such as personality) alienate them. In other words, if Black people are having problems in White society, they bring it upon themselves. The professor should have provided the students with an analysis of racial oppression—how, why, through which processes, and through whom it operates. Without an antiracist epistemology, including *Letters to Marcia* in the curriculum was an act of violence.

These interactions demonstrate that without a pedagogy for understanding and challenging racism, one's well-intentioned practice is rendered *poisonous*. These interactions manifest patterns that I have seen time and time again. First, White liberal academics often "include" Black texts on their reading lists and even invite Black people as guest speakers. But that is not enough for theirs to be considered an antiracist curriculum or pedagogy. It is often surprising how often, in such courses, there rarely is enough time to discuss these texts, which are often relegated to the latter part of the semester. Moreover, the practice of bringing in Black guest speakers allows White people to avoid working through any kind of antiracist pedagogy. Such malpractice demonstrates a clear message about the lack of political commitment to antiracist work. It also demonstrates how Black people are organized in such a way that such contractual work keeps them in a tenuous position economically and politically as indentured workers.

Because of such racism, I would hope that as educators who participated in the "Gender In/forms Curriculum" conference, which I found most disturbing, we would interrogate our own theory and pedagogy of antiracist practice. The conference exemplifies that although there is a semblance of a more just society, there has not been any radical shift concerning who is at the center and who is in the margins in the larger scheme of things. Indeed, at the conference, there were moments of resistance; voices were struggling to be heard on their own terms. But what have each of us done since then, in our practice, to precipitate dismantling the very structures of domination within which we were entangled in that house? As Audré Lorde (1984) reminded us in *Sister Outsider*, "The master's tools will not dismantle the master's house."

I am encouraged that, almost a year later, this painful process has not been sloughed off, or tucked away. It has precipitated many further and ongoing conversations among smaller groups of people. It has incited colleagues to understand collaborative exchange as conflictual. Some movement forward has taken place. The outcomes of this conference have renewed my hope that perhaps new tools can be constructed to dismantle the "master's house."

REFERENCES

Lee, Enid. (1989). *Letters to Marcia: A teacher's guide to anti-racist education.* Toronto: Cross-Cultural Communications.

Lorde, Audré. (1984). *Sister outsider.* New York: Crossing Press.

CHAPTER 1

So We've Got a Chip on Our Shoulder! Sexing the Texts of "Educational Technology"

MARY BRYSON AND SUZANNE DE CASTELL

PROLOGUE

> Lesbian Lovers Gunned Down
> A Detroit man ended his long and bitter dispute with a lesbian couple who lived next door by shooting the women to death on their driveway. Susan Pittman and Christine Puckett were killed May 5 as they were building a fence along their property line. James Brooks, 65, was arrested and charged with the crime. Brooks allegedly told a neighbour that he was bothered by the lesbian couple's open display of affection, such as when they "kissed and hugged on a blanket . . . in plain view of Brooks' kitchen window." Pittman's niece said police were called several times a year, "they would always say there was nothing they could do until he did something." When police arrived, both Pittman and Puckett were declared dead at the scene. ("Lesbian lovers," 1992, p. 6)

The work that we are doing here is about survival, not "enrichment," or "setting a positive and constructive tone." Sometimes, even purportedly radical pedagogical notions such as "transformation," "dialogue," or "possibilities" can seem like wolves in sheep's clothing (Bryson & de Castell, 1993b), seductive tropes that exist, intertextually, in an awkward, distant, and, finally, ambivalent "virtual" relationship with the stark reality of our everyday working worlds, filled as they invariably are with heterosexism, racism, homophobia, and other daily assaults. A collective sense that things could—indeed, should—be otherwise is possibly a place to begin the work that lies ahead.

INTRODUCTION

> Above all, a feminist assessment of technology must recognize technology
> as an equity issue. The challenge to feminists is to transform society in order
> to make technology equitable and transform technology in order to make
> society equitable. A feminist technology should, indeed, be something else
> again. (Bush, 1983, p. 168)

Women have always had *access* to technologies—whether reproductive,
domestic, industrial, or educational. However, a historical overview of
the *relationships between women and technologies* (Benston, 1985; Edwards,
1990; Hartouni, 1991; Rothschild, 1983; and Wajcman, 1991) suggests
three tentative conclusions, all of which provide acute cause for both concern about and systematic inquiry into issues of en/gendered in/equities:

1. Women are usually involved significantly in the development and/or
    early uses of technologies and then squeezed out of the picture as
    "expertise" coalesces around male technocrats and there is a concomi-
    tant redistribution of attendant social relations and practices [for more
    on this, see, for example, the interesting accounts of the "ENIAC girls,"
    who probably were the first group of computer programmers/hackers,
    and Ada, Countess of Lovelace, who actually was responsible for the
    transformation of Babbage's decimal "analytical engine" into a proto-
    type of current binary computer systems (Perry & Grebe, 1990)].
2. The kinds of technologies made readily accessible to women—like the
    "Fabulous Mark Eden Bust Developer," the Hamilton Beach Food
    Mixer, the Wang Word Processor, or the Dalkon Shield—have tended
    both to reify, and to produce, gender effects; effects which, in fact,
    consolidate already inequitable class and race positionings. Those new
    technologies that are construed as "power tools"—such as lap-tops
    (now, of course, palm-tops), cellular phones, and automobiles—typi-
    cally are targeted specifically to a male audience (read, also, White
    and middle class). *Time* magazine, after all, named the computer "Man
    of the Year." A past director of educational Marketing for Apple Com-
    puter summed up this exclusionary marketing strategy very well.
    Gregory Smith was quoted as saying, "The buyers of Apple computers
    are 98% male. We do not feel that women represent any great un-
    tapped audience" (Sanders, 1985, p. 24).
3. Perhaps most damning of all is the frequent observation that the ef-
    fects of new technologies (whether reproductive, domestic, or work-
    related) on women, as they consolidate inequitable divisions of labor,
    in fact increase the subjection of "gendered" bodies to surveillance,

chemical and physical damages, and other regulatory and extraordi-
narily destructive and demeaning practices.

Typically, educational reformers identify female students as a disenfranchised group whose members are systematically denied opportunities for equitable access to educational technologies, and who therefore
represent a high priority target for the construction of nondiscriminatory
policies. Paradoxically, instructional practices that are designed to promote gender equity embody exclusionary values that, we have argued
elsewhere, are more likely to entrench discriminatory practices and to
reduce their range of possible relations to technology than to empower
the oppressed (de Castell & Bryson, 1992).

SEXING THE TEXTS OF EDUCATIONAL TECHNOLOGY: A CONCEPTUAL FRAMEWORK

Centrally at issue here is the conceptualization of *gender* implicit in
contemporary discourses on the intersecting topics of gender, equity, and
technology. One procedure useful for explicating and critiquing such implicit presuppositions is to order the conceptual field by means of a preliminary classification of conceptions of gender in terms of four distinct
theoretical discourses, more or less historically represented in the order
of their emergence in textual accounts of technology and sexual difference (Table 1.1). First, we consider a *positivistic* conception of gender as
equivalent with biological sex; second, a *constructivist* conception of gender as socially produced and sustained; third, a *critical* conception of gender as the ideological product of a repressively patriarchal hegemony;
and fourth, a *postmodern* conception of gender as a noncohesive, open-
textured pastiche of characteristics, aptitudes, and dispositions whose
ongoing construction and reconstruction it is a central task of feminist
praxis to enable and encourage.

In this chapter, then, we describe four kinds of accounts, which are
implicit in academic texts dealing with issues of sexual difference and
educational technologies, in terms of how these accounts contribute to
the constitution of distinct "textual communities" (Stock, 1983), or groups
of interpreters whose function is to generate theoretical accounts (and
related research strategies and pedagogical practices) that situate
computers equitably within educational environments. In taking this
approach, we are choosing to focus on the necessarily conflictual social
terrain within which expert knowledge is contested and negotiated following the introduction of any significant new technology. This analysis,

	Positivism	Constructivism	Critical Analysis	Postmodernism/s
	Biology (nature) facts…	*…Sociology (culture) paradigms…*		*…Semiotics (virtual reality) discourses*
Gender	Biology is destiny: "The two genders"; sex is gender	Gender as socially constructed: Sex vs. gender	Gender as ideology: "Battle of the sexes"; social relations and practices as gendered; reproduction/resistance	The "differently gendered": Post-feminism/s; being any gender is a "drag"
Equity	Quantitative balancing	Qualitative levelling	Critique; dialogue; reconstruction; liberal pluralism	Irony/mimicry; problematics of gender; heteroglossia; carnival; radical pluralism
Technology	Thinking man's tools	"Convivial" tools for cultural amplifications	Technologies of normal-ization	Postbiological technologies of mutation; cyberware; morphing; technosubjectivity

Table 1.1. Conceptions of Gender/Equity/Technology

then, constitutes an explicitly antideterminist and "openly ideological" (Lather, 1986) stance that Carolyn Marvin (1988) has addressed in terms of the struggle for position:

> Here, *the focus of communication is shifted from the instrument to the drama in which existing groups perpetually negotiate power, authority, representation, and knowledge with whatever resources are available.* New media intrude on these negotiations by providing new platforms on which old groups confront one another. Old habits of transacting between groups are projected onto new technologies that alter, or seem to alter, critical social distances. . . . New practices do not so much flow directly from technologies that inspire them as they are improvised out of old practices that no longer work in new settings. . . . In the end, it is less in new media practices, which come later and point toward a resolution of these conflicts (or, more likely, a temporary truce), than *in the uncertainty of emerging and contested practices of communication that the struggle of groups to define and locate themselves is most easily observed.* (p. 5)

We argue (in greater detail in Bryson & de Castell, 1994) that the kinds of accounts that are provided of equity and educational technologies reflect differently ordered sets of assumptions about the nature of knowledge and sexual difference, the purposes of schooling, and the scope—and limits of—technologies in the classroom. In selecting texts for this analysis, we make no pretensions to an exhaustive or adequate inclusionary policy. Most texts about educational technologies written prior to 1985, or thereabouts, manage to completely omit considerations of the problematics posed by sex, equity, race, class, or gender in their analyses. Rather, we chose frequently cited texts within which the author/s explicitly commit themselves to engaging seriously with the goal of creating equitable technological environments for female students and teachers. Of necessity, then, we don't label any one kind of account as properly to be viewed as *feminist;* rather, *it is precisely the ongoing documentary evidences of contestation amongst groups of differently positioned academics for control of, and authority to speak from, this rocky, slippery terrain with which we want critically to engage.*

POSITIVISM/TECHNICISM—WOMEN AND COMPUTERS:
The Golden Opportunity (Deakin, 1984)

A dynamic way of dealing with intellectual abstractions over time, unbounded by the circumstances of any given facts but adaptable to new facts, new data, change. Well-structured problems that would require children to use a variety of computing tools at appropriate places would teach perhaps the most valuable skill of all, which is problem solving, beyond that, students acquire the confidence to deal with complexity, for even the simplest programs can transform a certain degree of messy, muddy detail into more clearly structured intellectual representations. (McCorduck, 1985, p. 229)

Positivistic/Technicist accounts of equity, probably more accurately described as accounts of "equality" (Sutton, 1991), provide a quantitative balancing model of "the two genders" in terms of differential access to, and usages of, educational technologies. With gender taken as equivalent to biological sex, *The problem* is construed as the numerical underrepresentation of female students in computer science classes, computer camps, in-class computer centers, and the like (for a synthesis of the empirical research, see Sutton, 1991). *The goal* is to increase the number of female users of technologies and to eliminate their apparent "attitude problems" in relation to new technologies. Two central assumptions made in these accounts are (1) that changes brought about by the advent of new educational technologies are necessarily positive in their effects, and (2) that female "resistance" to these changes can largely be attributed to psychological factors, such as fear, insecurity, and the social conditioning provided by "biased" media advertisements of computers portraying few (or no) appropriate female role models. This is a "value-neutral" account of educational technologies, whose pedagogical ideal is represented by the "Neuter Computer" (Sanders & Stone, 1986).

Much ink has been spilled delineating the perceived pedagogical challenges brought about by a clear pattern of empirical findings documenting the systematic underrepresentation of female students in school-based computer cultures (for comprehensive summaries, see Becker, 1986; Ragsdale, 1988; Sanders & Stone, 1986; Sutton, 1991). Collis (1985), for example, reports an oft-cited study, "Sex-related Differences in Attitudes Towards Computers," which exemplifies the explicit technicism of positivistic/empirical accounts of gender inequities and educational technologies. Collis begins her account by interspersing summaries of empirical studies, which provide quantitative "evidence" of female students' disinclination to avail themselves of opportunities to gain access to in-school computers, with citations from politicians' proclamations concerning the necessity for women to become technologically "literate." She reports that, for example, "As Canada's Federal Minister for the Status of Women, Judy Erola concurred that it was 'imperative' for Canadian women to develop technological skills ('Study Technology,' 1983). There is clearly a concern that women, through the lack of appropriate training, may seriously limit their options in a society dominated by computers"

(Collis, 1985, p. 121). The main argument Collis provides for the under-representation of female students in school-based computer activities is couched in a psychological model of "negative attitudes" and "poor self-efficacy." Collis presents these as "factors that influence women to resist occupations typically associated with men" and as "self-limiting stereotypes held by contemporary adolescents towards computers" (p. 122). Collis speculates that "women may choose to be professionally disenfranchised because of the influence of attitude patterns similar to those they have traditionally shown toward mathematics and science" (p. 122). Drawing on data collected by administering an "Attitudes Towards Computers" survey to nearly 2,000 students in Grades 8 and 12, Collis reports on the degree of disassociation:

> The results . . . support low self-confidence among girls with regard to computers. The typical girl believes that women in general are capable, but that she, as an individual, is not competent or likely to be a computer user. . . . This study confirmed the presence of negative attitudes of women toward computer users. Throughout the survey girls tended to endorse a stereotyped, somewhat negative view of computer users. Girls were more likely than boys to associate certain characteristics with computer users, to view these users as bright and studious but not personable, and to associate computer use with only a few courses in school and only game playing at home. (p. 129)

Ironically, what Collis interprets as "negative attitudes" about computers and computer users are beliefs reported by female students which appear, in fact, to be a close to accurate characterization of the culture of computers and their users in and out of schools (Turkle, 1984). But Collis's main recommendations for reducing gender inequities in school computer use involve school-based counselors' "working to change girls' attitudes" and "expanding on the positive attitudes girls have about themselves and their writing abilities" by having them use computers in "English composition and information handling steps," with which Collis finds girls to be more confident (1985, p. 129).

CONSTRUCTIVISM—WOMEN AND COMPUTERS: EPISTEMOLOGICAL PLURALISM AND "WOMEN'S WAYS OF KNOWING"

Strategies of teaching and methods of evaluation are rarely examined by faculty to see if they are compatible with women's preferred style of learning. . . . We believe that connected knowing comes more easily to many women than does separate knowing. We have argued . . . that educators can help women develop their own authentic voices if they emphasize connection over separation, understanding and acceptance over assessment, and collaboration over debate; if they accord respect to and allow time for the knowledge that emerges from firsthand experience. (Belenky et al., 1986, pp. 5, 229)

Several intellectual perspectives suggest that women would feel more comfortable with a relational, interactive, and connected approach to objects, and men with a more distanced stance, planning, commanding, and imposing principles on them. . . . Epistemological pluralism is a necessary condition for a more inclusive computer culture. (Turkle & Papert, 1990, pp. 150, 153)

Constructivist accounts of equity provide a qualitative leveling model both of "the two genders" (different, but equal—*vive la différence!*) and of optimal strategies for equalizing access to, and usage of, educational technologies. That is, biological sex is no longer taken as determining gender; rather, gender is posited as socially constructed and historically contingent. The *problem* is construed as women's lack of access to a computer culture that could accommodate a diversity of "styles" (Turkle & Papert, 1990) or "women's ways of knowing" (Belenky et al., 1986). The *goal* is to figure out how to accommodate female users and eliminate their problems in relation to new technologies by promoting and supporting diversity through a liberalizing process of admitting to the "inner sanctum" those modes of engagement with computers that are qualitatively distinct from the dominant or "approved" approach.

Turkle and Papert (1990) report results from a longitudinal study of the programming styles of both children and university students. They interpreted these results within a constructivist framework purported to provide a theoretical model capable of supporting the creation of equitable technological environments. In their words, "epistemological pluralism is a necessary condition for a more inclusive computer culture" (p. 153). Turkle and Papert (1990) declare their longstanding intellectual connections with Piaget in their usage of the notion of "*epistemologies*" as a conceptual tool for elucidating key components involved in the interactions between users and technologies. They caution, however, that "where he saw diverse forms of knowledge in terms of stages to a finite end point of formal reason, *we see different approaches to knowledge as styles, each equally valid on its own terms*" (p. 129). Turkle and Papert propose that students' approaches to programming can be categorized as either "personal and concrete" or "abstract and formal" and that "the concrete approach, [was] favored in our study by more women than men" (p. 131).

The authors include qualitative case study data from four students whom they determined to favor a "concrete style," three of whom are female (the reader isn't provided with any information about race, ethnicity, or class). Lisa and Robin, for example, are 18-year-old Harvard University students enrolled in a first year programming course where, "there is only one right way to approach the computer, a way that emphasizes control through structure and planning. . . . Lisa and Robin have intellectual styles at odds with it. Both have to deny who they are in order to succeed" (pp. 134–135).

In constructing an argument in support of the notion that a "concrete style" is important and valid, Turkle and Papert draw on the developmental work of Piaget (1976), who used this term to characterize the thinking demonstrated by children prior to the acquisition of "formal" logic, and on Lévi-Strauss's (1968) concept of *bricolage*, "a perspective that encourages looking for psychological and intellectual development within rather than beyond the concrete and suggests the need for closer investigation of the diversity of ways in which the mind can think with objects other than the rules of logic" (p. 143). Needless to say, there is a lingering problem posed for the authors by the fact that for Lévi-Strauss, the concept of *bricolage* characterized the cognitive capacities of "the savage mind." It is both interesting and troubling to observe Turkle and Papert arguing unproblematically that their strategy of demarcating and reifying ways or styles peculiar to women (read all women) will prove to be equitable or empowering despite the fact that in so doing, they draw directly on the labels devised by privileged White adult males to generate essentialist accounts of perceived differences in the favorite "Others" of anthro-imperialist researchers—children and native peoples!

Turkle and Papert's concept of "thinking style" and its significance in pedagogical interventions implemented in the name of equity has appeared in other research. Emihovich and Miller (1988), for example, claim to have matched minority students' so-called "learning styles" with LOGO instruction. Echoing Papert, they suggest that: "Ethnic differences are an important determinant of students' learning styles" (p. 474). The purpose of this study was to remediate what the authors construed to be a lack of "higher-order thinking" in Black American children. Citing a report from the Carnegie Corporation, the authors write that:

> One way for the United States to retain its competitive edge is for children to use a highly prized learning style called metacognitive thinking . . . minority children often lack opportunities to display metacognitive skills. . . . Programming builds upon the learning strengths of black students, such as high responsiveness to visual and auditory stimuli and desire to collaborate with

and pass on information to peers. By encouraging minority children to talk and share their ideas and to use the "turtle" as a concrete representation of their thinking, a learning environment can be constructed that may make these students more aware of their thought processes. (p. 476)

Papert's ongoing research on technology and "at-risk" students' learning processes in Project Headlight, which involves an intensive LOGO-based implementation in an inner-city school in Boston, focuses directly on the relationship between certain thinking styles (exhibited by minority and female students) such as "narrative" or "concrete" thinking and low levels of educational achievement (Goldman-Segall, 1991; Motherwell, 1988). The direct linkage by Turkle and Papert (and others) of the constructs of "thinking style" and "gender" constitutes essentialist ontological categories out of what are far more plausibly seen as vastly unequal access to power in school and in society (and in school *because* in society). This is a serious species of "category error," which results in extraordinary "oversights" in the reporting and interpretation of otherwise interesting work conducted within the LOGO/Papert context.

One extensive and innovative video-based ethnographic study conducted within the "LOGO constructionist culture" at Papert's Hennigan School, for example, provides case study data on three children, who are described as follows, "Josh, a predominantly empirical thinker; Andrew, a narrative thinker; and Mindy, a social thinker" (Goldman-Segall, 1991, p. 240). As it turns out, Josh is doing very well in school, whereas Andrew and Mindy are experiencing serious difficulties; difficulties which are attributed to the discordance between their "thinking styles" and that valued by the "culture of schools." Andrew, the storyteller, was "struggling to distinguish between fantasy and lies" (p. 256). Mindy, on the other hand, was "mostly interested in thinking about boys" (p. 263) and "making girls" by drawing female forms on the computer using LOGO, for which Goldman-Segall offers the following account:

> Women from the age of young childhood, knowing they will probably become mothers, never question their ability to make girls (and boys). . . . What could have happened to Mindy had she been able to develop her interest in "making girls" to the extent where her girl/boy skills became the guiding force for a class project? What would happen to many young girls who are physically experiencing strong hormonal changes in grades four, five and six if they could use their skills of understanding people to follow their interests within a curriculum? (p. 265)

As it happens, Josh is White and both Mindy and Andrew are Black. Andrew, apparently, ended up in a residential institution. But the children's racial identities are never once mentioned as constituting an important contextualizing element in this analysis which, importantly, is replete with interesting and richly textured, "thick descriptions" of children's sense-making within the complex world of institutional schooling.

There seem to be fundamental dangers/problems with constructivist accounts of difference as "style" and of equity as a species of "liberal pluralism" (Sawicki, 1991). The metaphor of "thinking style" serves in such accounts, rhetorically, to reduce political inequities and contextually variable differences in functions and uses to matters either of (1) *individually*-determined preferences, idiosyncrasies, and misfortunes as in "Mindy's father had recently married a young woman from Haiti" (p. 262) or (2) *categorically*-deterministic and essentializing accounts of the putatively universal impact of so-called biological processes—as in the connection of adolescent girls and "strong hormonal changes"—on all females, irrespective of class, race, or sexual orientation. Such analyses manage to obscure critical observations by the likes of John Ogbu (1981), whose own analysis of the persistent and disproportionate school failure of what he calls "subordinate minorities" is much more the result of their "caste-like" status, than their thinking styles.

It is one thing, of course, to suggest that students' performance on complex tasks is mediated by varying epistemologies. It is quite another to account for the ontogeny of such mediations. From the emerging perspective provided by sociocultural accounts of cognition (Wertsch, 1991; Walkerdine, 1988), "ways of knowing" are themselves now seen as construed as collaborative products of particular social and cultural settings. In the context of formal schooling, profound inequities demarcate differences between groups that appear, but only superficially, to manifest themselves as individual differences. Confusing these matters is the fact that both Turkle and Papert's and Goldman-Segall's accounts unproblematically juxtapose qualitative accounts of individually-mediated performances (e.g., Robin, Lisa, Andrew, and Mindy) and arguments positing relationships between group membership and epistemological propensities—between women and concrete thinking, for example.

Indeed, substantial empirical evidence already exists to the effect that these seemingly cognitive/dispositional differences are, in fact, constructed in the context of institutional schooling by the differential treatment of students according to their group membership, where group could refer to social class, race, ethnicity, gender, or sexual orientation. Accordingly, what is required is greater emphasis on the ways in which differences are produced through social relations and institutional practices, rather than on how to create, reify, and consolidate differences (perceived somehow as either natural or desirable) by liberalizing curricular options or increasing the number of legitimated "ways of knowing" from one to two. The complete absence of an analysis of institutional power or of oppression, and of the existing hegemonic organization of social relations and practices within the context of formal schooling, makes the prescription of "epistemological pluralism" both politically naive and potentially quite debilitating for all members of minority groups who are ostensibly admitted through the front door, but quickly escorted to their "proper place."

CRITICAL THEORY—WOMEN AND COMPUTERS: JUST SAY NAY!

I am writing with a mechanical pencil
I am sitting in an institution
I am hiding somewhere in my brain
I miss myself
                    —From a poem written by a woman while in an otherwise
                              all-male electricians' trades course. (Tica, 1991)

Critical accounts of equity provide a model of gender as ideologically and materially produced and sustained sets of differences manifested across groups within the social relations and practices particular to specific institutional settings, such as schools, differences that ought properly to be considered dynamically in relation to other key sites of both difference and oppression such as race and class. The goal is to figure out how to identify and characterize existing inequities, or oppressions, through the tools provided by critical analysis and how to radically intervene in the existing web of social relations and institutional practices to produce transformative and liberatory changes in otherwise inequitable or hegemonic contexts of work.

A significant body of critical research on educational technologies has accumulated over the past decade, the results of which document systematic inequities in both access to, and utilization of, technology by members of marginalized groups. These critical discourses focus at the first level on technology as a material commodity unequally distributed and hence only differentially accessible, and at a second level on how those in power adapt and channel innovation to retain control over emerging forms of knowledge. Persell and Cookson (1987), for example, report a study of the prevalence and usage of computers in a range of American schools, including coeducational schools and boys' and girls' elite boarding schools. Their findings suggest that: (1) larger, better-endowed schools were more likely than smaller, and less well-endowed schools to have computer centers; (2) boys' schools and coeducational schools were more likely than girls' schools to have computer facilities; and (3) White boys were much more frequent computer users than were any other subgroup. These findings mirror those reported in a national survey of 1,082 schools using microcomputers reported by the Center for Social Organization of Schools (1983/1984), which reported the following:

1. More computers are being placed in the hands of middle- and upper-class children than poor.
2. When computers are placed in schools for poor children they are used for rote drill and practice instead of for the cognitive enrichment they provide for middle- and upper-class students.
3. Female students have less involvement than male students with computers in schools, irrespective of class or ethnicity. (LCHC, 1989, p. 74)

Apple and Jungck (1990) characterize the "deskilling" effects of institutional power as it operates through specific gendered relations and practices in a study of teachers and their involvement and re/actions to the development and implementation of a seventh grade Computer Literacy Unit (CLU). The authors point out the importance of the district's policy to involve teachers directly in the curriculum development process:

Because teachers have always sought ways to retain their day to day control over classroom reality, and are not passive receivers of top-down strategies, complexity must be recognized. . . . Teachers may indeed still have space to maneuver. However, these pressures may actually also create a context that makes it seem unrealistic and not in their immediate interest for many teachers to do other than participate in recreating conditions that foster continued difficulties in their own labor. (p. 237)

The CLU was developed by two male teachers, one of whom was a math instructor and the other a district computer "expert." The three other math teachers, all of them women, had no part in the development of the CLU. In the words of one of the developers, "You have to remember that we have faculty in this department who don't know much about computers. We needed a program that everyone could teach . . . a canned Unit" (p. 238). The CLU was prepared as a "curriculum-on-a-cart" that was whizzed through the Grade 7 classrooms under severe time constraints imposed by the school's standardized testing schedule. Most of the CLU lessons consisted of students listening to tapes and filling out worksheets on topics such as "history and parts of a computer" or "flow-charting." Teachers rarely deviated from the prescribed sequence of activities in order to stay within severe time constraints.

Reactions by teachers to the CLU were mixed. Some enjoyed the time made available while students listened to tapes because it allowed them to catch up on other work. Others expressed some concern about the imposed structure. In the words of one female teacher, "You don't have to be a teacher to teach this Unit." Apple and Jungck interpret the reactions by female teachers, such as using the extra time provided by CLU to catch up on other work, as indicative of their capacities for creating *resistance* in the face of oppressive relations and practices:

> When a new curriculum such as computer literacy is required, women teachers may be more dependent on using the ready-made curriculum materials than most male teachers. Intensification here does lead to a reliance on "outside experts." An essential understanding of the larger structuring of patriarchal relations, then, is essential if we are to fully comprehend both why the curriculum was produced the way it was and what its effects actually were. (Apple & Jungck, 1990, p. 249)

It is not clear from this critical text how the authors construe the implications of this key concept of resistance in the development of a pedagogical context within which women (and female students) might be endowed with agency and voice in relation to educational technologies.

There is a tendency on the part of adherents to critical theory "accounts" to minimize expectations, for both female teachers and students, of what the technology can do for them and what they can do with the technology. The traditionally gloomy posture of the critical tale—an essentially tragic tale of preordained and hence inevitable misfortune—has been mitigated in recent years by postcritical stories about the pedagogic "possibilities" opened up in virtue of the contradictory and contested terrain of educational praxis, such that the critical tale's tragic predictions of inevitable reproduction of educational inequities are disclosed as a species of mechanistic determinism that construes female (and other minority) subjects as the unwitting dupes of an inexorable hegemonic process (Aronowitz & Giroux, 1991). Contestation and resistance by both teacher and students are proposed within a "logic of possibility" capable of transforming traditionally reproductive education into a new, postmodern pluralism whose leveling of all traditions, even the previously sacrosanct, holds out the promise of a new educational equity within which educational technology, because of its unique capacities for blurring male/female or human/machine binaries, plays a central role.

POSTMODERNISM—WOMEN AND COMPUTERS:
CYBORGS HAVE MORE FUN!

This is a dream not of a common language, but of a powerful infidel heteroglossia. It is an imagination of a feminist speaking in tongues to strike fear into the circuits of the super-savers of the new right. It means both building and destroying machines, identities, categories, relationships, space stories. Though both are bound in the spiral dance, I would rather be a cyborg than a goddess. (Haraway, 1991, p. 181)

We must insist that high technology is for, among other things, the liberation of all women, and therefore usable by women for their self-defined purposes. . . . Feminists must find ways to analyze and design technologies that effect the lives we all want without major dominations of race, sex, and class. These goals will sometimes lead to insisting on small, decentralized, personally-scaled technologies. Such technologies are not synonymous with soft, female, and easy. (Aronowitz & Haraway, 1985, p. 107)

Postmodernist accounts of technology and opportunities for "agency amongst the oppressed" are located in ironic, "enfant terrible," or "bad attitude" models for the reconsideration of received notions of "equity." In these accounts, "being any gender is a drag," and carnival and a dis/continuous shifting amongst and between identities is the order of the day. The problem is construed as the need to dissolve the impasse created by conceptual dualisms, such as male/female gender models, natural/artificial ontological systems, or for/against intellectual frameworks for thinking about educational technologies. As Donna Haraway put it, "It's about being in the belly of the monster and looking for another story to tell" (p. 9). The *goal* is to figure out how to conceptualize/materialize new and "politically articulate" (Penley & Ross, 1991) relations with/in technologies, by reflecting critically on, and making fundamental changes in, conceptualizations about both the discursive categories of "gender," "technology," and "difference," and related practices.

Postmodernist discourses (Barthes, 1977; Baudrillard, 1983; Bordo, 1990; Derrida, 1978) displace the fixed subjects of both modernist and critical theorizing; that is, both the notions of (1) the individual (e.g., "woman") as constituting a unified *subject* whose true or essential "nature" can be determined under the penetrating gaze of science, and (2) bodies of knowledge, such as "mathematics," as constituting coherent *subject matters*, with clear epistemological boundaries, appropriate methodologies, truth conditions, and so on. Accordingly, it comes as no surprise that in postmodern discourses about technology, there is a deliberate blurring of the boundaries between fixed slots in binary categorization schemes that refer to "natural kind" distinctions, such as "male and female," "teacher and student," "the natural and the artificial," or "person and machine." In "true" postmodern style, then, Donna Haraway (Aronowitz & Haraway 1985), in "A Manifesto for Cyborgs," suggests that:

> . . . the boundary between science fiction and social reality is an optical illusion. . . . We are all chimeras, theorized and fabricated hybrids of machine and organism; in short, we are cyborgs. The cyborg is our ontology; it gives us our politics. The cyborg is a condensed image of both imagination and material reality, the two joined centers structuring any possibility of historical transformation. . . . This is an argument for pleasure in the confusion of boundaries and for responsibility in their construction. (p. 191)

One of postmodernism's main contributions to theories of *difference* has been the deconstruction of the kinds of essentialist theorizing about sites of oppression in traditional and critical theorizing, such as in constructionist accounts of gender in terms of "women's ways of knowing" (Belenky et al., 1986), for example, as fundamentally racist, heterosexist, classist, and probably politically unproductive in an ongoing struggle for equity, voice, and empowerment (Bordo, 1990). Haraway's cyborg "women," for example, embody fractured identities that are contested on multiple sites of oppression including age, race, sexual orientation, and so on.

In educational discourses, postmodernist theorizing has cast doubt on the monolithic claims of latter-day critical theorists to be able to identify the ideological underpinnings of oppressive pedagogies and therefore, from a safe distance, to restructure educational environments in such a manner as to realize the goals of their "liberatory" or "emancipatory" projects. Elizabeth Ellsworth (1989) paints a complex portrait of her practices as a White middle-class woman and professor engaged with a diverse group of students developing an antiracist course. She describes her experience of the contradictions inherent in actively engaging with liberatory pedagogy:

> Our classroom was the site of dispersing, shifting, and contradictory contexts of knowing that coalesced differently in different moments of student/professor speech, action, and emotion. This situation meant that individuals and affinity groups constantly had to change strategies and priorities of resistance against oppressive ways of knowing and being known. The antagonist became power itself as it was deployed within our classroom—oppressive ways of knowing and oppressive knowledges. (p. 322)

It is difficult, though perhaps not impossible, to determine the relevance of postmodern theorizing about technology and pedagogy, such as the terrain of contradictions traversed by Haraway and Ellsworth, for reconstructing praxis in the domain of educational technologies. Perhaps a brief account (for a more complete account, see Bryson & de Castell, 1993a) of a recent and very challenging instructional task involving the protopolitical production of, and critical engagement with, "technologies of gender" will suffice as a place to begin tying these postmodern threads into some kind of useful web. We include this example because it represents a material context of educational practice within which we were attempting to deal simultaneously with issues of equity, gender, and technologies.

We recently cocreated and cotaught a Women's Studies undergraduate course at the University of British Columbia entitled, "Lesbian Subjects Matter: Feminism/s From the Margins?" We deliberately made use of (invited to our classes and/or arranged for equipment and instruction in the uses of) a wide range of technological resources (both products and producers in radio, video, photography, desk-top publishing) so as to reconstruct the typically limited opportunities for both access to, and production of, nonstereotypic representations of lesbian identities and cultures. We chose to focus on two major themes in constructing the course—representation and identity. These themes generated two central questions: First, whether the claiming of cultural representation and voice necessarily entails the inevitability of essentialism. And second, whether the politics of identity, especially an identity constructed "on the margins," could be a viable strategy, either theoretically or politically.

We arranged for student access to, and instruction in, the use of a range of technologies in video production, photography, desk-top publishing, and the like and encouraged students to make use of nontextual media for some part of their coursework. They were asked to do a project during the course either individually or collaboratively, exploring some aspect of lesbian identity/representation and making use of any available technology. The curriculum included a wide range of kinds of presenters and texts, our purpose being to engage students with the ways in which the sliding signifier "lesbian" would be differently constructed as a function of age, ethnicity, race, class, body size, and other key axes that could/ do function as sites for "systems of domination," as bell hooks (1992) describes the interlocking forces of oppression.

For many participants in the course, the specific liberatory contribution of technology, then, was the provision of tools providing the means for (1) reconstructing the division of labor in classroom tasks that are historically assigned to, and completed by, individual students; (2) restructuring power relations between participants in educational contexts

who typically occupy very unevenly positioned discursive roles in relation to power; and (3) transforming received knowledge, texts, and images through ironic acts of mis/representation, mimicry, collage, mon-
tage, and re/degendering.

What we saw in much of the work created by the students were
examples of the kinds of "politically articulate" uses of technologies of
cultural production characteristic of postmodernism, specifically, the
postmodernist practice of "recycling," which salvages icons, images, and
artifacts resurrected from within their original socio-historical context,
and reinserted into another, within which this "detritus" can take on a
new, significantly greater cultural value. Correspondingly, postmodern
pedagogies can find videos, photographs, posters, and paper dolls capable of articulating sophisticated and complex theory, while formal essays
and conventional book reviews may be relegated to the margins. Inversion indeed!

CONCLUDING THOUGHTS

> Do we really need a true sex? With a persistence that borders on stubborn-
> ness, modern Western societies have answered in the affirmative. They have
> obstinately brought into play this question of a "true sex" in an order of
> things where one might have imagined that all that counted was the reality
> of the body and the intensity of its pleasures. (Foucault, 1977, p. vii)

It has frequently been asserted that technology is "always already"
gendered, and that its gender is masculine (Rothschild, 1983; Benston,
1985). That being so, the practical strategies for effecting "gender equity"
can be seen to have, hitherto, involved adjustments directed at a regenderment of the relation of female students and technology: whether that
be a resocialization of girls and women (the modernist/positivist view)
in terms of their attitudes towards that technology, a pluralist reorganiza-
tion of pedagogy and curriculum for girls and women in accordance with
"women's ways" (the constructivist paradigm), or repudiation of that technology as pregendered (and raced and classed) and therefore inherently
undermining goals of women's empowerment (the critical account). Thus
each approach to technology and gender leaves the gender of technology
intact and operates in different ways on the regenderment of women.

Postmodern theorizing brings about a significantly different set of
possibilities, for on this account, "gender" is degendered altogether, as
dichotomies are exploded, practices are disrupted, roles and rules reversed, positions and directions inverted, and accordingly, technologies

assume novel forms and functions with/in reconfigured sets of social relations and practices. In place of a mythologized "gender identity" there is a fluid and changing set of "gender effects" (see Butler, 1990) based upon a politics of location; a politics which, moreover, refuses to ignore the always intersecting differences of ethnicity, class, and material conditions in its acknowledgement of the realities of gendered positionality. Postmodernism offers, too, a correspondingly novel blueprint for change: construing the skills hitherto the usual preserve of males as themselves only apparently gendered, but in fact merely contingent effects of the privileged positionality of males in institutionally produced relations to technology. Postmodern pedagogies, then, would recognize the tactical insufficiencies of contending approaches to intervention, based as they are on preservationist strategies equating technology with masculinity. A pedagogy of salvage and recycling might accordingly appropriate traditional skills, simultaneously abandoning the traditional (gendered) meanings, functions, and uses of those skills in a species of mimicry of (thus far usually masculine) competences which, because of its self-conscious playing with positions, thence its parodying of the fixity of position, is at last capable of truly disrupting hegemonic relations between learners and technology. The "inner truth" of gender is by this means enacted as the outward manifestation of position, as the product of particular relations socially constructed between power and knowledge (Foucault, 1980).

It is important to acknowledge that these brief remarks, though they may hopefully suggest new trajectories for practice, give little by way of concrete pedagogical direction. This is because our attempt in this chapter has not been to specify in practical terms *the best approach* to remediating inequitable relations between gender and technology in education. Instead we have focused principally on elucidating the pedagogical significance of forms of classification within which and by means of which modes of domination have been effected, and how these have been located far from their productive origins and instead have been embedded within the sexed bodies of the gendered subjects of technology. As Foucault (1980) strongly urged, there is often more "liberation" to be effected by asking "what is the greatest danger?" than by colluding in the "history of solutions." And we have wanted to suggest that, perhaps with the aid of protopolitical technologies, things could be otherwise.

Coda

A word here on feminine funnels: These devices to facilitate a women's peeing are obtainable in washable, reusable plastic . . . there are several designs, some accompanied by various lengths of hose. They are delighting women sailors who could use them to avoid going below in order to go. . . . The funnel entails no dropping of drawers—only an unzipping of shorts or pulling aside of a bathing suit. Women could stand tall, hip to hip, with the men and pee over the rail. I pass along the following funnel story related to me by an employee of a Sausalito yachting supply house: After carefully selecting a pink plastic funnel, an elderly white-haired couple arrived at the cash register, whereupon the woman sweetly inquired whether a longer hose might be attached for her. Her request was gladly granted and the funnel whisked away to the back workroom. Then, lifting her gentle, wisdom-aged face toward her husband, with a cherubic wink she crooned, "Now dear, mine will be longer than yours!" (Meyer, 1989, p. 63)

REFERENCES

Apple, Michael, & Jungck, Susan. (1990). "You don't have to be a teacher to teach this unit": Teaching, technology, and gender in the classroom. *American Educational Research Journal, 27*, 227–251.

Aronowitz, Stanley, & Giroux, Henry. (1991). *Postmodern education: Politics, culture, and social criticism*. Minneapolis: University of Minnesota Press.

Aronowitz, Stanley, & Haraway, Donna. (1985). A manifesto for cyborgs. *Socialist Review, 80*, 65–108.

Barthes, Roland. (1977). *Roland Barthes by Roland Barthes* (Richard Howard, Trans.). New York: Hill & Wang.

Baudrillard, Jean. (1983). *Simulations* (Paul Foss, Paul Patton, & Philip Beitchman, Trans.). New York: Semiotext/e.

Becker, Henry Jay. (1986). Our national report card: Preliminary results from the new Johns Hopkins' survey. *Classroom Computer Learning, 6*, 30–33.

Belenky, Mary Field, Clinchy, Blythe, Goldberger, Nancy, & Tarule, Jill. (1986). *Women's ways of knowing*. New York: Basic Books.

Benston, Margaret L. (1985). The myth of computer literacy. *Canadian Women's Studies, 5*, 20–22.

Bordo, Susan. (1990). Feminism, postmodernism, and gender-skepticism. In Linda Nicholson (Ed.), *Feminism/postmodernism* (pp. 133–156). New York: Routledge, Chapman & Hall.

Bryson, Mary, & de Castell, Suzanne. (1993a). Queer pedagogy?/I: Praxis makes imperfect. *Canadian Journal of Education, 18*, 285–305.

Bryson, Mary, & de Castell, Suzanne. (1993b). En/Gendering equity. *Educational Theory, 43*, 341–355.

Bryson, Mary, & de Castell, Suzanne. (1994). Telling tales out of school: Modern, critical, and postmodern true stories about educational technologies. *Journal of Educational Computing, 10*, 199–221.

Bush, Corlann Gee. (1983). Women and the assessment of technology: To think, to be; to unthink, to free. In Joan Rothschild (Ed.), *Machina ex dea: Feminist perspectives on technology* (pp. 151–170). New York: Pergamon Press.

Butler, Judith. (1990). Gender trouble: Feminism and the subversion of identity. New York: Routledge, Chapman & Hall.

Collis, Betty. (1985). Sex-related differences in attitudes toward computers: Implications for counselors. *School Counselor, 33,* 121–130.

Deakin, Rose. (1984). *Women and computing: The golden opportunity.* London: Macmillan.

de Castell, Suzanne, & Bryson, Mary. (1992). En/gendering equity: Emancipatory discourses or repressive regimes of truth? *Philosophy of Education, 48,* 226–241.

Derrida, Jacques. (1978). *Writing and difference* (Alan Bass, Trans.). Chicago: University of Chicago Press.

Edwards, Paul. (1990). The army and the microworld: Computers and the politics of gender identity. *Signs: Journal of Women in Culture and Society, 16,* 102–127.

Ellsworth, Elizabeth. (1989). Why doesn't this feel empowering? Working through the repressive myths of critical pedagogy. *Harvard Educational Review, 59,* 297–324.

Emihovich, Catherine, & Miller, Gloria. (1988). Effects of LOGO and CAI on black first-graders' achievement, reflectivity, and self-esteem. *Elementary School Journal, 88,* 473–487.

Foucault, Michel. (1977). *Language, counter-memory, practice.* Ithaca, NY: Cornell University Press.

Foucault, Michel. (1980). Afterword. In Hubert Dreyfus and Paul Rabinow (Eds.), *Michel Foucault: Beyond structuralism and hermeneutics* (pp. 217–227, 2nd ed.). Chicago: University of Chicago Press.

Giroux, Henry. (1981). *Postmodern education.* Minneapolis: University of Minnesota Press.

Goldman-Segall, Ricki. (1991). Three children, three styles: A call for opening up the curriculum. In Idit Harel (Ed.), *Constructionism* (pp. 235–268). Norwood, NJ: Ablex.

Haraway, Donna. (1991). A cyborg manifesto: Science, technology, and socialist feminism in the 1980's. In Donna Haraway (Ed.), *Simians, cyborgs and women: The reinvention of nature* (pp. 149–182). New York: Routledge, Chapman & Hall.

Hartouni, Valerie. (1991). Reproductive discourses in the 1980s. In Constance Penley and Andrew Ross (Eds.), *Technoculture* (pp. 27–56). Minneapolis: University of Minnesota Press.

hooks, bell. (1984). *Feminist theory: From margin to center.* Boston: South End Press.

hooks, bell. (1992). Representing whiteness in the black imagination. In Lawrence Grossberg, Cary Nelson, & Paula Treichler (Eds.), *Cultural studies* (pp. 338–346). New York: Routledge, Chapman & Hall.

Lather, Patti. (1986). Issues of validity in openly ideological research: Between a rock and a hard place. *Interchange, 17,* 63–84.

LCHC (Laboratory of Comparative Human Cognition). (1989). Kids and computers: A positive vision of the future. *Harvard Educational Review, 59,* 73–86.

Lesbian lovers gunned down. (1992, April). *Angles,* p. 6.

Lévi-Strauss, Claude. (1968). *The savage mind.* Chicago: University of Chicago Press.

Marvin, Carolyn. (1988). *When old technologies were new.* New York: Oxford University Press.

McCorduck, Pamela. (1985). *The universal machine.* New York: McGraw-Hill.

Meyer, Kathleen. (1989). *How to shit in the woods.* Berkeley: Ten Speed Press.

Motherwell, Lise. (1988). *Gender and style differences in a LOGO-based environment.* Unpublished doctoral dissertation, Massachusetts Institute of Technology, Boston.

Ogbu, John. (1981). School ethnography: A multilevel approach. *Anthropology and Education Quarterly, 12,* 3–29.

Penley, Constance, & Ross, Andrew. (1991). Introduction. In Constance Penley and Andrew Ross (Eds.), *Technoculture.* Minneapolis: University of Minnesota Press.

Perry, Ruth, & Grebe, Lisa. (1990). Women and computers: An introduction. *Signs: Journal of Women in Culture and Society, 16,* 74–101.

Persell, Caroline, & Cookson, Peter. (1987). Microcomputers and elite boarding schools: Educational innovation and social reproduction. *Sociology of Education, 60,* 123–134.

Piaget, Jean. (1976). *The grasp of consciousness.* London: Routledge & Kegan Paul.

Ragsdale, Ronald. (1988). *Permissable computing in education: Values, assumptions, and needs.* New York: Praeger.

Rothschild, Joan. (1983). Introduction: Why machina ex dea? In Joan Rothschild, (Ed.), *Machina ex dea* (pp. ix–xxx). New York: Pergamon Press.

Sanders, Jo Shuchart. (1985). Making the computer neuter. *Computing Teacher,* April, 23–27.

Sanders, Jo Shuchart, & Stone, Antonia. (1986). *The neuter computer: Computers for girls and boys.* New York: Neal-Schuman.

Sawicki, Jana. (1991). *Disciplining Foucault.* New York: Routledge, Chapman & Hall.

Stock, Brian. (1983). *The implications of literacy.* Princeton, NJ: Princeton University Press.

Sutton, Rosemary E. (1991). Equity and computers in the schools: A decade of research. *Review of Educational Research, 61,* 475–503.

Tica. (1991). *Images, 11* (4).

Turkle, Sherry. (1984). *The second self: Computers and the human spirit.* New York: Simon & Schuster.

Turkle, Sherry, & Papert, Seymour. (1990). Epistemological pluralism: Styles and voices within the computer culture. *Signs: Journal of Women in Culture and Society, 16,* 128–157.

Wajcman, Judy. (1991). *Feminism confronts technology.* University Park: Pennsylvania State University Press.

Walkerdine, Valerie. (1988). *The mastery of reason.* New York: Routledge, Chapman & Hall.

Wertsch, James. (1991). *Voices of the mind.* Cambridge: Harvard University Press.

CHAPTER 2

Art Education as a Negative Example of Gender-Enriching Curriculum

GEORGIA C. COLLINS

In the editors' initial call for papers for this book, I found two general assumptions about our shared project. Although these ideas have evolved with the development of the project, I begin by posing the original assumptions as questions that are still in need of answers: *Has feminist research reached a point where we might now recommend its positive application across the public school curriculum? Will the application of feminist research entail using gender to enrich the curriculum?*

Like feminists in other fields of culturally valued endeavors, feminists in the visual arts have questioned the historical dominance of males and masculine values, and the discrimination against women and feminine values at the upper reaches of their discipline. After more than 20 years of systematic inquiry, they have produced an impressive body of research documenting and analyzing gender-related inequities in the teaching, content, production, history, criticism, and philosophy of Western mainstream art (Soucy, 1991). Prompted by a continuing desire for sexual equality, feminist scholars have also made positive suggestions regarding the application of their findings to the advanced study and practice of art. Many of these applications parallel those recommended by feminists in other disciplines. They include the development of special courses, support groups, exhibitions, and publications devoted to women's issues and concerns in art; the use of political pressure to increase the number and power of women in art-related positions and the proportion of women's work in exhibitions, galleries, and museum collections; the demand for equal attention to and treatment of women students and artists in art courses, historical texts, and critical reviews; the reevaluation of feminine-identified media, forms, subject matter, sensibilities, styles, and traditions in art; and the critical examination of masculine-identified career models, conceptions of art, notions of creativity, and other potential sources of sexist bias in the Western mainstream art tradition.

Feminist research in art along with its application at university and professional levels open the possibility of extending and adapting these ideas to public school art education—where to date little has been done in terms of application.[1] Art teachers ready to move from a critical to a constructive stance with regard to the lack of sex equity in American elementary and secondary school art might expect to find precedent, direction, and encouragement in the work their sisters have accomplished at adult levels of education and practice. The first assumption of this book—that feminist research has reached a point where we might now recommend its positive application across the public school curriculum—seems, therefore, to be well-founded in the area of art.

To some, the idea of using gender to enrich the curriculum might seem harmless enough, even calculatedly so. Nevertheless, the notion immediately set off alarm bells for me. The notion of enrichment seems to ignore situational problems peculiar to a feminine-identified subject such as art. Although a general critique of this concept was mounted by a number of participants in this project, as reported in the book's introduction, there are specific aspects of the concept related to the nature of art education that are worth reviewing. What would using gender to enrich curriculum actually mean in such a subject?

A major manifestation of sexism in a masculine-identified subject is an exclusionary focus on males and masculine values. In this instance, using gender to enrich the curriculum could mean, among other things, adding feminine perspectives and values to the study of that subject. Adding feminine perspectives and values to a feminine-identified subject, however, would be redundant and questionable even as a ploy for raising feminist consciousness. A reverse approach to enriching a feminine-identified subject with gender might be to add masculine perspectives and values to its study. But viewed as an application of feminist research for the purpose of bringing about sex equity, gender enrichment as the addition of the masculine seems strangely paradoxical if not altogether perverse.

Perhaps for the feminine-identified subject, then, we might consider taking a contextual approach to gender enrichment, one that promises to avoid either redundancy or paradox. If the general school curriculum is heavily weighted toward the masculine, the addition of a subject such as art might enrich the overall curriculum by contributing a counterbalance of feminine values. But the thought of that possibility reveals the source of my initial alarm: Art is already being used as a form of gender-based curriculum enrichment in public schools. From an art educator's perspective, the results have been less than satisfactory. If the term *enrichment* has often been used to praise art's unique educational value, it has also been used to rationalize art's degraded role and marginal status in the public school curriculum. I think it unwise, therefore, to assume that feminine values added to the curriculum for the purpose of enrichment will automatically empower or preserve the integrity of activities associated with these values. I do not think we should ignore the possibility that our efforts to apply feminist research to public school education will be self-defeating if they do not challenge the assumption that the value of gender is to be found in its capacity to "enrich."

A closer examination of art's role and status, as these relate to the notion of gender-based curriculum enrichment, should keep open the question of how feminist research might best be applied in our effort to bring about sexual equality in this society and its schools. I have argued elsewhere that achieving equality for women in art will require questioning not only their role in art, but art's role in education, and education's role in our society (Collins, 1979). An understanding of how assumptions about gender have influenced our society's view of art and its place in the curriculum suggests the need for new conceptions of education that give equal attention to the values associated with feminine ways of experiencing the self and the world.[2] My thesis in this chapter is that feminine-identified subjects, individuals, occupations, institutions, and spheres will not be fully empowered until the values associated with them are held to be as valid in their own right as masculine values and are viewed as equally applicable to all subjects, individuals, occupations, institutions, and spheres.

After suggesting how art as a feminine-identified subject has been used to enrich the curriculum with feminine values, I will describe how this use is related to four major problems in art education and look at our field's most recent attempt to deal with these problems. I will conclude by suggesting that feminist educators will need to take a more confrontational approach than using gender to enrich the curriculum if we intend to bring about sex equity in our schools and society.

Forced to say which is more masculine, the fork or the spoon, most people would say the fork. Compare the fork to a knife, however, and the fork suddenly reveals its more feminine aspects. While gender in the abstract tends to be defined in absolute terms, when it comes to people, things, and activities, it is always a matter of more or less.[3] Compared to many culturally valued activities in our society, the gender identification of art clearly falls within what is commonly taken to be the feminine.

Most feminist scholars in art have focused on sexism as a by-product of male dominance and masculine bias within the Western art establishment and tradition. Early in the women's art movement, however, at least two authors gave serious attention to the facts and effects of art's popular feminine identification: June Wayne in her 1974 article "The Male Artist as Stereotypical Female" and Mary P. Garrard in her 1976 article "Of Men, Women, and Art." These authors pointed out how closely art and femininity are associated in our society. Concrete associations between women and art occur at local, highly visible levels: women work as volunteers in art museums, women take community arts and crafts classes, women join art associations and patronize art events. Until quite recently, art reviews were placed on the women's pages of the newspaper. Poetic personifications, analogies, and myths in our culture have depicted art as feminine. Psychological studies and tests of personality have used an interest in art as an indicator of femininity. On a more subtle level, art has played a similar role and shares a similar stereotype with women in our society. Hence the virtues and weaknesses of women and art are described by the same "flock" (Hughes, 1972) of adjectives: decorative, emotional, sensuous, frivolous, and, in their place, quite desirable.

At higher levels of education and practice, levels where male dominance and masculine bias are most palpable, feminists have tended to dismiss the popular feminine identification of art as an ironic stereotype, just as they have attacked the burden of the aforementioned adjectives as defining the feminine in a singular sense. At the public school level, however, where art is less insulated from public belief and assumption, the popular feminine identification of art cannot be viewed with similar dispassion.

ART EDUCATION IN NORTH AMERICAN PUBLIC SCHOOLS

Art education slipped into American public schools as copybook drawing for the purpose of training individuals to fill our country's need for industrial designers (Eisner & Ecker, 1970). Art teachers soon abandoned such pragmatic concerns to vocational training in the industrial arts, however, and turned their pedagogic attentions to what we in Western societies refer to as "fine art." For many interesting historical reasons, Americans have exhibited a good deal of ambivalence in their response to fine art, regarding it as, at once, the profoundest expression of human idealism and yet, somehow, a sign of moral decadence; as a serious pursuit worthy of the genius and yet, somehow, a lighthearted concern; as a harmless, even healthful pastime and yet, somehow, a dangerous, subversive activity. Perhaps the typical American's most abiding and hopeful conviction about fine art is that it is a feminine cultural frill, a desirable but frivolous cultural enrichment.

Opinions of fine art within American public schools more closely resemble those held by the general public than those held at upper levels of education and in the professional art world. Except in the case of experimental art-centered schools, the lay public and its departments of elementary and secondary instruction generally view art as an educational frill—a subject embodying feminine qualities capable of enriching the basic public school curriculum. And it is as an educational enrichment that art has survived if not thrived in American public schools, where the basic business of curriculum and instruction is the socialization of children for a future of responsible, competent, and competitive citizenship in our democratic, materialistic society.

Some art educators might argue that teaching art as a curricular enrichment has nothing to do with art's popular feminine identification and that treating art as a curricular enrichment has had only positive effects on this subject by assuring a great deal of educational freedom for art teachers and students. I suspect, however, that most art educators would be willing to consider the possibility that art's feminine identification and its use as a curricular enrichment are not unrelated, and that, taken together, they have had a negative impact on the theory and practice of art education. Among the problems caused or complicated by using art as a feminine-identified curricular enrichment are art's low curricular status, the degraded feminine role it is likely to play within the curriculum, its discontinuity and isolation from other subjects and levels of education, and the excessive time art educators feel they must spend arguing the educational value of their subject (Chapman, 1982).[4]

Art's Low Curricular Status

Because art is an enrichment rather than a basic, it is one of the first programs dropped and one of the last to be added in response to the fluctuations in educational budgets. Because art is an enrichment, when monies for space, equipment, personnel, and materials are divided, art teachers are less likely than those who teach basic subjects to get what they need to maintain a quality program. At the elementary school level, relatively little instructional time is devoted to the teaching of art. When classroom teachers are responsible for teaching all subjects including art, they are less likely to schedule it during prime instructional time and more likely to slate it for late Friday afternoon. At the high school level, art is more likely to be offered as an elective than as a course required for graduation or college entrance.

Art teachers experience many painful reminders of what it means to teach a subject that is an enrichment rather than a basic subject. Attending art class may be treated as a reward for work completed in other subject areas, and students may be required to stay in the classroom to finish other assignments rather than being "allowed" to attend their scheduled art class. Teachers of basic subjects feel free to ask art teachers to adjust their art lesson plans to correlate with what is being studied in these subjects while the reverse would be almost unthinkable. No matter how desirable, a curricular enrichment is less essential than a basic subject, by definition, and the inessential has low curricular status in American public schools. If that enrichment happens to be a feminine-identified subject, it is likely to assume a feminine role within the school, further diminishing its status.

Art's Feminine Role in the Public School

The feminine qualities ascribed to art are often exploited by parents, administrators, teachers, and students who expect art to play a feminine role in the life of the school. Viewing art as a feminine-identified curricular enrichment, they believe art's value lies in its ability to provide for the catharsis and articulation of emotion, to enhance the self-concepts of the young, and to offer a maternal refuge from an otherwise demanding patriarchal curriculum. For example, in schools where basic subjects have high and rigid standards for academic achievement, all concerned expect art to provide a supportive atmosphere and permissive environment where students can release tension, experience success, and increase or reclaim their self-esteem. School counselors send students with intellectual, social, emotional, and/or physical problems to art classes, trusting they will find nurturance there. To meet such expectations, art teachers must prepare courses and programs capable of accommodating children who are, for one reason or another, at a disadvantage in their academic course work. Art's feminine role in the school may also extend into the realm of domestic service when art teachers and students use their work to decorate the school and use their class time to recreate reassuring images and symbols to accompany traditional celebrations of seasonal cycles and holidays. In a society that devalues feminine activity, expecting art to play a feminine role in the school not only assumes but reinforces its low curricular status. Its helpmate role and precarious status produce predictable effects on the way art educators justify the educational value of their subject.

Art Education's Obsession with Rationales

Given the marginality and feminine role of public school art education, art educators have had to give inordinate attention to the development, articulation, and updating of rationales for its continued inclusion. The first historical surveys of art education were often not much more than chronological accounts of the many justifications that have been put forth to maintain art's credibility as an educational enrichment.[5] Art educators have shaped and reshaped the particulars of these rationales in response to current events, trends, and fads, seizing every opportunity to argue art's relevance to solving or mitigating the problems of an ever-changing society. In one way or another, however, all have tended to focus on the enrichment or enhancement value of art for children's development, for the teaching of other subjects, and/or for the creation of an attractive school environment. In these rationales, art educators have asserted many things, including art's ability to improve penmanship, elevate taste and morals, promote transferable creativity, provide a spot in the curriculum for freedom and self-expression, maintain mental health and self-esteem, increase patriotic feeling, increase ethnic pride, make productive use of leisure time, encourage environmental and ecological awareness, and create intelligent consumers. The precarious status of an enrichment in the public school curriculum encourages its practitioners to make many different and often exaggerated claims for the subject's enriching powers. Changing rationales in quick response to changes in the larger society, art education's practice rarely has time to catch up with its rhetoric, and its credibility in its own and perhaps others' eyes has suffered as a consequence. Obsessive changing of rationales, like rearranging furniture, reinforces stereotypes of feminine flightiness. That this obsession with self-justification is neither shared nor sympathetically understood by those who teach basic subjects is often remarked on by art educators, adding a sense of isolation to the other frustrations of playing a marginal, feminine role in American public school education.

Discontinuity and Isolation

For art to play its nurturing role in public school education, art teachers have had to focus on art's more therapeutic aspects. They have had to deemphasize the type of concept and skill teaching associated with basic public school subjects. Doing otherwise would undermine art's feminine value and role. In many ways, public school art education finds itself in the proverbial double bind of the feminine-identified. Art has a male-dominated tradition and history—its discipline is difficult and competitive and its successful practice requires intellect and skill. Although art teachers are capable of teaching the concepts and skills associated with art's masculine-identified mainstream tradition, they tend to ignore or disguise those that conflict with art's feminine role. On the other hand, if they stress what are imagined to be the feminine values and behaviors associated with art, they generally take care to confine and trivialize these so they do not pose a threat to the values of the basic school curriculum. The cost of keeping art in public school curriculums as a feminine enrichment has been a field that knows its place and keeps it.

Art's role as a feminine enrichment in the public school curriculum requires art teachers to exaggerate the differences between art and other subjects. Teaching measurable content would conflict with art's feminine identification and role, so the mechanisms of accountability supporting and constraining the teaching of basic subjects are less likely to be used in public school art. Public school art teachers typically avoid textbooks, exams, and tough grading practices, and typically are not required to conform to standardized curriculum guides or teach for standardized tests. The accoutrements of academic procedure and accountability, if applied to the teaching of art, would be counterproductive to encouraging therapeutic creative self-expression and to maintaining the air of frivolity that is thought to surround this activity. If these differences between art and other subjects allow individual art teachers to design curricula in response to their own and their students' needs and interests, they also make public school art more vulnerable to spurious criticism, capricious revisionism, and arbitrary cutbacks in program support.

Being used and shaped as a curricular enrichment isolates public school art not only from the concerns of those who teach basic school subjects, but from those of art faculty at colleges and universities. While the purposes of education at elementary and secondary levels make the teaching of any subject at these levels somewhat discontinuous with its teaching at the university, such differences are even more dramatic in art. Art at the university level emphasizes the concepts, skills, and values of the masculine-identified Western art tradition, and art at the public school level emphasizes the feminine values associated with therapeutic creative self-expression. As a result, art teachers and programs in the public schools often receive more criticism than support from university art teachers and professional artists. Students initially attracted to art at the public school level are often unprepared for or disappointed in the way it is taught at the university level. Many of these same students opt to return to the public schools as certified art teachers more interested in teaching art as a feminine curricular enrichment than in pursuing masculine-identified artistic careers. In many instances, this is because they have internalized enough mainstream-art attitudes to know that their only choice is, in effect, to pursue a feminine-identified art career with very low status in the artworld, closing the circle, as it were.

CONFRONTING ART EDUCATION AS FEMININE CURRICULAR ENRICHMENT

Based on their own experience as public school art students, the vast majority of past and present art teachers believe in art's capacity to enrich the lives of children, the school, and the society. If for this reason they have been content to teach art as an enrichment, their efforts to do so have been frustrated by art's low curricular status, the constant need to justify and improve art's place in the curriculum, the fragmentation of energies associated with playing a feminine role, and the isolation from the concerns of other subjects and art at higher levels. In response to recent changes within the field, art educators have begun to wonder if there might not be some connection between their willingness to teach art as a curricular enrichment and the frustrations that have attended their efforts to do so.

Art education is a young field, and only recently have its practitioners become interested in exploring its past. The increasing number of publications devoted to historical studies in American public school art education provide art educators with a new sense of their own professionalism, and a new vantage point from which to view their field in terms of trends and patterns.[6] In the past, each generation of art educators devised new rationales for art as an educational enrichment, tending to blame art's curricular status on the inadequacy of the preceding rationale. From a historical perspective, each of these rationales has promised but failed to increase art's curricular status. Inevitably, art educators have begun to question the whole attempt to teach and "sell" art as an educational enrichment.

The historical study of the rationales for art education has encouraged art educators to look for significant similarities and differences among them. The majority of rationales for art education have been, to use Tyler's characterizations, child-centered, a lesser number have been society-centered, and very few have been subject-centered.[7] Child-centered rationales have encouraged art teachers to focus on studio-based activities, to use media and methods that promote children's creativity, and to treat children's work as artistically valid expressions of their experience, personality, and general development. Society-centered rationales have encouraged art teachers to focus on studio-based activities, using media and methods related to art in everyday life outside of school, and to call attention to the social functions of art in this and other cultures as exemplified by applied, commercial, popular, mass media, and folk art, as well as fine art forms. Subject-centered rationales have not dissuaded art teachers from their traditional focus on studio-based activities but have encouraged them to show slides of famous artists' works and discuss the art elements and principles that might be related to such activities. Art educators can see that the notion of art as a curricular enrichment is closely related to the field's preference for child- and society-centered over subject-centered rationales for art education. These orientations do not challenge the assumption that art is to be valued as an educational enrichment, because they point to how this subject might be taught for the purpose of enriching something other than itself.

The recent research on the history of art education, then, encourages art educators to begin to distance themselves from the rationales that have been used to support art as an educational enrichment, to acknowledge that these have not won for art anything more than a marginal role in education and to give more consideration to a subject-centered approach that might allow teachers to spend more time teaching art and less time justifying it. Although foreshadowed by proposals made by art educators in the 1960s who were attuned to the "structure of disciplines" movement (Mattil, 1966), a serious consideration of a subject-centered approach to art in education began in the 1980s with a powerful and well-funded movement called "discipline-based art education."[8]

Discipline-Based Art Education

Advocates of discipline-based art education (DBAE) argue that art education has had a low curricular status because it has been taught as a child- or society-centered curricular enrichment (Getty Center for Education in the Arts, 1985). Emulating those who teach subjects with high curricular status, DBAE proponents assume or assert that art is a basic subject and do not try to justify art's value as an educational enrichment. Instead, they propose to solve the problems of art education's role and isolation by eliminating exaggerated differences between the way art and other subjects are taught and between the content of public school art education and art at higher levels of education and practice.

DBAE proponents say that public school art education ought to derive its form and content equally from the disciplines of studio art, art history, art criticism, and aesthetics; that art teachers ought to teach the concepts, skills, and values found at professional levels of practice; that teachers ought to expose students to the works of exemplary art professionals and stop thinking that children are already artists; that teachers ought to teach using a written, sequential curriculum; and that teachers and their students ought to be held accountable by a system of standardized evaluation and testing (Clark, Day, & Greer, 1987; Eisner, 1990; Greer, 1984). Their arguments imply that by eliminating unnecessary discontinuities between public school art and other subjects, and between public school art and art at higher levels, DBAE would eliminate (or at least allow us to ignore) art education's problems with curricular status, role, isolation, and justification.

A DBAE approach to art education would obviously require radical changes in the way art has been taught in the public schools. To overcome the inertia of tradition in art education, the Getty Center has promoted DBAE by sponsoring research projects and invitational seminars, by funding the revision of public school art curricula and pre- and inservice programs for art teachers, by offering fellowships, and by supporting the publication and distribution of books and journal issues devoted to DBAE (Dobbs, 1988; Smith, 1987). Art educators sympathetic to DBAE tend to welcome Getty Center contributions of money, energy, and expertise, feeling these are effective expressions of public-minded concern on the part of a wealthy and powerful private institution. Others resent and fear these contributions for much the same reasons. Some art educators who oppose DBAE support a child-centered approach to art education because this approach is most compatible with their romantic understanding of art and its unique values.[9] The most vocal opposition to DBAE, however, comes from critical theorists, multiculturalists, feminists, and others who believe art education should not be used to disenfranchise any group or individual nor require them to deny their differences in order to be enfranchised. These art educators fear that DBAE would perpetuate ethnic, class, racial, sexual, and gender biases in art education because DBAE's emerging versions of art history, criticism, and aesthetics, along with its more tough-minded approach to art studio, tend to enshrine the art, heroes, practices, and values of the Western mainstream art tradition, an art tradition dominated by a White, European, heterosexual, middle- or upper-class male worldview. From a feminist perspective, DBAE might be understood to promise, among other things, the defeminization of art education (Collins & Sandell, 1988), which would initially seem to offer some fringe benefits.

Defeminizing Art Education?

Were DBAE instituted, feminists might find it easier to describe the need for gender equity at this level—a need obscured by the present feminine identification and role of art in the public schools. We might also find that the types of enrichment used to achieve gender equity in other subjects or at higher levels of art education and practice would become newly plausible at the level of public school art education. For example, if DBAE were successful in achieving a defeminized, subject-centered approach to art education, art education would then include the study of Western art history. Under such circumstances, feminists might easily argue for the enrichment of art education with feminine perspectives and values. We could point out that if art education includes the study of male artists in Western mainstream art, then it should also include the study of women artists who have participated in this tradition, and that if it includes the study of the mainstream Western art tradition, it should also include the study of women's art traditions in this culture, as well as the study of men's and women's art traditions in non-Western cultures, and so forth.

As a feminist art educator, I do not want to wait until public school art is defeminized before arguing the need for gender equity in art education. And while I might be a little envious of the apparent ease with which an enrichment approach can be described as countering sexism in a masculine-identified subject, I believe there are important lessons to be learned from examining the relationship between a feminine-identified subject and its problems with status, role, justification, and isolation. One of these lessons is that, as a gender-equity strategy, curricular enrichment has severe limitations. The curriculum may indeed be enriched by adding feminine perspectives and values to it, but this enrichment will not necessarily enhance the status and role of the feminine, nor liberate it from isolation, nor alleviate the need for its endless justification.

Art educators have tried to improve the status of their feminine-identified subject by increasing its value as a curricular enrichment. Recognizing the futility of this effort, many would now defeminize art as a means of asserting its equality with masculine-identified subjects in the curriculum. What is common to both bids for art's improved status is that they reinforce assumptions that feminine-identified activities are less basic than masculine-identified activities, that these activities have a lesser value in our schools and society, and that the value they do have is limited to and defined by their ability to enrich education and life without threatening the primacy of the masculine. We cannot hope to gain equal status for feminine-identified activities without questioning these assumptions. This involves asking what schools would be like if we regarded the values associated with the feminine as equally valid, equally basic, and no more or less capable of "enriching" the curriculum than the values associated with the masculine.

In American schools, teachers, most of whom are women, are charged with the task of preparing children for future citizenship in an adult society dominated by males and masculine values. These schools could be described as feminine-identified, low-status institutions serving, as do most institutions in our society, masculine-identified and male-defined purposes. If schools were to serve the full range of feminine as well as masculine purposes, they would be more than bureaucratic organizations dedicated to the efficient preparation of individuals for citizenship in our larger society, they would be nurturing communities that accept individuals as they are in the present and encourage good relationships as ends in themselves. In such schools, feminine perspectives and values would not be treated as educational enrichments, but would receive attention equal to that given masculine ones in every subject. As a result, feminine-identified activities and attitudes would not be trivialized or exploited. And current practices that set aside either feminine or masculine ways of knowing as inappropriate for certain subjects, people, spheres, times, or places would be replaced.

Painting this pretty picture ought to evoke a few of the possibilities that curricular enrichment approaches to sex equity omit. This picture does not begin to suggest, however, what obstacles might stand in the way of achieving such a vision. For example, were we to claim that feminine values are as basic as masculine values and must therefore receive equal consideration in elementary and secondary schooling, these claims could be taken as a direct challenge to the integrity of the school as a masculine project. Many would see such a challenge as political in nature, and hence present a great deal of angry resistance. The bright picture of schools dedicated to feminine as well as masculine purposes also fades a bit when we consider the tensions and conflicts between the different sets of values associated with each gender, which, having surfaced, would be hard to resolve.

In anticipation of such difficulties, and despite the above review of art education's problems as an educational enrichment, some will nevertheless find virtue in an approach to sex equity that would use gender to enrich the curriculum. Using gender in this manner would be one way to avoid serious political confrontation between masculine and feminine values at the level of school purpose and function. Art educators have learned, however, that the peaceful nature of curricular enrichment can exact its own price. Enrichments are additions that enhance. They neither challenge nor change the basic qualities of that to which they are added— although they may make them easier to swallow. A little enrichment goes a long way, and too much is not good for you. Marie Antoinette to the contrary, enrichments will be offered only when the basics are secured.

NOTES

1. Suggestions for the application of feminist research to public school art education have been made, however. For examples, see Collins and Sandell (1984, 1987), and special issues of journals such as *Art Education, 45*(2), 1992 and *Studies in Art Education, 32*(1), 1990.
2. Using Simone de Beauvoir's (1949/1961) concepts of *immanence* and *transcendence*, I have argued elsewhere that masculine and feminine values derive from different but equally valid ways of experiencing the self and the world (Collins, 1977, 1987).
3. For a discussion of the implications of viewing the masculine and feminine as opposing universal principles, see Whitbeck (1976).
4. For a functional analysis of art's role in the public school see Efland (1976). Efland does not, however, use the term "feminine" to describe this role.
5. For an actual chronology, see Karen Hamblen (1985).
6. For examples, see Wygant (1983), Wilson and Hoffa (1987), Efland (1990), and Soucy and Stankiewicz (1990).
7. For descriptions of these orientations in an art education context, see Elliot Eisner (1972) and Gilbert Clark (1991).
8. W. Dwaine Greer (1984) is generally credited with naming this movement.
9. See Blandy and Congdon (1988); Burton, Lederman, and London (1988); Ewens (1988); Hamblen (1987); Huber (1987); and Sandell (1988).

REFERENCES

Blandy, Doug, & Congdon, Kristin. (Eds.). (1988). Special issue on DBAE. *Journal of Multi-cultural and Cross-cultural Research in Art Education, 6*(1).

Burton, Judith, Lederman, Arlene, & London, Peter. (Eds.). (1988). *Beyond DBAE: The case for multiple visions of art education.* North Dartmouth, MA: University Council on Art Education.

Chapman, Laura. (1982). *Instant art, instant culture.* New York: Teachers College Press.

Clark, Gilbert. (1991). Art education, DBAE, and traditional curriculum orientations. In *Examining discipline-based art education as a curriculum construct* (pp. 2–5, 24–25). Bloomington: Indiana University, ERIC Art.

Clark, Gilbert, Day, Michael, & Greer, W. Dwaine. (1987). Discipline-based art education: Becoming students of art. *Journal of Aesthetic Education, 21*(2), 129–196.

Collins, Georgia. (1977). Considering an androgynous model for art education. *Studies in Art Education, 18*(2), 54–62.

Collins, Georgia. (1979). Women and art: The problem of status. *Studies in Art Education, 21*(1), 57–65.

Collins, Georgia. (1987). Masculine bias and the relationship between art and democracy. In Doug Blandy & Kristin Congdon (Eds.), *Art in a democracy* (pp. 26–43). New York: Teachers College Press.

Collins, Georgia, & Sandell, Renee. (1984). *Women, art, and education*. Reston, VA: National Art Education Association.

Collins, Georgia, & Sandell, Renee. (1987). Women's achievements in art: An issues approach for the classroom. *Art Education, 40*(3), 12–21.

Collins, Georgia, & Sandell, Renee. (1988). Informing the promise of DBAE: Remember the women, children, and other folk. *Journal of Multi-cultural and Cross-cultural Research in Art Education, 6*(1), 55–63.

de Beauvoir, Simone. (1961). *The second sex* (H M. Parshley, Ed. & Trans.). New York: Bantam Books. (Original work published 1949)

Dobbs, Stephen. (Ed.). (1988). *Research reading for discipline-based art education*. Reston, VA: National Art Education Association.

Efland, Arthur. (1976). The school art style. *Studies in Art Education, 17*(2), 37–44.

Efland, Arthur. (1990). *A history of art education*. New York: Teachers College Press.

Eisner, Elliot. (1972). *Educating artistic vision*. New York: Macmillan.

Eisner, Elliot. (1990). *The role of discipline-based art education in America's schools*. Los Angeles: J. Paul Getty Trust, Getty Center for Education in the Arts.

Eisner, Elliot, & Ecker, David. (1970). Some historical developments in art education. In George Pappas (Ed.), *Concepts in art and education* (pp. 12–25). New York: Macmillan.

Ewens, Thomas. (1988). *In art education, more DBAE equals less art*. Washington, DC: Heldref.

Garrard, Mary P. (1976). Of men, women, and art. *Art Journal, 35*(4), 324–329.

Getty Center for Education in the Arts. (1985). *Beyond creating: The place for art in America's schools*. Los Angeles: J. Paul Getty Trust, Getty Center for Education in the Arts.

Greer, W. Dwaine. (1984). Discipline-based art education: Approaching art as a subject of study. *Studies in Art Education, 25*(4), 212–218.

Hamblen, Karen. (1985). An art education chronology. *Studies in Art Education, 26*(2), 111–120.

Hamblen, Karen. (1987). An examination of discipline-based art education issues. *Studies in Art Education, 28*(2), 68–78.

Huber, B. W. (1987). What does feminism have to offer DBAE? *Art Education, 40*(3), 36–41.

Hughes, Robert. (1972, March 20). Myths of sensibility. *Time*, pp. 72–77.

Mattil, Edward. (Ed.). (1966). *A seminar in art education for research and curriculum development*. University Park: Pennsylvania State University Press.

Sandell, Renee. (1988). *DBAE: From a teacher's point of view*. Paper presented at a seminar on DBAE, University of Maryland, College Park.

Smith, Ralph. (Ed.). (1987). DBAE [Special issue]. *Journal of Aesthetic Education, 21*(2).

Soucy, Donald. (1991). *Women & art: An annotated bibliography of books and articles*. Unpublished manuscript.

Soucy, Donald, & Stankiewicz, Mary Ann. (Eds.). (1990). *Framing the past: Essays on art education*. Reston, VA: National Art Education Association.

Wayne, June. (1974). The male artist as stereotypical female. *Arts in Society,* 2(1), 107–113.

Whitbeck, Caroline. (1976). Theories of sex difference. In Carol Gould & Marx Wartofsky (Eds.), *Women and philosophy* (pp. 54–80). New York: G. P. Putnam's Sons.

Wilson, Brent, & Hoffa, Harlan. (Eds.). (1987). *The history of art education: Proceedings from the Penn State conference.* University Park: Pennsylvania State University Press.

Wygant, Foster. (1983). *Art in American schools in the nineteenth century.* Cincinnati, OH: Interwood Press.

CHAPTER 3

Making It Work: Gender and Vocational Education

JANE GASKELL

The analysis of where women are in the workplace has been fundamental to feminist scholarship and to rethinking women's place in the world. Data on wage differences for full-time workers demonstrate women's disadvantage in an incontrovertible way. Women who work full time for pay earn on average less than two-thirds of what men earn, although they have more education than men in the labor force. Women work in different jobs from men, and these jobs are paid and respected less than the jobs men work in. While economistic approaches and Marxist theories, by starting and ending with the workplace, have often ignored the importance of culture, domestic labor, language, representations, and physical violence, in this postmodern moment (and in this climate of labor relations) we have to keep the labor market, and the position of women in it, firmly in mind. The material base counts.

When women as a group are compared to men as a group, the analysis risks forgetting differences among women. If statistics for "women" are not disaggregated by class, occupational sector, ethnicity, race, or sexual orientation, they conceal particular pockets of disadvantage or advantage, while claiming to represent the experience of all women. While programs like pay equity and employment equity or affirmative action are designed to help "women," they have worked mainly to the advantage of professional, White women. The gradual overall narrowing of the wage gap between men and women can be accounted for by the fact that the gap is closing at the higher end of the wage scale, while it is growing or staying the same at the lower end (Cohen, 1991; Fudge & McDermott, 1991). Analysis of women's experience at work is best carried out in relation to specific groups of women, in specific job categories, in order to avoid overgeneralizing from some groups of women to all. It is particularly important to look at the experience of the large majority of women who do not hold professional jobs.

The role of the school curriculum in reproducing women's disadvantage at work is multifaceted, and can be examined in any subject area. Schools prepare everyone for jobs in one way or another.[1] They put students into different subjects and document different levels of achievement to better feed them into the labor market. Researchers can ask how the work of women is portrayed and valued—in literature, in history, in technology, and in art. But in secondary schools, it is in vocational classrooms that students are explicitly prepared for the workplace. It is here that the curriculum deals directly with what employers want, what workers need to know, and how students should negotiate the social and technical relations of jobs. The jobs for which the secondary school directly prepares students are not professional jobs, for they require university education. They are not jobs that are considered to be particularly "skilled," for these require preparation at community colleges, junior colleges, or technical institutes. In secondary school vocational classes, those destined for poorly paid jobs in the society are taken aside and taught about work. In an increasingly polarized economy where there are "good jobs and bad jobs" (Economic Council, 1990), these are the students destined for the "bad jobs." The low status of the vocational students translates into low status for the instructors and the subject. These courses are filled with the students who have been least affected by the gains of a feminist movement too often focused on the concerns of professional, White, middle-class women (Cohen, 1991; Gunderson, 1990).

Vocational courses remain a bastion of single-sex education within the public school system because they reflect the divisions in the labor market. Courses in auto mechanics and metalwork and carpentry are filled with young men. Young women study hairdressing, child care, food, sales, and overwhelmingly, clerical skills. Thirty percent of all women in the labor force, and 50% of all women in the labor force with a high school education, are employed as clerical workers (Statistics Canada, 1991), and this translates into a large enrollment in courses labeled variously "office education" or "business education," courses preparing young women to work in office jobs as secretaries and clerical workers. Understanding the experience of the large number of women who work in the clerical sector is enormously important for understanding why women fare as poorly as they do in the labor force. The wages are low, the prospects for mobility few, and the working conditions are frequently terrible. The jobs are overwhelmingly filled by women, and this association with women has kept the wages low. The work also enjoys a kind of respectability and status not reflected in the wage rate because, historically, literate middle-class women could find work in offices—with social approval (Davies, 1983). The requirement for facility with language and for social interaction with the public meant that employers would rarely hire any but White, English-speaking women. Today, the residual status attached to clerical jobs, their wide availability and flexibility, the lack of available alternative employment, and the attractiveness of working with other like-minded women continue to make clerical work and office education courses a popular choice for young women (Gaskell, 1992).

In this chapter, I will work from an analysis of office education to draw some more general conclusions about vocational education. Fully considering the nature and contributions of women's work in secretarial and clerical jobs means rethinking what goes on and what should go on in office and business education. Work, especially women's work, has been conceived too often as a technical set of tasks done at the behest of others, which had been learned through imitation and recitation in training to be displayed in "real" settings. The work women have actually done as secretaries and clerical workers cannot be described this way. Their tasks are varied and the intellectual and social competencies they require are complex and learned over time. A narrow understanding of the nature of office work serves to keep class and gender distinctions clear, to belittle the work and the workers, and to restrict the training and education it entails. It misrepresents how work gets accomplished, trivializes the contributions of women, and finally, reduces the well-being of all workers. On the other hand, recognition of the broad social and intellectual competencies women have brought to their work is part of a struggle to increase women's status at work and to usher in major changes in how we conceive of vocational education. To prepare young people for work is to prepare them for their place in the economic structure and to prepare them for a large part of their lives. Vocational education needs to be conceived in this spirit.

THE SOCIAL AND THE TECHNICAL

Much of the discussion about what should be taught in vocational courses is about trying to construct accurately what jobs require so that it can be taught. This is particularly true in clerical courses, for they are described as necessary for finding a job, unlike many other practical courses in the high school that are avocational or exploratory. In the secondary school I studied in British Columbia, the course catalogue described the secretarial and clerical courses offered in the business department in clearly job-related ways. Courses will cover "as many types of written language projects as are relevant to office work"; students who graduate "should be capable of handling books in a small business firm"; and the course "qualifies a student for a high standard secretarial position" (see also Valli, 1986). Courses in industrial education, on the other hand, prepare students to embark on trades training after graduation ("recommended for students going on in engineering or architecture"; "designed to fulfill the requirements for admission to vocational school") or develop avocational skills ("the skills necessary to repair and maintain his own vehicle"; the skills required for "constructing a stereo"), and sometimes to do math or science ("to illustrate the fundamental principles of science").

There is a long tradition of public education for women being vocational, related to their future work as teachers, housewives, or secretaries. Employers were unwilling to invest in on-the-job training of women, as women were never considered long-term employees. Women themselves did not have the economic power to insist that employers provide on-the-job training.[2] But women's work has always been necessary in the workplace, so their training had to be done at public expense. The result is a pattern that continues today of vocational courses being provided in public educational institutions for work traditionally done by women, while little formal on-the-job training is available or required in the female sector of the labor market (Wolf & Rosenberg, 1978). The necessity for women to get vocational training in public educational institutions accounts for the apparent anomaly of women attending secondary schools in much larger numbers than men since the end of the nineteenth century.

But what does vocational preparation actually consist of? In the case of office workers, what do employers look for in an employee and what do workers say they need to learn? The question is not an easy one to answer, for it requires that the neat and tidy specification of a few "skills" be abstracted from the messy and complex world of the workplace. Although, as Ronnie Steinberg (1990) points out, "sociologists and political economists have tended to agree more than they disagree about what constitutes skilled work," notions of skill are constructed through social conventions and ideologies and the discourse of skill is a discourse of power. The specification of skills, while particularly complex in clerical jobs, is always and everywhere a judgmental process that involves reducing a varied set of activities to a few definable and rankable capacities. "Classifications of workers are neither 'natural' nor self evident, nor is the degree of skill a self evident quality which can simply be read from the labels given to various classifications" (Braverman, 1974, p. 428). As Phillips and Taylor put it, "far from being an objective economic fact, skill

is often an ideological category imposed on certain types of work by virtue of the sex and power of the workers who perform it" (1980, p. 79).
Any version of skill requirements is partial and serves someone's interests. Some workers have had more power to insist on the skilled nature
of their jobs than other workers. Skill designations are used to give status
and importance to some kinds of work, and to take it away from others.
They are also used to justify and specify the length and type of educational requirements. With pay equity legislation, which links skill rank-
ings explicitly to wages, they are suddenly more obviously a matter for
political negotiation.

Clerical and secretarial work involves a wide variety of types of jobs
and activities. There is a huge range of kinds of work labeled generally as
"clerical" or "secretarial." Typing, bookkeeping, formatting documents,
filing, and spelling are commonly part of what the work involves. But
many analyses of secretaries and clerical workers emphasize their role as
office "wives"—as smiling, quintessentially cooperative, and decorative
women who are helpmates in whatever tasks need to be done—answering the phone, receiving the public, making the coffee, anticipating the
needs of the boss, calming furious customers, pleasing everyone in the
office, remembering birthdays, and listening to personal stories. Standard
job descriptions are often hard to come by, and even when they are available, they underrepresent the variety and the social nature of many of the
tasks that are done (Benet, 1972; Meissner, 1991; Pringle, 1988). The technical skills themselves are not clear, as the debate about what happens to
the work with the introduction of new technologies indicates (Braverman,
1974; Glen & Feldberg, 1977/1978). The specific technical skills required
are inextricably entwined with the interpersonal competencies required.

While these interpersonal demands are particularly obvious in the
work and image of the secretary, they are present in many of the jobs
women do: teacher, waitress, librarian, shop assistant, nurse, domestic
worker. The jobs filled predominantly by women involve more social and
verbal tasks than jobs filled predominantly by men (England, Chassic, &
McConnock, 1982). *Caretaking* is often a part of the work women do and
it is rarely given the respect and rewards it deserves. The sex segregation
of jobs reinforces "the association of masculinity with mechanical and
technical skills and the association of femininity with patience and
selfless dedication to repetitive tasks" (Acker, 1988, p. 482). Men's work
is seen to demand skills; women's work is seen to demand a virtuous personality.

For the interpersonal work women do is not recognized as skill or
rewarded in salaries or status. It is treated as an aspect of femininity or
perhaps a personality attribute of the woman doing it. To judge the skills

involved in work is to engage in evaluations and political judgements that have never counted what women do seriously. Our common sense notions of skill arise in the context of male crafts, for these were the workers who had the power to regulate and define their work.[3] "Skilled workers" were craft workers who had gone through an apprenticeship. The census defined skilled workers as those who had learned to work with machinery (Braverman, 1974). The realm of the social is invisible and undervalued in these discussions of skill. In 1974, *The Dictionary of Occupational Titles* rated dog pound attendant, parking lot attendant, and zoo keeper as more complex jobs than nursery school teacher and child-care worker (Steinberg, 1990).

Vocational curriculum buys into this technical and industrial discourse, emphasizing technical skills, downplaying social skills. Vocational education became part of the school curriculum in the context of technological changes and industrialization in the early twentieth century. Its justification drew on the technical and industrial skills that workers needed to cope with these changes (Jackson & Gaskell, 1987). Today, the rhetoric of vocational education is still about the specification of skills of a technical nature, skills that can be defined clearly, graded "objectively," and traded profitably in the labor market. The education of clerical workers is forced into this mold.

The tensions around technical and social competencies are illustrated in interviews I have carried out with clerical instructors. They emphasize that employers care a great deal about how students present themselves socially. All the instructors indicate that what they usually refer to as appropriate "attitudes" are necessary for getting and keeping a clerical job. "If you have a girl who has been drilled and trained and whose attitudes are extremely poor, then she will always do worse than someone whose attitudes are good and who is slower in fact." But they do not really approve of this, for it underplays the skills they teach, and they have no clear mandate to teach students and especially to grade them on anything related to social competencies. "The policy is to base grading on technical competence only." "We aren't allowed to evaluate students on their attitude." "We always try to have 10% of the grade on attitude and that is very difficult . . . you can run into problems because some of them will say . . . well you are just prejudiced, you don't like me or whatever." "It's a pretty difficult thing to grade as such, because it would be very controversial." Or, as one teacher puts it, "There's this rotten human rights act where I can't tell a student that they are not acceptable." One of the instructors who is more sympathetic to the importance of interpersonal competencies defines them in terms of pleasing the employer:

All we can try to do is teach it, we can't necessarily grade it. We hope that some of what we are teaching will sink in and they will accept it. . . . We teach them what is most acceptable to the business community, and it really is up to them as to whether they listen to what we are telling them or not. . . . We try to build a good attitude into students about their work, so when they go out they have the right attitude, but it's so intangible that you don't know if you are being successful.

The interpersonal dimensions of women's work are central to the Western stereotype of the feminine. It is not surprising that women have an ambivalent relation to this interpersonal work, sometimes seeing it as an aspect of femininity that must be left behind in order to attain equality with men, and sometimes taking pride and pleasure in its accomplishment. Many important strands of feminist theory have tried to reclaim the interpersonal, the reproductive, the nurturant, the caring—not just for the sake of increasing the recognition due to women, but also because of its importance for all of us (Gilligan, Lyons, & Hanmer, 1990; Martin, 1985; Noddings, 1984). The public world depends on the domestic, as Jane Roland Martin (1985) points out. Men have only been able to marginalize the domestic and the reproductive because they can take for granted that women will do it. But it is not just the domestic world that depends on women's interpersonal work. The workplace has been run on the backs of women who get the coffee, look after the emotional needs of clients and workers, share personal stories, create a sense of community, smile, and handle complaints. Not all women do it, or do it without resistance, but it is a critical part of getting work done. It is not something women do "naturally." It is learned, stressful, difficult. This work has been trivialized by men who don't do it, but depend upon it. It is important work and must be recognized as such.

There are strands of feminist scholarship that are uneasy with the link between women and nurturing and caring, pointing to the culturally limited basis of these images as well as to the way they are used to limit, control, and exploit women's labor. Not all women are or want to be nurturing and warm. The association of women with interpersonal, relational work has always been used to limit their access to positions of power, and to reinforce their association with the domestic realm. It can be argued that it is Western, White, middle-class images of the mother that underlie a feminism dedicated to reclaiming caring in the name of the women's movement (hooks, 1984). In the workplace, these representations have been used to identify particular tasks—secretary, nurse, primary school teacher—with women, and to trivialize them. It is not surprising that women want a break from the relational and interpersonal work they have been held responsible for, and that unions of clerical workers have fought for clear technical job descriptions and hiring policies that make "personality" and "attitude" illegitimate bases to judge the work or the worker. It is an attempt to combat the devaluation of the work that is a consequence of its association with women.

This is understandable, but ultimately self-defeating. Interpersonal work has got to be done in universities, offices, and factories, as well as at home. Threatening as the idea may be to a liberal, individualist ideology, no person functions outside a human community that must be sustained by lots of interpersonal work. Clearly men as well as women should do it, but the low status of the work is self-perpetuating. Recognizing and valuing interpersonal work is necessary to produce equality for women, to get men to share in it, and to increase the well-being of everyone in the domestic sphere as well as in the workplace. Having this work ignored or reviled threatens both productivity and happiness. Instead of trying to turn clerical and secretarial work into a conglomerate of technical tasks with specified typing speeds, computer competencies, and bookkeeping knowledge, those concerned for its recognition must rethink and revalue the interpersonal tasks involved. The social and interpersonal work women do is rarely specified and recognized, but it is vital to any workplace. It has been a freebee, part of what everywoman does, and therefore taken-for-granted. It needs to be specified not as something personal and idiosyncratic, but as a set of behaviors we can talk about and teach, and upon which the workplace depends.

Pay equity schemes have been one mechanism for putting the discussion of skill back on the table and trying to revalue the things women do (England & Norris, 1985; Gaskell, 1990). There is an increasing amount of research on the invisible skills of women at work that emphasizes the social (MacKeracher, 1990; Meissner, 1991). But vocational educators, themselves low in status in the school hierarchy, have been reluctant to ally themselves with the interpersonal, the female, the low status.[4] Vocational discourse is already devalued in the school setting. Reforms to vocational education have been aimed at bolstering its status by attaching it to high status images and attracting material and symbolic resources (Goodson & Dowbiggan, 1991). Taking on the social realm seems to promise neither. Vocational education has been valued for its technical tasks, its machines, its scarce skills, and criticized for its lack of "serious" content, its emphasis on the "hidden" curriculum of social expectations. Increasing the number of specific technical skills required has been a way of demonstrating the status and importance of the work and of the instruction. The shift from technical skills to what has come to be called "life skills" in vocational courses suggests that the courses are fit only for those who are not coping with life and that the work demands only the same common skills that living demands. Social relations are considered private matters, and the public has been valued over the domestic; paid work has taken its status from not being private, not being woman's sphere, not being the everyday.

But, recognizing all this, vocational education has much to gain by expanding its understanding of what is necessary for work, what can be taught and how. Social skills can be reclaimed as real skills, ones that involve moral judgement and sophisticated emotional and intellectual work. They can be taught and learned, recognized and evaluated. Arlie Hochschild (1983) describes Delta airline's training for flight attendants as education in what she calls "emotional work." She notes the predictions that more and more jobs call for the capacity to deal with people and notes, "celebrants and critics alike have not inspected at close hand or with a social psychological eye what it is that 'people jobs' actually require of workers. They have not inquired into the actual nature of this labor" (p. 10). When she looks, she finds the careful training that airlines provide for women in emotional labor, the stress that doing it entails, and the personal consequences of always being cheerful and upbeat because it is part of the job.

There are of course dangers, contradictions in the project. Teaching social skills, like teaching most curriculum content, can be used to oppress, discriminate, and invade the legitimately private. Hochschild is critical of airline training because of the way it estranges people from their feelings. Human rights codes properly restrict the social bases on which hiring judgements can be made. But debate about what kinds of interpersonal competencies are required can be carried on only when the social is not smuggled into job definitions and the curriculum illegitimately. In the vocational program I studied, there was disagreement about what kinds of "attitudes" should be fostered. Most instructors stressed the needs of employers for docility, doing what is asked quickly and efficiently: "Employers . . . are praying always for the bright girl who is pleasant and outgoing and can answer the phone. Is polite, but speaks up." "Employers still rely on the employee to come in and care about getting the job done on time, accurately. Stay a little longer if you have to because it has got to be done." These instructors put a lot of emphasis on being "professional," "helpful," and "cooperative." The good student is "dependable, well-groomed, professional."

But another version, stressing the needs of women as workers and citizens, was also articulated. "Students are not independent enough. They are afraid to ask why."

If nobody coaches them otherwise, they will be subservient to their bosses and I don't think they should be like that. I try to get them to argue with me . . . for example . . . to argue with me about marks, and I tell them why I do that, that it is a role playing situation. . . . We've got to train people to be thinking adults and to recognize bad treatment and to recognize their union rights.

You have to give a lot of reinforcement and encourage them as they go through, because a lot of them are very shy. . . . There are women that all of a sudden have to go back to the workplace, they've had traumas in their lives.

These disagreements about what kind of social skills should be taught and why and how need to be aired in public, just like debates about what kind of knowledge or technical skills should be taught. The public debate will clarify the meanings of terms, and the appropriate ends and means of education for interpersonal competence. The alternative is treating social skills as personality characteristics, immutable and only incidentally important to the work that is accomplished. This obscures much of what happens in offices, fails to give public recognition to those areas of competence where women make major contributions to the economy, and continues the devaluation of women and the activities associated with them.

THE MENTAL AND THE MANUAL

Clerical work has been portrayed as a set of deskilled tasks that simply involve following orders. It has also been portrayed as the center of power and knowledge in the office. As one trainee put it, "I don't think a lot of people realize that a lot of the work done in the offices isn't done by the boss. Most of it is done by the staff and everybody doesn't look at it that way. I feel that it's the staff that runs the whole office more than the boss does." Vocational education can reflect a deskilled version of work that involves little thought or understanding on the part of the worker, or it can reflect a version of the worker as thoughtful actor in a complex world. It can produce a vision of a skilled job where knowledge is important, or a deskilled one where rote repetition of technique is required. The two versions become self-fulfilling, for workers trained in technique expect to follow orders, whereas those educated to understand their work can challenge its organization. As John Dewey put it in 1915 in a debate with David Sneddon, a professor at Columbia and the influential commissioner of education in Massachusetts, vocational education should not be designed to fit young people efficiently into the fabric of the workplace, "for I am not sufficiently in love with the regime for that" (Drost, 1977).

Feminists are not sufficiently in love with it either, for a curriculum that fits women into the slots they are expected to fill in the workforce recreates both class and gender privilege and power. A feminist critique of vocational education must ask how a curriculum that represents "really useful knowledge" for women in the workplace might be conceptualized and put in place. To educate for work as a feminist means to encourage young women to think about the conditions and organization of their work. It does not mean just getting them to practice specific skills, whether formatting a letter or welding a metal box or answering the telephone properly.

There are many studies of vocational classrooms that show this is primarily what the vocational curriculum consists of. Tanguay (1985) and Grignon (1971) show how vocational classrooms reproduce rather than challenge the existing relations of production through reifying manual skills. "The organization of production serves as a backdrop against which the techniques used in production are presented as neutral and natural facts. This exclusion of societal concerns from technical curricula leads to a neutralization of techniques and a reification of social production" (Tanguay, 1985, p. 27). Students learn how to do tasks, without reference to the division of labor that might explain why "the future worker, unaware of the why and the wherefore, learns only to use them." Jackson (1987) also points to the dangers of what she dubs "competency-based vocational education" as a way of conceiving of the outcomes of training: "This form of learning has built into it the subordination of the worker to the employer, not as a matter of proper attitudes or discipline, but as a feature of the division of working knowledge itself" (p. 358). Valli (1986) points out how the authority relations that are encouraged in a high school coop class and the technical construction of skills correspond to the relations of the workplace.

> The ideological messages the students received were fairly congruent with the gender-specific patterns and relations they had become accustomed to both in their homes and at school. In the process of elaborating their lives at work, the students utilized a fairly conventional culture of femininity which identified them not as "raw labor power," but as sex objects, on the one hand, and as office wives and mothers on the other. (p. 169)

The vocational teacher in a business program concerns herself with preparing students for office jobs. Students' "employability" dominates curriculum discourse, but its meaning is constructed, just as the meaning of "skills" is constructed, for it is quite unclear what kinds of knowledge, skills, beliefs, and attitudes it entails. The version of office work reflected in the curriculum will reflect notions of what work entails, how capable students are, and what the responsibilities of employers are to educated workers. What is "needed" by the employer to get the work done faster is different from what is "needed" by the worker herself to get some control of the work process. What women need to cope with sexual harassment and take advantage of promotion opportunities is different from what men need to preserve their privileged access to power. Each of these accounts of what is needed might be different again from what is needed by the consumer of the services that are produced by the company. Whose needs count? This is a question that instructors implicitly or explicitly decide in arriving at a curriculum.

There are many structural pressures forcing educational institutions to take a narrow view of vocational training and turn out minimally educated workers able to carry out specific tasks. One instructor who emphasizes correctly filling out legal forms in her class stresses the need to please the business community:

> If you can match the students to the firms, you keep the firms happy. That then enhances the program . . . by putting a good student out, they [employers] are happy and they'll come back again. They will tell their friends and their friends tell their friends. That's the way it works. In this way we keep our own program marketable . . . my program will crunch if I don't get the support of the business community.

She emphasizes specific manual tasks in class, and stresses the importance of keeping the forms and equipment she uses similar to those used in downtown offices. She simulates the office in her classroom, treating her students as employees who are graded on speed and accuracy. Many vocational instructors in business areas have been supervisors or employers of clerical workers. Increasingly they have been educated in faculties of commerce, and they identify with the problems of management.

On the other hand, instructors see themselves as educators, helping students to learn and ultimately to lead more satisfying lives. Some have worked in clerical jobs. They are in close contact with students, and often empathize with their problems and frustrations. They also have an interest in upgrading the status of the occupation, a status that they as instructors come to share:

> I don't believe that the college's responsibility is to turn out workers who will be able to be re-plugged in on the 5th floor of the Bentall Centre. . . . [The employer's] description of what a student would need to know is based on their point of view of standing in their office wanting to get more work done faster for less. . . . I think they are looking for a person who will almost come ready made so it makes their interviewing easier . . . like they can measure them up on the wall and see if they are exactly the right shape and it can completely absolve them of the responsibility for on-going training in that person's working life. That makes me angry. I think it is their responsibility.

This instructor wants to broadly educate her students, ask them questions, provoke them to think. Echoing Dewey, she says, "the most important thing for you to know is what values you are looking for in order to make a reasonable decision; I guess I secretly hope that if I plant enough of those ideas that they will agitate for the right to make those decisions, rather than just accepting."

Gender relations can also be reproduced in a rote way or introduced as a social issue for reflection. As one instructor explains, "Last week someone phoned me up and said, 'I need somebody and she's going to have to be good looking'—and I went 'Oh!' I mean they say these things to me that they would not say to a lot of other people because it is against all human rights and the rest of it." But knowing the importance of dress in the workplace, the instructor tells students how to dress while they are in training. "I tell them basically what to wear . . . isn't that awful? But I do." She describes the students who will not get a job:

> She had a disgusting attitude, she dressed poorly and her attitude was obnoxious. . . . She has dress problems . . . her hair sticks out like this, she looks like the Wild Woman of the West, she is not going to get a job, it's as easy as that. Forget it. She isn't even going to be looked at for 20 seconds.

On the other hand, a different instructor takes up feminist issues in class, encouraging students to take their careers seriously and discussing the devaluation of women's work. She talks about issues in the workplace, safety standards, and ergonomics. She sees dress as an issue to be "discussed" in class and "negotiated" between employer and worker. She talks about the dilemmas this poses, not wanting to "take the responsibility of making students feel that they ought to stick up for their rights in a way that might just put them right out of the job market altogether."

But ultimately she wants to help her students by encouraging them to transform the nature of secretarial work.

When vocational education focuses on technique and doing what someone else requires, it reifies working activities, takes them out of their context and makes them an end in themselves. It separates the execution of tasks from thinking about them. It reflects a workplace where some people conceive of action and others act, a workplace where male managers make the decisions and female clerical workers carry them out. The distinction between a vocational education and a liberal one arose in the class system of the Greeks. Aristotle prescribed a liberal education for the citizens, and a vocational education for the slaves, the foreigners and the women. As women's role was to serve men, their education was to remain practical in its orientation, firmly separated from men's and lower in status. Dewey pointed out as much years ago as one who had developed notions of vocational education in his laboratory school in Chicago:

> Women are classed with slaves and craftsmen as factors among the animate instrumentalities of production and reproduction of the means for a free or rational life . . . slaves, artisans and women are employed in furnishing the means of subsistence in order that others, those adequately equipped with intelligence, may live the life of leisurely concern with things intrinsically worth while. (Dewey, 1916, p. 253)

It is this underlying separation of the hand and the head, the practical and the theoretical, that pervades vocational education as well as the class and gender system of the workplace. And it is this separation that must be reconstructed. Both academic education and vocational education suffer from the distinction. Any educated person must be educated for action or for some "community of practice," to borrow from the language of cognitive psychology. The sphere in which people will act makes a difference to the kind of education they will find useful, but it does not change the importance of thoughtful reflection on practices that involve physical, emotional, and social work.

CONCLUSIONS

What has been typically cast as "women's work" is crucial for the workplace, for production, for all of us. It has been trivialized and denigrated and devalued in a myriad of ways, in vocational programs as well as in the workplace. In this essay, I have set out two arguments about how the construction of training programs for women's work in offices fails to give women credit for what they do and could do more of with appropriate education. First, vocational education has tended to buy into technical skills talk and to draw on images of "skilled," male blue-collar work to garner respect. But the work women do in offices, and increasingly all the jobs we do, put a higher premium on interpersonal sensitivity and understanding the social relations of the office. There is no place for this in a classroom dedicated to technical proficiency. Education generally, and vocational education in particular, needs to find ways to incorporate social skills into the curriculum. Second, vocational education has assumed that workers carry out predetermined tasks, when a closer look at working knowledge shows how complex and contextual an understanding people need to perform well. What is taught in vocational classrooms needs to be rethought as contextual knowledge, where understanding of the whole is necessary for understanding of the parts (see Simon, Dippo, & Shenke, 1991). It needs to equip young people with the knowledge to analyze work critically, to challenge the existing relations of power and value. In this, it moves toward challenging the way all subject areas are defined, for it insists on the relevance of thinking for doing.

Gender is implicated not just in the overt messages young women receive about how to be feminine and dress appropriately, but in the ways they come to conceive of what is involved in "women's work." For the problem women have had in the workplace is not that they do not have skills and knowledge, but that their skills have not been counted. Women's jobs pay much less than men's jobs for the same level of education. Women's contributions to the economy are undervalued by every official measure that is used—the GNP excludes unpaid labor and undervalues women's paid labor, the "labor force" excludes unpaid labor, "skills" and "human capital" are defined in such a way that what women know and can do are not part of them. Women have not had the economic or ideological clout to insist on the economic value of their education, even when it is credentialed.

Vocational education will not solve these problems, but is a site of struggle over them. Vocational teachers need not reflect uncritically the taken-for-granted gender inequality that is built into the relations of work. A feminist vocational curriculum is part of a strategy to recognize and value the contributions women make to the work of the society. While taking on "women's issues" may seem a risky strategy for a subject that is already low in status, it can provide new resources and draw on the tradition of a progressive vocational education that was articulated at the turn of the century.

NOTES

1. All public education is linked to preparation for the workplace. A liberal education has substantial exchange value in the labor market, and students know it. Most students take liberal arts courses for the economic advantages they promise, not for the intellectual fascination of English poetry or Chinese history. However, in the secondary school, vocational courses are the ones that say they prepare students for work, and this gives a particular salience in the vocational curriculum to the "needs" of the workplace.

2. In contrast, apprenticeships were protected by some of the powerful male trade unions, and these unions were also able to negotiate other kinds of opportunities for training. As Cockburn (1983) shows, eventually the deskilling of the job weakens unions, but unions are able to insist on training and skilled status well beyond their necessity in the workplace.

3. Women were excluded from the skilled trades, at least by the late nineteenth century in Europe and North America. Women worked in their own trades as well as in the home. They were less often organized, less often explicitly trained for their work, and their skills, instead of being mysterious and esoteric, became the skills of "everywoman."

4. See Georgia Collins's discussion, in this volume, of art educators taking on the feminine for a similar concern in another marginal subject area.

REFERENCES

Acker, Joan. (1988). Class, gender and the relations of distribution. *Signs, 13*(3), 473–497.

Benet, M. K. (1972). *Secretarial ghetto.* New York: McGraw-Hill.

Braverman, Harry. (1974). *Labour and monopoly capitalism.* New York: Monthly Review Press.

British Columbia Ministry of Education. (1990). *Gender equity: Distribution of females and males in the British Columbia school system.* Victoria, BC: Author.

Cockburn, Cynthia. (1983). *Brothers: Male dominance and technological change.* London: Pluto Press.

Cohen, Marjorie. (1991). *Restructuring of women's employment opportunities: Policy implications for feminist organizing.* A paper presented at the OISE, Toronto.

Davies, Marjorie. (1983). *Women's place is at the typewriter: Office work and office workers.* Philadelphia, PA: Temple University Press.

Dewey, John. (1916). *Democracy and education.* New York: Free Press.

Drost, Walter. (1977). Social efficiency reexamined: The Dewey-Sneddon controversy. *Curriculum Inquiry, 7*(1), 19–32.

Economic Council of Canada. (1990). *Good jobs bad jobs.* Ottawa, Ontario: Author.

England, Paula. (1982). The failure of human capital theory to explain occupational sex segregation. *Journal of Human Resources, 17*, 358–370.

England, Paula, Chassic, M., & McConnock, L. (1982). Skill demands and earnings in female and male occupations. *Sociology and Social Research, 66,* 147–168.

England, Paula G., Farkas, B., Kilbourne, M., & Dau, T. (1988). Explaining sex segregation and wages: Findings from a model with fixed effects. *American Sociological Review, 53*(4), 544–558.

England, Paula, & Norris, Bahar. (1985). Comparable worth: A new doctrine of sex discrimination. *Social Science Quarterly, 66,* 627–643.

Eyre, Linda. (1991). Gender relations in the classroom: A fresh look at coeducation. In J. Gaskell & A. McLaren (Eds.), *Women and education* (pp. 193–220, 2nd ed.). Calgary, AB: Detselig.

Fudge, Judy, & McDermott, Pat. (1991). *Just wages: The politics of pay equity.* Toronto: University of Toronto Press.

Gaskell, Jane. (1990). What counts as skill. In Judy Fudge & Pat McDermott (Eds.), *Just wages: The politics of pay equity* (pp. 141–159). Toronto: University of Toronto Press.

Gaskell, Jane. (1992). *Gender matters from school to work.* Milton Keynes, UK: Open University Press.

Gilligan, Carol, Lyons, Nona, & Hanmer, Trudy. (1990). *Making connections: The relational worlds of adolescent girls at Emma Willard School.* Cambridge, MA: Harvard University Press.

Glen, Evelyn, & Feldberg, Roslyn. (1977/1978). Degraded and deskilled: The proletarianization of clerical work. *Social Problems, 25,* 52–64.

Goodson, Ivor, & Dowbiggan, Ian. (1991). *Subject status and curriculum change: Commercial education in London, Ontario 1920–1940.* Paper presented to workshop no. 2 of the Transition from School to Work Network, London, Ontario.

Grignon, Claude. (1971). *L'ordre des choses.* Paris: Minuit.

Gunderson, Morley. (1990). *Women and labour market poverty.* Ottawa, Ontario: Canadian Advisory Council on the Status of Women.

Hochschild, Arlie. (1983). *The managed heart: Commercialization of human feeling.* Berkeley: University of California Press.

hooks, bell. (1984). *Feminist theory: From margin to center.* Boston: South End Books.

Jackson, Nancy. (1987). Skill training in transition: Implications for women. In J. Gaskell & A. McLaren (Eds.), *Women and education* (pp. 351–371). Calgary: Detselig.

Jackson, Nancy. (1991). Skill training in transition implications for women. In J. Gaskell & A. McLaren (Eds.), *Women and education* (pp. 371–387). Calgary, AB: Detselig.

Jackson, Nancy, & Gaskell, Jane. (1987). White collar vocationalism: The rise of commercial education in Ontario and B.C. *Curriculum Inquiry, 17*(2), 177–201.

MacKeracher, Dorothy. (1990). Women's on the job procedural knowing. *Proceedings of the Canadian Association for the Study of Adult Education.* Victoria, British Columbia.

Martin, Jane Roland. (1985). *Reclaiming a conversation.* New Haven, CT: Yale University Press.

Meissner, Martin. (1991). *Savoir et faire: Structures de la connaissance pratique dans le travail des femmes au bureau et au domicile.* Paper presented at the Centre for Policy Studies in Education, University of British Columbia, Vancouver.

Menzies, Heather. (1989). *Fast forward and out of control: How technology is changing your life.* Toronto: Macmillan.

Noddings, Nel. (1984). *Caring: A feminine approach to ethics and moral education.* Berkeley, CA: University of California Press.

Oppenheimer, Valerie K. (1970). *The female labour force in the United States* (Population Monograph Series No. 5). Berkeley: University of California, Institute of International Studies.

Phillips, Anne, & Taylor, B. (1980). Sex and skill: Notes toward a feminist economics. *Feminist Review, 79.*

Pringle, Rosemary. (1988). *Secretaries talk: Sexuality power and work.* London: Verso.

Simon, Roger, Dippo, Don, & Shenke, Arlene. (1991). *Learning work.* Westport, CT: Bergin & Garvey.

Statistics Canada. (1991). *Women in Canada* (2nd ed.). Ottawa, Ontario: Author.

Steinberg, Ronnie. (1990). Social construction of skill: Gender power and comparable worth. *Work and Occupations, 17*(4), 449–482.

Tanguay, Lucie. (1985). Academic studies and technical education: New dimensions in an old struggle in the division of knowledge. *Sociology of Education, 58*(1), 20–33.

Tyack, David, & Hansot, Elizabeth. (1990). *Learning together: A history of coeducation in public schools.* New Haven, CT: Yale University Press.

Valli, Linda. (1986). *Becoming clerical workers.* London: Routledge & Kegan Paul.

Wolf, Wendy, & Rosenberg, Rachel. (1978). Sex structure of occupations and job mobility. *Social Forces, 56*(3), 823–844.

CHAPTER 4

Reading and the Female Moral Imagination: "Words Mean More Than What Is Set Down on Paper"

FRANCIS E. KAZEMEK

While her sisters are vying with false protestations of love to secure their father's kingdom in the opening scene of *King Lear,* Cordelia says in an aside, "I am sure my love's / More ponderous than my tongue." When King Lear asks his "joy" to speak publicly of her love for him, Cordelia tells him that she has nothing to say. Lear threatens her with loss of fortune, and she says, "Unhappy that I am, I cannot heave / My heart into my mouth. I love your Majesty / According to my bond, no more nor less." Lear asks, "So young, and so untender?" She responds, "So young, my lord, and true." The king then disowns and banishes her. This misunderstanding between a father and daughter who love each other deeply leads eventually to their deaths. Lear is a proud, impulsive, and pigheaded man who gauges love according to the *quantity* of its expressions, however false. The love and moral bond between him and his daughters is something that can be counted. Cordelia, on the other hand, understands the love and moral bond between Lear and herself in *qualitative* terms; it is a relationship that cannot be measured.[1]

We can explore the moral confusion that Shakespeare represents as arising between Lear and Cordelia in terms of contemporary views of moral development. Lear's moral stance is a "male" morality, albeit a misguided version, which arises out of his experiences as a man and is concerned with universal principles, rights, rules, and hierarchies of value, as expounded, for example, by Kohlberg (1981). This orientation emphasizes a principled reciprocity among people (for example, "Do unto others as you would have them do unto you") that allows each person to develop as a moral *individual*. Cordelia's stance reflects a "female" morality, which arises out of women's experiences and is less concerned with abstract principles and separation than it is with the development of concrete, contextual, and caring connections among individuals as selves-in-relation (Gilligan, 1982; Jordan, Kaplan, Miller, Stiver, & Surrey, 1991; Noddings, 1984).

In this essay I explore what I call the "female moral imagination" and its implications for reading education. The relationship between Lear and Cordelia, with all of its reticence, denial, suffering, love, and reconciliation, will serve as an introduction and exemplar. Cordelia embodies an outlook that is central to the female moral imagination, education in general, and reading education in particular. The central thesis of my essay is straightforward: *Reading education is a moral endeavor and not simply the transmission and acquisition of some set of amoral skills.* It entails the creation of a moral and social intelligence among teachers and students. Reading is always *for* something, and at the center of that something is the moral community. The stories we read, as Robert Coles (1989, p. 205) tells us, can help us as we try "to find a good way to live this life."

FEMALE MORAL IMAGINATION

Feminist scholars and writers from a variety of disciplines have explored different dimensions of the female moral imagination and its implications for education. For example, in developmental psychology we find the work of Carol Gilligan (1982) and Mary Belenky and her colleagues (Belenky, Clinchy, Goldberger, & Tarule, 1986); in the philosophy of education, Maxine Greene (1988a), Nel Noddings (1984), and Sarah Ruddick (1989); and in literacy research, the groundbreaking work of Jennifer Horsman (1990). These researchers and scholars highlight the fact that relatedness is the basic human reality and not separation or some form of unhealthy, typically "rugged," individualism. Relatedness is manifest in (1) concrete and contextualized thinking, acting, imagining, and ways of being moral; (2) the care, concern, and mutuality that people exhibit in their daily work, for example, the work of mothers; and (3) the manner in which truth is integrally tied not only to reason but also to the body, feelings, and imagination, and is socially constructed. Let's look in a little more depth at these dimensions of relatedness.

Noddings (1984, p. 24) says that morality involves the caring relationship between "one-caring" and "one-cared-for." To care is not to act by fixed rules but by affection and regard: "To act as one-caring, then, is to act with special regard for the particular person in a concrete situation." Caring involves stepping out of one's own personal frame of reference and into that of the "one-cared-for"; likewise, it requires the recognition and response of the "one-cared-for." In these terms we can fault both Lear and Cordelia for their failure to maintain a caring relationship. However, the difference in their moral orientations is clearly seen toward the end of the play when Cordelia returns and kneels at the side of the physically and spiritually crushed king. Lear, still perceiving the world in terms of rights and rules, says to her:

> If you have poison for me, I will drink it.
> I know you do not love me; for your sisters
> Have (as I do remember) done me wrong.
> You have cause, they have not.
>
> (Act IV, Scene VII, lines 72–77)[2]

Cordelia responds with one of the most beautiful lines in Shakespeare: "No cause, no cause." Cordelia thus demonstrates her love for Lear and her moral beauty in a specific situation. She was incapable of her sisters' abstract and empty expressions of love but is able to act in a difficult context. Her care and concern are grounded in the particular work she does as the now-queen of France and daughter-*cum*-mother to her "child-changed father." She embodies the maternal thinking and protectiveness that begins in the mother-child relationship and then expands into the wider world through webs of relationships (Ruddick, 1989, p. 79). Ruddick says that this "female" way of being in the world is very different from an overtly "male" way of being that is manifest by "especially 'masculine' men (and sometimes women)": "They imagine a truth abstracted from bodies and a self detached from feelings. . . . Fearful of the dependencies in which connection begins, they become attached to detachment, developing ideals of objectivity that turns on separation and distance" (Ruddick, 1989, p. 132).

It is through connections, dependencies, and circles of caring, these feminist scholars tell us, that we arrive at tentative, often conflicting truths. Reality and truth are not fixed and bodiless abstractions that can be arrived at through some set of controlled procedures and objective detachment. Rather, they are inseparably connected to our bodies, experiences, cultures, imaginations, and interactions with others (Johnson, 1987; Ruddick, 1989). The female moral imagination, rooted in relatedness, opens the world to us, offers us possibilities, allows us to question and challenge, and encourages us to consider other ways of being in the world:

The web of relationships need not weaken or deflect from the pragmatic or worldly concerns. But it may well make it possible for that worldly interest to be transformed into something pulsating, alive, and forever open to more and more perspectives, to more and more dialogue, to more and more interruptions by persistent, unfailing life. (Greene, 1990, p. 377)

Lear learns of humanity by going out onto the storm-wracked heath and enduring physical, spiritual, and mental suffering. Truth and love he discovers are not abstract or quantifiable things that can be called up on demand. They are learned and earned by opening oneself to others, by establishing living connections with humankind. The night Lear spends with the Fool and Edgar masquerading as Tom O'Bedlam forces him to consider the plight of others:

> Poor naked wretches, wheresoe'er you are,
> That bide the pelting of this pitiless storm,
> How shall your houseless heads and unfed sides,
> Your looped and windowed raggedness, defend you
> From seasons such as these? O, I have ta'en
> Too little care of this.
>
> (Act III, Scene IV, lines 28–33)

At last he learns that morality means we take care of ourselves by taking care of others.

MULTIPERSPECTIVAL VIEW OF LIFE

A major focus of the feminist research and scholarship I have cited is the importance of being open to alternative ways of seeing the world. Belenky, Clinchy, Goldberger, and Tarule have explored five epistemological perspectives from which women view and know the world (1986). Moving from perspectives in which they either have no voice or simply accept the world as described for them by others (quite often men), women who have gained control over their lives tend to see the world from a position of "constructed knowledge" in which they "view all knowledge as contextual, experience themselves as creators of knowledge, and value both subjective and objective strategies for knowing" (p. 15). Operating from a perspective of constructed knowledge, women understand that there are always alternatives to prescribed ways of being or doing, that the world is beautiful, various, and new.

Maxine Greene (1988a) contends that the primary purpose of education is to foster this multiperspectival view of life. Children and young adults need to see life as rich, complex, and tentative—and to understand that they have multiple options, that there are *versions of truth*. Such a perspective fosters dialogue about and exploration of how to be and act in different situations. For example, through dialogue and careful examination, teachers and students can study the "abstractness that characterizes military discourse as a whole" (Ruddick, 1989, p. 146). Why are expressions like "collateral damage," "smart bombs," and "clean bombs" used? Who uses them? What kind of reality is being constructed and defended through the use of such language? Are there alternatives to this language and reality?

I must caution that what I am calling the female moral imagination is not necessarily gender-specific. Gilligan (1982) and Noddings (1984) have stressed the fact that males may make moral judgments based on caring and connection while females may make judgments based on rules, rights, separation, and reciprocity. In our society, however, this tends not to be the case. The emphasis on caring, nonviolent conflict resolution and tolerance of divergent perspectives are ideals that these feminist scholars find women striving toward. A particular woman qua woman is not necessarily tolerant, nonviolent, and caring. Women actively participate in hate groups (Zia, 1991), and as the Persian Gulf War and its aftermath have shown us, women as well as men can be cheerleaders for death and destruction: "War is exciting; women, like men, are prey to the excitements of violence and community sacrifice it promises" (Ruddick, 1989, p. 54).[3]

A multiperspectival view of life recognizes the importance of the imagination and respects it. The imagination is recognized as creative, transformative, and potentially subversive because it allows us to construct alternatives to dominant perceptions and ways of being in the world. The imagination and its primary instrument, metaphor, are thus fostered as inseparable components of an education for moral and social intelligence:

> To learn, after all, is to become different, to see more, to gain a new perspective. It is to choose against things as they are. To imagine is to look beyond things as they are, to anticipate what might be seen through a new perspective or through another's eyes. (Greene, 1988b, p. 49)

Education with the moral imagination at its center accordingly values the stories we hear, tell, read, and write (Bruner, 1984, 1986). Lear finally realizes the importance of dialogue, of being open to the other, as he and Cordelia are being led to prison.

Come, let's away to prison.
We two alone will sing like birds i' th' cage.
When thou dost ask me blessing, I'll kneel down
And ask of thee forgiveness. So we'll live,
And pray, and sing, and tell old tales . . .
And take upon 's the mystery of things
As if we were God's spies

(Act V, Scene III, lines 8–17)

READING EDUCATION FROM A FEMINIST PERSPECTIVE

What implications does the above discussion of female morality, with its emphasis on caring and connections, and of a multiperspectival view of life, with its emphasis on the creative power of the imagination, have for reading education? There are several implications, which I will explore in this part of the essay. Let's look briefly at a work of literary and moral power that will serve as a touchstone for this section. In her autobiography, *I Know Why the Caged Bird Sings*, Maya Angelou describes the impact that an old woman, a Black "aristocrat" of Stamps, Arkansas, had on her as a sexually and spiritually wounded African-American child (1969). She says that the woman, Mrs. Flowers, "threw me my first life line" (p. 77). The lifeline that Mrs. Flowers threw was literature, language, and an understanding of the connection between life and books. She offered her own books to Maya and guided her reading; talked with her about the wisdom of books and the wisdom of common, uneducated people; and modeled the importance of the reader in the reader-writer transaction:

Your grandmother says you read a lot. Every chance you get. That's good, but not good enough. Words mean more than what is set down on paper. It takes the human voice to infuse them with the shades of deeper meaning. (p. 82)

When Mrs. Flowers read *A Tale of Two Cities* aloud to her, Maya says, "I heard poetry for the first time in my life." This sharing of books with a wise and caring woman saved her. It gave her a chance "to exchange the Southern bitter wormwood for a cup of mead with Beowulf or a hot cup of tea and milk with Oliver Twist" (p. 84).

The relationship between Mrs. Flowers and Maya offers us a touchstone for reading education. First, Mrs. Flowers cares for the individuality of Maya and all of the complexity that this particularity entails. Second, she models for the child the importance of language, books, and reading; she demonstrates how imaginative literature can help us participate in and understand other lives and times while helping us learn how to live our own lives. Third, Mrs. Flowers shares the books *she* treasures with Maya; her love for them is contagious. Fourth, Maya learns of the importance of hearing the language of literature and of actively re-creating the author's voice. Fifth, Mrs. Flowers connects literature to the universal nature of storytelling. She honors community stories and storytellers:

> As I ate she began the first of what we later called "my lessons in living." She said that I must always be intolerant of ignorance but understanding of illiteracy. That some people, unable to go to school, were more educated and even more intelligent than college professors. She encouraged me to listen carefully to what country people called mother wit. That in those homely sayings was couched the collective wisdom of generations. (p. 83)

The relationship between Mrs. Flowers and Maya embodies the female moral imagination and provides us as reading/language arts teachers with a set of guideposts as we attempt to develop a viable curriculum. Let's look at these guideposts and some examples that embody them.

Reading Education as a Moral Endeavor

If we believe that form should follow function, then we must distinguish between the form and function of reading education. The work of the feminist researchers and scholars already cited and that of the philosopher-educator John Dewey helps us see that the function of reading education is to help develop the moral, critical, and social intelligence of our students and ourselves. In a world dramatically divided into those with too much or enough and those with little if anything, reading should foster caring, compassion, and responsibility for those less fortunate than ourselves. This certainly is not the only function of reading and reading education, and I am not promoting reading as a propagandistic or crudely didactic tool. However, as the ancients tell us, the purpose of reading and literature is to delight and instruct. Without delight, there will be little instruction; without instruction, delight can become shallow and self-indulgent. Regardless of what various literary critics contend to the contrary, we cannot dismiss the shaping power of what we read. The novelist John Gardner (1978) argued for the importance of "moral fiction," and critic Wayne Booth (1988) contends that it *does* indeed make a difference what "company we keep" in our reading. The function of reading and reading education that I would advocate entails developing what I have called the female moral imagination, with its emphasis on relatedness, and the multiperspectival view of life, with its emphasis on the imagination: "Our definition of relationship implies a sense of knowing oneself and others through a process of mutual relational interaction and continuity of 'emotional-cognitive dialogue' over time and space" (Surrey, 1991, p. 62).

The *form* of reading education must therefore reflect its primary function. Packaged programs, reading series, basal readers, and the like, for the great part ignore this function and instead emphasize a neutral or amoral form. Thus, we see reading education divided into so many scope and sequence charts, skills lists, and so forth. "It is about effectiveness, not truthfulness or rightness in the moral sense" (Brown, 1991, p. 234). Children spend 3 to 4 years supposedly "learning how to read" and then the next 8 years or so supposedly "reading to learn." The content of what they're reading is secondary. This emphasis on form is so encompassing that to discuss the moral function of reading with teachers, administrators, and curriculum developers is to encounter quizzical expressions, vigorous expressions about "not teaching morals," or exegeses of the "upper levels" of Bloom's Taxonomy.

Literature That Fosters a Multiperspectival View of Life

How are we to emphasize the function of reading education and not sacrifice it to form? Our second guidepost points the way: a path that continues to be discussed—the literature-based curriculum. From a feminist perspective, however, we are not satisfied with any literature, no matter how "whole language" it might be. Rather, we are eager to build our reading program around the wealth of children's and adolescent literature that fosters a caring, tolerant, nonviolent, messily-complex, and imaginatively-rich society and a multiperspectival view of life. Like Mrs. Flowers, we want to share with our students the books that *we* treasure and that have helped to shape *our* lives.

The company we keep in our reading as teachers will have a decided impact upon the company our students keep. It is impossible to prescribe a list of books that "foster a multiperspectival view of life." Such a list necessarily will be idiosyncratic, depending upon the particular teacher's own life experiences, and interests. Moreover, such a list would negate the particularity and contextuality of reading. In effect, it simply would be another reading series or anthology. The important thing is that we as teachers *do* have such idiosyncratic and ever-growing lists that we develop through our personal and professional reading, discussions with colleagues, and interactions with students. I'm almost embarrassed to write this because it is so obvious, but the reading curriculum ultimately depends upon what teachers read and not upon skills lists, comprehension strategies, and universal lists of "good books" for children at particular grade levels. Teachers who don't read quite obviously are held captive by the opinions, tastes, and ideologies of others, for example, textbook publishers.

Let's look at some examples of books that foster this feminine commitment to a caring, nonviolent, and imaginatively-rich society and a multiperspectival view of life. As exemplars, I've selected works that I enjoy and that deal with homelessness in contemporary society. The Newbery Award winning *Maniac Magee* by Jerry Spinelli (1990) takes us into the world of a homeless orphan who lives in a deer shed at the zoo, abandoned cars, empty garages, and a band shell in the park. He is a larger-than-life character capable of prodigious athletic feats. His history, the author tells us, is "one part fact, two parts legend, and three parts snowball" (p. 2). In the novel, we see how Maniac connects, often humorously, with those around him, whether they are Black, White, young, or old. Through his actions antagonistic individuals and racial groups are brought together. In Noddings's (1984) terms, he acts both as "one-caring" toward others and as "one-cared-for" who is able to receive and acknowledge the love and concern of others. He thinks at one time:

> Whites never go inside blacks' homes. Much less inside their thoughts and feelings. And blacks are just as ignorant as whites. What white kid could hate blacks after spending five minutes in the Beales' house? And what black kid could hate whites after answering Mrs. Pickwell's dinner whistle? (p. 159)

This kind of particular and grounded understanding combined with wonderful dialogue and plenty of action makes *Maniac Magee* a joy to share and explore with intermediate and middle school students.

A more grittily realistic novel of homelessness is Virginia Hamilton's *The Planet of Junior Brown* (1971). In it we meet Buddy, a tough African-American street kid in the eighth grade. Buddy is wise beyond his years because he has had to survive on his own. He understands that there are many kids like himself in the city: "It was not that no one cared about them, Buddy knew. It was simply that no one had any idea they existed" (p. 64). Buddy knows they exist and that even those who live in comfortable homes, like his friend Junior Brown, can be psychologically homeless. More importantly, he cares, and acts. In almost Biblical language he addresses a group of homeless boys at the end of the novel:

"We are together," Buddy told them, "because we have to learn to live for each other. . . . If you stay here, you each have a voice in what you will do here. But the highest law for us is to live for one another. I can teach you how to do that." (p. 217)

Diane Duane's short story, "Midnight Snack" (1984), metaphorically explores the horrors of being homeless and hungry. Two teenagers go down into the subway system to feed the starving unicorns who live in its hidden recesses. Their shock of understanding and commitment to do something, however small, to help the starving creatures reflects a complex moral engagement:

He just stood there looking at the black, while it [a unicorn] tugged at the Danish and gazed back at him with those deep, sad eyes. I know that look. My eyes started burning, and my nose filled up. Nothing that lives in a subway should be that proud, and that hungry, and feel that helpless. Nothing that lives anywhere should. (Duane, 1984, p. 27)

As these three examples demonstrate, we cannot explore in our reading program works that foster a feminine commitment to care, concern, and a multiperspectival view of life without also exploring serious and complex social and political issues. Homelessness is simply one topic, on which Carey-Webb (1991) should be consulted for a detailed discussion of incorporating the theme into the language arts curriculum and an accompanying annotated bibliography of books and films. Unless our reading curriculum is based on works of "lulling blandness" (Engelhardt, 1991, p. 60), it is impossible for it to be anything but ideological. Even such seemingly "safe" or mindless (depending on one's perspective) romance novels for female adolescents as the *Sweet Valley High* series embody particular models of femininity and reflect particular racial/ethnic and sociopolitical ideologies (Christian-Smith, 1990). And ideology is perhaps even less acknowledged and discussed among educators than morality.

Yet, clearly, reading, literature, and language education from a feminine perspective must be embedded within, promote the exploration of, and foster the clarification of the social and moral context of our time. As Paulo Freire and others have pointed out many times, literacy is always political and ideological; it is never neutral. Thus, the reading curriculum is based not only on what teachers themselves read but also on how they then explore their reading with other educators and, necessarily, with parents who often articulate different ideological perspectives. It is only through such exploration and debate, and some tentative agreement, that we can hope to arrive at a vital reading curriculum. It is only then that we can begin to help children and young adults engage a great variety of works that not only delight, but also instruct.

Individualizing the Reading Program

If children and young adults are to have a great many opportunities to read widely and explore different contexts, lives, perspectives, and alternate ways of being in the world, then some form of individualization is necessary. A multiperspectival view of life will be developed only by exploring multiple perspectives, some of which may be antithetical to the teacher's, and perhaps parents', own moral and sociopolitical orientation. Fortunately, that's what reading education for critical, reflective, and caring citizenship entails: the self-selection and exploration of books and other reading materials and the right to choose "dangerous" texts. Wayne Booth (1988) advises us to always attend carefully to the situation of our reading:

> [W]e must both open ourselves to "others" that look initially dangerous or worthless, and yet prepare ourselves to cast them off whenever, after keeping company with them, we must conclude that they are potentially harmful. Which of these opposing practices will serve us best at a given moment will depend on who "we" are and what the "moment" is. (p. 488)

Such preparation is a lifelong affair. It begins with models who, like Mrs. Flowers, help us see how our lives and literature are complexly intertwined, for the better or the worse.

The kind of individualized reading program I am discussing here is grounded in a clearly articulated moral, sociopolitical, and ideological base. It is not simply another reading methodology or way of organizing the classroom for effective instruction (though there certainly is nothing wrong with that). The elements of an individualized program outlined by educators like Veatch (1978) and Holdaway (1979)—for example, self-selected reading, conferences, learning centers, and so on—may be necessary but are not sufficient for a program that has a moral purpose. In themselves, such elements are morally and ideologically neutral. They can be used to help children become bigots or champions of civil rights. We as educators should be concerned with helping students respond sympathetically to Cordelia's "No cause, no cause" and to Mrs. Flowers's admonition to be intolerant of ignorance but understanding of illiteracy.

What, then, is the teacher's role in such a program? How can the teacher have a moral and ideological orientation and at the same time allow students to explore and develop their own ideas, beliefs, and perspectives? Many educators contend that this cannot be done and thus advocate a neutral stance. Others, for example, from religious schools, overtly acknowledge the teacher's role as indoctrinator. We should reject the first position because it is based on a naive understanding of classroom interaction and learning; an attempt to be morally and ideologically "neutral" in the classroom is itself a moral and ideological stance. Likewise, we should reject the second because we are attempting to help students become caring, compassionate, and critically-thinking individuals but are not proselytizing any particular set of doctrinaire beliefs.

The teacher's role in such a reading program is to serve as a model, guide, and coach. (Again, it is nearly impossible to be any of these if one does not read widely, continuously, and have one's own idiosyncratic list of "good" books.) The teacher's responsibility is to share, suggest, clarify, listen, challenge, teach strategies where necessary, and provide a classroom context in which books and ideas can be explored and tested. If reading is basically learned by reading (Smith, 1988), then the emphasis must be upon the students' reading and not upon the teacher's teaching:

> Your structuring best comes when you organize a classroom library, provide directions for reading activities, and confer with individuals about choices of texts. If you predigest form and content for your students, you will rob them of their education by short-circuiting their thinking. (Moffett & Wagner, 1991, p. 70)

The amount of guidance provided by the teacher will vary, as Booth says, depending upon who "we" are and what the "moment" is: first graders will undoubtedly need more modeling, guidance, and coaching than twelfth graders.

Reading as a Social Process

Philosophers (Dewey, 1976), developmental psychologists (Vygotsky, 1978), sociologists (Goffman, 1959), and feminist scholars (Belenky et al., 1986) have all highlighted the social nature of the self. We are to a great extent who we are because of others and our interactions with them. Similarly, literary and literacy scholars, especially Rosenblatt (1978, 1991), have stressed the social as well as the personal nature of reading. The reading of a text involves both private and public meanings. Thus, to foster the feminine webs of care and concern and the multiperspectival orientation to life discussed by Greene, the reading program must not only recognize the social nature of literacy but also must highlight it. This means that students need plenty of opportunities to share their readings and personal meanings with others.

There are a number of classroom activities that allow students to act on their reading in a social manner, and I will discuss some of them in the next section. It is all too easy, however, to lose the forest for the trees by focusing too much on often ingenious reading "extension" activities. (There seem to be an unlimited number of these if professional journals, teachers' magazines, and "whole language" idea books are any indication.) The best and most natural way of helping students share their personal meanings and encouraging them to test their own ideas, beliefs, and interpretations is through talk. Small group discussions among students and between a few students and the teacher provide opportunities for spirited talk, clarification, disagreement, and perhaps consensus. The purpose of such talk is not to arrive at the "right" answers or meanings but to help students see that reading and ideas *do* matter. The poet Adrienne Rich says that "Reading and writing/aren't sacred yet people have been killed/as if they were" (Rich, 1986, p. 109). Like Maya Angelou, students will experience the poetry and power of books and reading only when they share them with others.

It is through such discussions that the teacher can help students focus on the moral and sociopolitical issues, questions, and quandaries found especially in imaginative literature. Katherine Patterson's recent novel, *Lyddie* (1991), provides a case in point. Lyddie is a poor Vermont farm girl of the 1840s who has been "hired out" as a servant by her mother for 50 cents a week. She eventually leaves the job and makes her way to Lowell, Massachusetts where she gets a job as a "factory girl" in one of the mills. The relative independence and disposable income she gains from the job are contrasted with this vivid description of nineteenth-century corporate exploitation: "We're working longer hours [13–14 hours a day], tending more machines, all of which have been speeded up to demon pace, so the corporation can make a packet of money. Our real wages have gone down more often than they've gone up . . ." (p. 92).

This novel allows intermediate and middle school readers to enter into the life of a tough, working-class teenager and to explore questions of fairness, female solidarity, union organizing, blacklisting, and reading as a means of *both* liberation and control. (See Stuckey, 1990, for an examination of the "violence" of literacy.) When older and in senior high school, students who have enjoyed this novel might then be guided to Melville's chilling indictment of nineteenth-century capitalism, "The Tartarus of Maids" (1966).

The value of stories is that they allow us to enter into an almost infinite number of lives, times, and contexts. They allow us to experience vicariously what we might not want to or are unable to experience in our everyday lives. They will not foster by themselves the kind of compassion and understanding I have been discussing, however. The multiperspecti-val view of life is developed by sharing these vicarious experiences with others. As students read about Whites and African Americans, straights and gays, males and females, middle class individuals and those in pov-erty, young and old, and so on, they need to share these experiences with peers and the teacher. Through such ongoing dialogue, the *chances* of connections being made with the "other" are more likely. Reading and discussion alone may not change the way students perceive and act to-ward others. A much more comprehensive school-home-community pro-gram may be needed. It is beyond the scope of this chapter to elaborate such a program. Others have done so from varying viewpoints, as for example, Jonathan Kozol (1991). I am describing what the *individual* teacher can do in her or his classroom, recognizing all the while that it is this very structural individualism that contributes to isolation and alien-ation in our schools.

Stories that we read and explore with others can also serve as cata-lysts for our own stories. Scholars from a number of diverse disciplines have emphasized over recent years the importance of the narrative (Bruner, 1986; Schank, 1990). We are to a great extent the stories that we tell. Gossip, that form of narrative that is often associated with women and usually disparaged (by men), Spacks (1982) tells us, can be wise, "healing talk" that embodies the distinctly human: "Yet the immediacy and reality of gossip's material often generate deeper humanity, more penetrating analysis that one finds in any but the best fiction: the moral risks of gossip accompany real moral possibility" (p. 38). Thus, talk about books should also lead to talk about students' own lives, experiences, loves, dislikes, hopes, fears, and so forth. Such small group talk and more intimate partner-to-partner talk conjoined with writing about their expe-riences and feelings in journals, *Foxfire*-type reminiscences, and poetry will help students make the connections between their own lives and those in literature.

SOME ACTIVITIES

While talk is the best way of sharing the private and public meanings of texts, testing ideas and perspectives, and discovering connections with other, often diverse, people, there are related activities that should form a key part of an individualized program. The important thing, once again, is that these activities follow naturally from the reading and help students further explore the text; they must not become an end in themselves. Response activities should be opportunities for students to retell, extend, and transform what they have read by engaging with their peers in creative representations of the material (Squire, 1983). The best way of responding to a work of imagination is by creating another work of imagination. Role playing or spontaneous drama provides one such opportunity. After reading, students select a chapter or scene—or, for younger students, even a whole book—and plan how to reenact it. The discussion involved; the probing of characters' motivations; the assumption of different points of view; and the active, physical engagement with the text foster the content and context for developing understanding, care, concern, and a multiperspectival view of life.

For example, Alice Childress's novel, *A Hero Ain't Nothin' but a Sandwich* (1973), presents the inner-city world of African Americans through first-person accounts of the various characters involved. It is the story of a 13-year-old heroin addict, his family, friends, and neighborhood. In an unflinching manner, it deals with the dangers, despair, yet love and hope of a ghetto community. Benjie, the heroin addict, is tentatively rescued at the end of the novel by his stepfather, Butler Craig. Butler is a quiet hero who embodies Noddings's notion of "one-caring": "To act as one-caring, then, is to act with special regard for the particular person in a concrete situation" (Noddings, 1984, p. 24). He struggles with his own fears, doubts, and weaknesses to save Benjie:

> Had to get me another few days off from work. That's no big thing because the time can come offa my vacation. Afterall, I did get picked by Benjie, to be his father one hundred times [a note Benjie secretly wrote]. A chosen man so to speak. Well, some might say that me and circumstances ain't quite good enough for the job. But I know better. I can do what social worker, head shrink and blood kin can't—give a boy back to himself, so he can turn man. You better believe it. (Childress, 1973, p. 124)

In the context of this story, Butler's assertion is as powerful and moving as Cordelia's "No cause, no cause." This is the kind of text we want to encourage our students to creatively dramatize. Butler is the kind of man we want our students to "try on."

Readers' theater interpretations of texts and other oral performances also encourage students to look closely and think carefully about texts. Through discussion and rehearsals, they have to determine who particular characters are, why they act in certain ways, and how they can best present them in an oral interpretation. For example, we need to determine how to present the words of the ugly water-troll in Walter Wangerin, Jr.'s beautiful tale, *Elisabeth and the Water-Troll* (1991): "'Ohhh, pretty Beth,' he sighs, 'I did not want thee sad. I wanted to tell thee, this life is lovelier than bad'" (p. 36). The water-troll has stolen Elisabeth because, in Noddings's terms, he "feels with" and is "engrossed" in her sorrow and suffering over her dead mother. So we must consider how to interpret these words of the town mob who set out to save Elisabeth and to kill the troll:

> "God save the children!" roars the Sheriff. "Evil given, evil gotten, right?"
> "Right!"
> "A slasher—" the Sheriff cries.
> And the whole crowd answers, "—should be slashed!"
> "A killer—" the Sheriff howls.
> With the thrill of conviction the people thunder: "—should be killed!" (pp. 47, 50)

Group projects that encourage students to re-present a narrative in the form of a poem, a poem in the form of a narrative, a story in the form of a visual interpretation (murals are best here), or a story or poem in conjunction with a piece of popular or classical music help students to respond creatively to an author's work and perhaps to learn something about the culture whose art forms they are using, for example, Mexican murals, African-American raps, Japanese flute music, and so on. (Shuman and Wolfe's little 1990 booklet is a good place to begin reading and thinking about such activities.) These activities affirm the importance of the imagination and social collaboration and place reading among the other means of expression and communication. It helps students to place literacy within a broader context.

In the course of this chapter, I have explored the boundaries of reading education by considering various feminist lines of thought and research. I have focused on what I have called the female moral imagination and Maxine Greene's contention that we must help our students to develop a multiperspectival view of life. The key point I have argued for is a view of reading and reading education as moral endeavors dedicated to the ongoing development of the caring, compassionate, and critical individual and community. Feminist scholars such as Noddings, Gilligan, and Ruddick best help us see these moral connections. I have presented some examples of children's and adolescent literature that allow us and our students to engage in moral discourse. Lastly, I offered some classroom activities that I believe help our students to explore the worlds of texts. I want to affirm one last time my conviction that it *does* make a difference what "company we keep" in our reading program. The moral stance and actions of people like Cordelia, Mrs. Flowers, Buddy, the water-troll, and Butler Craig are what we want to celebrate with our students. For as Nel Noddings (1984, p. 49) maintains, "The greatest obligation of educators, inside and outside of formal schooling, is to nurture the ethical ideals of those with whom they come in contact."

NOTES

1. Typically we are critical of Lear for his irrational and hard-hearted behavior, but Cordelia herself is not blameless. Instead of telling him of her deep and continuing love after marriage, she uses Lear's own quantitative language: "Haply, when I shall wed, / That Lord whose hand must take my plight shall carry / Half my love with him, half my care and duty" (*King Lear,* 1.1.102–104). Thus, she unfortunately gives Lear the impression that her love for him will be less.
2. References are to act, scene, and line.
3. I recently gathered data for a follow-up study to that of Golden and Guthrie (1986). In "Convergence and Divergence in Reader Response to Literature" they examined the relationships between reader-based (personal beliefs and empathy) and text-based (plot events and plot conflict) factors in the construction of the meaning of a literary text by ninth graders. In addition, I was concerned with the ways that "moral stance," gender, age, and social interaction might affect the way a reader responds to a literary text. I had whole classes of students in Grades 6, 7, and 10, and at the freshmen level of college, read and respond to the short story "Reverdy" by Jessamyn West. I am just beginning to look at the data; however, I did scan the different moral stances adopted by readers in response to the text. Readers were asked to select from the three moral positions to follow and to explain why they did so: (1) a Kohlbergian "Golden Rule" stance, (2) a Kohlbergian "rights and rules" stance, and (3) a feminist stance of care and concern. It is interesting to note that the majority of students, both male and female, at all of the grade levels, chose the feminist moral stance.

REFERENCES

Angelou, Maya. (1969). *I know why the caged bird sings.* New York: Bantam Books.
Belenky, Mary F., Clinchy, Blythe M., Goldberger, Nancy R., & Tarule, Jill M. (1986). *Women's ways of knowing.* New York: Basic Books.
Booth, Wayne. (1988). *The company we keep: An ethics of fiction.* Chicago: University of Chicago Press.
Brown, Roger G. (1991). *Schools of thought: How the politics of literacy shape thinking in the classroom.* San Francisco: Jossey-Bass.

Bruner, Jerome. (1984). Language, mind, and reading. In Hillel Goelman, Antoinette Oberg, & Frank Smith (Eds.), *Awakening to literacy.* Portsmouth, NH: Heinemann.

Bruner, Jerome. (1986). *Actual minds, possible worlds.* Cambridge, MA: Harvard University Press.

Carey-Webb, Allen. (1991). Homelessness and language arts: Contexts and connections. *English Journal, 80* (November), 22–28.

Childress, Alice. (1973). *A hero ain't nothin' but a sandwich.* New York: Avon Books.

Christian-Smith, Linda K. (1990). *Becoming a woman through romance.* New York: Routledge, Chapman & Hall.

Coles, Robert. (1989). *The call of stories: Teaching and the moral imagination.* Boston: Houghton Mifflin.

Dewey, John. (1976). From the public and its problems. In J. Gouinlock (Ed.), *The moral writings of John Dewey* (pp. 230–251). New York: Hafner Press.

Duane, Diane. (1984). Midnight snack. In D. R. Gallo (Ed.), *Sixteen: Short stories by outstanding writers for young adults* (pp. 22–29). New York: Dell.

Engelhardt, Tom. (1991, June). Reading may be harmful to your kids: In the Nadirland of today's children's books. *Harper's Magazine,* pp. 55–62.

Gardner, John. (1978). *On moral fiction.* New York: Basic Books.

Gilligan, Carol. (1982). *In a different voice.* Cambridge, MA: Harvard University Press.

Goffman, Erving. (1959). *The presentation of self in everyday life.* Garden City, NY: Doubleday.

Golden, Joanne M., & Guthrie, John T. (1986). Convergence and divergence in reader response to literature. *Reading Research Quarterly, XXI,* 408–421.

Greene, Maxine. (1988a). *The dialectic of freedom.* New York: Teachers College Press.

Greene, Maxine. (1988b). What happened to imagination? In K. Egan & D. Nadaner (Eds.), *Imagination & education* (pp. 45–56). New York: Teachers College Press.

Greene, Maxine. (1990). Relationality in the humanities: A perspective on leadership. *Language Arts, 67,* 370–378.

Hamilton, Virginia. (1971). *The planet of Junior Brown.* New York: Collier Books.

Holdaway, Don. (1979). *The foundations of literacy.* Sydney: Ashton Scholastic.

Horsman, Jennifer. (1990). *Something in the mind besides the everyday: Women and literacy.* Toronto: Women's Press.

Johnson, Mark. (1987). *The body in the mind: The bodily basis of meaning, imagination, and reason.* Chicago: University of Chicago Press.

Jordan, Judith V., Kaplan, Alexandra G., Miller, Jean B., Stiver, Irene P., & Surrey, Janet L. (1991). *Women's growth in connection: Writings from the Stone Center.* New York: Guilford Press.

Kohlberg, Lawrence. (1981). *The philosophy of moral development.* New York: Harper & Row.

Kozol, Jonathan. (1991). *Savage inequalities: Children in America's schools.* New York: Crown.

Melville, Herman. (1966). The paradise of bachelors and The Tartarus of maids. In *Great short works of Herman Melville* (pp. 161–181). New York: Harper & Row.

Moffett, James, & Wagner, Betty J. (1991). Student-centered reading activities. *English Journal, 80* (October), 70–73.

Noddings, Nel. (1984). *Caring: A feminine approach to ethics and moral education.* Berkeley: University of California Press.

Patterson, Katherine. (1991). *Lyddie.* New York: E. P. Dutton.

Rich, Adrienne. (1986). Contradiction: Tracking poems. In *Your native and your life* (pp. 83–111). New York: W. W. Norton.

Rosenblatt, Louise M. (1978). *The reader: The text: The poem.* Carbondale: Southern Illinois University Press.

Rosenblatt, Louise M. (1991). Literature—S.O.S.! *Language Arts, 68,* 444–448.

Ruddick, Sarah. (1989). *Maternal thinking: Toward a politics of peace.* New York: Ballantine.

Schank, Roger C. (1990). *Tell me a story: A new look at real and artificial memory.* New York: Charles Scribner's Sons.

Shakespeare, William. (1969). *King Lear.* In William Shakespeare: The complete works (pp. 1065–1104). Baltimore: Penguin.

Shuman, R. Baird, & Wolfe, Denny. (1990). *Teaching English through the arts.* Urbana, IL: National Council of Teachers of English.

Smith, Frank. (1988). *Understanding reading.* Hillsdale, NJ: Lawrence Erlbaum.

Spacks, Patricia M. (1982). In praise of gossip. *Hudson Review, 35,* 19–38.

Spinelli, Jerry. (1990). *Maniac Magee.* Boston: Little, Brown.

Squire, James R. (1983). Composing and comprehending: Two sides of the same basic process. *Language Arts, 60,* 581–589.

Stuckey, J. Elspeth. (1990). *The violence of literacy.* Portsmouth, NH: Boynton/Cook.

Surrey, Janet L. (1991). The self-in-relation: A theory of women's development. In Judith V. Jordan, Alexandra G. Kaplan, Jean B. Miller, Irene P. Stiver, & Janet L. Surrey (Eds.), *Women's growth in connection: Writings from the Stone Center.* New York: Guilford Press.

Veatch, Jeannete. (1978). *Reading in the elementary school.* New York: Richard C. Owen.

Vygotsky, Lev S. (1978). *Mind in society: The development of higher psychological processes.* Cambridge, MA: Harvard University Press.

Wangerin, Walter, Jr. (1991). *Elisabeth and the water-troll.* New York: HarperCollins.

Zia, Helen. (1991, March/April). Women in hate groups. *Ms Magazine,* pp. 20–27.

CHAPTER 5

"The Feminist Trespass": Gender, Literature, and Curriculum

Ursula A. Kelly

> Literature, as a concept and a practice, is a particular selection and organization of texts . . . defined principally by its position and function in the curricular and pedagogic economy.
>
> (Batsleer, Davies, O'Rourke, & Weedon, 1985)

To begin to speak/write of the possibilities for a literature curriculum that contains and results from feminist analyses of literature and curriculum is to dream of disappearing daisies in a time of exciting theoretical reconceptualizations of history, culture, and identity. It is to wish for the eradication of both canons—literature and curriculum—as they each exist, hegemonically, as normalized, universalized, ahistorical, and elitist agents of the reproduction and continued reinsertion into discursive practices of conservative and oppressive sets of social relations. It is to argue for a shift from viewing reading as "an apolitical, internal, and individual activity to [viewing reading as] a socially and historically situated social practice" at work in the production and reproduction of certain community forms of human subjectivity (Christian-Smith, 1990, p. 141). Finally, it is to encourage the practice of reading production, meaning-making, as the focus of literature (and) curriculum whereby "our reading of the text becomes the curriculum," which "draws attention to the variety of readings, the partiality of any one view and our implications in historical social relations" (Lather, 1991, p. 145).

It is both a difficult and pressing question of which curricular and pedagogical practices might keep faith with these reconceptualizations while they remain sufficiently open to the ever-evolving insights gleaned out of the struggles, ambiguities, contradictions, and progressions of such practices. Arranged against a current backdrop of rationalism, ultraconservatism, and antifeminism, the questions raised by feminist poststructuralism about that edified subject of cultural imperialism, literature, seem all the more important and pressing. The terrain of culture is always the site of gender production; the state purveyor of literary culture, the literature classroom is where that work is done daily, often unnoticed, and usually unnamed but never uncontested by those subjected to and subjugated by the subject of literature.

CONTESTING THE "LITERARY" TERRAIN

The overwhelming preoccupation with what "they say we are" and "what we are not", our "otherization" by "them" precludes much exploration or importance of who we actually are. (Himani Bannerji, 1991)

For the desire to change life for the better may not be concentrated into a single conscious political channel, but may be dispersed into many rivulets and deltas, the network of available forms. (Jean Radford, 1986)

In discussions of feminist poststructuralism, literature, and curriculum, it seems necessary, somehow, to restate constantly and consistently, to recover and rediscover, renewed visions of an old history. It is as if we are always starting from the beginning, yet again, while hoping to move beyond the last time of speaking/writing about this. This must surely be a predicament, a condition, of speaking from the margins. Thus, it seems necessary to say, again, more vehemently, "ritualistically, in the way of chants and evocations" that, yes, the notion of "literature" is problematic for many, many reasons (Meese, 1986, p. 5). To continue to use it is, in many ways, to continue to assert its validity and to reproduce the characteristic privileges of gender, sexuality, class, race, and nation so violently etched in its history and use. To speak/write of literature is to speak/write of unbridled elitism, discrimination, exclusion, objectification, voyeurism, and what Janet Batsleer and her cowriters call "academic terrorism" sanctioned in and through the curriculum of educational institutions (1985, p. 28).

Feminists have long challenged the constitution of the literary canon, reclaiming from the dark corners of male literary history the voices of powerful women writing, and writing well, despite their pervasive and deliberate exclusion from the domain of legitimized public discourses of literary culture (Gilbert & Gubar, 1985; Spender, 1989). These efforts by feminist critics and literary historians have not resulted in any significant broadening of the literary canon. Instead, the double-edged result has been, for the most part, the establishment of a still marginalized "canon" of women writers whose works have found their way mainly into university courses on women and literature, women's studies, and women and writing. In public school curricula in Canada, for example, women writers are still severely underrepresented. Efforts to supplement and counteract this underrepresentation are hampered by unsupported costs and strict and limiting copyright laws.

These obstacles aside, it is in this domain of liberal feminism that the most common curricular intervention has been developed to address gender and literature. Such intervention, as important as it is, merely scratches the surface of the problem with literature, leaving largely uncontested more insidious aspects of the debate. With or without women writers, the notion of a canon of literature remains contentious, for "literary canons appear not just as selections but as hierarchies" (Batsleer et al., 1985, p. 29) of literary forms, genres, writers, representations, and cultures. The historical uses and present-day effects of these taken-for-granted and normalized discriminations must be the beginning of the project of literature undoing itself in its own classroom.

Furthering this project of undoing is the practice of "reading against," of giving voice, in classrooms of literature, to "resistant readers" and resisting readings (Fetterley, 1978). If "one of the major powers of the muted is to think against the current," then one of the ways in which gender consciousness can attempt to upstage the sanctioned readings of literature is through claiming dialogic space for resistance to these readings (Duplessis, 1985, p. 196). This strategy has been and continues to be one of survival not just for women, but for many disenfranchised groups, including communities of women who name their politics as falling within the spectra of feminism, for example, many lesbians (Warland, 1990), Afro-Canadian women (Nourbese Philip, 1990), and First Nations women (Maracle, 1990). Thus it is that women readers often find ourselves "reading against" objectifying, essentializing, and universalizing notions and representations of "woman" as White, heterosexual, dependent, subservient, and so on, a practice which, at once, seeks to name how a literary text works and to establish a counterposition, a resistant reading as political strategy.

Without undermining the importance of either of these fairly common feminist forms of curriculum/literary criticism, it remains necessary to point out their limits in terms of establishing a proactive practice aimed at naming the complex ideological relationship among texts, reading, and gender construction and identifying potential transformative disruptions in the terms and conditions under which this relationship takes place. The availability to students of more women writers, in all our social, sexual, and cultural diversity, and the insertion into curricula of feminist readings of canonical texts are absolute necessities in the face of legislated curricula in which are presented limited possibilities of "the way it is" in gendered relationships. As well, such measures leave untouched the more striking questions of what is read to fulfill notions of desire and pleasure in unlegislated contexts. Inserting such discourses is one of the major challenges of enriching curricula in and through feminist poststructuralism, a challenge that necessitates deconstructing the popular as well as the privileged texts of culture.

Challenging the sanctity of literature and its bolster, male-stream criticism, then, begs more compelling questions, the responses to which draw from a wider range of cultural spheres and cultural forms—questions of what culture, whose culture, in what form, under what circumstances, for what purposes, and with what meanings. These are questions pertaining to power, social relations, and human subjectivity. These are questions about readings that have at their heart a different agenda, one counter to the project of literature, that is, "to address the ideological and political concerns of the present-day reader" (Weedon, 1987, p. 163). Such critique is the groundwork of a larger, more interesting and, undoubtedly, more fruitful project for feminism and literature, the project of literature/literary studies/English studies as informed by feminist poststructuralism: literature as a cultural politics of gender, sexuality, class, race/ethnicity, ability, and nation.

REDEFINING READING AS PRAXIS

One of the most effective ways in which forms of eminence, for example, White heterosexual male privilege, are maintained in literary studies is through the guarded production of the "discriminating reader" of "discriminating texts," the major subject position offered the student of "literature." This reader/subject, for the most part, must accept the terms and conditions of the institution of "literature," based largely in White, heterosexual male knowledge and experience, as put forth by its critics and teachers. Those readers who will not accept fully these terms, whose desires, pleasures, and pains are fashioned differently, through different (yet, perhaps, similarly interested) discourses, fall by the wayside into the large pool called "the majority of readers" (often thought to be nonreaders), reading what Margaret Atwood (1991) sardonically calls "true trash," as the sanctity of "the reader" remains intact.

Literature is seen predominantly as the material basis of the development of "the life of the mind" (Arendt, 1977). Indeed, this argument is, in large part, the commonsense justification for the subject, literature, in a curriculum. This view of literature, as with most common sense views of any institution, has little to do with its actual history, that is, with any accounts of what literature does, how it works as only one form of knowledge. Reading, for its part, is predominantly seen as an activity of the insular variety, rarely understood, often theorized, and usually decontextualized. Where reading is more contextualized, as in mainstream reader-response criticism, reader responses are still often located and understood through the ideology of individualism. Less often is reading seen as the social practice it is, a practice in which the subjectivities of the readers, the conditions of reading, and the choice of texts are part of a larger set of social relations in which desire, pleasure, identity, community, culture, and politics are all players. As for readers, they, too, are isolated, individualized, stable, centered, and unified. And the reader is usually implicitly understood to be male, heterosexual, bourgeois, Christian, abled, and White: a reader/subject position I now call the "man advantage." The sociality of readers' multiple selves, fraught with the contradictions and tensions that make gendered subjectivity a struggle, ever contested, is often ignored.

In all of these juxtapositions, literature and reading work to produce certain political effects at the level of the gendered subject. These effects are mystified, hidden, and even misrepresented in dominant ideologies of literature and reading, those forms of theorizing and practice perpetuated in most official curricula. To challenge such hegemony, it is necessary not only to see literature as a political construct but, as importantly, to see reading itself as a politics. Within this politics, "literature is realized as praxis [for] [l]iterature acts on the world by acting on its readers" (Schweikert, 1986, p. 32). In what specific ways literature acts on its readers, in this case, the implications for gendered subjectivities of various readings of texts, of texts as various readings of the world, is a question in many ways begged in the dominant discourses of literary study.

To proceed from the theoretical position of reading as praxis, the political agenda of which is the resistance to and transformation of gender oppression, necessitates the recognition that the literature classroom is a complex and contradictory as well as a strategic site from which to operate. Legislated readings, the sort students produce for teachers (even though sometimes under the guise of producing them for themselves, for example, through the use of reading journals, response journals, and the like), will always be contaminated with the expectations, real or perceived, of authority. To make this point is not to argue that there are uncontaminated readings; to the contrary, the expectations of literary studies quite likely follow readers throughout their lifetimes, impacting not just on how readers read but also on how readers feel about their readings, the ghostly strains of indoctrination into literature. However, undeniably and unavoidably so, it seems, readings produced in formalized settings have in them the mediation of all sorts of desire and fears, not the least of which, particularly for women, may be the need to protect, in the face of literary authority, our tenuous control of those spaces in our lives where desire, pleasure, and satisfaction are read, if not actually lived, for example, in romance novels and romance magazines.

Focusing on how all readings are produced as mediations of competing and often conflicting discourses and on how texts are produced as partial readings of our worlds provides the groundwork for an understanding of how ideology works, socially, materially and personally, in the formation of subjectivity. This approach contrasts sharply with that of literature as the container and purveyor of "universal truths," of insights into an essential "human nature," and of "the best of what has been thought and said." Instead, its fundamental starting point is the well-grounded suspicion that Catherine Belsey identifies:

> Literature as one of the most persuasive uses of language may have an important influence on the ways in which people grasp themselves and their relation to the real relations in which they live. (Belsey, 1982, p. 66)

What feminist poststructuralism suggests to educators interested in the cultural ground of readers and texts, then, is to pursue in our classrooms "ways of reading which see texts for what they are—partisan discursive constructs offering particular meanings and modes of understanding" (Weedon, 1987, p. 172). Through such practice, readers can at least come to see how it is that texts suggest their readings, the possibility of reader positions in reading texts, and the suggestions of texts for gendered subjectivity and social relations. As well, as educators who share these classrooms, we need to be constantly aware of the insertion of our own institutionalized power and position into the production of any reading. It is necessary, too, to recognize that to understand readers more fully, and to mount effective political platforms based on a cultural politics of reading, means a foray into the readings conducted elsewhere than our classrooms, those readings and those texts relegated to the margins of dominant literary discourses, the so-called popular readings and popular texts.

PRODUCING THE GENDERED SUBJECT

[T]he power of all forms of subjectivity relies on the marginalization and repression of historically specific alternatives. (Weedon, 1987, p. 91)

At the crux of effective gendered subject production are the constructs of desire and pleasure. Tied to any forms of identity are deep and abiding senses of what women have come to want and to find pleasurable and how we women see ourselves being able to secure these wants in a smotheringly sexist, heterosexist, and racist world. Rosalind Coward (1985) describes this as the lure of privileged discourses:

> Feminine positions are produced as responses to the pleasures offered to us; our subjectivity and identity are formed in the definitions of desire which encircle us. These are the experiences which make change such a difficult and daunting task, for female desire is constantly lured by discourses which sustain male privilege. (1985, p. 16)

The work of literature in a curriculum is, in large part, to secure certain forms of "feminine positions" through the use of select texts, the encouragement of certain forms of readings, and the refusal to acknowledge the kind and degree of vested interests in the dominant discourses of criticism. The effect of such policing is tantamount to suggesting, through literature and criticism and the privileging of sexist and heterosexist discourses, that "That's just the way it is," while hiding behind the curtain of "fiction" which, for the doubtful, at least allows for the resistant rejoinder, "Not really."

Contesting the literary terrain and establishing a politics of reading practice, that is, recognizing the ideological basis of all discourse, text, and subjectivity, enhances the possibilities for challenging established notions of gender and sexual difference while creating spaces for the articulation of less oppressive gender positions. In other words, different discourses of literature and reading do allow for different subject positions, for it is within discourse that subjectivity is constituted. This argument is all the more important when we consider the array of often competing desires, for example, autonomy and heterosexual relationship, which arrange our gendered lives. With so much expectation of pleasure attached to the latter, the subject position of woman as heterosexual partner/lover/mother, it is little wonder that the initial desire for autonomy is quickly compromised, deferred, and, for many women, left unsatisfied. It is precisely this hierarchization of desire and pleasure that is most often circulated and "read with" in literature curricula, and reiterated in most other cultural forms (Gannett & Kelly, 1992). The very real sense with which these discourses of desire compete for our embrace is the pivotal ingredient for change. Chris Weedon suggests that the plurality of identities is the other key to this change: "Our sense of ourselves and of our femininity may be at times contradictory and precarious but only a conscious awareness of the contradictory nature of subjectivity can introduce the possibility of political choice between modes of femininity in different situations and between the discourses in which they have their meaning" (1987, p. 87). The literature classroom is certainly not the only site on which such consciousness may be nurtured. But in a subject area the specific agenda of which is human subjectivity, it is reasonable to expect that women should have some opportunities to examine and to assess the implications of varying ways of being and becoming feminine. In particular, speculating on how literature and readings work in this process of constructing gendered identity is a necessary critique of literary knowledge and its mediation by subjects that must also include those forms that compete with and/or work with the discourses of literature, for example, employment, family, media, and school (Gannett & Kelly, 1992). How any discourse is read and taken up by a subject should be the domain of the literature classroom.

To encompass these challenges to literature, feminist poststructuralism does demand a broadening of the scope of what can be discussed, of what is read, and of what curricular and pedagogical practices organize literary studies. If the political project of gender analyses of literature and curriculum has any worth at all it is in its commitment to work in the production of more conscious gendered subjects who see how all facets of culture work on, with, and against us; who are in touch with the contradictions and changing character of our struggles around subjectivity; and, most importantly, who can confront the ways in which we are implicated in our present circumstances while celebrating and acting on the desire to be agents in (re)shaping our present.

PRACTICES TO (AND FOR) THE CONTRARY

The transformation of literature and criticism as cultural institutions demands a language of defiance rather than the silent or unquestioning mimetic complicity expected of us in order to sustain phallocentrism. If it is any good, feminist criticism, all feminist writing, and from my view all criticism, is guaranteed to offend the mighty. Its contrariness is essential to its value, a barometer of its ultimate effectiveness. (Meese, 1986, p. 17)

Central to the project of gender, literature, and curriculum is the transformation of gendered lives and the social conditions in which those lives are lived. What is constituted as "literary" and the "curriculum" (as an official transmitter of this literary knowledge) are more than telltale signs of real, dominant social relations; they also have real political effects. Cora Kaplan argues that "the 'stuff' of the literary, its narratives, and its poetics, is steeped (one might say mired) in the contemplation and elaboration of sexual difference and inequalities" (1986, p. 60). Readings, as (re)productions of texts, are a quagmire in which are located the mediations of these ideologies, of readers' wants and desires, and, as well, of the historical and social contexts in which readers read. Whether resistant to and/or accommodating of the positions offered them, readers are still materially affected by what and how they read.

Working from this theoretical position, then, what are the effective curricular and pedagogical interventions and strategies that propel the project of teaching to critique and to transform dominant gender relations and which, simultaneously, critique and transform the subject, literature? What follows are sketches of/nudges toward a curriculum and a pedagogy for and of difference:

1. Never beg the question of literature and its history. Studying literature should be about studying its effects, both past and present, on human subjectivity and its insertion into social relations at the level of gender, sexuality, class, race, nation. In a wider gesture, this aspect of the study of literature is about resurrecting and revising some other "stories" of literature, stories as fascinating, beguiling, infuriating, and forming as any sanctioned literature, and certainly as important.

2. The study of texts and readings must always be recognized as an exclusionary practice. To study/speak/write of some people and things is, at once, to impose a silence on other people and things. What and who is included in literary studies, through reading, discussion, and writing, must always be gauged by a discussion of what and who is excluded. Such practice points to the partiality of all texts, all readings, including those of (those in) the classroom.

3. Encourage readings that both deconstruct texts and construct transformative texts. That is, teach students to address the gendered assumptions of any text, to identify the subject positions offered the reader through texts, and to resist the persuasive power of texts as gender ideology. Such "reader power" works in the formation of a more politically conscious reader/subject with a wider array of discursive positions available from which to choose (Belsey, 1980, p. 29).

4. Recognize that readings are a site of struggle on which are mediated all sorts of often conflicting and competing discourses of desire and demand. Teach to and for multiplicities of readings and encourage an interrogation of readings that allows space for the reader to hold fast to the precarious ground, built on desire, negotiated daily and expressed materially in readings.

5. Choose (and make available) texts (as readings of the world) that are more open and do offer and affirm a wider range of discursive subject positions. It is necessary to give space to those writings, historically silenced, which represent a variety of human potential and struggle and challenge the oppressive sexual, racial, and cultural hegemony of literature.

6. Any discussion of genre must include the gendered character of genre and the ideological work of such "a social contract between writers and readers" (Radford, 1986, p. 9). Tracing genre—for example, women's romances, detective stories, or westerns—is tracing the evolution of discursive relationships in the world, as read and as lived (McRobbie, 1982; Radstone, 1988; Willinsky & Hunniford, 1986).

7. Connect cultural forms whose discourses are compatible and/or conflictual. Working with a variety of cultural texts encourages students to see the (un)conscious, often contradictory, work of culture and the interconnectedness of cultural forms in the reproduction of social divisions. The work of juxtaposing competing and conflicting forms provides opportunities to determine which discursive forms work together to establish, to maintain, or to challenge hegemony.

8. Encourage the establishment of "reading groups" whose political interests are similar. Readers need to be encouraged to explore the social relations of the production, distribution, regulation, and consumption of a particular cultural form to see the ways in which texts, readings, and subject positions are determined. More effective campaigns to challenge the sexist, heterosexist, and racist institution of literature in all its guises may then be launched.

9. Create spaces where alliances may also be formed on the basis of race, sexual preference, class, region, and so on—problematics that permeate all cultural forms. As a politics of sharing and caring emerges, not only is solidarity built but the interconnectedness of cultural forms as sites of regulation and transformation are also identified.

10. Forge links among readers and community-based groups whose political interests affirm and extend the struggles of readers to define themselves and their readings of the world as oppositional to the present status quo. Disenfranchised readers need to identify their

choices and to claim spaces in which their choices are affirmed and realized as lived practice.

11. Sustain a critique of the text of the classroom. Part of this critique includes an articulation of the ways in which the insertion of the teacher's own experience of privilege or powerlessness is yet another dimension in the politics of reading (Gannett & Kelly, 1992). For example, what questions are raised by the presence of a lesbian teacher in a classroom critique of heterosexual romance ideology? Such critique must be seen as both a constraining and an expanding of possibilities as the limits of subjectivity are exposed and confronted through the determination of discourses privileged in the classroom.

The complexities and contradictions of this work need not be underestimated. Terry Lovell (1987) notes that "The transmission of literary culture from generation to generation depends on women; on their wholesale induction into that culture; but under the tutelage of men who remain its custodians and primary producers" (1987, p. 13). However, it is also worth noting that the induction is never "wholesale" at all. Feminist poststructuralism offers us many fronts from which to determine the conditions of our subjugation and to assert our agency in creating "other" stories of literature. There is much work to be done before literature becomes the "common ground" Virginia Woolf so long ago asserted it to be. On the terrain of literature, "the feminist trespass" (Batsleer et al., 1985) is not temporary. Nor is the intent merely to "find our way freely," as Woolf, too, would have us do. Rather, our intent must be to transform the landscape completely.

REFERENCES

Arendt, Hannah. (1977). *The life of the mind.* New York: Harcourt Brace Jovanovich.

Atwood, Margaret. (1991). True trash. In *Wilderness tips* (pp. 7–37). Toronto: McClelland & Stewart.

Bannerji, Himani. (1991). But who speaks for us? Experience and agency in conventional feminist paradigms. In Himani Bannerji et al. (Eds.), *Unsettling relations: The university as a site of feminist struggle* (pp. 67–107). Toronto: Women's Press.

Batsleer, Janet, Davies, Tony, O'Rourke, Rebecca, & Weedon, Chris. (1985). *Rewriting English: Cultural politics of gender and class.* New York: Methuen.

Belsey, Catherine. (1980). *Critical practice.* London: Methuen.

Belsey, Catherine. (1982). *Re-reading the great tradition.* In Peter Widdowson (Ed.), *Re-reading English* (pp. 223–236). London: Methuen.

Christian-Smith, Linda K. (1990). *Becoming a woman through romance.* New York: Routledge, Chapman & Hall.

Coward, Rosalind. (1985). *Female desires: How they are sought, bought and packaged.* New York: Grove Press.

Duplessis, Rachel B. (1985). *Writing beyond the ending: Narrative strategies of twentieth-century women writers.* Bloomington: Indiana University Press.

Fetterley, Judith. (1978). *The resisting reader: A feminist approach to American fiction.* Bloomington: Indiana University Press.

Gannett, Susan G., & Kelly, Ursula A. (1992). *Romancing the stone: Or, "sweet dreams are made of this, and who am I to disagree?"* Paper presented at the annual conference of the Canadian Society for the Study of Education (CSSE), Charlottetown, Prince Edward Island.

Gilbert, Pam, & Taylor, Sandra. (1991). *Fashioning the feminine: Girls, popular culture and schooling.* Sydney: Allen & Unwin.

Gilbert, Sandra M., & Gubar, Susan. (1985). *The Norton anthology of literature by women: The tradition in English.* New York: W. W. Norton.

Kaplan, Cora. (1986). *Sea changes: Culture and feminism.* London: Verso.

Lather, Patti. (1991). *Getting smart: Feminist research and pedagogy with/in the postmodern.* New York: Routledge, Chapman & Hall.

Lovell, Terry. (1987). *Consuming fiction.* London: Verso.

Maracle, Lee. (1990). Just get in front of a typewriter and bleed. In The Telling It Book Collective (Eds.), *Telling it: Women and language across cultures* (pp. 37–41). Vancouver, BC: Press Gang.

McRobbie, Angela. (1982). Just like a Jackie story. In Angela McRobbie & Trisha McCabe (Eds.), *Feminism for girls* (pp. 113–128). London: Routledge & Kegan Paul.

Meese, Elizabeth A. (1986). *Crossing the double-cross: The practice of feminist criticism.* Chapel Hill: University of North Carolina Press.

Nourbese Philip, Marlene. (1990). The disappearing debate: Racism and censorship. In Libby Scheier, Sarah Sheard, & Eleanor Wachtel (Eds.), *Language in her eye: Writing and gender: Views by Canadian women writing in English* (pp. 209–219). Toronto: Coach House.

Radford, Jean. (1986). Introduction. In Jean Radford (Ed.), *The progress of romance: The politics of popular fiction* (pp. 1–20). London: Routledge & Kegan Paul.

Radstone, Susannah. (Ed.). (1988). *Sweet dreams: Sexuality, gender and popular fiction.* London: Lawrence & Wishart.

Schweikert, Patricia P. (1986). Reading ourselves: Toward a feminist theory of reading. In Elizabeth A. Flynn & Patricia P. Schweikert (Eds.), *Gender and reading: Essays on readers, texts, contexts* (pp. 31–62). Baltimore: Johns Hopkins University Press.

Spender, Dale. (1989). *The writing or the sex? Or, Why you don't have to read women's writing to know it's no good.* New York: Pergamon.

Warland, Betsy. (1990). Where our loyalties lie. In The Telling It Book Collective (Eds.), *Telling it: Women and language across cultures* (pp. 191–202). Vancouver, BC: Press Gang.

Weedon, Chris. (1987). *Feminist practice & poststructuralist theory.* New York: Basil Blackwell.

Willinsky, John, & Hunniford, R. Mark. (1986). Reading the romance younger: The mirror and fears of a preparatory literature. *Reading-Canada-Lecture,* 4(1), 16–31.

CHAPTER 6

Tone Deaf/Symphonies Singing: Sketches for a Musicale

Roberta Lamb

AN INTRODUCTION TO THE TEXT

As a discipline music education is tone deaf—it does not know how to sing feminist, it refuses to hear the symphonic chorus murmuring beneath the surface. This chapter illustrates the difficulty of speaking directly to the very issues problematic to gender and music education. In this way, it is not unlike the "Gender Enriches Curriculum" nonconference described in this book's introduction, where White lesbians and heterosexual women of color raised the politics of speaking directly, of who speaks and in what context. Just as I was both participant in and critic of what began as "Gender Enriches Curriculum," I am at once a participant in and feminist critic of music education (making me both tone deaf and a symphonic singer). This doubled position focuses my interest on finding the means for artistry, research, and pedagogy to be integral to musical sense-making in ways that consider the varied realities of students, teachers, and musicians in those contested sites where music is made. As was evident at the nonconference, this is a very real struggle.

"Tone Deaf/Symphonies Singing" does not utilize a linear argument because to do so would misrepresent and oversimplify the gender question in music, since neither music nor gender is linear. Like the oversimplified but pleasant commercial jingles that numb the creative mind, easy answers to complex pedagogical and political questions do not suffice. Although there are innumerable patterns in which this text on gender and music curricula can be read—because it is not linear—the textual motives have been assembled here in a particular order because that is necessary for a book; therefore, you will read my specific version from a particular time, a particular political act.

THE TEXT

(1) GOLDEN SPACES LACUNAE

. . .

(6) THE SOUND OF THE SINGING VOICES
(7) THE DEAD WOMEN THE DEAD WOMEN

. . .

(19) THE CRIES THE LAUGHS THE MOVEMENTS
(20) THE WOMEN AFFIRM IN TRIUMPH THAT
(21) ALL ACTION IS OVERTHROW[1]

MOTIVE
ON AN
OCTAVE

> Nicole Brossard calls this kind of work "fiction theory"[2]
>   . . . spinning, highly speculative, and exploratory.
> Voice, that will not be silent as would be expected from one
>   in my position: insider-outside.
> Voices, engaging biomythography,[3] embodied.
> In my theoretical work I attempt to challenge aesthetic theories
>   and the arts in a manner that is aesthetically satisfying. A
>   labyrinthine task.

There is the necessity of being highly speculative and exploratory because integration of feminist theory into the music curriculum is in its early stages, whether it is the music curriculum of the elementary or graduate school. This lack of sophistication is especially noticeable when music is compared to other disciplines in the humanities. The development of theory in this text, though rooted in practice and moving towards praxis, is provisional. It is provisional because this voice still struggles with silence as a form of resistance, even as greater politicization enables the theory to be tried out, tried on, worn, and altered; wandering through many "creepy detours"[4] before the "Material girl['s] in Bluebeard's castle"[5] enriches the music education curriculum.

My musical design: to improvise "fiction theory" so that a critical feminist music education informed by feminist music criticism and theory could be composed, seen, and heard. I want this improvisation to lead to "theoretical fictions organized into a pedagogy that would collapse the distinction separating teaching, research and art."[6] I envision a palindromic form, circling back on itself, not unlike the title of this musicale, though probably not to where it began. My ideal would be to do so in a musical-poetic form that is both self-reflexive and disruptive. I, and many of my women colleagues—teachers, musicians—experience these fiction theories as doubled illustrations of our contradictory locations.

> This is not a story my people tell. It's something I know myself.
> And when I do my job I am thinking about these things.
> Because when I do my job, that's what I think about.[7]

MOTIVE
IN THE
DORIAN MODE

The difficulty with this text, the reason for not knowing/seeing/ hearing the score is that gender cannot *add* to the music curriculum. Male heterosexual gender, White and exercising class privilege, *is* the music curriculum. The gender of the music in the classroom, the music that becomes the curriculum in the Ministry of Education guidelines, the music-read-from-the-score, is male: Bach, Beethoven, and the boys (yet evidence points towards the boys being neither as White nor as heterosexual as we were taught to believe, e.g., Beethoven may have been mulatto; Schubert homosexual). Though undoubtedly less monolithic than it often appears to be, this male-gendered curriculum claims a technical rationalism, demonstrated in the quest for perfect performance and the emphasis on the scientific aspects of music cognition and psychological development in music education research. Thus, interruptions to this curriculum (ethnic, creative, etc.) are identified as play music or school music, not as *real* music. Gender cannot enrich the curriculum until women and others are present, authentically, in the music, and as musicians; however, currently women do not exist as women in music itself, let alone the music curricula. In fact, for a music teacher to ask "How could a woman be in music as a woman?" is to invite laughter and derision from both peers and students.

Women as music teachers signify the angel-in-the-house of the nine-

Pauline Alderman * Vittoria Aleotti * Anna Amalia von Preussen *
Grazyna Bacewicz * Agathe Backer-Grøndahl *
Amy Beach (Mrs. H. H. A. Beach) * Beatrice de Dia * Lili Boulanger *
Nadia Boulanger * Laura Bovia * Antonia Brico * Francesca Caccini *
Julie Candeille * Madalena Casulana * Cecile Chaminade * Rebecca Clark *
Ruth Crawford Seeger * Mabel Daniels * Sophie Drinker *
Louise Farrenc * Amy Fay * Peggy Glanville-Hicks *
Maria Margharita Grimani * Fanny Mendelssohn Hensel *
Hildegard von Bingen * Augusta Holmes * Hroswitha *
Elisabeth Claude Jacquet de la Guerre * Josephine Lang * Isabella Leonarda *
Ethel Leginska * Elisabeth Lutyens * Alma Mahler * Marianne Martinez *
Tarquinia Molza * Undine Smith Moore * Caroline B. Nichols *
Maria Theresia von Paradis * Frederique Petrides * Priaulx Rainier *
Louise Reichardt * Camilla de Rossi * Clara Schumann * Corona Schröter *
Julia Smith * Ethel Smyth * Barbara Strozzi * Maria Symanowska *
Germaine Tailleferre * Phyllis Tate * Pauline Viardot-Garcia *
Maria Walpurgis * Beatrice Witkin *

* * * *

Kathryn Alexander * Kristi Allik *
Yardena Alotin * Birgitte Alsted * Godelia Alverio * Avril Anderson *
Beth Anderson * Laurie Anderson * Violet Archer * Elinor Armer *
Deborah L. Austen * Lydia Ayers * Heidi Bader-Nobs * Ruth Bakke *
Françoise Barriere * Debra Barsha * Joyce Barthelson * Janet Beat *
Irene Becker * Eve Beglarian * Elizabeth Bell * Ilia Bergh * Adele Berk *
Christine Berl * Nicola Bernardini * Ginette Bertrand * Alma Bethany *
Laura Bianchini * Susan Bingham * Renate Birnstein * Susan Blaustein *
Carla Bley * Marilyn Bliss * Tamara Bliss * Patricia Blomfield-Holt *
Esta Blood * Sanchie Bobrow * Carolyn Bock * Sylvie Bodorov *
Harriet Bolz * Maria Luisa Bon * Victoria Bond * Marian Borokowski *

teenth century, a continuity, a stability in the late twentieth century where all else has changed.[8] Women music teachers, at all levels, are expected to uphold patriarchal standards of piety and excellence in the affective training of children.[9] We do not have to remember very far back to recognize the influence of Lowell Mason in our public rationales for teaching music in school: discipline; cooperative group endeavor; lifting the spirit to more noble, transcendent human character; self-expression. Women teach children right from wrong, morally and musically. Women teach children to work together, socially and musically. Women teach children to express themselves, through drill and practice. Still, women mediate male-dominated music curricula, often in the name of virtue, sometimes in the name of creativity. Sometimes women teach children to express themselves creatively through musical composition, but how often do women teach composers? How often do women become composers?

> To date, most discussions concerning women in composition have centered on the issue of equal opportunity. The idea is that given the same access to training and education, women too will emerge as composers, *indistinguishable from their male colleagues.* . . . Unwittingly, young women composers often find themselves committed to further "dissemination" . . .
>
> For what are the alternatives? A time-honored strategy practiced by many other groups marginalized by a musical mainstream is that of creating a stylistic synthesis: appropriating components of that mainstream but blending them with elements of their own readily recognized idiom. . . .
>
> . . . There is . . . no traditional woman's voice. . . . Worse yet, there is a bogus tradition of "how women sound" in European classical music—a code developed and transmitted by men, in which women are either docile and passive . . . or else man-hating harpies. . . .
>
> Because these pernicious images of women—the madonna or the whore have been the only ones available, generations of women training to be performers or composers have learned not to let themselves "sound like women" in their playing, conducting, or composing. In order not to resemble the passive ideal of femininity, we have learned how to write (how often have we gloried in this compliment!) *with balls;* and yet we have also learned not to play *too* aggressively for fear of terrifying . . . Thus not only do women not have a musical language of their own upon which to rely, but they often have internalized a strong distaste for the idea of permitting their identities as women to be apparent in their music. The category "woman" is already colonized and is overcrowded with caricatures concocted by male artists. . . .
>
> Music . . . rarely has dimensions that are readily identified with aspects of the material or social world. . . . If music is music is only music, then how does the woman composer enter into composition *as a woman?*[10]

Katarzyna Bortkun * Linda Bouchard * Anne Boyd * Nancy Briggs *
Jeannie Brindley-Barnett * Rosemary Broadbent * Jane Brockman *
Elisabetta Brusa * Joanna Bruzdowicz * Dawn Buckholz * Barbara Buczek *
Brio Burgess * Diana Burrell * Ann Callaway * Karen Campbell *
Carmen Maria Carmenci * Eva de Castro-Robinson * Augusta Cecconi-Bates *
Valerie Capers * Nancy Laird Chance * Chen Yi *
Mary Ellen Childs * Rhona Clarke * Rosemary Clarke * Laura Clayton *
Sheree Clement * Louise Cloutier * Gloria Coates * Linda Robbins Coleman *
Sarah J. Coles * Gia Conolli * Constance Cooper * Eleanor Cory *
Jean Coulthard * Cynthia Cozette * Tania Cronin * Joan Crowell *
Migdalia Cruz * Marilyn Currier * Tina Davidson * Margaret K. Davies *
Pamela Decker * Royce Dembo * Marilyn Boyd DeReggi *
Yvonne Desportes * Michelle Dibucci * Emma Lou Diemer *
Tamar Diesendruck * Maria Consuelo Diez * Violeta Dinescu *
Magdalena Dlugosz * Lucia Dlugoszewski * Lori Dobbins *
Deborah Drattell * Judith Dvorkin * Dorota Dywanska * Cecile Effinger *
Jutta Philippi Eigen * Karólina Eiríksdóttir * Michelle Ekizian *
Szilvia Elek * Ethel Ennis * Elaine Erickson * Siegrid Ernst * Pozzi Escot *
Eibhlis Farrell * Nancy Plummer Faxon * Maria Helena Rosas Fernandes *
Beatriz Ferreyra * Joan Finnigan * Elena Firsova * Susan Fisher *
Tsippi Fleischer * Jacqueline Fontyn * Jennifer Fowler * Erika Fox *
Mary Elizabeth Franklin * Sherilyn Fritz * Yuri Fujibayashi *
Nancy Galbraith * Mary Gardiner * Kay Gardner * Margaret Garwood *
Ada Gentile * Miriam Gerberg * Pamela Gerke * Rosalie Gerut *
Miriam Gideon * Ruth Gipps * Janice Giteck * Sylvia Glickman *
Ida Gotovsky * Janet Graham * Suzanne Grant * Beverly Grigsby *
Alicja Gronau * Sofia Gubaidulina * Amanda Guerreño * Lily Hood Gunn *

MOTIVE
ON A FIFTH

Is it possible that where women set out to write music *as women* or to create music *as women,* the resulting music may in some way be different from the malestream? Ethnomusicologists certainly find differing musical practices by gender when looking at the other; when that ethnographic gaze or ear is turned to our own cultural sites, is it not possible that we, too, will hear some *différance?* If gender is to enrich the music education curriculum, then it is important to dis/cover and listen to those musics women create, expanding our definition past the boundaries of the White, heterosexual, upper-class, northern world, so as to not be limited to the dominant music in which women may be participating. Although many women compose using the exact same sound system as their male counterparts, some women clearly, perhaps self-consciously, compose in "feminine" forms, leading some feminist music critics to suggest that women make use of different sound-images, often related to female life and body cycles, such as childbirth and menstruation. It has been hypothesized that cyclic or circular forms (rounds, canons, rondos, drones) are common in music of or by women from diverse cultural origins.[11] Some critics see a deliberate inverting of the narrative order in women's music (an example of this would be the static, lyric "feminine" phrase as the primary theme, interrupted by the more aggressive, directional, "male" one; or music that appears to lack direction).

Perhaps these compositional techniques are one form of resistance to the universalizing of the transcendent in aesthetic theory. Resistance is found also in criticism that draws our attention to these alternative readings of the musical text. Therefore, feminist music criticism suggests that we examine women's music as it exists on the margins of patriarchal society and attempt to define the values that the many musics created by women contribute to musical experiences and cultures on their own aesthetic and political terms. The feminist music teacher who wishes to join women composers/performers/critics in defining, creating, and valuing music can draw on the methodologies of feminist music composition and feminist music criticism while struggling with the meanings and practices necessary to constitute a feminist music pedagogy.

> I must have been about 11 or 12 when Elvis became for me a fulltime hobby. . . . I saved pocket money to buy his records, see his films, buy fan magazines and stick posters on my bedroom walls. . . . If I spent large amounts of time in my (shared) bedroom alone fixing pictures in my scrapbook, this was OK. . . . So it was also a way of spending a consider-

Frances Hadden * Tina Hafemeister * Carol McClure Hahn * Helen Hall *
Sarah Fuller Hall * Brooke Halpin * Ann Hankinson * Joan Hansen *
Kazuko Hara * Holly Harris * Ruth Berman Harris * Sadie Harrison *
Linda Tutas Haugen * Sorrel Hays * Åse Hedstrøm * Barbara Heller *
Sharon Hershey * Cirley de Holanda * Dulcie Holland * Kristin Holm *
Carita Holmström * Adriana Holszky * Katherine Hoover * Eleanor Hovda *
Hsu Wen-Ying * Elaine Hugh-Jones * Denise Hulford * Susan Hurley *
Miriam Hyde * Memrie Innerarity * Chizuko Ise * Jean Eichelberger Ivey *
Viera Janarcekova * Barbara Jazwinski * Kerstin Jepsson *
Irene Johansen-Sawatzky * Betsy Jolas * Helge Jung * Patricia Jünger *
Laura Kaminsky * Laura Karpman * Elena Kats * Minna Keal *
Winifred Keane * Ann Kearns * Mary M. Kelley *
Stefania Maria de Kenessey * Margaret Fairlie Kennedy *
Minuetta Kessler * Michelle Kinney * Antoinette Kirkwood * Juna Kirlin *
Vera Polenova Kistler * Yayoi Kitazume * Dorothy Klotzman *
Megumi Koga * Celina Kohan de Scher * Barbara Kolb * Nagako Konishi *
Laura Koplewitz * Grazyna Krzanowska * Mayako Kubo *
Hanna Kulenty * Harue Kunieda * Renata Kunkel * Yoko Kurimoto *
Larysa Kuzmenko * Christina Kuzmych * Joan LaBarbara * Ann LaBerge *
Nicole Lacharte * Lam Bun-Ching * Marta Lambertini * Maria Lamburn *
Libby Larsen * Julie Davidson Larson * Maria Lattimore * Anne Lauber *
Elizabeth Lauer * Beatrice Laufer * Mary Jane Leach * Joëlle Leandre *
Anne LeBaron * Nicola LeFanu * Vania Dantas Leite * Tania León *
Julie Lyonn Lieberman * Lanette Lind * Anne Linnet * Beatriz Lockhart *
Annea Lockwood * Ruth Lomon * Alexina Louie * Gudrun Lund *
Janice Macaulay * Kim McCarthy * Judith McGuire * Diana McIntosh *
Marian McLaughlin * Priscilla McLean * Jennifer McLeod * Cindy McTee *

able time alone in an overcrowded household which was accepted as legitimate by my family.[12]

... the problem is not to discover who we are but to refuse who we are. . . . Being someone else . . . creating new subject positions for us to occupy. . . .

. . . what playing the piano meant for me was not an opportunity to express my "creativity" but to have some control. . . . By engaging in a public and visible act, I could gain control over my time and thoughts while at the same time appearing to be under my mother's control and supervision. . . .

The same practices which constituted me as a "creative" subject also . . . worked to make me a "bourgeois subject," and a "female subject." . . . In my case, girls who played the piano became teachers, not musicians. We became music teachers, perhaps . . . but we did not enter the "bohemian" world of the musician. . . .

Playing the piano is an "appropriate" activity for young girls, an indication of "culture" and "femininity" *and* an alternative way to spend time that might otherwise be spent in more "negative" pursuits. . . . "playing" still meant sticking to the music-as-written: any effort on my part to play in a way which might be "inventive" or "imaginative" . . . was quickly censored by my mother, who would ask, "Is *that* practicing?" . . .

. . . I felt, on the one hand, somehow "gifted" and "special" and "competent," and on the other quite thoroughly fraudulent, since I did not really occupy the subject position "creative" as it was defined for me. I had learned that my abilities were somehow public property, yet I was sure that, given enough opportunity to display myself publically, my lack of ability on the piano—my lack of "creativity" or "talent"—would display itself for all to see.[13]

MOTIVE
ON A
MINOR SECOND

. . . Dance and music play an important role in these small daily *evasions*, partly because they are so strongly inscribed, in our culture, within the realms of feeling and control. They are associated with being temporarily out of control or out of the reaches of controlling forces. . . .

. . . Dance therefore signifies intertextually across different discourses. What brings these spheres together is their emphasis on the body and the pleasure they promise, which will bear not only on the body but on the "imagined other." They also offer simultaneously an escape from work and an opportunity to make something of work.[14]

Elizabeth Maconchy * Mary Mageau * Ursula Mamlok * Myriam Marbe *
Ada Belle Marcus * Bunita Marcus * Tera de Marez Oyens *
Kikuko Masumoto * Bernadetta Matuszczak * Melinda Maxwell *
Marilyn Mazur * Beth Mehocic * Margaret Shelton Meier * Joyce Mekeel *
Hanne Methling * Ruth Meyer * Agata de Mezar * Elma Miller *
Meredith Monk * Dorothy Rudd Moore * Junko Mori * Reiko Morohashi *
Chase Morrison * Krystyna Moszumanska * Minta T. Mulhare *
Marie-Louise Muller * Thea Musgrave * Amina Claudine Myers *
Yoko Nakamura * Yukimo Nishida * Alison Nowak * Jane O'Leary *
Vivienne Olive * Jocy de Oliveira * Pauline Oliveros * Kazuko Osawa *
Blythe Owen * Lynne Palmer * Isabelle Panneton * Hilda Paredes *
Alice Parker * Wilma Paterson * Maggi Payne * Janet Peachy * Polly Pen *
Barbara Pentland * Diana Pereira * Anita Perry * Byrony Phillips *
Alina Piechowska * Alexandra Pierce * Elizabeth Faw Hayden Pizer *
Katalin Pocs * Maria Pokrzywinska * Claire Polin * Wendy Prezament *
Grazyna Pstrokonska * Marta Ptaszynska * Laurie Radford *
Natalia Raigorodsky * Theresa Rampezzi * Shulamit Ran *
Elizabeth Raum * Karin Rehnqvist * Sarah (Sally) Johnston Reid *
Wendy Reid * Marisa Resende * Marie Rhines * Marga Richter *
Sylvia Rickard * Lolita Ritmanis * Lou Rodgers * Sarah L. Rodgers *
Betty Roe * Helen Roe * Carol Roes * Amelia Rogers * Patsy Rogers *
Carol Rohr * Hanne Rømer * Ann Ronell * Muriel Roth * Amy Rubin *
Anna Rubin * Diana Elena Rud * Vivian Adelberg Rudow *
Kaija Saariaho * Judith St. Croix * Kathleen St. John * Alice Samter *
Rhian Samuel * Deborah Sandoval * Elizabeth R. Scheidel * Annette Schlünz
* Mia Schmidt * Ruth Schonthal * Betsy L. Schramm *
Linda Schwartz * Amanta Scott * Ilona Sekacz * Daria Semegen *

Women's secret stories of a fan's scrapbooks, piano lessons, music teacher education, compositional strategies, and professional apprenticeship in music speak to the colonization of women intertextually in several music curricula. Although this is not a story my people tell (publicly), it is also not the whole story; the grand narrative of the master's music is not the only one experienced. There is great pleasure and solace in music for women. Music provides women with opportunity for integral time, space, and energy, wherein the contradictory becomes multi-dimensional, full with the possibility of in/corp/orated wholeness. It is from this volume of our thought that *l'intégrales* rises up.[15] The place of a woman's private thoughts is a site and strategy of resistance as, for example, when dance functions as sexual expression for young women, these "daily evasions" where daydreams are beyond control (and yet she *appears* to be controlled), where the freedom to make something of music and her "work" with/in it is possible; thereby marking an area in which she cannot be totally colonized.

This space of daydream and dance may be wonderful for the student (it could also be lonely, full of anguish), but it is definitely problematic for the woman teacher. How is she to respect such abandon and still teach? Does attempting to incorporate music that is so real in the dancing daydream infringe on boundaries of intimacy and deny agency? What is the cost of ignoring or trivializing the *real* music of daydreams? What is the curriculum and pedagogy of musical daydreams?

4.
Piano lessons   The mother and the daughter
Their doomed exhaustion   their common mystery
worked out in finger-exercises Czerny, Hanon
The yellow Schirmer albums   quarter rests   double-holds
glyphs of an astronomy   the mother cannot teach
the daughter because this is not the story
of a mother teaching magic to her daughter
Side by side I see us locked
My wrists your voice   are tightened . . .
The daughter struggles with the strange notations
—dark chart of music's ocean flowers and flags
but would rather learn by ear and heart   The mother
says she must learn to read by sight   not ear and heart
5.
Daughter who fought her mother's lessons— . . .

Judith Shatin * Kim Sherman * Alice Shields * Melissa Shiflett *
Shih-Hui Chen * Mieko Shiomi * Clare Shore * Marilyn Shufro *
Laura Shur * Ann Silsbee * Sheila Silver * Faye-Ellen Silverman *
Jeanne Singer * Pril Smiley * Allison Sniffin * Pamela Snow * Ann Southam *
Bernadette Speach * Mira Spektor * Jennifer Stasack * Lynne Steele *
Dorothy Strutt * Elizabeth Swados * Gloria Wilson Swisher * Ewa Synowiec *
Iris Szeghyova * Katalin Szekely * Caroline Szeto *
Erzsebet Szonyi * Olga Szwajgier * Yuko Tagashira * Akemi Takahashi *
Louise Talma * Sawako Tamura * Karen Tanaka * Hilary Tann *
Nancy Telfer * Etsuko Teraoka * Alizia Terzian * Ivana Themmen *
Augusta Read Thomas * Karen P. Thomas * Marilyn Taft Thomas *
Diane Thome * Shirley Thompson * Joan Tower * Tui St. George Tucker *
Sara Scott Turner * Ludmilla Ulelha * Irma Urteaga * Julia Usher *
Galina Ustvolskaya * Mary Jeanne Van Appledorn * Janika Vandervelde *
Nancy Van de Vate * Elizabeth Vercoe * Persis Vehar * Lois V. Vierk *
Melinda Wagner * Elizabeth Waldo * Gwyneth Walker * Joelle Wallach *
Wang An-Ming * Elinor Remick Warren * Judith Weir * Ellen Weller *
Hildegard Westerkamp * Barbara White * C. B. White *
Gillian Whitehead * Beth Wiemann * Eva Wiener * Inger Wikström *
Greta Wilens * Margaret Lucy Wilkins * Linda Williams *
Ann Rivers Witherspoon * Julia Wolfe * Sabine Wüsthoff-Oppelt *
Jeanette Yanikian * Jeanne Zaidel-Rudolph * Judith Lang Zaimont *
Anna Zawadzka * Isidora Zebeljan * Lidia Zielinska * Magrit Zimmerman *
Ellen Taaffe Zwilich

These names are from "Part I: Gazette" of Judith Lang Zaimont
(Ed.), *The Musical Woman, Vol. 3, 1986–1990* (Westport, CT:
Greenwood Press, 1991).

your daughter   whom you taught for years
held by a tether over the ivory
and ebony teeth of the Steinway
                    It is
the three hundredth anniversary of Johann
Sebastian Bach   My earliest life
woke to his English Suites   under your fingers
I understand a language I can't read
Music you played streams on the car radio
in the freeway night
You kept your passions deep   You have them still
I ask you, both of us
—Did you think mine was a virtuoso's hand?
Did I see power in yours?
What was worth fighting for?   What did you want?
What did I want from you?
1985–1988[16]

LYDIAN
MOTIVE WITH
DESCENDING TRITONE

The site where students and teacher begin to engage meanings in music is that place where the master's tools[17] are put away and the lively knowledge unpacked by feminist theory and translated through feminist music criticism permeates the classroom, embodied. I understand why we attempt to maintain the master's house with his tools and just freshen it up with a coat of "add women" paint. This embodied site of multiple realities, where women are truly present and alive, settling our scores with knowledge;[18] this site is one of great risk. The risk sneaks through the space created by feminist theory that allows lived experience into a normally calcified existence. Feminist theory questions and alters the relations of ruling[19] through its reflexive approach.

> It presupposes an insider's . . . [music], that is, a systematically developed consciousness of [music in] society from within, renouncing the artifice that stands us outside what we can never stand outside of. . . . This doesn't mean working subjectively; rather it means working from the site of knowing that is prior to the differentiation of subjective and

objective. It means an explication of the actual practices in which we are active.[20]

As women begin to work from this site of knowing where power relations intertwine with the gendered discourse of music, we begin to hear and speak, and maybe sing. What is heard repeatedly in this place where we are active as musicians (often in response to examples illustrating theoretical paradigms, such as the virgin/whore dichotomy facing women in music) are stories of sexual harassment and abuse. As these women students engage feminist theory, particularly in a setting where they are thinking about becoming music teachers, as they look at what power means in their musical lives, they come to similar conclusions: *Sexual harassment is part of the daily life of women in music.* We are stunned, silent, and I wonder that we have not seen how power is vested in the relations of ruling so that sexual harassment is a commonplace within music. I wonder at the ways we women music teachers participate in this structure when we do not speak out against this violence perpetrated in the names of artistry and talent.

The Ninth Symphony
of Beethoven Understood At Last
As a Sexual Message

A man in terror of impotence
or infertility, not knowing the difference
a man trying to tell something
howling from the climacteric
music of the entirely
isolated soul
yelling at Joy from the tunnel of the ego
music without the ghost
of another person in it, music
trying to tell something the man
does not want out, would keep if he could
gagged and bound and flogged with chords of joy
where everything is silence and the
beating of a bloody fist upon
a splintered table
1972[21]

MOTIVE WITH
A MAJOR SEVENTH

> They assume the moral and political values of the discourses of which
> they are part . . . the dilemmas and contradictions and anxieties they give
> rise to. *And above all they take for granted the silences of those who do not hold*
> *these positions, who are outside* . . . those who occupy and appropriate those
> positions are men.[22]

The relations of ruling assume the silence of women in music. They
take for granted that women will not speak about sexual harassment because women are outside the positions of power. In addition, the prevalent model for *real* music education continues to be the master-apprentice
model. In this monastic model, the student practices in religious solitude
to reach the perfection of performance acceptable to the best teacher/
professional so that he may earn the possibility of becoming the master
himself. The outdated moral and political values of music education, under the guise of scientific objectivity and transcendent aesthetics, assume
that no musician is female,[23] yet for nearly a century women have been
the majority of music students (though not of professionals). The intimate
teaching context of the master-apprentice situation, in which the woman
student is dependent on the master's favorable appraisal of her performance for her future success, ensures her silence.

Speaking of harassment disrupts the relations of ruling because we
question our ways of participating in musical practice. Men ignore what
is said or accuse us of hysteria. Women speak to me in private, individually, or in the safety of all-women groups. "You were brave to say those
things. Someone has to—it's the truth—but I'd be scared," are their first
words, followed by "I could tell you stories." The stories we women tell:
how we changed instruments or schools to get away from harassment,
how we won't graduate because of one man's mark, how we lost an audition, how we quit music altogether, how they didn't believe us, how
health-related problems ensue.

> Musical ideologies and practices, together with musical products, form a
> little social system, or musical world: a network of functions both mental
> and material, supporting and legitimating one another. . . . This social sys-
> tem does not survive autonomously, but is reproduced through a recipro-
> cal relationship with the wider social system. . . . [24]

MOTIVE ON
A UNISON

A philosophy of aesthetic education as the basis for music education has dominated school music education for the past 25 years. One educator notes that "[s]everal countries outside North America have embraced this formulation more recently."[25] Expressionist and phenomenological aesthetic philosophies (particularly as presented by Langer, Meyer, Beardsley, Goodman, Roger, and Dewey) have been adapted by education writers (especially Reimer, Broudy, and R. Smith) to legitimate the study of music within the school curriculum based on the premise "that the essential nature and value of music education are determined by the nature and value of the art of music."[26] These philosophers draw their discussions of aesthetics, and consequently the pedagogical emphasis within an aesthetic music education based on their work, from exemplars of primarily European art music composed by White men. Music by women and non-White men does not meet the exemplar criteria, primarily because such music has not been constantly in the art music repertoire past its initial generation. Such music, as some would say, has no staying power. Aesthetic education, by virtue of its omissions, hierarchical criteria, and positivistic process reinforces Western art music as grand narrative.

To further complicate the issue, the codes of music and the codes of music education frequently conflict around concepts of art. The conventions structuring music education neither run parallel to nor intertwine with the structures of music as discourse. Music education is rationality, control, and indoctrination into a knowledge of music, primarily through performance. We music educators do not even encourage feeling-and-thinking performance; the emphasis is on doing it. We do not encourage direct feeling in the broad range of possible musical experiences but rather a version of knowing-feeling, what some have called "feelingful."

> [M]usic ideology perpetrates the same distortion of historical reality under which we all labour in our day to day experiences . . . the assumption that music is the atomised and fragmented creation of isolated individuals, and that it achieves greatness when it transcends this apparent singularity and pertains to the universal, the timeless, the ahistorical.[27]

MOTIVE IN
C MAJOR

Most music education research follows a model of scientific inquiry whose underlying project appears to be the establishment of music as science,[28] as a body of knowledge worthy of study, as an academic entity that in spite of its reputation for softness, fuzziness, and femininity, can "walk like a man."[29] It appears that this definition of music as a science, and the socialization of students, function as a politics of dominance. Beliefs about the proper socialization of young students are betrayed in the way inquiry into music cognition is framed. The following educators disclose an unacknowledged socialization process organizing the conception of musical thinking, in which there is no realization that conceptualization occurs within a societal context; rather, the assumption is cognition is pure and rational.

> As music teachers, it is crucial that we not lose sight . . . of our ultimate mission—to help our students grasp the deeper meaning of musical structure and thus gain the ability to use music as a metaphor of reality.[30]

> . . . the key to musical independence lies in metacognition—in learning to monitor one's own thinking, to maintain control.[31]

> . . . to develop self-control by channeling their energies to attain a common goal.[32]

> The critical [creative musical] thinker must understand the elements of music.

> The critical [creative musical] thinker must have high-quality resources available for comparison.[33]

Throughout the literature of music cognition there is an assumption of universality and a grand narrative, that there is a general and definable music learner, and that the music under consideration is Western. The concerns with self-control, musical independence, the elements of music, and so forth focus on Western values. If music is a metaphor for reality, and yet differences of location, history, and experience are not identified, then whose reality is heard in this musical metaphor? If the central, culture-specific structure of "music" is not placed in the foreground of research in which it is clearly operating, there is not much likelihood of creating an empowering possibility of music.[34]

MOTIVE
IN THE
PHRYGIAN MODE

Despite decades of aesthetic education as *the* philosophic model for music education, the practice of music pedagogy—especially in many high schools, conservatories, and universities—stubbornly clings to this very traditional performance-based model. University music schools and conservatories place a great emphasis on the performance audition and conservatory exam results when admitting students for further study. A student who is marginal academically but a good performer will be accepted before a student who is strong academically but a marginal performer—even in those schools that espouse a nonperformance perspective, that is, an emphasis on composition or music history or music education. Evidence of music education as the practice of performance is demanded by the general public in the numerous music festivals and the continuing reliance on prizes and conservatory exams as a measure of musical achievement: If the student musician, orchestra, band, or chorus win honors, awards, prizes, and trophies, then music education has been successful. Additional evidence of the practical predominance of performance in music education can be found within official curriculum documents that reify performance, with little real-time attention paid to other aspects of music education.

Musical performance is untheorized practice. It is not praxis; it is what we musicians do because it is what we do. Performance is very much a male-constructed model for music. The master-apprentice relationship of most professional musicians toward their students exemplifies this model. Performance is about control by a master, a conductor, usually male, usually White. Historically, cross-culturally, women who have performed music outside of strictly defined feminine roles have been named as prostitutes or unnatural women.[35] When I began my music teaching career in 1975, I was denied the opportunity to interview for a band director's position because a woman would (should?) not have the authority to control a high school band. Later, in 1980, when I was conducting, people were amazed at the performance quality and my pleasant demeanor. Clearly, a woman was not expected to capably present the appropriate public image in musical performance.

MOTIVE IN
SARASWATI RAGA

Like other fields of human endeavor, the "[i]mages, vocabularies, concepts, knowledge of and methods of knowing the [musical] world are integral to the practice of power"[36] within it; therefore, the concert piece itself may "serve to order, legitimate, and organize social relations and the socially relevant aspects of experience"[37] in an ideology of music. The production of music within this ideology takes for granted the conditions of the relations of ruling, their experiences, interests, and relevances; yet feminist theory in music creates the possibility of opening the walls of the relations of ruling so that women, children, and marginalized men have a chance to attempt to produce the means of thinking and imaging music. Music education then could invoke the examination of music as a symbol system constituted within the ideology of institutions/practices as relations of ruling.

Prior to the appearance of the *texts* of feminist music criticism, there were few strategies of overt resistance within music. Even with the appearance of feminist texts-one-can-read, most of these strategies have been borrowed from other disciplines, especially literature and history. We are, at this time, in the process of defining a truly musical *and* feminist critique. This is the point at which I write theoretical essays in musical forms, making use of "cyclic fragmentarity"[38] I wonder about this particular piece as if it were a public melody, full of lyric hope and dramatic interaction, as well as private sounds and silences. Its opening motive might be the often unsung, hidden curriculum in music education. Perhaps the melody could be transformed through various themes to resolve in alternative feminist music pedagogies. And yet, I am hampered by the hegemony of the very theory of music education that I critique. I am always looking over my shoulder, always ready.

> I have, however, attended to what Derrida (1978) speaks of as "writing under erasure." What this means to me is that to write "postmodern" is to write paradoxically aware of one's complicity in that which one critiques. Such a movement of reflexivity and historicity at once inscribes and subverts.[39]

MOTIVE ON A
PERFECT FOURTH

> ... The appearance that music arises naturally out of its own materials and their relations fails to recognize the social and historical roots of musical laws; style is not understood as a learnt and historical construction necessary for musical experience, but as the natural, unconventional expression of music....
>
> ... Great music is made to appear, and required to appear, eternal, natural and universal ... hence the refusal to recognise style, the continual attempt to get to "music itself"; to rid music of all its social constructs, is at the root of musical ideology.... The ideology of autonomy encapsulates music's absence from the material world....[40]

It is *in the way* in which music is learned/taught that we are so oblivious to our *practice* of music education. We put a lot of stock in correct teaching methods, yet we ignore the meaning of the *way* we teach. Mary

Hookey acknowledges this issue after interviewing Native teachers in Ontario, some of whom had been students in her music education courses. Her Native teacher-education students "remind us of the negotiated nature of what we teach and the factors that define acceptable music in a culture."[41] These Native teachers tell us: how the specificity of musical experience in particular times and places affects the definition of music, how it is inappropriate to examine all music by the organizational principles of Western music, about the many differences among Native communities as well as between Native and Western musics, how the meaning of performance in Western music is at odds with the meaning of participation in many Native music experiences, and about the unsuitability of many of the curriculum materials currently available in schools. Hookey notes that "political and musical traditions are not always congruent" such that "there appears to be an uneasy match between the music education of the school system and the informal sharing of elders and Native musicians."[42] This uneasiness becomes apparent in the concerns raised by Native teachers/education students about content, process, and the participating subjectivities. Hookey concludes, "In designing a program, we would be wise to remind ourselves that education is a political process."[43]

MOTIVE ON A
MAJOR SECOND

One recent, and possibly hopeful, shift in music education integrates music into daily life—music while doing other things, more drama, more visual arts, more ethnic and popular musics. I wonder, is it not likely that gender constructions will be reproduced in these musical interpretations? When children write their own operas or produce their own music videos, when they characterize their lives musically, it seems likely that the structures of class, race, gender, and sexual orientation will be implicit at the least, if not explicit, within those productions. The creative processes and concepts of art as life/life as art[44] may demonstrate possibilities toward antiracist, antisexist music education, but only when the social structure of music itself is foregrounded as problematic. If music is left unmediated, as pure expression untouched by culture, rather than identified and examined as a process and object produced by, as, and in culture, then any new methodology or philosophy will be no more empowering than what has gone before.

I envision a radical change in music education content and process. In terms of pedagogy we could begin with perceptions of composing as a woman, of hearing with a female ear, of experiencing music as a woman performer, critic, or student and ask: How do we make sense of this world of music as women?[45] And because that sense is found in multiple subjective sites, these discursive practices of making sense will constitute and reflect social reality in differing musical discourses. Feminist theory suggests a praxis of music education informed by feminist music criticism wherein both men and women speak in resistance to the relations of ruling; women's silence is not taken for granted. There would be an emphasis on critical participation and empowerment. In pragmatic terms this results in an integration of women into music *and* a specialized scholarship of women in/and music. It means giving attention to the meanings of the ways we teach and learn. It means finding alternatives to the master-apprentice model. It means changing the definitions of music and theorizing about music education as we know them. It means we listen to feminist music criticism, hear, and respond, in ways that open up the score rather than close it down.

(3) NO / SYMBOLS TEARING
(4) ARISE VIOLENCE FROM WHITENESS
(5) OF THE UNDYING BEAUTIFUL PRESENT
   . . .
(11) ARISE NO / SYMBOLS MASSED
(12) EVIDENT / THE DESIGNATED TEXT
   . . .
(14) FAULTY
(15) LACUNAE LACUNAE
(16) AGAINST TEXTS
(17) AGAINST MEANING
(18) WHICH IS TO WRITE VIOLENCE
(19) OUTSIDE THE TEXT
(21) IN ANOTHER WRITING
(22) THREATENING MENACING
(23) MARGINS SPACES INTERVALS
(24) WITHOUT PAUSE
(25) ACTION OVERTHROW[46]

HOW I READ THIS TEXT

Selections from Monique Wittig's *Les Guérillères* (1971) begin and end this arrangement of the text as introduction and coda. She speaks of golden lacunae that in my reading become the women absent from the musical canon and the theoretical basis of music education, even as we are so very present as music teachers and students. The coda again invokes the gaps, the void, the margins, the spaces, intervals among the unfamiliar names. This piece is a text-outside-the-text of music and music education. It is a text against the dominant meaning, that is, written about the violence in music and music education that contributes to such meaning even as that violence is outside the same overriding text.

The first list of women's names are those of dead women, musical ancestors—composers, performers, historians, conductors—being a most partial list from the herstory of women in music, a respectful chant, the reading of the names (Wittig, too, listed women's names, disrupting her story of the women warriors). The singing voices of these dead women, only recently heard in a contemporary world, constitute movement toward change (overthrow). Their names define a motive, developed and repeated as the principal theme of an oscillating rondo, through the subsequent lists of names of living women who compose music.

Other motivic themes alternate with the starkness and steady rhythm of the composers' names in this rondo form. During the first half of the piece three examples—the memoirs from two different women who describe what music meant as a girl and the poems by Adrienne Rich—replace the names as the piece moves toward the central, crucial, and permeating theme of violence against women carried out through the structures of music education.

There should be a grand pause (silence) after the *Motive with a Major Seventh* and before the reading of the women's names continues because, even though violence against women in the form of sexual harassment and abuse has been recognized previously in other places, its common and constant presence has not been acknowledged within music education. Naming harassment interrupts the movement of music through time; yet, it is a delayed or echoed silence not actually heard when it first occurs (in the Lydian motive), but rather somewhat later (in the seventh). While other themes are heard throughout the following motives, none is so disruptive; therefore, the rest of the work oscillates with less intensity. This is also the midpoint of the piece. The names of the women composers continue after the *Major Seventh* with more regularity than before; they are more persistent, more prevalent, perhaps soothing, definitely surviving.

This rondo almost forms a mirror image (palindrome) with related themes on each side of the grand pause. At the center, close to the mirror-image line, the violent aspects of music education are reflected and still hidden in its narrative tracks of aesthetic educational philosophy and the very real emphasis on musical performance. The experiences of young women as students in music of pianos, Elvis, dance, and daydreams contrast with the other, official, side of the practice of performance. Similar to the fourth being the inversion of the fifth, the inversion of the problem of composing as a woman becomes awareness of some structures and processes of resistance in music education. Just as the themes near the beginning speak of the improbability of gender enriching music curricula, those near the end look toward the possibility.

The following brief statements include definitions of the musical motives, the themes. (Here I acknowledge Kay Gardner's work [1990] as influential in my definitions.)

The *Motive on an Octave* indicates the unison plus the same tone an octave distant, a great leap, a pure tone, doubledness—being a music teacher, a musician, a teacher-of-teachers, a thinker, a lesbian, an activist in a context that does not have room for such expansion or contradiction. An octave is where I can hear the first response of a rich overtone.

The minor third and flatted seventh characterize the *Dorian mode*, making it relatively easy for beginning musicians to use. Frequently the basis of Gregorian chant, the *Motive in the Dorian Mode* can seem religious or magical and, like traditional music teaching, many find it uplifting and serene.

The *Motive on a Fifth* wanders through possibility and potential. The perfect fifth interval characterizes "otherness" or a center, so it seemed logical to "compose as a woman" with this interval. It is a round, full, complete sound; and yet, within its roundness, it is possible to hear rich overtones, especially the third and octave.

The *Motive on a Minor Second* is filled with the secrets of otherworldly daydreams and dance, since the minor second interval is often described as busy or mysterious, as if anticipating resolution.

The *Lydian Motive with Descending Tritone* is expressively lyric, yet disturbing in its particular repetition of the descending tritone. The descending tritone shows a malevolent character, traditionally called "diabolus in musica" (an apt signifier in conjunction with sexual harassment). Some identify this sound as deep, suspenseful, or weird. The tritone is found between the fourth tone and the first of the Lydian mode. Plato forbade use of the Lydian mode, fearing it would make men effeminate. Yet, when the ascending tritone is emphasized, the expression can become prayerful, pastoral, and lyric.

The *Motive with a Major Seventh* expands on the Lydian mode making the seventh structurally significant. This large leap is a strange, discordant, and eerie interval, most often resolving to the octave, but sometimes heard as the unison.

Motive on a Unison is where everyone is singing or playing the same tone. It produces a great sense of solidarity, yet it can become quite boring if not moderated by different tones; the unison is hegemonic in this motive.

The *Motive in C Major* relates to the unison. C major is the Ionian mode, the white keys on the piano from C-to-C, known commonly as the major scale. The Ionian mode formed the basis of "common practice" harmony, which controlled Western music for at least 300 years and continues within music curricula.

The *Motive in the Phrygian Mode* feels dramatic, passionate, perhaps tinged with sadness, an emotive performer. Like the Dorian it has both a minor third and a flatted seventh, but it also has a minor second and flatted sixth, both intervals leaning towards the tonic and fifth, pulling the mode to dramatic passion, rather than letting it soar.

Motive in Saraswati Raga, comprised of the tones of the harmonic sequence of the fourth octave above the fundamental, is named after Saraswati, Hindu goddess of music and the sciences. To Western ears, this is the first four tones of the Lydian mode plus the last four of the Mixolydian, a hybrid of the two characteristically "feminine" modes.

The *Motive on a Perfect Fourth* is the inversion of the fifth and can claim balance to the center, or with the "other." Its sound tends to serenity, clarity, contraction, and is often expressed in non-Western music as a return to the mother and balance.

The major second is a mild dissonance, yet it often seems to sound happy, hopeful, or open. The *Motive on a Major Second* takes a step away from the unison and looks toward the possible.

NOTES

1. Wittig, (1971), p. 1 (unpaginated).
2. Brossard, 1988, in "The aerial letter," pp. 67–89.
3. Biomythography concept from Lorde.
4. This comment comes from Deborah Britzman in her discussion of "guilty readings" in her (1990) paper.
5. Introductory chapter in McClary, 1991.
6. Ulmer in Lather, 1991, p. 12.
7. L. Anderson, *United States,* as quoted in S. McClary, 1991, p. 132.
8. See Solie, 1991, for a discussion of the angel-in-the-house in relation for her feminist critical reading of R. Schumann's *Frauenliebe* songs; see also McClary, 1991, for a compelling analysis of music in terms of its role in perpetuating social structures and its resistance to change.
9. See Grumet, 1988, Chapter 2, "Pedagogy for Patriarchy," for discussion of these ideals in relation to the elementary school classroom teacher.

10. McClary, 1991, excerpts from pp. 114–116.
11. Gardner, 1990.
12. Wise, 1990, p. 137.
13. Heald, 1991, excerpts from "From pianos to pedagogy," pp. 129–135.
14. McRobbie, 1984, pp. 134 & 140.
15. See Brossard, 1988, pp. 103–119, and especially "From radical to integral," pp. 114–115.
16. Rich, 1989, excerpts from the poem, "Solfeggietto," pp. 4–5.
17. Lorde, 1984, pp. 110–113, "The master's tools will never dismantle the master's house."
18. See Brossard, 1988, "I have a score to settle with knowledge," in "The Turning Platform," p. 39.
19. Relations of ruling concept from D. Smith, 1989.
20. Smith, p. 38, 1989.
21. Rich, 1973, p. 43.
22. Smith, 1991, p. 237, emphasis in original.
23. See Walker, 1990, for a description of the medieval monastery as the ideal institution for education in Western art music.
24. Green, 1988, p. 11.
25. Elliott, 1989, p. 10.
26. Reimer, 1989, p. 1.
27. Green, 1988, p. 5.
28. Within the last 5 years, the major music education research journal prefaced an essay explaining ethnography to music educators and an action research study with disclaimers that they don't normally print this type of research, but that music education researchers might want to familiarize themselves with these "new" methodologies. Although some historical and qualitative work is being published, these follow very orthodox paradigms.
29. This is from a song by Bob Crewe and Bob Gaudio, Saturday Music, recorded by The Four Seasons in 1963 (Shapiro, 1967).
30. Boardman, 1989, p. 5.
31. Boardman, 1989, p. 6.
32. Pogonowski, 1989, p. 12.
33. Deturk, 1989, pp. 23, 30.
34. This grand narrative in music education becomes even more obvious after reading the current literature of critical pedagogy in other disciplines, for example, the work of Freire and of Giroux. See Ellsworth (1989, 1990) for an examination of the problematic of critical pedagogy when assumptions are not questioned and the politics of location and voice are not considered.
35. Koskoff, 1989.
36. Smith, 1991, p. 233.
37. Smith, 1991, p. 236.
38. Lather, 1991, p. 10.
39. Lather, 1991, p. 10.
40. Green, 1988, p. 82, 101.
41. Hookey, 1991, p. 11.

42. Hookey, 1991, pp. 18–19.
43. Hookey, 1991, p. 23.
44. See Schafer, 1976, for a discussion of "art as life/life as art" in elementary school music.
45. This is a paraphrase of Brossard, 1988, p. 112, "How then to make sense collectively?"
46. Wittig, 1971, p. 143.

REFERENCES

Boardman, Eunice. (1989). The relation of music study to thinking. In E. Boardman (Ed.), *Dimensions of musical thinking* (pp. 1–8). Reston, VA: Music Educators National Conference.

Britzman, Deborah. (1990, October). *Could this be your story? Guilty readings and other ethnographic dramas.* Paper presented at the Bergamo conference, Dayton, OH.

Brossard, Nicole. (1988). *The aerial letter* (M. Wildeman, Trans.). Toronto: Women's Press.

Derrida, Jacques. (1978). Structure, sign and play in the discourse of the human sciences. In *Writing and difference* (Alan Bass, Trans.) (pp. 278–293). Chicago: University of Chicago Press.

Deturk, Mark. (1989). Critical and creative musical thinking. In E. Boardman (Ed.), *Dimensions of musical thinking* (pp. 21–32). Reston, VA: Music Educators National Conference.

Elliott, David J. (1989). Key concepts in multicultural music education. In *Multicultural music education: The "Music means harmony" workshop* (pp. 9–18). Toronto: University of Toronto, Faculty of Music, Institute for Canadian Music.

Ellsworth, Elizabeth. (1989). Why doesn't this feel empowering?: Working through the repressive myths of critical pedagogy. *Harvard Education Review, 59*(3).

Ellsworth, Elizabeth. (1990). The question remains: How will you hold awareness of the limits of your knowledge? *Harvard Educational Review, 60*(3), 297–324.

Freire, Paulo. (1970). *Pedagogy of the oppressed.* New York: Continuum.

Gardner, Kay. (1990). *Sounding the inner landscape: Music as medicine.* Stonington, ME: Caduceus.

Giroux, Henry. (1988). *Schooling and the struggle for public life: Critical pedagogy in the modern age.* Minneapolis: University of Minnesota Press.

Green, Lucy. (1988). *Music on deaf ears: Musical meaning, ideology, education.* Manchester, UK: Manchester University Press.

Grumet, Madeleine. (1988). *Bitter milk: Women and teaching.* Amherst: University of Massachusetts Press.

Heald, Susan. (1991). From pianos to pedagogy. In Himani Bannerji et al. (Eds.), *Unsettling relations: The university as a site of feminist struggle* (pp. 129–149). Toronto: Women's Press.

Hookey, Mary. (1991, May). *Native pre-service music education: Searching for a framework*. Paper presented at the Canadian Music Educators National Conference, University of British Columbia, Vancouver.

Koskoff, Ellen. (Ed.). (1989). *Women and music in cross-cultural perspective*. Urbana: University of Illinois Press.

Lather, Patti. (1991). *Getting smart: Feminist research and pedagogy with/in the postmodern*. New York: Routledge, Chapman & Hall.

Lorde, Audré. (1984). *Sister outsider*. Freedom, CA: Crossing Press.

McClary, Susan. (1991). *Feminine endings*. Minneapolis: University of Minnesota Press.

McRobbie, Angela. (1984). Dance and social fantasy. In Angela McRobbie & Mica Nava (Eds.), *Gender and generation* (pp. 130–161). London: Macmillan.

Pogonowski, Lenore. (1989). Metacognition: A dimension of musical thinking. In E. Boardman (Ed.), *Dimensions of musical thinking* (pp. 9–20). Reston, VA: Music Educators National Conference.

Reimer, Bennett. (1989). *A philosophy of music education* (2nd ed.). Englewood Cliffs, NJ: Prentice Hall.

Rich, Adrienne. (1973). *Diving into the wreck, poems 1971–1972*. New York: W. W. Norton.

Rich, Adrienne. (1989). *Time's power, poems 1985–1988*. New York: W. W. Norton.

Schafer, R. Murray. (1976). *Creative music education*. New York: Schirmer.

Shapiro, N. (Ed.). (1967). *Popular music: An annotated index of American popular songs, Vol. 3, 1960–1964*. New York: Adrian Press.

Smith, Dorothy. (1989). Sociological theory: Methods of writing patriarchy. In R. A. Wallace (Ed.), *Feminism and sociological theory* (pp. 36–64). Newbury Park, CA: Sage.

Smith, Dorothy. (1991). Analysis of ideological structures. In Jane Gaskell & Arlene McLaren (Eds.), *Women and education* (rev. ed., pp. 233–256). Calgary, AB: Detselig.

Solie, Ruth. (1991). Whose life? The gendered self in Schumann's Frauenliebe songs. In S. P. Schor (Ed.), *Music and text: Critical Inquiries* (pp. 219–240). New York: Cambridge University Press.

Walker, Robert. (1990). *Musical beliefs: Psychoacoustic, mythical and educational perspectives*. New York: Teachers College Press.

Wise, Sue. (1990). From butch god to teddy bear? Some thoughts on my relationship with Elvis Presley. In Liz Stanley (Ed.), *Feminist praxis* (pp. 134–144). London: Routledge & Kegan Paul.

Wittig, Monique. (1971). *Les guérillères* (P. Owen, Trans.). New York: Viking Press.

Zaimont, Judith Lang. (Ed.). (1991). *The musical woman, Vol. 3, 1986–1990*. Westport, CT: Greenwood Press.

CHAPTER 7

Now You See It, Now You Don't: Gender as an Issue in School Science

Arlene McLaren and Jim Gaskell

I think it's equal here. Like I said, I've never seen any discrimination between females and males. Of course there is some, but you don't see it.
—Girl in a Grade 12 physics course

This quotation illustrates the difficulty many girls have in articulating their experience of inequality in schools. It's there but it isn't. It's equal but there is some discrimination. In the context of liberal discourse about equality, gender neutrality pervades the schools; girls and boys are supposed to be treated alike. Schools are supposed to be meritocracies that make no distinctions based on gender, race, class, sexual orientation, able-bodiedness, and so on. But as many commentators have pointed out, even if girls and boys were treated the same, they would not receive the same education (Howe, 1984; Rich, 1979). Girls and boys bring their gender-connected conventions and expectations into the classroom and these continue unaltered, indeed, strengthened, if they are not addressed (Houston, 1987). In this chapter we will examine the accounts girls construct of their gendered experience in school science and look at the implications of these accounts for developing a more gender-sensitive pedagogy.

In spite of the official discourse of gender neutrality, and the reluctance of schools to directly address issues of gender, there is substantial evidence that gender makes a difference in schools. In school science, researchers have identified differences between males and females in course enrollment, participation in teaching, activities of students, and relations in the classroom (Kahle, 1988; Kelly, 1985; Whyte, 1986). Moreover, the curriculum reflects what men do. In a walk around a physics lab or classroom you typically see pictures of rockets, motor cycles, cars, and posters of the great men of modern science. Pictures of women are hard to find. Sjøberg and Imsen (1988) present evidence that of the myriad possible activities that could be used as possible starting points for school science, or as concrete examples in the treatment of science topics, most school science, especially physics, builds on activities with which boys are more likely to have had experience than girls. Science, in the minds of students and in the perceptions of their teachers, is masculine (Kahle, 1988), and, amongst the sciences, students rate physics as more masculine than chemistry and chemistry as more masculine than biology. This perception may be one of the reasons why girls tend to avoid science in school, particularly physics (Kelly, 1985). Those girls who take science are faced with patterns of classroom interaction in which boys tend to dominate discussion and monopolize the equipment (Whyte, 1986). Alison Kelly (1985) comments on how this pattern can pass without notice:

> The ordinary, everyday, taken-for-granted ways that boys behave form a link between masculinity and dominance in science. These behaviours are commonplace—so commonplace that they are virtually invisible. (p. 141)

Such studies show ways in which school science takes place within a gendered social context and represents dominant male values. Despite the ideology of gender neutrality, school science is highly gendered in practice.

Commentators have suggested a variety of solutions to gender inequality in school science. Early work focused primarily on understanding why girls could not do science as well as boys. A major problem in such an approach is that it tends to blame the victim (Kelly, 1987). Later work has shifted to examining how the structure and organization of school science lead girls to avoid the subject. This perspective has led to recommendations for enriching or transforming school science by making it more girl-friendly through including real-life applications and career opportunities (Smail, 1987) or by making it more feminine through creating a classroom environment that places value on caring, cooperation, ethical issues, subjectivity, and the quality of life (Manthorpe, 1982). Bentley and Watts (1986) argue that this repackaging of school science is too narrow and leaves the masculinity of science unchallenged. They argue that school science should support a feminist science that is "particularly humanistic" and revisions the investigative nature of science itself. Such a feminist science would stress the importance of wisdom, subjectivity, holism, and mystical forms of thought. The authors confidently claim,

"Our view is that girls are seeking a school science that is consistent with our outline of feminist science" (p. 130).

We will argue in this chapter that no attempt to change school science can ignore the responses of girls themselves. We are particularly concerned with how girls make sense of their experiences in school science within a contradictory context that simultaneously denies the significance of gender (by believing that schools should be and in fact are gender neutral) and embodies gender (and its interaction with race and class) as a major element of experience. We examine the responses of 19 girls who in 1989–1990 were enrolled in a variety of math and science courses that included Physics 12, the second year of a two-year senior physics course in British Columbia. We focus on senior physics because so few girls pursue this course. The interviews are part of a larger study that sought to understand the reasons for the participation or nonparticipation in senior math and physical science courses of Grade 12 students in 12 schools throughout British Columbia (Gaskell, McLaren, Oberg, & Eyre, 1992). The study looked at the experiences of both girls and boys, but focused primarily on girls. The small minority of girls enrolled in Physics 12 were mostly from White middle-class families.[1] This underlines the fact that access to physics is not just a gender problem, but also one of social class and race.[2]

Although there is considerable evidence of differences in girls' and boys' experiences in science classes, we know little about the girls' responses to these differences, especially about the responses of those who choose to remain with the subject into the last year of high school. To what extent do girls "see" gender? What does it mean to them? How do they think it affects their school science experiences? We focus, in particular, on girls' interactions with teachers and boys. This is an important component of the hidden curriculum in which girls learn about science and their relation to it. This focus illustrates how gender differences get constructed in schools and the difficulties that girls have in "seeing" the male-dominated nature of their schooling in science.

RESPONSES TO PHYSICS

The girls we consider here were, on the face of it, successes of the school system. They were taking Physics 12, a male-dominated subject, in which almost all the teachers were male, and that had the reputation of generally being the hardest of all the courses. Although one might assume girls enrolled in it would feel successful, most felt ambivalent or negative about the subject and did not feel that they were doing well in it. A few, however, were very enthusiastic about physics:

> Physics is the one that I enjoy the most because I know I'm interested, and we do quite a few experiments, and our teacher is really good. So it's fun.

> Physics, I've got a great teacher and I really like rationalizing skills—like having a problem and trying to work through it and try different things and come down to an answer.

Both these girls related their enthusiasm for physics to the inspiration and encouragement of their physics teachers. They attended highly academic schools, were planning to continue with physics in university, and were thinking about pursuing engineering, medicine, or teaching.

Most of the girls, however, were ambivalent about or did not enjoy Physics 12 and were not planning to continue with physics after high school. For example:

> Physics, I find that kind of boring, but I'm struggling through it. It can be fun, but it's harder to compare it to real world situations. Like with biology you can figure out how the muscles work and things like that, and with physics you're dealing with situations that they have to be almost perfect for you to work with—like air has no friction—so it's harder to take the things that you've learned and look at the real world with it. So it's not as exciting, I don't find, as using formulas and things like that. We do some lab work but not a great deal of lab work. . . . In physics, amazingly enough, I've always gotten Bs which is a surprise, because I don't know what I'm doing.

> For physics, I think you need to really understand what's going on, especially for those experiments. You're not just doing it but you need to understand it, and I think physics is the most difficult one amongst those. I don't like anything in physics.

> Physics 12 is really tough. Sometimes I wonder why I took it since I didn't do that badly in Physics 11, but I didn't do exceptionally well either.

Even when the girls were obtaining As and Bs, they did not necessarily feel that they were doing well in physics. Most felt that physics was boring or that they had difficulty grasping the concepts. What is left unsaid is whether the concepts might be easier to grasp if they were more related to the girls' experiences. The idea that school physics might be different, more related to the diversity of women's interests, is not raised. In trying to understand why they were not more positive about physics relative to other courses, many blamed themselves for their lack of effort and some blamed their teachers. Rarely did the girls frame the discussion around questions of gender—not unless we asked them directly whether or not gender made a difference in their experiences with school math and science.

QUESTIONS OF GENDER

Initially most of the girls responded to questions about gender by saying that boys and girls were treated equally, that schools were gender neutral. However, as the interviews proceeded and the questions became more direct, many of the girls identified ways in which their experiences were different from, and less positive than, those of the boys. Some identified gender bias in their teachers; some talked about put-downs by some of the boys in the classes. However, even when they identified such problems, the girls tended to stress that changes were occurring and that the problem was "taking care of itself." No particular action needed to be taken to highlight the issue. They did not connect their struggles in physics with the gendered context of science.

The girls generally did not spontaneously bring up issues related to gender and even when we asked them directly about whether gender made a difference, some girls insisted that they were not discriminated against in schools or that they did not have different experiences from boys. For example:

> *Interviewer:* Have you faced any particular obstacles in this school as far as doing things in math or science?
> *Student:* They're not discriminating against anybody in this school. They're really good.

Many of the girls thought of an obstacle only as a deliberate form of discouragement and were quick to deny that discrimination existed in their schools.

Some girls distinguished their experiences from those of girls who did not take physics by referring to differences in their cultural backgrounds. When asked if she thought the girls' reactions to the science courses were any different from the boys' reactions, a girl replied:

No, I mean, although like in my physics class there are definitely more boys than girls, no, I don't think so. I think it's within your own family. Like I know a lot of friends, you know, they are not encouraged to take, you know, with a certain cultural background, like some of the Asian background, some of the Indian background, they are not really encouraged to take, you know, to take physics. You know, maybe it's better that they take sewing. I think that's up to a young person's background, what their parents encourage them to do, what their culture encourages them to do. Whereas from my background, there are no expectations. I'm not expected to stay at home; I'm not expected to take sewing or cooking. And so I have a total choice of what I want to do, but no expectations to meet or anything like that.

Here, gender is seen to interact with ethnicity. Gender is a problem for girls in certain cultures but it is not a problem in mainstream, White Canadian culture, which has "no expectations" and "total choice." Gender is not an issue to be addressed by schools. Again, for this student, as for the previous, equality is the absence of active discouragement:

There's nothing to discriminate against me or discourage me from taking science or math; there's nothing. And why the statistics are down, I don't know, but it's not like there's a big discrimination out there or something that we have to fight. It's just maybe old ideas that are subconscious in the back of our mind. There's nothing, you know, big force of people. I mean there are some weird people who go shoot women in Montreal, but generally there's no idea, like counsellors don't discourage girls from taking certain courses.

Overall, this student did not feel discriminated against because discrimination was something "big" that implied coercion, physical force, or violence. Since nothing like this was part of her school experience, there was nothing "to fight" against. The fact that not as many girls as boys took physics is a result of old, subconscious ideas; it is the individual's responsibility to get rid of these ideas on her own. There is no responsibility of teachers in the school to help to surface these ideas and to examine them. There is a sense for this girl that if the school had addressed any of these issues and made her experience in physics any easier then her own achievements and her own sense of herself would have been diminished. Many of the girls valued this gender neutrality in which teachers and counselors seemingly left course choice up to individuals and there was little pressure one way or the other. It was not up to schools to discuss gender and its impact upon girls' lives.

Despite the voluminous literature on the gender biases of teachers (Kelly, 1987; Sarah, 1980), few of the girls referred to sexist treatment by their science teachers. If they noted differential treatment, they often dismissed it. Sometimes this occurred in the jokes told by teachers:

> *Interviewer:* Do you think the teachers treat boys and girls any differently in the class?
>
> *Student:* I think as a joke they might. Jokingly they'll say something but they really never treat anyone . . . I don't think seriously they would. There's, you know, some little wisecrack sometimes, but nothing very serious.

The girls' assessment of their school science experiences took place within a social context in which teachers and students shared cultural expectations about how normal behavior is defined differently for males and females. Only occasionally would incidents occur that girls would identify as showing "double standards" and sexism. The difficulty of identifying and talking about sexism is captured in the following comment:

> *Interviewer:* What about the teachers, do you feel they treat girls . . . do they encourage the girls as much as the boys?
>
> *Student:* I think it's equal here. Like I said, I've never seen any discrimination between females and males. Of course there is some but you don't see it. Like, I've always had my eyes closed, it seems, to things like that. Let's say a guy will just get suspended or something, but a girl can be expelled for something like, say, swearing at a teacher or something. And it's quite obvious, I mean, guys in this school they push each other and, you know, they'll get a warning, but a girl does that, you'll see that they get a lot harsher treatment because they don't expect them to act that way. They're expected not to, they're not to bully around, they're not to push, and not to swear. And you know, they're put in their place, it seems. But you don't see that much, it just depends on who the teacher is and whether it's a girl or a guy.

This passage eloquently describes the taken-for-grantedness of different expectations for boys and girls and the way these unequal expectations make unequal treatment appear normal and, therefore, difficult for girls to talk about.

The sensitivity of this particular girl to these issues can be partially understood by an incident she recounted later in the interview in which one of her teachers accused her of being a racist (he was White; she was Black):

> At one of the meetings I remember him saying something like, "When you look at me you don't look at a teacher, you look at a white teacher." And I don't know where he got that, but even if I did, I didn't. Like I don't say, "You are, whatever." I wouldn't do that. Like I just . . . I was interested in [black power literature].

> You know, his attitude is probably what made me realize that there was discrimination between females and males. If it wasn't for him my eyes would probably be like closed and I would never know. So it was just, it was him and [the principal] who really opened my eyes. I'm more aware and not so ignorant as I was before. I think because I didn't treat him the way he wanted to be treated, it reflected on me as being, first of all a girl, second of all a young girl, like "Who do you think you are telling me what to do?"

This girl was fortunate in that she performed well in her subjects and had a sympathetic counselor to help her sort out the confrontations with her teacher. As she said over and over again in the interview, discrimination was there, but you often did not recognize it. Because she had dealt with racial as well as sexual discrimination, she saw problems of discrimination more than most of the other girls:

> Well, there's always racial discrimination, but uhm, it depends on who you are. If you kind of go into the white crowd and become white then you're looked upon, "You're white," and you don't feel that discrimination. But if you're just a person who follows their religion, they get a lot more discrimination. And it's so evident that nobody seems to want to look at it. Just like men and women, nobody seems to want to look at it, but it's there and you can feel it, but you know, it's just something that society wants to keep under the carpet and wants to sweep it away and say they haven't seen and don't talk about it.

For some girls, the stereotyped ideas that some science teachers held about girls being less able to do science than boys, ideas that led science teachers to talk more to the boys, "really got to them." In a context where issues of gender were not part of the institutional discourse, however, it was difficult for girls to talk about them without their behavior appearing abnormal. The fact that their science teachers were usually men added to the silencing of some of the girls. They were "afraid" to ask questions:

> *Student:* I think, for example, if the teacher is a male, he will talk more to a guy rather than to a girl and they will communicate more to a boy, but if the teacher is a female, I think she would like girls more than boys. Boys, they ask a lot of questions, especially during physics and chemistry and, I don't know, but I think they are more active. Boys, they are more active. But for girls, sometimes they are afraid to ask, right.
>
> *Interviewer:* I wonder why girls are afraid to ask?
>
> *Student:* For myself, I'm afraid to ask. Sometimes I want to ask my friends rather than teachers. If I think, for example, if I have any question about physics I didn't want to ask Mr. X at all, I preferred to ask my friend or others who could help. But, for example, if I have any problem with chemistry I will ask Mrs. Y because I think I have a feeling that she can help me and she didn't mind to do it.
>
> *Interviewer:* So what is it that makes you feel comfortable about asking Mrs. Y and not so comfortable about asking Mr. X?
>
> *Student:* Maybe I think I was fond of Mrs. Y and I like her teaching and her personality so I prefer to ask her so sometimes it depends on the teacher and I don't feel nervous or afraid to ask her. I just feel so friendly. Most of my friends, they don't ask at all, they just ask their friends rather than teachers if they have any questions. They didn't dare to ask their teachers.

This girl felt "friendly" with her female chemistry teacher but not her male physics teacher. Some girls felt positively encouraged by women science teachers, especially if they were sensitive to issues of gender stereotyping:

> *Student:* And then my teacher, when I came here she really persuaded me to . . . she didn't like persuade me but she got me into more like involvement in it. She didn't say, "Well, no, you're no good at it. Don't do it." She [said], "You can do this, so do what you want to do."
>
> *Interviewer:* So after you had a course with her in Grade 11, you felt encouraged to go on in Grade 12?
>
> *Student:* Uh huh. And because she's a woman, she knows what it's

like to have the stereotyping of the, like man only in science. So she helped a lot.

This chemistry teacher encouraged this girl to continue with science and even to plan to become a science teacher herself one day.

Although some girls talked about their experiences in physics being different from and unequal to boys because of the preconceptions and practices of teachers, more girls identified the source of the differences as the ways the boys treated them. The extent to which boys in science teased and harassed the girls, the way it was handled, and the effect it had on girls (and boys) varied. Several girls talked about the ways in which the boys made them feel as if they did not belong in physics. For example, a girl said:

Well, this is an example: in our class there is one guy and he is really, really smart; he has a 90% average and over and he kind of looks at me as if I'm not supposed to be in that class. And he kind of thinks that he's smarter than me and that I'm wasting my time in that class. And then when I get a good mark on my test, I feel really good because I proved to him that I'm not stupid, that I can do it too.

The girl, discussed previously, who had insisted there were "no discrimination" and "no gender differences" in her school, when asked about how boys and girls got along together in physics class, began by continuing the "no difference" theme but then painted a more problematic picture:

Student: Oh! fine. I mean, you know, it's just like working with another girl, working with a guy, you know, there's no difference, I wouldn't say. The only thing sometimes you do something wrong and the guy would look at you and go, "Air head." I mean, occasionally you get comments like that, but it's not really that much of a problem, you know. We work, like I mean, let's say we've been in a program so long with the same people that we know these people, you know, all the people in class are really good friends so that you're so used to the people, you know them so well, that there's no tension or anything like that.

Interviewer: When they say something to you like "air head," what do you say? How do you respond?

Student: That depends, usually I tell them off. I don't know, I guess I'm used to it by now.

Interviewer: What other kinds of things might they say as well as air head?

Student: Well, they usually just say that one, because they're not used to . . . well because what happens is, I guess, traditionally girls in [this school] are very what they would consider nerd-like and study, and all that stuff. And now my friends, I mean, we go in there, you know, we have light-colored hair, and, you know, blond or whatever and we do other things and we go out and party and do what regular teenagers do. A lot of people sort of react to that, "That's weird, she does that and she does well at school?" So a lot of times you do get called air head and stuff like that, I don't know, I mean, I'm used to it.

"No difference" dissolved into a choice between being considered "nerds" or "air heads." Since she and her friends had "light-colored hair" and could "party," this girl was able to establish her difference from other girls, who were "nerds." She had accepted, or at least had gotten "used to," being called an "air head." Her comment was particularly revealing given the ethnic composition of her school, in which a large proportion of the students were Asian or East Indian who had what she considered to be traditional values about female roles. She seemed to imply that being White ("blond") placed her in a preferred category. She was able to use her race and culture to gain an advantage over many of the girls but she could not stop the boys from asserting their own power by labeling her as an "air head."

The fact that being an "air head" was something that you had to get "used to" suggests that it was not desirable. However, in this context she was not prepared to identify it as a problem. To do so might have jeopardized her determination to do well in science and math while still remaining friends with the boys—an essential element of not being called a "nerd." She had resolved to her satisfaction the cultural contradiction between femininity and science, using her race and social class to facilitate this resolution. She was one of the few girls who felt unequivocally positive about physics and planned to pursue this area of science at university.

Many of the girls had contradictory relations with the boys in physics classes. Though they often talked about their difficult relations with the boys, they also recognized that their friendships with the boys were important and that boys who were "fair" often outweighed the others:

Interviewer: Do you feel that sometimes there is unequal treatment in this school?

Student: Uh huh. Well, not really. I guess not, no. No. There isn't any unfair treatment for sciences, like for girls and guys, you know. They've all been treated equally. Just the guys the way they think they're better than the girls. Even that, there's not much here because everyone's friends with everyone. It seems to me, like maybe someone else, maybe not.

Interviewer: So that the guys are pretty fair-minded with the girls?

Student: Well, of course, there's some egotistical, you know, chauvinistic ones, but uhm, the ones that are fair, they outweigh the ones that aren't, so you don't see them as much.

Although most of the boys were fair in not actively putting down the girls, it did not appear that the girls were generally prepared to take on the boys who drew on social resources to assert the power of men over women.

Some girls did not, however, dismiss so easily the way that boys "ganged up" on them in science classes:

Well there's only . . . there's four girls in my physics class this year and like last year in Physics 11 a lot of the guys, you know, they have this thing, you know, we're better than girls, so that discouraged a lot of them because they didn't. . . . "Well, so and so can do this better than I can because he's a guy. I can't do this so I'm not going to bother." So there's like out of one class, there's only one class of Physics 12 and there's four girls.

She insisted that the lower enrollment of girls in Physics 12 was not because of the teachers: "The teachers encourage everything; encourage it all. They treat us all equal." But with the boys:

I don't like guys telling me that I'm not as good as they are in whatever area it might be. It's like . . . that was a long time ago, you know, women were, you know, stay home, and do the housework but now . . . maybe if they say it as a joke but it really gets to me. I don't know why. Whatever we're doing, they're always making comments about how women are inferior and stuff like that.

Just having the teachers encourage the girls was not enough when the girls were being discouraged by the boys. The behavior of some of the boys, who often put down the girls, needed to be taken on. In her chemistry class, the female teacher "dished it out too" when the boys joked around with her about females and science, but this did not resolve the problem of harassment for the girls. Such a response led to a contest to see who had the quickest wit; it did not throw the power and authority of the school behind a position that the jokes were illegitimate to begin with. For this particular girl, it was the response of a girlfriend who stuck up for the girls that she most appreciated:

> Well, there's this one girl in my class, like she's one of my good friends, and she's really strong-willed, and she's determined. And no matter who it is in the class that says something about putting women down, she just rips their head off practically, because she's used to it, you know, she's got, you know, I guess some of her family may be putting her down, or whatever, but it's good to hear her. Like it's good to hear anybody with . . . and sometimes even some of the other guys stick up for us.

Despite the fact that the teacher was sensitive to questions about gender, she played a minor role when the boys picked on the girls.

Even though many of the girls saw through the put-downs of the boys, the frequency of the negative comments could lead to self-doubts:

> Like there's some I know, there's some guys, you know, smarter in our class, right, and they have the saying that, you know, they automatically take women as a lower thing in life or whatever. And I think whether you mean to or not, that does get in the way and you start thinking, "Oh well, he's smart; he must know," kind of thing, right? And you start thinking, in all the textbooks and stuff all you see is guys. . . . In the textbook you see, this guy invented this sort of thing, a lot in the math and sciences. That's all you really see. You start thinking, "Oh, maybe it's because females can't really do that," and I think, that sort of affects it, maybe not because they really particularly think about it, but I think that it may have something to do with it unconsciously or whatever. I just sort of get that impression.

Boys may feel freer to harass girls in science than in other classrooms. By reading the culture, which suggests that science is a male domain, boys can easily reproduce these messages. Because the problem of harassment of female students by male students is not part of the official curriculum, students have to deal with it informally. What does not seem to happen is a serious discussion about gender, how it is organized in the culture, how it affects students' lives, and how girls should respond to sexist comments, curriculum, and pedagogy.

How can one make gender an issue in science classrooms without also destroying friendships and patterns of work that help the girls learn science? Several of the girls with whom we talked referred to the help they received from the boys in science rather than from their teachers. One of the girls above was bothered by the boys ganging up on the girls:

> *Student:* I'm starting to learn (physics) better now. I'm going in for extra help.
> *Interviewer:* And so it's to the teacher you go in for extra help?
> *Student:* And some other students who know what they're doing. Some of the guys know, like, what they're doing, so lots of times I go ask them for help.

Later she explained the apparent contradiction in her relations with some of the boys:

> I find myself working more with the guys because, even though they tease me about not knowing it, once they get serious, they will sit down and help me.

Once the power relations are made clear, help can be given! Other girls also emphasized the help they received from the boys in their classes, for example:

> Last year I asked the teacher all the time. I had the same teacher last year as this year. This year, on either side of me, there are two guys who are really smart, so I usually just ask them.

> Well, I try to participate in class by asking questions. Then, I'm not really, I'm not usually satisfied with the teacher's answers so I ask other guys. They explain it better and they have different, easier ways too. The guys, sometimes they find shortcuts. They know an easier way to the question. I try to listen to the teacher even though he's boring.

One reason some girls relied on boys was because the girls were fearful of their science teachers or were dissatisfied with the teachers' responses. Though the boys may have intimidated and harassed them, the boys were also often friends, and were more approachable than the teachers. Some girls had little choice but to turn to the boys.

It is interesting to see how this process of turning for help to some boys who were smart led to language on the part of some girls that made all boys smart in physics.

> It seems like guys are smarter because we have these two scholars in the physics class, and they did really well. They got 90% throughout the year. And I was just going, I got my A but I was, you know, fluctuating. My marks were fluctuating, right.

> I think the guys are having an easier time in physics, it seems. Just looking at some of the marks that they're getting. A lot of the guys in our class are really smart and it comes easily to them and some of us girls are, we have to work at things, getting high marks and being smart. Seems that most of the guys in our class, it just comes really easy to them.

One way that boys seemed to maintain their status in science classes was to harass the girls and make them feel as if they did not belong. Though many of the girls performed well, they still felt that they were not good enough. Many of the girls had doubts about their abilities and felt "dumb" relative to the boys. The fact that gender issues may have been involved was rarely addressed explicitly in science classrooms.

Nonetheless, not all girls were intimidated by the boys and not all believed that the boys were smarter than the girls:

> I walked in that class the first time and looked at them and they looked totally smart. All the guys, they were all the smart people that take all maths and science and calculus. That was at first. But now I ask questions and all that, so it's not that hard or different. I think the girls try more. The guys seem to be lazy.

> The girls in physics class, most of them are doing really well or doing their best anyway. There are boys that are doing equally as well, but there's a lot of them that aren't even interested in physics but they're still there. It's just a course, it's a credit.

These girls were able to overcome and transcend the pressures of bantering, intimidation, discouragement, and discrimination. Their ability to withstand such pressures belied the daily struggles that many faced, and ironically, reinforced the assumption that gender was not a problem in school science.

Given the lack of attention to gender in the official curriculum, most girls could see little choice but to tough it out. They dismissed as much as possible the boys' harassment and believed that times were changing, that things were getting better for women, and that, if they really worked hard, they could achieve what they wished:

> I think that in a couple of years, [girls' and boys' participation in science classes] will be 50/50.

> But now a lot of girls are being doctors, so they want those courses. It's looking after itself. You don't have to encourage people that much. It's getting better.

> I think it's a lot better now because I know a lot of girls who are taking sciences.

> Like I'm interested in going into aviation, and I can do that now because they're letting women fly and become pilots. In that way people are thinking, well I may as well go into say physics or something because women are being allowed into such and such a field that interests me that maybe awhile ago you wouldn't have been able to get into.

Despite the fact that most of them were having difficulties in physics and did not intend to continue with it, they were optimistic that the problem of girls and science was "taking care of itself." The girls were able to identify some fields that had opened up more for women. They had a sense of wider options for their future education and careers. They had cause for optimism and assumed that an overt challenge was not needed.

In our study, the girls struggled to meet the demands of school science on its own male-defined terms. They did not disrupt the classroom to ensure that the curriculum addressed their needs. Their responses contrast with those of boys documented by researchers (Eyre, 1991; Sarah, 1980; Walkerdine, 1981). These authors found that boys tend to draw upon the cultural authority of being male to negotiate power with teachers, especially if the teachers are female. The boys had more power in the classroom than the girls in their relations with the girls and with the teachers. Eyre (1991) found that home economics teachers made special efforts to ensure that the curriculum would attract the attention of boys. Several had changed the curriculum to accommodate the boys: "I do just cover the basics because the boys would get a little lost," "I want to get boys more comfortable with the things women have traditionally done," "I say, 'This is a machine. It has a clutch . . .' All these similarities to things that are masculine help. I think I joke with the boys more than I do with the girls. . . . They need to feel secure in what is traditionally a girls' area" (p. 200). This kind of accommodation did not seem to happen to the girls.

The girls taking senior physics had less power than the boys in the class-room. They were harassed by some of the boys and were generally con-fronted with at least two layers of authority—teacher as expert and teacher as male.[3] The girls were reluctant to challenge the behavior of the male harassers and saw few alternatives to the present construction of school physics. They could not, when asked, envisage how physics could be transformed to reflect their interests.

> I don't really know, I guess, there is no way. It's the same subject; you can't change it. Movies or something, I don't know, there is nothing you can really change about it.

> I don't think they can. I think it's just the people who want to take them. If you don't think you're capable of doing those courses you shouldn't be pushed into it, because some people just don't understand.

A few girls did suggest changes such as having better science teachers, having more female science teachers, using labs more, incorporating real life examples into the curriculum, showing students more ways to use math and science in their everyday lives, and integrating arts with sci-ence. Still, most felt that nothing could be done to transform the curricu-lum itself and did not see how the curriculum related to gender.

TOWARD A GENDER-SENSITIVE, CRITICAL PEDAGOGY OF SCIENCE

Questions of gender arose in our discussions with the girls in Physics 12, but in complex, contradictory, and limited ways. Sometimes the girls saw it; sometimes they did not. Many of the girls we talked to down-played the differences in experiences between females and males, or at least pointed to the improved conditions for girls and women that made their experiences increasingly similar to those of boys and men. Many also referred to various other forms of gender differences such as biologi-cal, psychological, and cultural differences.

Overall, however, the girls did not articulate issues related to gender as a major problem in school science. This was not just because they were "blinded" by patriarchal, meritocratic, and scientistic ideologies, but be-cause they had to make the best of their situation. Little official acknowl-edgement was given in their schools of the gender-related difficulties they faced. They were mainly left to their own resources. Given the cultural perception of physics as male (reinforced by posters, textbooks, exercises, examples, etc.) and the male dominance of their classes, it made sense to downplay gender. To highlight gender differences in experiences might exacerbate even more the girls' status of being the "other." Thus the girls tended to dismiss their harassment by some boys as a joke and to point to the help that other boys were prepared to give. The discourse of gender neutrality seemed to be more powerful—safer, simpler, easier to express, and having greater official recognition—than a discourse of gender difference.

Thus these girls' persistence and successes, ironically, masked the struggles that they encountered. Since struggles of gender (as well as race, class, sexual orientation, etc.) were not part of the official curriculum, they were generally ignored, and few attempts were made by the girls to overcome them. Without official status within the curriculum, problems of gender remained individualized: it was almost impossible to raise questions about the different social worlds for girls and boys, about how physics could be transformed to reflect different interests and concerns, and about how girls' difficulties in physics were connected to classroom dynamics of males' harassment of females.

The girls' portrayal of gender differences draws attention to the necessity of making gender (in all its differences) an explicit part of the science curriculum. In addition, their concerns about gender neutrality reveal the complexity of this task because discussing gender differences has both liberatory and retrogressive implications. It can revalue female experiences and provide visions of a more promising future for both males and females, but it can also reinforce sexual stereotypes, patterns of subordination, and conflicts between the sexes. This means that neither a stress on gender similarities nor a stress on gender differences is a panacea for feminist reform or transformation (see Scott, 1990). As Snitow (1990) suggests, this tension between gender similarity and gender difference is as old as Western feminism and is at the heart of its meaning. This tension is always with us. We need to embrace the paradox, which will only change through historical process and not dissolve through thought. We need to conceive of this paradox as a dynamic force that not only divides very different women and men in unsettling ways but also unites them.

Our study suggests that school science must take into account the kinds of concerns, ambivalences, and tensions that are voiced by girls about their school science experiences. What is needed is a gender-sensitive perspective on the curriculum that allows for taking gender into account when it makes a difference in furthering sex equality and ignoring it when it does not (Martin, 1985; Vertinsky, this volume). Specific approaches from such a perspective will necessarily vary from context to context.

While it is important to take on explicitly the structure of gender relations in the classroom, it is also important to look at the construction of science as male. Several writers have attempted to imagine a feminist science education by first outlining what a feminist science might look like. Rosser (1990), for example, lays out a variety of characteristics of feminist science based on Belenky, Clinchy, Goldberger, and Tarule's (1986) alternative ways of knowing and then uses these characteristics for suggesting a feminist pedagogy in science.

The idea of a feminist science, however, has encountered resistance. Longino (1989) cautions against a view of feminist science that encodes a particular worldview and assumes a particular female sensibility or cognitive temperament. Such a view denies the diversity of women's experiences and, therefore, frameworks. Keller (1989) also cautions against the hasty embrace of a "different science" that would necessarily replace current science and argues, instead, for a notion of "difference in science" that reclaims a richer, more multifaceted approach to doing science. Longino and Keller resist the collapsing of the complex experiences of people and science to simple dualities: masculinist science or feminist science. Following Longino, we suggest that the issue needs to be reframed from a concern with constructing a feminist science to one of constructing science as a feminist.

When constructing science as a feminist, issues of gender, race, class, and so on are a conscious and central component of classroom and curriculum discourse; issues of gender, science, and school science are made problematic. In approaching this goal, it is important to understand the views of girls, boys, and teachers concerning gender in school science in order to be able to work with those views. Rather than imposing our views about gender difference upon girls, we need to look, first, at the concerns and ambivalences girls (and boys) and men and women teachers have about gender as an issue in science. Ultimately, we need to bring all these concerns (in all their diversity) into the curriculum and to ensure that pedagogy enables this.

In a male-dominated context, such a program of action, needless to say, will not be easy. As Lewis (1990) found, engaging in a feminist critique of classroom dynamics may lead to the reproduction of exactly the practices that are being criticized. Feminist practice/politics, rather than ameliorating women's feelings of threat, may exacerbate them. There are no simple techniques for achieving equity in school science. The different voices of girls need to be heard. The ways in which gender and science affect girls' lives need to be understood so that girls do not take on the blame for their difficulties. The gendered experiences of girls and boys need to be part of the official curriculum.

NOTES

1. The relationship of girls' (and boys') enrollment in physics with social class has been noted elsewhere. See, for example, Kelly, Whyte, and Smail (1987).
2. The mandate of our study was to examine the significance of gender, not race or class. But because of the importance of the latter dimensions in the girls' lives, they became part of our analysis, though not as fully as we would have liked.
3. Depending on the students, they may be confronted with many other layers of authority: teacher as White, teacher as middle class, teacher as heterosexual, teacher as able-bodied, and so on.

REFERENCES

Belenky, Mary, Clinchy, Blythe, Goldberger, Nancy, & Tarule, Jill. (1986). *Women's ways of knowing: The development of self, voice and mind.* New York: Basic Books.

Bentley, Di, & Watts, Mike. (1986). Courting the positive virtues: A case for feminist science. *European Journal of Science Education, 8*(2), 121–134.

Eyre, Linda. (1991). Gender relations in the classroom: A fresh look at coeducation. In Jane S. Gaskell & Arlene McLaren (Eds.), *Women and education* (pp. 193–219). Calgary, AB: Detselig.

Gaskell, P. James, McLaren, Arlene, Oberg, Antoinette, & Eyre, Linda. (1992). *The 1990 British Columbia mathematics assessment: Gender issues in student choices in mathematics and science.* Report submitted to the British Columbia Minister of Education. Victoria: British Columbia Ministry of Education.

Houston, Barbara. (1987). Should public education be gender-free? In G. Nemiroff (Ed.), *Women and men: Interdisciplinary readings on gender* (pp. 134–149). Toronto: Fitzhenry & Whiteside.

Howe, Florence. (1984). *Myths of coeducation.* Bloomington: Indiana University Press.

Kahle, Jane. (1988). Gender and science education: 2. In P. Fensham (Ed.), *Development and dilemmas in science education* (pp. 249–265). New York: Falmer Press.

Keller, Evelyn. (1989). The gender/science system: or, is sex to gender as nature is to science? In N. Tuana (Ed.), *Feminism and science* (pp. 33–44). Bloomington: Indiana University Press.

Kelly, Alison. (1985). The construction of masculine science. *British Journal of Sociology of Education, 6*(2), 133–154.

Kelly, Alison. (1987). *Science for girls?* Milton Keynes, UK: Open University Press.

Kelly, Alison, Whyte, Judith, & Smail, Barbara. (1987). Girls into science and technology: Final report. In Alison Kelly (Ed.), *Science for girls?* (pp. 100–112). Milton Keynes, UK: Open University Press.

Lewis, Magda. (1990). Interrupting patriarchy: Politics, resistance, and transformation in the feminist classroom. *Harvard Educational Review, 60*(4), 467–488.

Longino, Helen. (1989). Can there be a feminist science? In N. Tuana (Ed.), *Feminism and science* (pp. 45–57). Bloomington: Indiana University Press.

Manthorpe, Catherine. (1982). Men's science, women's science or science: Some issues related to the study of girls' science education. *Studies in Science Education, 9*, 65–80.

Martin, Jane R. (1985). *Reclaiming an education: The ideal of the educated woman.* New Haven, CT: Yale University Press.

Rich, Adrienne. (1979). Taking women students seriously. In Adrienne Rich, *On lies, secrets and silence* (pp. 237–245). New York: W. W. Norton.

Rosser, Sue. (1990). *Female friendly science.* New York: Pergamon.

Sarah, Elizabeth. (1980). Teachers and students in the classroom: An examination of classroom interaction. In D. Spender & Elizabeth Sarah (Eds.), *Learning to lose: Sexism and education* (pp. 155–164). London: Women's Press.

Scott, Joan. (1990). Deconstructing equality-versus-difference: Or, the uses of poststructuralist theory for feminism. In M. Hirsch & E. F. Keller (Eds.), *Conflicts in feminism* (pp. 134–148). New York: Routledge, Chapman & Hall.

Sjøberg, Svein, & Imsen, Gunn. (1988). Gender and science education: 1. In Peter Fensham (Ed.), *Development and dilemmas in science education* (pp. 218–248). New York: Falmer Press.

Smail, Barbara. (1987). Encouraging girls to give physics a second chance. In Arlene Kelly (Ed.), *Science for girls?* (pp. 113–118). Milton Keynes, UK: Open University Press.

Snitow, Ann. (1990). A gender diary. In M. Hirsch & E. F. Keller (Eds.), *Conflicts in feminism* (pp. 9–43). New York: Routledge, Chapman & Hall.

Walkerdine, Valerie. (1981). Sex, power and pedagogy. *Screen Education, 38*, 14–23.

Whyte, Judith. (1986). *Girls into science and technology: The story of a project.* London: Routledge & Kegan Paul.

CHAPTER 8

The Radical Future of Gender Enrichment

JANE ROLAND MARTIN

How does the study of gender enrich curriculum? Let me count the ways.

I

The androcentrism of the disciplines of knowledge is by now an established fact. Thanks to the study of gender, we know, for example, that the field of history, that comprehensive study of the past, misrepresents when it does not entirely skip over the lives, works, and experiences of women.[1] We know that instead of being universal, as claimed, psychology's norms and its narratives of human development have been derived from studies of boys and men. We even know that biology's accounts of nature have mapped society's sex stereotypes onto the animal "kingdom," its studies of primates have consistently made the male the main actor of the troop and the linchpin of that small society, its predominant account of human cultural evolution has done likewise although there is no more evidence for the theory named "man-the-hunter" than for the one called "woman-the-gatherer."

In addition, research on gender has cast doubt on the very objectivity of the judgments by which some works of art, literature, history, science, and philosophy have been deemed valuable, or even great, and others have been put in the scrap heap. I do not simply mean that scholars have recovered long lost works by women and that recent research challenges the portrayals of women enshrined in science and history as well as in literature and the arts. Accepted definitions of what constitutes great art and literature and even good science have been called into question

157

by the study of gender and so has the idea of canonizing any set of works.

Insofar as school's course of study draws its subject matter from fields such as history, literature, mathematics, the natural sciences, the human and social sciences—as of course it does to a great extent—it repeats these distortions. But to recognize that the gender bias of the disciplines is reflected in the subject matter of school is one thing and to improve the school curriculum is another. If this end is to be achieved, more accurate representations of women's lives, works, and experiences must be incorporated into the school curriculum.

The question is, how? Even as some scholars have begun to reconstruct the intellectual disciplines, others have distinguished different stages of curricular change and have debated the pros and cons of making the study of women a separate subject as opposed to integrating subject matter about women into existing school subjects. The question is also, which women? Do we introduce into the school curriculum a few famous ones or do we attempt to bring in all women? And whichever course we adopt, do we unthinkingly cast our net so as to include only middle-class, White women or do we make sure to reach out to all women?

As participants in the National Seeking Educational Equity and Diversity (SEED) Project on Inclusive Curriculum[2] and other groups attempting to transform the school curriculum, we all know that the task of subject matter inclusion is as challenging as any curriculum maker could wish. Yet it would be a mistake to think that the androcentrism of the school curriculum is due solely to the fact that its subject matter mirrors the gender biases of the intellectual disciplines. By alerting us to the contamination in one of curriculum's wellsprings, the study of gender allows us to shut off a major source of distortion and misrepresentation. But school's subject matter normally comes wrapped up in those neat bundles we call "subjects" and even a quick survey of these by one wearing gender-sensitive lenses reveals another kind of bias.

II

At a time when we are continually being reminded that gender is a social construction, it is not always remembered that school subjects are constructions too (Martin, 1982). Our subjects were never just "out there" in the world waiting to be brought into school's course of study. On the contrary, those bundles of subject matter that are so often treated as God-given were actually made by human beings. This does not mean that curriculum development is a capricious enterprise or that school subjects are nothing but arbitrary collections of subject matter. It does, however, signify that one of the most important decisions curriculum makers face is that of determining which of the innumerable things there are should serve as the points of departure for our school subjects.

That every school subject takes something in the world as its starting point is seldom acknowledged, perhaps because a subject usually derives its name from what, for want of a better term, I will call its *subject-entity*. Thus, the school subject physics draws its name from the science physics, the school subject French draws its name from the language French, the school subject reading draws its name from the activity of reading. Quite clearly, despite the sameness of name, a subject is not identical with its subject-entity. On the one hand, the subject French, for instance, has an educational function that the language French does not; on the other, the subject matter belonging to the subject French can be drawn from a whole range of sources that includes the French language but goes beyond it to, for instance, linguistics, literature, history, and geography.

Now I can think of only one subject, and it is very much to the point that I am not sure what name to give it—should I be calling it home economics, family studies, or something else altogether?—that clearly and unequivocally draws its subject-entity from "the world of the private house," to use Virginia Woolf's phrase (Woolf, 1938, p. 18). Need I say that, historically, this world has been considered women's domain? Need I add that even in the best of times this school subject tends to be situated much closer to the margins of curriculum than to the center, and that when there are budget crises, the subjects on the margins are the first to go?

The devaluation of home economics—or family studies, if you prefer—is not news. Study the social construction called gender, however, and one sees that the negative assessment is part of a larger pattern of discrimination against a whole class of subject-entities.

The very different treatment in the school curriculum of the strikingly similar cases of politics and education illustrates the double standard by which subject-entities are judged (Martin, 1992, p. 139). As activities in the real world around which institutions have grown up, education and politics would each seem well-suited to be a subject-entity of a school subject. Nevertheless, one and not the other has been welcomed into the general or liberal curriculum in this capacity. Notice that in becoming a subject-entity the activity called "politics" has been converted from an occupation to be undertaken into an object of study. Students are taught theory, history, and research *about* politics, not politics itself. Success in the subject that sometimes goes under the name "political science" and sometimes "government" is judged by the comprehension of a body of knowledge and perhaps the ability to undertake relevant inquiries, not by the efficacy of action taken in the real world. But the activity we call "education" can also be recast. It too has inspired its fair share of theory and research, some of it as enlightening and profound as one could wish. And despite disclaimers, education is no less interesting than politics. Indeed, from the standpoint of the survival of both the individual and society, not to mention the planet, it is surely as important a set of activities and institutions as any.

Why have curriculum makers favored politics as a subject-entity over education? The advantage politics has is that, considering it one of society's "productive" processes, North American culture has situated it in the public world and placed it in men's care. Education's problem is that even though school has moved it out of the private home and into the public world, it is seen as a "reproductive" societal process whose "natural" practitioners are still assumed to be women (Martin, 1985).

Just to recognize the unequal treatment of subject-entities drawn from society's reproductive processes or associated in our cultural consciousness with home and family is to enrich curriculum making. After all, calling attention to the unrepresentative nature of our subject-entities, and hence our subjects, is a necessary prelude to redressing the curricular imbalance. However, I do not see how the double standard can be abolished if the gap in school's goals is not filled in.

III

Don the lenses of a student of gender and one sees not only the absences and distortions in the content of today's course of study and a serious subject-entity imbalance. One notices for perhaps the first time the telling omission in the list of goals curriculum is supposed to further (Martin, 1990, 1992).

It has been said that "the stated goals of education in modern democratic societies remain constant: the development of each person as (1) a worker, (2) a citizen, and (3) an individual" (Waks & Rustum, 1987, p. 24). A case for adding (4) a keeper of the cultural heritage can be made, and the list with this emendation seems correct. To be sure, the four goals are not given equal time in every discussion of education. Still, together they represent the full range of what education is expected to do. That these expectations fail to take account of a basic function of education in a modern or post-modern society, namely, (5) the development of each person as a member of a home and family, escapes everyone's notice.

Let me make it clear that in adding (5) to the list I am not presupposing any particular type of home and family, let alone some traditional form with its gender inequalities. Lesbian families, interracial families, stepfamilies, single parent ones: whatever the type, education is needed for life therein. Yet, for example, in the spate of reports published in the 1980s on the condition of education in the United States, home and family were all but ignored. Granted, the reports did advise parents to support the teacher's authority and warn them against dereliction in their duty to monitor homework. The thought that school might be derelict in *its* duty to prepare young people to live in those private homes and families from which they exit each morning did not occur to the authors of these tomes. It did not occur to their many critics either.

An analysis that recognizes that institutions as well as individuals are gendered explains the gap. One major assumption underlying educational thought in the United States today, and presumably in other Western nations as well, is that the function of school in a modern democratic society is to prepare children, practically all of whom are born into the domestic environment of the home and who spend their earliest years in close contact with its ongoing reproductive processes, to take their places in the larger society—in the "public world" of politics, economics, and "high" culture. To be sure, almost all those who enter the larger world continue to live their lives in private homes as members of private families, albeit in homes and families of many different sorts. Yet my compatriots do not seem to think that the tasks and activities carried out in the latter or the personal qualities one needs in order to function well there require education. Holding onto the by now discredited perception of home and family as "natural" institutions, retaining the outmoded custom of assigning women primary responsibility for running them, and persisting in the mistaken belief that whatever knowledge and skill are needed are either innately female or will be picked up informally by girls and women as they mature, they assume that these things will take care of themselves.

The evidence suggests otherwise. Although the statistics on domestic violence in the United States vary considerably depending on which reports one reads, it seems safe to say that at least 2 million women are beaten by their husbands each year and that as many as 600,000 are severely assaulted by their husbands four or more times a year. Violence in the other direction—by women toward their husbands and lovers—does occur, but in comparison to these figures its incidence is negligible (Breines & Gordon, 1983; Langone, 1984; Reynolds, 1987).

If the incidence of wife beating is staggering, so is that of child abuse. Recent studies suggest that 38 million adults were sexually abused as children and that, in all, 22% of Americans are victimized, with this proportion quite possibly on the rise. Investigators are now discovering that males as well as females are victims of child sexual abuse and that women as well as men are the victimizers. There is not equal representation in the two categories, however. Female victims far outnumber males and the great majority of offenders are men. Interestingly enough, despite our ever-present fear that a stranger will molest our children, the vast majority of child sexual abuse cases occur in or close to home. Nearly 8 million of those victimized as children were abused by a family member. When the abuser is not a family member, he or she—but far more likely he—is very probably a family friend or else a neighbor, the family physician, or someone standing in loco parentis: a baby-sitter or day-care worker, a teacher or coach, a foster parent or a member of the staff of an institution for abused and neglected children (Breines & Gordon, 1983; Crewdson, 1988).

Include in this picture the statistics on divorce and desertion and one sees clearly the folly of assuming that in American society, at least, being a person who contributes positively to home and family comes naturally.

The reasons for adding (5) to the list of educational goals and for restructuring the school curriculum accordingly are many, but a nagging question remains. If education for family living is really needed, is it not home's responsibility rather than school's? School and home are indeed partners in the education of a nation's young (Martin, 1992). Moreover, it is correct to say that, in the past, (5) was assigned to the hidden partner whose continuing contributions to a child's development are both relied on by school and society and refused public recognition. But home and family have been transformed in the last decades. As John Dewey pointed out almost a century ago in connection with the changes in the American household wrought by the Industrial Revolution, when conditions change radically "Only an equally radical change in education suffices" (Dewey, 1943, p. 12).

Dewey's answer to the question he posed in *The School and Society* of what radical change in school suffices when home changes—namely, placing the occupations of the once traditional home at the center of the school curriculum—does not address the problems created at century's end by the most recent transformation of our private homes. The issue today is not the removal of work from the household into factories but the domestic vacuum that is created when mothers as well as fathers leave home each day to go to work. To be sure, it is not just in the last decades that women have left their own homes to go to work—often in other women's homes. But in the past it was primarily the very poor who did not return home once they had children.

Let me emphasize that to acknowledge this new reality is not to blame mothers for going out to work. After all, if fathers had not already done so there would be no domestic vacuum. However, the evidence I have cited suggests that in the United States, at least, the changed and changing home is not adequately handling the assignment of teaching young children to live at home in families and preparing older ones for their future lives there. There would seem, then, to be no alternative but to respond to Dewey's challenge by adding (5) to our list of the goals of schooling.

That curriculum will thereby be enriched goes without saying. Why is so little space presently reserved in the general curriculum for subject-entities and subject matter associated with home and family? The curricular gap is explained by the gap in our goals. Why learn about home and family, why study society's reproductive processes, if school's function is to equip students to take their places as workers and citizens in the world outside the private home? Granted, education's goals do not dictate the details of curriculum. But just as the exclusion of (5) from the list accounts for its extraordinary absence in school's course of study, its inclusion will insure the presence of what has been left out—or at least *some* of what is missing, for (5) can all too easily be interpreted very narrowly. It can be construed as mandating simply that curriculum space be given over to theories and narratives *about* home. It is equally important, however, that boys and girls alike learn to exercise the virtues that our culture thinks of as housed in our private homes.

IV

Basic knowledge about home and family—for instance, about their histories and their different cultural forms, indeed, the fact that they have histories and take different forms—has been missing from the school curriculum because of the gap in school's goals and the prejudice against subject-entities drawn from society's reproductive processes. But that is not all. In the reports issued in the 1980s on American higher education, lower education, teacher certification, and professional preparation, one finds repeated demands for proficiency in the 3Rs; for clear, logical thinking; and for higher standards of achievement in science, mathematics, history, literature, and the like. One searches in vain for discussions of love or calls for mastery of the 3Cs of care, concern, and connection.

Once again, a gender analysis explains the omission (Martin, 1992, pp. 136–137). Associated in our cultural consciousness with home and with the reproductive processes housed there, and viewed as women's exclusive property, the 3Cs are thought to have no bearing on the activities of the public world. Those reports on the condition of American education testify, however, to the preoccupation of educators with life in that domain. Giving home the silent treatment, they view boys and girls as travelers to the public arena, and school as the place they stop en route in order to acquire the knowledge, skill, attitudes, and values that they will presumably need when they reach their destination.

Once children enter school they do not go home again in this unexamined scenario—not ever, not even as adults. True, the authors of the reports expected children to do something called "homework," but the term is a misnomer. Designed by teachers as part of the ongoing work of the classroom, these assignments have no more to do with the business of the home than the briefs a lawyer reads on the commuter train each evening or the papers a teacher corrects after dinner. Homework is schoolwork done after school hours. The worksite may be the private home, but the home represented in the script is a house in which the silence of school prevails and parents act as proctors for their offspring.

The reports turn school's partner in the educational enterprise into an antagonist ever ready to subvert its mission. The idea that because home has changed school might have to change did not occur to the authors of these tomes. The thought that school should take over its partner's responsibility of preparing young people to live in those homes and families from which they exit each morning first to go to school and then to go to work in the public world was the furthest thing from their minds.

Obviously, to go beyond is not necessarily to leave behind. Nevertheless, in the United States, if not in all Western societies, people tend to think of becoming educated not just as a process of acquiring new ways of thinking, feeling, and acting. They also assume that it is a matter of casting off attitudes and values and patterns of thought and action associated with domesticity.

Does it matter? In May 1989 a courageous 16-year-old wrote to the *Boston Globe* expressing concern about the rise in teen violence (cf. Martin, 1992, pp. 44–45; Naples, 1989). He said he had gotten used to kids carrying knives, but now they were carrying guns. "There are a couple of reasons for this rise," he said, "but the main one is to be tough or respected. They feel power when they have that deadly piece of steel in their hand. Another reason is that they are so easy to get." Since he had observed this change in just 6 months, he wondered what the world would be like in 6 years. Would it turn into "a combat zone" controlled by kids with guns?

Historians have shown that when the Industrial Revolution irrevocably changed the American household by removing both work and workers from it, home—specifically the White, middle- and upper-class home—came to be viewed as a haven in a cold, cruel world: the place to which men retreated after spending a long day in the greedy, pugnacious, possessive, jealous public arena. Whether or not it ever actually fit this description, its presumed ethos of love and intimacy and the values of care, concern, and connection it was said to embody were thought to be conducive to the rest and renewal required by the husbands and sons who were expected to reenter the fray each morning. But home's culturally assigned task was not merely to refresh and invigorate. It was expected to play a moral role as well. Besides inducting infants into human culture and teaching young children the basics of American life, it was supposed to provide its members with an ongoing education in the very kindness and cooperation, affection and sympathy that were also considered to be the prerequisites of life in a harmonious society.

According to Dewey (1943), before the Industrial Revolution, industry, responsibility, imagination, and ingenuity were the basic elements of home's curriculum. Perhaps so, but after that cataclysmic event it was considered home's particular function to teach what Carol Gilligan has called an "ethics of care." Serving to curb the selfishness and dampen the pugnacity of men who spent their days in the public world of work and politics, the moral education extended by the home was supposed to keep society as a whole from slipping into a war of every man against every man. As the nations of nineteenth-century Europe were deemed able to keep the peace so long as the balance of power among them was maintained, the individuals in a society were considered able to live together harmoniously so long as the moral equilibrium between private home and public world was preserved.

Whatever efficacy that delicate balance of home and world might once have had, the changes in both make our continued reliance on home for a curriculum in an ethics of care anachronistic. That the 3Cs are vital to the well-being of the world beyond the private home and essential to the maintenance of life on earth makes this outdated arrangement all the more reprehensible. Yet even as research on gender exposes this curricular absence, thus paving the way for curriculum improvement, it uncovers the scorn that boys have for girls and women. For an ethics of care to be a genuine part of the curriculum of boys as well as girls, school will have to address the misogyny of its male inhabitants.

V

For 4 years in the 1970s, Rafaela Best watched a group of elementary school children in the Central Atlantic region of the United States learn what she called the "second curriculum"—the one that teaches each sex "how to perform according to conventional gender norms" (Best, 1983, p. 5). Coming to know the children intimately, she reported in *We've All Got Scars* that although most of the boys did not master this material by the end of first grade, in the next 2 years the majority became proficient in it. The ones who did not grasp the norms or were simply unable or unwilling to meet them were scorned by the other boys and excluded from their club. These outcasts were not necessarily shunned by the girls in the class, but they were perceived as losers both by themselves and by those who had passed the various tests of masculinity with flying colors.

Tracing the mastery of the second curriculum by 6-, 7-, and 8-year-old boys, Best showed how closely the macho ideal to which they aspired was linked to a scorn of girls and women and a fear of feminization. The excluded boys "were regarded as being like girls and not like real men," she reported (Best, 1983, p. 24; cf. Martin, 1992, pp. 72, 102). For a third grader to be called a sissy "was a fate worse than death" (Best, 1983, p. 22). To be a cry-baby or to be oriented to one's mother or female teacher was inexcusable. Kenny, one of the "losers" in the class, liked doing housekeeping tasks in school for his teacher and enjoyed receiving her hugs in return. Jason, another "loser," cried frequently. And Edward, whose behavior in school was far too perfect, was not good at games. Fighting, or at least the willingness to fight when challenged, was one essential ingredient of masculinity in the "winners'" eyes. Playing well and playing rough was another. Engaging in "antiestablishment" activities ranging from throwing mudballs at houses and cars to stuffing paper in the school locks was a third. All three aspects of 7- and 8-year-old machismo were valued in large part because their opposites betokened femininity.

Can we disregard Best's boys? In 1989 Derrick Jackson told *Boston Globe* readers about sixth graders in a public school who had been asked to say the first word that came to mind about the other sex. The girls said: "Fine. Jerks. Conceited. Ugly. Crazy. Dressy. Sexy. Dirty minds. Boring. Rude. Cute. Stuck up. Desperate. Sexually abusive. Punks." The boys said: "Pumping ('big tits'). Nasty. Vagina. Dope bodies (big breasts and behinds). Door knob (breasts). Hooker. Skeezer (a girl who will 'do it' with 50 guys)" (Jackson, 1989).

There is nothing idiosyncratic about these images. Here is what Margaret Clark, in *The Great Divide*, reported that primary school girls in Australia have to say on the subject:

> There's a group of boys in our class who always tease us and call us—you know, dogs, aids, slut, moll and that. (Clark, 1989, p. 25)

This boy used to call us big-tits and period-bag and used to punch us in the breasts. (Clark, 1989, p. 25)

They take things off us and drag us into the boys' toilets. (Clark, 1989, p. 39)

They call us rabies, dogs, aids. (Clark, 1989, p. 39)

They reckon I'm a dog. My brother gave me to them. He said, "Oh, come here, I've got a pet for you. Do you want my dog?" And he gave me to them as a pet dog. (Clark, 1989, p. 40)

According to the female teachers in Clark's report, the girls were not the boys' only targets, however:

I've been here for four years, but at the beginning of this year the whole school blew up with some problems. Boys that I had visited at home, taught in my class and been on camp with—I thought I had a good relationship with them—put their fingers up at me and then stood there as if to say, "What are you going to do about it?" I was horrified. I could not believe it. (Clark, 1989, p. 22)

I used to spend a lot of time on the basketball court, to get the girls involved but last year I was bullied off the court, by one of my boy students. I was in tears. He bullied me off. (Clark, 1989, p. 22)

Almost any day of the week I see boys using sexuality as a way of exerting power. You know boys going up to a female teacher and sticking two fingers up at her. (Clark, 1989, p. 23)

There's a case of a little boy in this school. Now he didn't know that I was the principal. I guess he just assumed it would be a man. He was sent to me for being obnoxious and obscene with one of the children in the playground. So I went and spoke to him, treating him fairly gently because he does have a lot of problems. He just stood there and was quite defiant. I just said to him "now listen. I am the boss of this school". Now that child just changed. (Clark, 1989, p. 24)

Female teachers are nothing to some male children. (Clark, 1989, p. 23)

By comparison, the experience of 16-year-old Kathy, an Inner London comprehensive school student, seems mild:

Sometimes I feel like saying that I disagree, that there are other ways of looking at it, but where would that get me? My teacher thinks I'm showing off, and the boys jeer. But if I pretend I don't understand, it's very different. The teacher is sympathetic and the boys are helpful. They really respond if they can show you how it is done, but there's nothing but "aggro" if you give any signs of showing them how it is done. (Spender, 1980, p. 150)

Yet other reports cited by Spender resemble these given by Clark:

> A group of year 6 students were walking across the school yard from the library to the classroom. One of the boys ran up behind one of the girls, rammed a rule between her legs and called her a slut. (Clark, 1989, p. 25)

> Well, as the music started, without a word spoken, the girls lined up at the back and the boys all moved together and sort of faced the girls. The girls started to move and sing but the boys stood in the line and started singing very loudly and moving in a very sexual way, you know swinging their hips and their arms and legs and walking slowly towards the girls as they did it, staring at them. It was an aggressive and threatening situation. The girls immediately stopped moving, stopped singing and just looked at each other with very stunned expressions. (Clark, 1989, p. 42)

Studies of gender relations in classrooms leave little doubt that boys need training in the 3Cs. The reports of male violence point to the same conclusion. Yet how can we expect boys and men to appropriate for themselves traits and values that both they and their culture associate with girls and women? Why would anyone want to adopt an ethic belonging to a despised people?

Given the misogyny that stands in the way of teaching the 3Cs to boys, it is tempting to renounce the undertaking. Yet insofar as both our private homes and public spaces are plagued by violence, the policy of excluding an ethics of care from the school curriculum or including it only in the curriculum of girls is a recipe for disaster. Yet what can we do?

The studies cited here make it quite clear that misogyny is learned in school as well as in society at large. One response to a hidden curriculum of school or society or both is to do nothing, to act as if it does not exist (Martin, 1976). But nonaction scarcely seems defensible when the hidden curriculum at issue dehumanizes half the population. A better response than inaction to an offensive hidden curriculum is to raise it to consciousness by bringing it into the curriculum proper as an explicit topic of study. Besides making it possible to reduce the misogyny, this step would enrich the school curriculum by introducing subject matter about the psychological and cultural construction of gender and even perhaps by making gender itself the subject-entity of a school subject. Yet although it would also help to pave the way for the entrance of the 3Cs, it is not enough.

VI

If the goal of preparing young people to live in private homes as family members does not assure space for the 3Cs in the curriculum of boys as well as girls, neither does it guarantee that domesticity will be made the business of both sexes (Martin, 1992, pp. 106–107, p. 150). In 1975, one of Best's boys said to her, "I'll starve to death before I'll cook" (Best, 1983, p. 80). When asked how he planned to keep his house clean and have food to eat he replied, "I'll get a wife for that." This scorn for things domestic finds an echo in Anne Machung's report on a survey of the expectations of graduating seniors at the University of California at Berkeley (Machung, 1989). The overwhelming majority of those studied hoped to marry, have children, and pursue a career. Of the women, nearly nine-tenths planned to acquire graduate degrees and half thought they would earn at least as much as their husbands. Few anticipated getting divorced or raising their youngsters alone. Each one believed she would rear two or three children and expected to interrupt her career for anywhere from 6 months to 12 years to do so. While in Machung's words the women were "talking career but thinking job" in order to be in a position to take care of the children they wanted to have, the men were talking family but thinking career. They were willing to "help out" at home but they did not want to be told what to do or have their contributions measured against their wives', let alone share housework equally. As for child care, most not only believed it to be the wife's responsibility, but could barely see themselves making day-care arrangements or missing work when the children were sick.

If Machung's college seniors sound like Best's boys grown up, they also bear a close resemblance to the young men in the philosophy of education course I recently taught. Like many of the women students in my class, I had started to think that American culture was no longer in the clutches of those traditional gender stereotypes that place women in the home and put them in charge of society's reproductive processes. Then, in connection with our study of Rousseau, I played the song "William's Doll" from the recording *Free To Be You and Me* and was forced to change my mind. Young William wanted a baby doll to hug and hold and wash and clean and dress and feed. As the song proceeded and William continued to ask for a doll against his father's wishes and his friends' taunts, the young men in my class began exchanging looks. By the time Grandma had come to William's rescue, saying that he wanted the doll so that when he was a father he would know what to do, they were beside themselves. Why? It turned out that, to a man, they believed that if you give a small boy a doll to play with—not a GI Joe but a baby doll—he will grow up to be homosexual, in their eyes something definitely unnatural and abnormal. That he will ultimately contract AIDS seemed also to be a foregone conclusion.

Although I did not know this at the time, a decade earlier Best had played the same song for the young children she was studying and to similar effect. The boys in Grades 1 to 3 did not look askance—they crawled under their desks and hid under the coats on the rack. Commenting that some years later those boys could listen to "William's Doll," "without experiencing trauma," she said that for fifth graders gender "stereotypes were no longer so urgent" (Best, 1983). Quite possibly her 10-year-old boys were beginning to make some accommodations to girls because of her interventions in their classrooms, but the scene in my classroom attested to the staying power of the stereotypes. It also bore witness to young men's continuing resistance to domesticity.

Whatever gains women may have made in the last decades, the cultural conviction that caring and concern are womanly virtues and that domesticity in general and the nurture of children in particular are primarily, if not exclusively, women's business persists. So does the belief that the activities and tasks associated with society's reproductive processes are too trivial to command men's attention and too menial to warrant their participation.

Although boys do not learn to devalue and resist domesticity only in school, the silences about home and family in the curriculum proper constitute a hidden curriculum in antidomesticity. As gender research has long since demonstrated, the power of curricular silence is immense. The British philosopher R. S. Peters was right: whether or not what is taught in school is in fact worthwhile, in calling something "education" we place our seal of approval on it (Peters, 1967, p. 3). Not that education always lives up to its reputation. Peters knew that some teaching is good and some bad, that some curricula are well designed and others are not. His point was that although the content of education differs from one culture to the next, whatever it is that a culture chooses to call "education" will comprise the information it designates as important for young people to know and the activities it considers worthwhile. Peters did not pursue the logic of his own argument but it is easily done. Just as the inclusion of something in the curriculum—a topic, a body of fact and theory, a perspective—signifies the value placed on it, exclusion of something bespeaks the culture's devaluation of it. In addition, the act of exclusion serves to reinforce that assessment.

The devaluation of domesticity is so widespread that it might seem the prudent course to forego the hope of bringing it into the curriculum as everyone's business. The problem is, men's resistance to domesticity is taking its toll on society. "I've had 4,000 arrests on nonsupport, and this guy was the smoothest I've seen. All he talked about was how he loved sailing and couldn't wait to get back to it," a State Department of Revenue investigator told a news columnist (English, 1989). The man's ex-wife who at one time held two jobs so as to stay off welfare said, "Now, I hope Chip can finish college. He's such a nice kid. I just do not understand how a father could leave a child like that."

What with many fathers leaving home altogether, the majority of men who remain there being unwilling to do more than a tiny fraction of home's work, and mothers as well as fathers going out to work each day, children are being left to their own devices and women are becoming "bone-weary" (Landers, 1990). Gender roles have changed considerably in the last decades and our cultural construction of domesticity has not kept pace. To bring domesticity into school as the business of both sexes will not just enrich curriculum. It will help bring both the concept and the practices of domesticity into alignment with the new realities of family life. "I have a little difficulty being a househusband," an unemployed coal miner told *Time* correspondent Melissa Ludtke. "But I love being with the kids. I also believe it is good for them to see me doin' housework, so they don't keep believin' that outside work belongs only to the man and inside is the woman" (Ludtke, 1988).

VII

Needless to say, if the curriculum is really to teach boys as well as girls to shoulder responsibility for the tasks and functions of the private home, our cultural construct—or perhaps I should say constructs—of domesticity and the hidden curriculum in antidomesticity will both have to be raised to consciousness. The links between misogyny and the denigration of domesticity will also need to be addressed for, as the attitudes of Best's boys make clear, the scorn of things domestic and of females are closely linked. And, of course, school will have to take to heart the fear of feminization that lurks behind these phenomena.

Even this listing suggests that it may well be a mistake to speak of curriculum "enrichment," as I have been doing. And if the domain of the 3Cs is to be enlarged, curriculum makers will also have to take steps to counteract the stereotypical images of the private home and the public world—and of society's reproductive and productive processes—as polar opposites. Connoting mere addition—as when milk is enriched by an injection of vitamins—the term does not begin to capture the radical implications for curriculum of the study of gender. Actually, "enrichment" is doubly misleading: it masks the transformative potential of research on gender as it implies that there is nothing really wrong with curriculum, that curriculum only needs a bit of fortification. Add up the misrepresentations of and silences about women in curriculum's subject matter, the double standard by which its subject-entities are judged, the gap in its goals, its failure to save space for an ethics of care and to reserve room for the tasks and responsibilities of domesticity, however, and it becomes quite clear that curriculum as it stands is failing to transmit to the next generation one-half of the cultural heritage.[3] This in itself should be enough to undermine the faith that curriculum requires only minor improvement. Take into account the misogyny and antidomesticity that are now being passed along by curriculum's silences and distortions, and any lingering doubts that curriculum needs to be radically revised will surely be dispelled.

As I hope I have shown here, the study of gender is as germane to the reconstruction of curriculum as to its deconstruction. I do not want to leave the impression, however, that curricular enrichment and radical curriculum revision are incompatible and that attempts to accomplish the former will necessarily subvert the latter. On the contrary, I have become increasingly convinced that the radical reconstruction of curriculum we so badly need will come about not in one fell swoop but as the "emergent" outcome of massive doses of enrichment, each one of which may require a small act of courage.

ACKNOWLEDGMENTS: I wish to thank Ann Diller, Susan Franzosa, Barbara Houston, Susan Laird, Michael Martin, Beatrice Nelson, Jennifer Radden, Janet Farrell Smith, and members of the Gender Enrichment Conference Workshop for their helpful comments and suggestions on an early draft of this essay.

NOTES

1. History and the other disciplines of knowledge also misrepresent the lives, works, and experiences of minority men. However, because the conference topic is gender I will not discuss this gap here.
2. The project is based at the Wellesley College Center for Research on Women in Wellesley, Massachusetts. Peggy McIntosh and Emily Style are its co-directors.
3. When one counts the omissions relating to minorities, it turns out that it is actually transmitting much less!

REFERENCES

Best, Rafaela. (1983). *We've all got scars*. Bloomington: Indiana University Press.
Breines, Wini, & Gordon, Linda. (1983). The new scholarship on family violence. *Signs, 8*, 490–531.

Clark, Margaret. (1989). *The great divide*. Canberra, Australia: Curriculum Development Centre.

Crewdson, John. (1988). *By silence betrayed: Sexual abuse of children in America*. Boston: Little, Brown.

Dewey, John. (1956). *The school and society*. Chicago: University of Chicago Press. (Original work published 1943)

English, Bella. (1989, May 15). No support, but nice tan. *Boston Globe*, p. A7

Jackson, Derrick Z. (1989, June 2). The seeds of violence. *Boston Globe*, p. A1

Landers, Ann. (1990, February 26). A few survival tips for working parents. *Boston Globe*.

Langone, John. (1984). *Violence*. Boston: Little, Brown.

Ludtke, Melissa. (1988, August 8). Through the eyes of children. *Time*.

Machung, Ann. (1989). Talking career, thinking job: Gender difference in career and family expectations of Berkeley seniors. *Feminist Studies, 15*, 35–58.

Martin, Jane Roland. (1976). What should we do with a hidden curriculum when we find one? *Curriculum Inquiry, 6*, 135–151.

Martin, Jane Roland. (1982). Two dogmas of curriculum. *Synthese, 51*, 5–20.

Martin, Jane Roland. (1985). *Reclaiming a conversation*. New Haven, CT: Yale University Press.

Martin, Jane Roland. (1990). Filling the gap: The goals of American education revised. *International Review of Education, 36*, 145–157.

Martin, Jane Roland. (1992). *The schoolhome: Rethinking schools for changing families*. Cambridge, MA: Harvard University Press.

Naples, Robert. (1989, May 26). Letter to the editor. *Boston Globe*.

Peters, RS. (1967). *Ethics and education*. Glenview, IL: Scott, Foresman.

Reynolds, Pamela. (1987, March 29). Violence at home. *Boston Globe*, pp. A15, A17.

Spender, Dale. (1980). Talking in class. In Dale Spender and Elizabeth Sarah (Eds.), *Learning to lose*. London: Women's Press.

Waks, Leonard, & Rustum, Roy. (1987). Learning from technology. In Kenneth D. Benne & Steven Tozer (Eds.), *Society as educator in an age of transition*. Eighty-sixth Yearbook of the National Society for the Study of Education. Chicago: University of Chicago Press.

Woolf, Virginia. (1938). *Three guineas*. New York: Harcourt, Brace & World.

CHAPTER 9

Family Studies: Transforming Curriculum, Transforming Families

LINDA PETERAT

Family studies/home economics has been a recognized part of the curriculum of North American schools for over 100 years. Wilson (1966) traces its beginning as a school subject to the beginning of women's formalized education. Thompson states "the idea of home economics can be traced to antiquity in the Bible (Exod. 18:17–18), the writings of Pythagorean women philosophers, Book I of Aristotle's *Politics*, Xenophon's *Oekonomicus,* and Francis Bacon's 'Salomon's House' in The New Atlantis" (1992, p. 171). Its recognition as a legitimate part of the North American school curriculum coincided with and grew out of women's gaining access to secondary and postsecondary education in the late nineteenth century. Family studies/home economics curricula gained legitimacy through alliances with the early women's movement, the manual training movement, vocational and practical arts, progressive education beginning with Dewey, and more recent curriculum reconstructionist movements.

In Canada, family studies/home economics is known by both names, with some provincial educational systems using "family studies" and others using "home economics" to designate programs. Family studies is considered by some to be a title evolving from home economics and a more apt description of courses since about the 1940s, when child studies and human relationships and development became a common part of courses. In this chapter, I use family studies to refer to recent curricula, and home economics to refer to older or traditional programs and philosophies and when it is the title used by contemporary authors. In Canada, family studies is commonly an elective course in schools and a part of general rather than vocational education. This is unlike the situation in the United States, where the links with vocational education are more direct. It is also unlike in Great Britain, where it has been called "housecraft" or "domestic science" and, more recently, placed within the Design and Technology curriculum.

The awkward use of "family studies/home economics" in the opening paragraphs attests to the difficulty this subject has had in truly naming itself and being recognized as a legitimate school subject in an educational system. That home economics was founded on the concerns of and for women is clear. Adelaide Hoodless, Canadian activist and promoter of home economics in public schooling, stated: "It is women's work and must have women associated in its development" (Stamp, 1977, p. 21). In 1841 in the United States Catharine Beecher first organized knowledge of daily home living into the text *A Treatise on Domestic Economy,* which influenced school programs until the late 1800s. Thompson (1986) interprets Beecher's efforts as intentions to secure and achieve for women a domestic/home economics of equal social value to the emerging public economics constructed and dominated by men. The evolving educational visions of Hoodless and Beecher during the past century and a half raise numerous questions about the politics, practices, and theories of women educators, and one purpose of this chapter is to articulate the current central questions emerging from a feminist perspective in the subject area. This chapter is written for family studies educators, teacher educators, and educators of other school subjects who wish to know more about the efforts made and the challenges emerging in the struggles with regard to gender that are affecting family studies. The chapter focuses on the past few decades and reviews the responses family studies educators have made to counter sexism and contribute to gender equity in education. These efforts are critically analyzed and the emerging questions are outlined.

Home economics formed and developed with the purpose of fostering social change, or "reformism" (Vincenti, 1982). Its concern was with improving the health and daily well-being of families and individuals, and the relationships of both in society. It has tended to be practical in the sense of expecting students to use knowledge and understanding to make changes in their lives, rather than fostering a more liberal or general knowledge about families as families (Brown, 1980). With practical and reformist purposes foremost, home economics has readily embraced student-centered ideologies in education and made a virtue of being responsive to the local and current "needs" of families and individuals. While numerous historical interpretations are offered of the evolution of home economics as a school subject, with a holistic perspective it can be understood as constituted of a number of contesting visions of its value and purpose.[1] Social conditions and power relations have served to support the domination of one or more visions in any historical moment.

In the context of schooling, home economics confronted well-established norms that defined legitimate knowledge and the purposes of schooling. Home economics advocates asserted that school curricula ought to be practical, experiential, and related to the problems of everyday life. They argued that a quality life in homes and families does not occur naturally, and therefore should be a part of schooling. They assumed that knowledge about daily living can be articulated and can have a positive impact on the well-being of families.

Home economics as a part of schooling has had a constrained existence (Peterat, 1983). While accepted as part of the established curriculum, what it has been able to do, in what ways, and in whose interests are fundamental questions. Thompson states: "Home economics is an invisible part of the curriculum. Its practitioners are routinely denied the opportunity to speak 'in their own voice'" (1986, p. 276). This point is reinforced by Anna Maria Puissi, writing about women's experience in education in general: "Entry into the world of culture and education means being deported into the male social and symbolic order, thus finding their original female humanity deprived of power" (1990, p. 85). The general picture of home economics in schooling is as a school subject focused on the concerns of daily home and family living, striving for betterment in the quality of daily lives and women's conditions, and asserting the relevance of different ways and contents of knowing. In this introduction, I have sketched an outline of the context and founding of home economics as a school subject that situates the next sections of this chapter, which review recent efforts to address gender equity issues. In the last section of the chapter, I return to the larger context of schooling and the emerging challenges for home economics in the current times.

GENDERED PARTICIPATION

It was not always intended that home economics should be a subject only for women (Vaines, 1981). Periodically over the years, arguments were made as to why it was a necessary subject for men as well as women (Peterat, 1986; Schaffer, 1965). However, women in postsecondary home economics programs believed they had worked hard to secure their own profession and were ambivalent about encouraging men's participation. This feeling is made explicit by Howden (1968) when she reacts to recent administrative appointments made in Canadian Universities: "Let us be more vocal in our anger and dismay at this unworthy usurpation by men of the administrative positions held by women in Home Economics" (p. 44). She continues:

There were at the time and still are women with the requisite degrees, experience and personality available for such appointments. . . . We all recognize the well-developed encroaching trend and practice—women do the spade work—men take over the profession when it has become a success. One wonders if this is not the beginning of an attempt to alter the name, meaning and content of Home Economics in favor of abstruse science and research. (p. 29)

The "takeover" by men has been in the administrative positions in postsecondary education, and not as either students or professors. In secondary schools, men's participation was of less concern (Lawson, 1977); however, the decisions of male administrators have very directly influenced the subject. When home economics became increasingly accepted as a school subject at the end of the 1800s, it was in the context of mass immigration, urban growth, and labor unrest. Male educational administrators often supported the program for its potential as a domesticating and stabilizing force in the lives of women, families, and society (Peterat, 1983), while home economics educators argued for its acceptance as an applied science. For administrators who readily accepted manual arts education for boys, home economics solved the problem of what to do with the girls while the boys did manual or industrial arts. Although it was not the original vision, home economics evolved a separatist politics and became by the 1960s a clearly female-dominated although marginal profession, postsecondary discipline, and school subject.

In the early 1970s, attention in schools turned to the high schools, and coerced the enrollment of girls in family studies courses, and to the accusation that family studies was a major oppressive force in the lives of young women. That women dominated the subject in number and that it provided education for unpaid service labor in families were viewed as central problems. Robin Morgan accused the home economics curriculum of being "the final icing on the cake, the nail in the coffin, after which she [the female student] is a limp, gibbering mass of jelly waiting for marriage" (What Robin Morgan Said, 1973, p. 13).

In schools, the practice of splitting school classes and streaming girls into home economics while boys studied industrial education was common until the 1970s. It was largely accepted without question that the purpose of schooling was to prepare young people for their adult lives, and that the majority of girls would be primarily responsible for home and family life and therefore ought to be educated for this responsibility.

Whether home economics was a school subject appropriate for boys as well as girls has been an ongoing question (Lawson, 1977). The number of boys enrolled in home economics courses steadily increased over the years (Lawson, 1977), but the justification of courses for boys changed. Until the 1950s, girls and boys were likely to be enrolled in separate courses specifically designed for their different future roles in families. Common arguments were that boys should be in home economics courses to learn to appreciate women's work in the home and to be able to help if necessary (Mack, 1933; Sunderlin, 1933). By 1965, Schaffer argued that family roles had become fluid and negotiable for women and men. Thus "boys need as strong a background in all areas of family relationships as do girls" (p. 29). Lawson (1977), in a comprehensive review of the history of secondary school home economics for boys in the United States, concluded that school programs:

> Continued to reinforce traditional sex-role stereotypes. Despite the increasing participation of males, home economics has remained female in orientation, ostensibly preparing women for the traditional role of housewife-homemaker. Males have not been included from any commitment to a long-term shift in the roles of either males or females. (p. 223)

When educational mandates of the 1970s insisted that no student could be denied access to any school program, the practice of streaming females into family studies and males into industrial education changed. In some jurisdictions students are given a choice of which subject they wish to study; in some, all students are required to study both family studies and industrial education, and in some, there is a return to special courses designed for either boys or girls. There was some anticipated and real reluctance by teachers to having boys in family studies, as well as the perceived reluctance of boys to enroll. A major effort of family studies educators has been to encourage boys to enroll (Dobry, 1977; Kelly & Morgan, 1979; Sheppard, 1983; Spurrier, 1977). Efforts have been made to understand boys as learners in home economics and to reorient courses to their interests (Allard, 1984; Fleck, 1972; Spurrier, 1977; Weis, 1974). In the attempt to encourage reluctant teachers, comparisons have been made between boy and girl students and girls have become the negative reference group as boys: "[are] more mechanically minded" (McLeod, 1977), "want and need more responsibility" (McLeod, 1977), "did better work than girls" (Lawson, 1977), "[are] more adventurous" (Allard, 1984), and "[are] more competitive" (McLeod, 1977). Enrollment of boys has continued to increase. MacMartin (1991) reports that up to one-third of the students enrolled in family studies courses today are boys. Some schools report participation rates of boys at 40 to 50% (Pierce, 1989).

While boys' presence in family studies classes is desirable, there are indications that it has done little to assure gender fairness or equity in learning for girls and boys. In her 1-year study of a class of Grade 8 boys and girls in home economics and industrial education classes, Linda Eyre (1992) describes how some boys in the class secured power to dominate other boys, the girls, and the female teachers, as part of the classroom teaching and social relations. She states: "Treating students 'the same' meant catering to the perceived interests and experiences of boys . . . the curriculum supported a particular kind of masculinity, one interested in authority, technology and control" (p. 147).

As in other school subjects, the presence of boy students in family studies has led to their dominating the classroom and controlling curriculum content in ways that may make it less relevant and meaningful for girls. In addition, the identification of family studies with women leads to open denigration of the female teachers and curriculum content. As one 18-year-old male student states: "Its . . . sort of gay, for guys to take something to do with families. Guys think that all that feeling stuff is sort of silly. . . . It's seen as a girl's area because they are going to be mothers and all that"(Malone, 1989, p. 4).

That girls and boys together take family studies courses can give the appearance that it serves everyone equally well. This new reality, however, raises new questions. How can a school subject identified with women come to be valued by young male students who are constructing their identities in opposition to anything "feminine" or "female" identified? In what ways can a school subject about the daily lives and experiences of diverse young people truly incorporate and enlighten all participants? In what ways must gender relations constitute the explicit curriculum to assure equitable learning experiences for all?

COUNTERING BIAS AND STEREOTYPES IN CURRICULUM CONTENT

Until the 1960s, female and male gender stereotypes were widely unchallenged, as was the intent to educate for different and stereotypical roles. Encouraging boys' participation in family studies classes became the central way of countering the main stereotype that family studies was only for girls and that family and home responsibilities were girls' only. Attention also turned to the sexist stereotypes and bias contained in the language, pictures, and illustrations of textbooks and teaching materials. Hutton (1976) examined six texts recommended in one of the states in the United States and argued that books needed to change to show a realistic portrayal of the "multidimensional roles for both men and women" (p. 30). Weis (1979) examined 100 texts published between 1964 and 1974. She found sex bias in language usage and in pictures portraying male and female role environments and the role behaviors and expectations emphasized. She argued for portraying multiple role behaviors, for equal inclusion of female and male photographs and pronouns, and for adherence to the many recently available guidelines for eliminating sexism in texts. Texts began to incorporate nonsexist portrayals of girls and boys and different races and classes.

Recently, Bernice Hayibor (1990) examined three family studies texts published in the 1980s and commonly used in Canadian schools. She found that the concern with making family studies appealing to and inclusive of boys led to boys dominating the photos and illustrations in some texts. She also found that in analyzing photos it was important to go beyond mere frequency counts of appearances to analyze the activities and the kinds of relationships between the girls and boys portrayed. In analyzing the texts of books, she found that the desire to include boys led to some topics and issues being presented from a typical male experiential standpoint rather than a female one. For example, in a discussion of divorce, one text described legal decisions as favoring women in terms of child custody and alimony, but did not mention women's difficulties in receiving alimony settlements or the lower standard of economic life that usually ensues for women and children following divorce. In another example, one text in an attempt to be neutral and inclusive described woman battering as "spouse abuse" and noted that "social stereotypes of manhood" may be one reason why fewer cases of abuse against men than women are reported. In this example, the attempt to be inclusive and neutral contributed to a distortion of the realities of women's and men's experiences.

When gender-neutral language was adopted in texts, it tended to mask, distort, and minimize gender differences. For example, language such as "parenting" masks the different experiences of mothers and fathers, particularly in events such as childbirth, and the language of "spousal abuse" distorts the real differences in men's and women's experiences. Hayibor (1990) found that non-White adolescents, and especially non-White girls were particularly underrepresented in the texts. Hayibor's work shows that the enthusiasm to include boys in family studies has led to boys dominating in number in the pictures and illustration of texts. This contributes to a new kind of bias because boys do not dominate in number in participation in the subject or in family responsibilities. Likewise, in making content appealing to boys, their perspectives prevail while the perspectives of girls were absent. There is an apparent reluctance in textbooks to question knowledge, to present human relations as problematic, and to confront students' beliefs and assumptions. Instead, "nonstereotypical" illustrations become unrealistic, or at least unrepresentative, as men are shown changing diapers and scrubbing floors. Familial relations are described in neutral, factual terms rather than as human interpretive narratives of conflict, contradiction, and partial, relational standpoints.

Attention to language usage in the classroom and consciousness about the assumptions behind the language used are also proposed as ways of countering bias and stereotypes in the classroom (Dobry, 1977, 1986; Kelly & Morgan, 1979). Dobry (1986) emphasized the need for an equitable number of verbal and nonverbal interactions between teachers and students as a way to make the classroom a more "equitable" and encouraging environment. Beyond textbook research, there is little research reported on teachers' efforts to counter bias and stereotypes through daily practices in the classrooms or schools. Other than Eyre's recent work (1992), there is an absence of research on student interactions or student and teacher interactions in the classroom. This absence of research can indicate an absence of effort in this area. How can a school subject based on the stereotypical role of women and dominated by women, counter the perpetuation of that stereotype?

What is taught in family studies courses has always been shaped by the perceived future life and family activities of students. It has been shaped by the perceived local needs and interests of students. Accompanying efforts to attract more boys into home economics was the call for changes in curriculum content. Weis (1974) stated that in order to avoid perpetuating sex stereotyping, the curriculum should include: managing home and family roles with an occupational role, sharing household and child-care responsibilities, home service and production, as well as buying and using out-of-home goods and services, and varieties in family life. She stated that home economics courses should minimize sex-differentiated standards in nutrition, grooming, and personal care. Weis's proposal was to add content to balance teaching about in-home production, for example, with consuming, and to become inclusive of boys' activities and interests, and of other minority perspectives in family living. While Weis believed sex stereotyping could be countered by making curriculum more balanced between girls' and boys' interests, and the private and public domains of experience, Clark and Murray (1984) believed home economics should be teaching about sex-role stereotyping. They saw sex and gender equity as legitimate content about which home economics educators should teach, through topics such as parenting, child development, and family relationships. Both arguments to change curriculum content suggest a peculiar distance from the topic, proposing to teach *about* sex stereotyping and how others experience it, rather than beginning with students' experiences in school and families (the situations of everyday life) and analyzing these for sex stereotyping, discriminating, and genderizing processes at work. In other words, the structural connections between family studies and gender inequities in schools and in society were not suggested as topics for analysis and critique.

Others have questioned whose knowledge constitutes home economics (Badir, 1989; Peterat, 1983). Home economics courses have not lacked men's perspectives, which have been present as men's theories and values. But they have lacked attention to women's and men's *experiences* in home and family living. That is, home economics courses have commonly incorporated men's theories such as those of Maslow, Freud, Erickson, and Kohlberg. In doing so, they have sought legitimacy through reliance on "reputable" science (Badir, 1989). Thus, home economics has been dominated by men's ways of knowing and men's knowledge. The humanities, human sciences, and feminist theories have been less a part of such courses. What counts as knowledge has not been widely problematized, nor has sufficient attention been given to people's diverse experiences in families, dating, parenting, life planning, and so on. Brown stated that family studies represents middle-class interests (1984) and in a critique of home economics research, Williams (1988) states:

> Little is known about Afro Americans, Asian-American, Native American, and Hispanic families . . . the knowledge created has been shown to be fragmented and atheoretical. . . . More detrimental, however, are implicit ideologies pervading some research about racial and ethnic diversity . . . pejorative ideologies based on race and class are apparent. (p. 74)

Ralston states that "messages from black home economists may have been dismissed, overlooked or . . . muffled by competing messages within the larger profession" (1992, p. 39). Eyre writes that "adherence to a technical rationality precludes education for emancipatory action" (1991, p. 103) in family studies, and describes the curriculum as "sexist, classist, racist, and heterosexist" (p. 103).

Since 1979, a new vision of home economics has been available to shape and influence school programs (Brown, 1980; Brown & Paolucci, 1979). This vision is of home economics as a critical science. It is founded on a thorough critique of home economics' overreliance on a technical-instrumental view of knowledge. It calls for vastly increased attention to interpretive and critical knowing as necessary for empowering individuals and families both individually and collectively to understand their condition in the world, and to influence change to improve their state of well-being and the conditions in society that influence this.

Efforts to counter gender bias and stereotypes in family studies/home economics have focused on becoming inclusive of boys and balanced by adding boys interests and activities into curriculum. But these efforts have largely ignored the fact that boys expect to dominate interactions and attention, assert their values and preferences in classrooms, and see little reason to take seriously a school subject identified with women. The politics of knowledge has not been a sufficiently conscious element in family studies curriculum, practice, and policies; and here politics means the power to define knowing and knowledge. But it is increasingly recognized that alternate modes of pedagogy are necessary to overcome the sexism, racism, classism, and heterosexism inherent in the school subject (Brown, 1980; Eyre, 1991) and that transformed views of knowledge and knowing are necessary to surpass the current constraints on family studies as a school subject (McLean & Peterat, 1984). These views will be discussed in the remaining section of this chapter.

TRANSFORMING CURRICULUM, TRANSFORMING FAMILIES

In this last section of the chapter, I gather the questions emerging from the review of efforts to create a gender equitable family studies. I reflect on these efforts and suggest actions needed for short-term changes and for the more long-term visions toward which family studies educators should struggle. The short-term changes are changes that family studies educators may be able to achieve as individuals and as a group. The longer term visions will necessitate struggles in concert with other educators, administrators, and parents. I refer to transforming curriculum because I find within the history of home economics a vision for education that through focusing on the practical problems of everyday life would be integrative and morally deliberative, and with a form and purpose counter to the prevailing beliefs about the purposes of education. The vision should be restored and the history understood so that practices relevant to the desires and realities of today can emerge. The purpose of family studies as a school subject has been the betterment of everyday lives in homes and families. Thus, transforming families refers to the intent of the school subject to improve family well-being by enabling families in their own becoming and in recognizing their potential as forces for change in other social institutions and in society in general. Thus, by titling this section "Transforming Curriculum, Transforming

Families," I wish to reexamine the foundations of the school subject and consider the ways in which they may be reenlivened for the present.

Probably no school subject has more potential to be effective in changing the gender outlooks, understandings, and practices of students than family studies. The influences of family and interpersonal relationships, pop culture, and mass media on identity formation are "natural" curriculum topics for family studies. In other words, extending Weis's (1974) and Clark and Murray's (1984) arguments for changing curriculum content would mean that the influences on gender identity formation would be a topic for consideration throughout family studies, in lessons on child care, food studies, textiles, and so on. Because family studies has had and still retains for many a gendered identification with women, opportunities for family studies educators and students to challenge each other's biases and misperceptions often occur naturally in the highly socially interactive format of family studies classes. Thus classroom organization, routines, expectations, and relations are all areas that can become opportunities to consider gender justice and fairness. Focused on daily living, family studies is a different form of knowledge with purposes different from or outside of the norms of schooling. If the value of educating for daily living can be accepted widely in schooling, family studies is positioned to substantially influence such a change. However, making family studies an effective force for gender equity requires awareness of the potentialities and visions of the possibilities.

In concluding the previous section, I proposed that transformed views of knowledge and knowing are necessary to surpass the current constraints on family studies as a school subject. These constraints arise from family studies curriculum being denigrated by many boy students and men, and some girl students and women. The dominant technical-factual form of knowledge accepted as the norm in schooling has perpetuated myths and misconceptions in family studies curriculum. It has contributed to a blindness that has rendered many "family processes (as) deceptive or invisible" (Zinn, 1992, p. 474). Marjorie DeVault proposes that families need to be understood as "mythologized" packages and analyzed to see the activities they perform as much as "the way the activity is constructed in public discourse" (1991, p. 230). Elsewhere, I have proposed that interpretive and critical sciences are appropriate to knowing daily life (McLean & Peterat, 1984). Stories have long been considered appropriate in learning about daily life and their potential for providing the vicarious experiences that can contribute to understanding multiple perspectives needs to be recognized.

Patricia Thompson (1992) proposes that home economics is a knowledge system that addresses the basic human needs of all people. As a knowledge system, she argues that the struggle for home economics is to secure epistemological equity, rather than gender equity. This means that the real struggle in schooling is to have an education for daily living valued equally with an education for employment. This is a point of view supported by Jane Roland Martin (1985), who argues for an equitable curriculum that would place an equal emphasis on educating for the re-productive processes of society (care, concern, and connections) *and* the productive processes of society (employment, commerce, and politics).

Attending to issues of gender equity in the curriculum requires a move beyond attending only to gender. Concerns with equity also raise concerns with racism, classism, heterosexism, and sensitivities to other identity categories of age, ethnicity, physical handicaps, and so on. John-nella Butler states that "Knowledge is identity and identity is knowledge. All knowledge is explicitly and implicitly related to who we are, both as individuals and as groups" (1991, p. 83). If this claim is true, it would mean that a true knowledge of daily life can only be possible through attending to the standpoints of the multiplicity of identities of the students participating. Elizabeth Spelman (1991) proposes that we need to understand the ways "gender identity exists in concert with other aspects of identity" (p. 223). She states: "It is only if we pay attention to how we differ that we come to an understanding of what we have in common" (p. 223). According to this claim, if we are to know daily life, it is important to know the partialities and commonalities in the meanings people give to it. It is important to explore the relationships between our knowing and our being. This encourages us to see knowledge being constructed not only in relation to the formal, explicit curriculum of the classroom but also in the social relations among students in the classroom, the hallways, and the school as a whole. In this way, teachers need to bring the social subtext of schooling into discussion in the classroom.

Viewing family studies as a different knowledge system is proposed in the writings of both Patricia Thompson (1992) and Marjorie Brown (1980), and is supported in much feminist writing (Butler, 1991).[2] This view is important for parents, administrators, educators, and students to understand if educating for daily and family living is to be valued in our schools, and if family studies is ever to surpass the constraints it endures when viewed and evaluated according to the dominant, White, middle-class, patriarchal values of schooling. Equity struggles must be directed toward equity among ways of knowing and knowledge forms.

Viewing family studies as a different knowledge system implies dif-ferent pedagogical practices. Ideas that inform feminist pedagogies are appropriate (Martel & Peterat, 1988). Important elements are the articula-tion (naming) and reexamination of experience, the critique of theories, and "teaching from multifocal, multidimensional, multicultural, pluralistic, interdisciplinary perspectives" (Butler, 1991, p. 73). Family studies educators need to see themselves as learners and inquirers, constantly bringing into dialogue human differences and similarities, in search for understanding and wisdom in daily living. Butler writes: "Essentially, transformation is the process of revealing unity among human beings and the world, as well as revealing important differences. Transformation implies acknowledging and benefiting from the interaction among sameness and diversity, groups and individuals" (p. 75). Pedagogies that enable learning from human differences and similarities could overcome the many biases currently perpetuated in curriculum and practice.

Family studies is both a part of and not a part of current school curriculum. As an elective course and as a course recognized as different (practical, active, nonacademic), it does not have the same status as "core" courses in the curriculum. We can say that it has a marginal existence in many schools. On the margins, it has been dominated by the knowledge and practice norms of the core courses, and largely unable to control its own definition and destiny. To overcome the oppressions of marginalization, the politics of the subject need to be more clearly recognized, debated, and strategized. The power of being both part of the curriculum and not part of it, of being insider and outsider, can be drawn from this dual existence. Family studies is positioned to assert itself as a different kind of knowledge and to transform the larger curriculum of schooling. But this is not something that family studies educators can accomplish on their own, rather it is where alliances must be formed with others of similar position: health educators, fine arts educators, women's studies educators, and individuals within all school subjects who are beginning to raise epistemological questions.

There is potential within the margins of the school curriculum to inform the long-term visions of what knowing and learning can be. But to leap forward as though such a transformation has already occurred will foster illusions of change and secure no change at all. For while there is the possibility for fundamental transformation in curriculum in the present, there is also a clear possibility for a stronger reassertion of the traditional purposes of schooling and modes of knowing. Evidences of the reassertion of values associated with the traditional core curriculum subjects are the return to government mandated examinations, international comparisons of test scores to determine economically progressive nations, the emphasis on outcomes and standards, and the encouragement of girls (and everyone) to study more mathematics and science. While I am generally supportive of the latter trend, one does have to wonder in whose interest this effort is, when no comparable effort is made to encourage boys to study nontraditional subjects. It is also naive to expect that educators can act unconstrained by the expectations of students, parents, and local communities. I am reminded of this point by Patricia Thompson when she states that it is textbook publishers' attention to public acceptance that shapes the texts they produce rather than their own unwillingness to incorporate more controversy in the texts.[3] In efforts to make schooling more equitable for all, educators must work more with parents and communities to have them understand possible changes, to engage again in debate about the kind of knowledge most worth having, and to learn from each other in choosing the right actions to make. Then family studies curriculum may be transformed and become a force in transforming families.

ACKNOWLEDGMENTS: I appreciate the assistance of the following people, who read and commented on an earlier draft of this chapter: Linda Eyre, Mildred Barnes Griggs, Patricia J. Thompson, Annabelle Slocum, and Gloria Williams.

NOTES

1. For a treatment of this view in relation to school curricula in general, see Herbert Kliebard (1985), Three Currents of American Curriculum Thought, in Alex Molnar (Ed.), *Current Thought on Curriculum* (pp. 31–44), Association for Supervision and Curriculum Development, Alexandria, Virginia. A supportive analysis of home economics curricula is provided by Marjorie East (1980), in *Home Economics, Past, Present, Future*, Allyn & Bacon, Boston. Contrasting interpretations of curricular ideals are present in the British writings of June Purvis—see Domestic Subjects since 1870 in Ivor Goodson (Ed.), (1985), *Social Histories of the Secondary Curriculum: Subjects for Study* (pp. 145–176), Falmer Press, Philadelphia; and Carol Dyhouse (1978), Towards a Feminine Curriculum for English Schoolgirls: The Demands of Ideology 1870–1963, in *Women's Studies International Quarterly*, 1, 291–311. In Canada, see Robert Stamp (1977), and Patricia Saidak (1987) in *The Inception of the Home Economics Movement in English Canada, 1890–1910: In Defense of the Cultural Importance of the Home*, unpublished master's thesis, Institute of Canadian Studies, Carleton University, Ottawa, Ontario.
2. Pioneering work particularly relevant to family studies are texts such as Marjorie DeVault's (1991) *Feeding the Family* and Dorothy Smith's (1987) *The Everyday World as Problematic*, University of Toronto Press; and Laurie Abraham, MaryBeth Danielson, Nancy Eberle, Laura Green, Janice Rosenberg, and Carroll Stoner's (1991) *Re-inventing Home*, Penguin Books, New York.
3. Personal communication, August 1992.

REFERENCES

Allard, Ruth. (1984). Why teaching boys is really different than teaching girls. *Forecast for Home Economics, 4*, 14–1.

Badir, Doris. (1989). Home economics and feminism. *People and Practice: International Issues for Home Economists, 1*(3), 1–21.

Beecher, Catharine. (1848). *A treatise in domestic economy* (rev. ed.). New York: Harper & Brothers. (Original work published 1841)

Brown, Marjorie. (1980). *What is home economics education?* Minneapolis: University of Minnesota, Department of Vocational and Technical Education.

Brown, Marjorie. (1984). Home economics: Proud past, promising future. *Journal of Home Economics, 76*(3), 48–54.

Brown, Marjorie, & Paolucci, Beatrice. (1979). *Home economics: A definition.* Washington, DC: American Home Economics Association.

Butler, Johnnella. (1991). Transforming the curriculum: Teaching about women of color. In Johnnella Butler & John Walter (Eds.), *Transforming the curriculum* (pp. 67–87). Albany: State University of New York Press.

Clark, Virginia, & Murray, M. Eloise. (1984). Equity: A perennial concern for home economists. *Illinois Teacher, 27*(3), 124–126.

DeVault, Marjorie. (1991). *Feeding the family.* Chicago: University of Chicago Press.

Dobry, Alberta. (1977). Title IX: What's all the fuss about? *Illinois Teacher, 20*(4), 154–158.

Dobry, Alberta. (1986). Creating a classroom climate of equity: A look at teacher behaviours. *Illinois Teacher, 30*(2), 42–45.

Eyre, Linda. (1991, March). A pedagogy for gender equity. In *Proceedings of a Canadian symposium: Issues and directions for home economics/family studies education* (pp. 98–113), Winnipeg, Manitoba.

Eyre, Linda. (1992). Re-visiting the co-education classroom. In Linda Peterat & Ellie Vaines (Eds.), *Lives and plans: Signs for transforming practice* (pp. 122–150). Mission Hills, CA: Glencoe.

Fleck, Henrietta. (1972). Boys in home economics. *Forecast for Home Economics, 9*, 150, 159.

Hayibor, Bernice. (1990). *Analysis of gender bias in home economics textbooks.* Unpublished master's thesis, University of British Columbia, Vancouver.

Howden, Elizabeth. (1968). Men are encroaching upon our profession. *Canadian Home Economics Journal, 18*(3), 29, 44.

Hutton, Sandra. (1976). Sex-role illustrations in junior high school home economics textbooks. *Journal of Home Economics, 68*(2), 27–30.

Kelly, Joan, & Morgan, Eddye. (1979). Combating classroom sex bias. *Journal of Home Economics, 71*(1), 36–38.

Lawson, Royston. (1977). Tigers amongst the roses: An historical review of home economics for secondary school boys in the United States. *Illinois Teacher, 20*(5), 215–225.

Mack, Fay. (1933). Evaluation of training for boys in home economics. *Practical Home Economics, 4*, 104, 124.

MacMartin, Joyce. (1991, March). Issues and directions for home economics. In *Proceedings of a Canadian symposium: Issues and directions for home economics/ family studies education* (pp. 9–12). Winnipeg, Manitoba.

Malone, Mary. (1989, August 26). Where the boys aren't. *London Free Press*, pp. 3–5, 16.

Martel, Angeline, & Peterat, Linda. (1988). Feminist pedagogies: From pedagogic romanticism to the success of authenticity. In Peta Tancred-Sheriff (Ed.), *Feminist research: Retrospect and prospect* (pp. 80–95). Montreal: McGill-Queen's University Press.

Martin, Jane Roland. (1985). *Reclaiming a conversation.* New Haven, CT: Yale University Press.

McLean, Carol, & Peterat, Linda. (1984). Knowing daily life: A reaction to education for families of the future. *Canadian Home Economics Journal, 34*(3), 153–155.

McLeod, Stella. (1977). Co-ed home economics. *Vista, 8*(3).

Peterat, Linda. (1983). Education, women and home economics. *Canadian Home Economics Journal, 33*(2), 67–74.

Peterat, Linda. (1986). Isabel Bevier: A different voice for women's education in the mid-west. In L. Peterat (Ed.), *The conversation and company of educated women* (pp. 24–32). Champaign: Illinois Teacher of Home Economics.

Pierce, Cathy. (1989). Where the boys are. *What's New in Home Economics, 22*(5), 4.

Puissi, Anna Maria. (1990). Towards a pedagogy of sexual difference: Education and female genealogy. *Gender and Education, 2*(1), 81–90.

Ralston, Penny. (1992). Distinctive themes from black home economists. *Journal of Home Economics, 84*(2), 39–44.

Schaffer, Ruby. (1965). Home economics for boys. *THESA Journal, 3*(1), 28–34.

Sheppard, Holly. (1983). How to get guys into child care classes. *Forecast for Home Economics, 29*(1), 96–98.

Spelman, Elizabeth. (1991). Gender in the context of race and class. In Johnnella Butler & John Walter (Eds.), *Transforming the curriculum* (pp. 201–226). Albany: State University of New York Press.

Spurrier, Patsy. (1977). Teaching the guys effectively! *Tips and Topics, 17*(4), 6–7.

Stamp, Robert. (1977). Teaching girls their God given place in life. *Atlantic: A Women's Studies Journal,* Spring, 18–32.

Sunderlin, Ida. (1933). Why not for boys, too? *National Education Association Journal, 12,* 255–256.

Thompson, Patricia J. (1986). Beyond gender: Equity issues for home economics education. *Theory into Practice, 25*(4), 276–283.

Thompson, Patricia J. (1992). *Bringing feminism home.* Charlottetown: University of Prince Edward Island, Home Economics Publishing Collective.

Vaines, Eleanore. (1981). A content analysis of the ten Lake Placid conferences on home economics. *Canadian Home Economics Journal, 31,* 29–33.

Vincenti, Virginia. (1982). Toward a clearer professional identity. *Journal of Home Economics, 74*(3), 20–25.

Weis, Susan. (1974). Home economics education: Sexism in the schools. *Illinois Teacher, 18*(2), 85–88.

Weis, Susan. (1979). Examination of home economics textbooks for sex bias. *Home Economics Research Journal, 7*(3), 147–162.

What Robin Morgan said. (1973). *Journal of Home Economics, 65*(1), 13.

Williams, Gloria. (1988). Race and ethnicity in home economics: Theoretical and methodological issues. In Herma B. Williams (Ed.), *Empowerment through difference* (pp. 46–86). Peoria, IL: Glencoe.

Wilson, Johanna. (1966). *A history of home economics education in Manitoba, 1826–1966.* Unpublished master's thesis, University of Manitoba.

Zinn, Maxine Baca. (1992). Reframing the revisions: Inclusive thinking for family sociology. In Cheris Kramarae & Dale Spender (Eds.), *The knowledge explosion* (pp. 473–479). New York: Teachers College Press.

CHAPTER 10

Out of the Cameos and Into the Conversation: Gender, Social Studies, and Curriculum Transformation

JANE BERNARD-POWERS

Like many children of my generation in the United States, I read for pleasure and to learn about life. Television became available only after my reading habits were well formed and so my lenses and knowledge about what it meant to be female came from life experience and from my reading. Rebecca of Sunnybrook Farm, Jo and Amy March of *Little Women*, Nancy Drew, Scarlett O'Hara, a young Queen Elizabeth I, and Clara Barton are feminine characters whom I befriended, counseled, and compared myself to in my imagination. My cast of characters reflects the seamless biases and blinders that were part of my experience growing up not only in the fifties but also in the Midwest. Class, race, and sexual identity were not explicit concerns in the informal curriculum that my pleasure reading constituted. But in my books and stories, girls and women had lives, made choices, and were immortalized in print. That was important in a world that proclaimed girls and women to be important but provided no evidence of it or even evidence contrary to it in the formal curriculum.

Women, notable or otherwise, separately or in relation with men, were virtually invisible in social studies texts and curricula and their absence was little noted until 1971 when Janice Law Trecker wrote her ovarian article, "Women in United States History Textbooks" (1971). This article was published when I was teaching eighth-grade U.S. history in Pacifica, California. The article raised questions for me that I had never considered and in the vernacular of the period, I experienced a small "click" that grew into a compelling need to know (O'Reilly, 1980). I realized that I had been teaching history that had little connection to women's lives and that I was virtually ignorant about women in history. Moreover, I didn't personally know anyone who was knowledgeable about women in history. The two decades that followed (1971–1991) gave rise to a remarkably vital, rich, and controversial room in the academy—women's studies. We can now study and teach women's history, anthropology, economics, political science, sociology, and psychology, along with feminist critique and theory. We appreciate and can question the experiences, histories, and myths that women share in common and that distinguish them from one another. But in the K–12 social studies curriculum, women of all classes, races, and ethnicities; women who are differently abled; women who are heterosexual; and women who are lesbian are still in the margins of the text, or invisible—along with their perspectives, experiences, and connections to each other, to men, and to children (AAUW, 1992). The K–12 curriculum has not been receptive to change.

The realization of gender equitable and gender fair social studies, and ultimately curriculum transformation, is a formidable challenge. The somewhat loose organization of the field is one major source of the challenge. Social studies is a combination of historical, geographical, anthropological, economic, and sociological concepts, generalizations, and topics; it also includes a number of special interest topics such as law related education, environmental education, and global education, all of which compete for classroom time. The absence of a uniform or national curricula, such as that of Norway or Great Britain, has been both a strength of the system because it allows for local and school-based curriculum decisions, and a source of difficulty when curriculum change is the goal.

Social studies curricula and assessment are currently under attack by proponents of "cultural literacy" and disciplinarians who are advocating the restoration of history and geography as the centerpieces of the curriculum. Advocates for gender-fair and culturally inclusive social studies have made limited progress in the past two decades and the climate is chilly in the circles of conservative educators who are pushing for social studies curriculum reform (Waugh, 1991).

Compounding the challenges that arise from social studies curriculum politics is the ascendance of a poststructuralist, postmodern critique that poses gender as a problematic cultural construct (Butler, 1990). According to Mary Evans, "voices are raised, inside and outside feminism, which suggest that women's studies is no longer necessary, that the category of 'women' is no longer viable and that the apparent maintenance of a concept of sexual division is no longer acceptable" (1991, p. 68). Moreover, Evans goes on to criticize the idea of gender on the grounds that it dilutes and alters women's studies and feminist studies. The debates over essential feminine identity—is there a woman's culture?—have shaped conversation and scholarship in women's studies and to some extent the social science disciplines in the last decade. What exists at present is a conspicuous tension between the need to construct and sustain gender as a category and a lens for understanding structures of knowledge in the social sciences and the experiences of students, on one hand, and the call to deconstruct notions of gender based on their inadequacy for explaining diverse human identities on the other. The tension between perspectives has caused considerable furor in women's history and is a potential problem for social studies educators who deal with the practicalities of curriculum and who have been lobbying for gender-fair curricula in public schools for years. Development of gender consciousness is a tentative enterprise in K–12 social studies curricula and it seems premature to talk about eliminating the lens and the topic even though the controversial conversation has enriched our understanding.

Avoiding the pitfalls of dichotomous choices in favor of a flexible and inclusive agenda seems appropriate to social studies. Understanding and sorting through gender influences and issues in the curriculum as it is currently structured is important in making informed decisions. At the same time, mining the richness of feminist scholarship and theory to inform the former and work towards curriculum transformation is a useful perspective. This chapter attempts to consider both. Framing questions include: What does gender equitable social studies mean in terms of content and method? How can it be realized? How can bridges between feminist research and scholarship and the K–12 curriculum be sustained? How can we foster the critique that illuminates our hidden and systemic biases? Moreover, what would curriculum transformation look like? The chapter is organized into two parts that address the broad issues outlined above. These are, first, considerations of equity and feminism in relation to the curriculum as it is currently structured—this is the unfinished business of the last decade and the challenge of the new decade. And, second, the more elusive fabric of potentially transformative feminist ideas and processes—especially the notion of citizenship education for the twenty-first century.

A note of caution for readers who prefer an even reading terrain: this field that encompasses gender and social studies is broad, uneven, and rocky. The domination of information in textbooks and the reality that the language of curriculum is essentially practical are biases that not only shape what we know but also the structure of the story. Moreover, this chapter is written by an educator who works in both public school and academe, thus the writing is bridgework.

GENDER POLITICS AND CURRICULUM PRACTICALITIES

Resilient conservatism in the face of potential change aptly characterizes social studies curriculum in the past two decades. This section addresses pressure points for change in curriculum reform and the politics of social studies curriculum. These potential sources of change include curriculum frameworks, textbooks, classroom processes, social studies content, and the research that informs notions of gender and social studies.

The 1990s have given rise to a remarkably conservative wave of curriculum reformation in social studies. In the United States, the conservative wave in social studies was solidified with the publication of three extended critiques of education. The most seemingly influential social studies critique is *What Do Our 17-Year-Olds Know?* This book reports on the results of a National Assessment of Education Progress test that found high school juniors to lack historical knowledge. Chester Finn and Diane Ravitch, coauthors of the report, call for the restoration of traditional literature and history to schools (Walker, 1990, p. 351). National curriculum documents in the United Kingdom, and particularly the document, "Charting a Course: Social Studies for the 21st Century," have identified history and geography, with an emphasis on the former, as the core subjects of social studies (History Working Group, 1990; National Commission on Social Studies in Schools, 1989). Both documents have been criticized for increasing the study of traditional history and excluding critical interpretations of history. In particular, Jack Nelson writes, "The proposed curriculum will ring hollow to those who read American history in terms of how our past values and ethical principles resulted in mistreating women, minorities, labor unions, suspected communists, radicals, anarchists, private farmers, small business owners, working class children, migrant workers . . ." (1990, p. 437). The apparent goal of conservative educators, as Elizabeth Genovese has observed, is to restore the canon of Western civilization by declaration—a gambit with poor prospects (Genovese, 1991). However, the conservatism that threatens to minimize considerations of gender and feminism is being translated into curriculum frameworks and proposed national standards.

Curriculum Frameworks

Curriculum frameworks are sources of both continuity and potential change. Frameworks and guidelines published by the state, county, community, or professional organization (National Council for the Social Studies) outline the order of topics or content knowledge, skills, values, and attitudes that students should acquire (Mehlinger & Marker, 1992). There are comparable frameworks in Canada and the United Kingdom (History Working Group, 1990; McKenna, 1986).

There are three key points to be made about curriculum frameworks and scope sequence documents. First, they are revised periodically and thus might reflect the watershed of scholarship published in the past 20 years that has focused on women's experiences and perspectives. But there is considerable evidence to indicate that curriculum documents have not been receptive to this "new" scholarship (Hahn et al., 1985; McKenna, 1989).

Second, they are political documents created through political processes. The California State Department of Education (1988) is a particularly important case in point. This document was to be written by a committee of social science educators representing different levels of education and diverse points of view. The process was derailed when the first draft was rejected by the State Department of Education. An adjunct professor of history, a state department staff person, and a member of the curriculum commission formed a new committee that was primarily responsible for the final framework document that was created "without substantive participation by the other members of the Curriculum framework committee" (Campbell, 1988, p. 403). For many, this document represents a major step toward state control of what knowledge is most valuable (Cornbleth, 1990). More specifically, the History Social Science Framework is a basically conservative document that minimizes women's history (Henry, 1989). Feminist groups in California lobbied to influence the document when it was still an idea, when it was drafted, and when the textbook series based on the document was selected. None of these were effective. While the lobbying for more representation of women and feminist scholarship continues in California, the influence of this document has expanded into the national picture (Waugh, 1991). National history standards and tests reflecting the seamless consensus history of the California framework are currently being developed.

Since frameworks specifically, and curriculum making generally, are political activities, social studies educators and feminists need to work together to influence the politics of framework committee appointments, and the content of documents. Feminist scholars in the social sciences are a particularly critical resource because they know the scholarship and the critique. They can argue with specific examples of curricula that accurately reflect the economics, politics, geographies, and histories of women's lives.

Lastly, the traditional scope and sequence process needs to be problematized as a method of curriculum design. The expanded environ-

ments approach to curriculum design, and scope and sequence documents that reflect the model, were not defensible based on research on
learning (Ehman & Hahn, 1981; Mehlinger & Marker, 1992). Yet the expanded environments approach held sway in social studies curriculum
design for decades. The tight relationship between key frameworks such
as California's and textbook markets distances the curriculum decision
making—at least in theory—from the seat of the most important elements in the curriculum-design process—this has been discouraging to
gender and multicultural inclusion. According to Audré Lorde, if ". . .
The master's tools will never dismantle the master's house," then we need
to reshape the tools (Noffke, 1992).

Textbooks

Curriculum frameworks can profoundly influence social studies curriculum because they shape textbooks. Moreover, textbooks are a fundamental source of content knowledge: "about half of all social studies
teachers depend upon a single textbook; about 90% use no more than
three" (Mehlinger & Marker, 1992, p. 849). Textbooks are also the most
systematically studied source of information about the social studies curriculum, and as such they constitute a reliable source of information of
the representation of women and women's experiences over the last two
decades (Mehlinger & Marker, 1992). Beginning with the "ovarian" work
done by Janice Law Trecker, there have been regular content analyses
documenting the quantity and quality of references to women's experiences in textbooks used in classrooms (Hahn & Bernard-Powers, 1985;
Light, Staton, & Bourne, 1989; Trecker, 1971).

One notable study published in the United States was done by Mary
Kay Tetreault on the extent and quality of scholarship in textbooks (Tetreault, 1986). Tetreault set up a framework of five "stages of thinking
about women in history" (1986, p. 215). Her framework begins with the
absence of women in stage one and then moves to compensatory history
where notable women are recognized. The third stage is "Bi-Focal History," which provides for inclusion of women's experiences as a comple-
ment to men's; the fourth is "Feminist History," which provides for a reconceptualization of history to encompass female experiences; and the
fifth, called "Multi-Focal, Relational History," provides for a holistic view
of human experience that is multidisciplinary.

Using the five stages as guidelines, Tetreault analyzed 12 popular texts
used in United States secondary history courses. Her findings indicated
that the percentage of visuals depicting women has increased dramatically,
ranging from 30 to 58% of all visuals, and that six of the texts had over 40%.

Yet the text and the overall narrative have changed very little. The percentage of copy devoted to women's experience does not exceed 8% in any of the textbooks and was under 5% in over half of the books.

The significance of Tetreault's work is that she has carefully looked for evidence of quality in the written text. She asks, whose histories are included in the text? Not surprisingly the histories are based on White male-centered frameworks with some female activities added. "Women's oppression and their contributions to wars, reform movements and women's rights organizations warrant space in these books . . . [but] the content of women's everyday lives is lost in high school textbooks" (Tetreault, 1986, p. 225).

A Canadian study done in 1989 by Beth Light, Pat Staton, and Paula Bourne found similar results. Women seemed to be present by virtue of photographs and art work in the 66 texts they studied, but they were marginal to the main text (Light et al., 1989). More recently, Darlene Clark-Hine, speaking to a National Council for Social Studies audience (1990), argued that her analysis of four currently used textbooks found that, "the authors . . . consistently fail[ed] to provide an appropriate social, political or cultural context for the Black Woman. People of color were marginalized and the dominant narrative requires a total reconceptualization" (Clark-Hine, 1990, p. 14).

The conversation and the state of feminist/gendered history and social sciences has advanced well beyond discussions of contributions and stark omissions to develop theoretical frameworks, multiple perspectives, and critiques of perspective. Yet while this rich body of work has developed over the last 20 years, feminist scholarship still has not made its way into the cornerstone of social studies curriculum—textbooks.

There are common sense explanations for this. First, it makes sense that if teachers know multicultural feminist history, economics, political science, and sociology, they will be able to teach from that perspective, critique curriculum frameworks from that perspective, and look for textbooks and supplementary materials that are inclusive. Thus the education and reeducation of teachers, and teachers of teachers, is a key point. Teachers are a critical source of the critique of textbooks and until teachers demand textbook change, it is unlikely to happen.

The academy, meaning undergraduate liberal arts courses where students acquire knowledge for teaching, has not caught up with the general flowering of research and scholarship on women and gender. To illustrate this point, I cite DuBois and colleagues, who reviewed articles on "women and women's issues" published in major journals from 1966 to 1980 in the fields of history, philosophy, education, literature, and anthropology. Less than 10% dealt with feminist and gender issues (DuBois et al., 1985). Farnham's edited work on the academy (1987) has also noted the paucity of feminist research and scholarship.

To change the fundamental questions, methods, and perspectives in social studies, the field must have social studies teachers educated in liberal arts courses that substantively include multicultural feminist content, theory, and method. Moreover, these teachers must also have textbooks written by people who know feminist scholarship.

Once teachers have left their preservice education programs, they need inservice education to keep them current or to update their educations, and the storefront enterprises and consciousness raising committees that set up shop on the margins of the field have been invaluable. The National Council for the Social Studies has a special interest group on Gender and Social Studies that has organized programs, materials, speakers, and general awareness of gender bias in the organization for a number of years. The National Women's Studies Association has a K–12 network that actively promotes social studies curriculum change, and the Canadian Committee on Women's History has supported a number of important efforts, including the linking of scholars with teachers ("Women's History Committees and Associations," 1989). Independent support groups and networks such as the National Women's History Project, the Upper Midwest Women's History Center, Women in World Area Studies, and Women Associated for Global Education, along with the special interest groups affiliated with organizations such as the National Women's Studies Association, the Association for Independent Schools, the Western Association of Women Historians, the Seeking Educational Equity and Diversity (SEED) Project at Wellesley, and the California Council for the Social Studies have in the United States been the primary agents for curriculum change in the last decade. Conferences, workshops, lobbies for publications, and annual gatherings such as the Gender Special Interest Group (SIG) Breakfast at the National Council for the Social Studies have provided basic education and resources that enable individuals to incorporate women's histories into the curriculum with support. Because of the work of individuals and networks, many of which began with funding from the Women's Educational Equity Act, we now have a wealth of classroom resources that span the K–12 curriculum in social studies. We have within our grasp the seeds of change.

Research on Gender

We have some evidence that gender-fair curriculum makes a difference. Kathy Scott and Candace Garrett Schau reviewed more than 100 studies for their chapter in *The Handbook for Achieving Sex Equity in Educa-*

tion, and reported that "Pupils who are exposed to sex-equitable materials are more likely than others to: (1) have gender-balanced knowledge of people in society, (2) develop more flexible attitudes and more accurate sex-role knowledge, and (3) imitate role behaviors contained in the materials" (Scott & Schau, 1985, p. 228).

In 1985 and 1986, 300,000 eighth-grade students in California were tested under the California Assessment Program (CAP). On the new history/social studies/science test boys did better on 467 of the questions, while girls did better on 253. Whereas "Boys did better on questions related to war, historical documents (such as the Declaration of Independence, the Constitution, the Bill of Rights), and questions involving geography or chronology. . . . Girls did better on questions related to interpretation of slogans, quotations (except those associated with war), women's rights or questions in which the focus of the question was a woman" (Kneedler, 1988).

Compelling evidence of the impact of gender-inclusive curriculum comes from an example of curriculum change in Dutch secondary schools. In 1990, approximately 40,000 secondary students received instruction in women's history of the Netherlands and the United States in preparation for compulsory exams. Whereas young women, who were in the majority, usually scored lower than young men on the history exams, the reverse was true on this test for a substantial percentage of the test takers (Grever, 1991).

Testimonies and stories provide inspiring evidence of the impact of gender-inclusive curriculum. For example, Geraldine Taylor and Stephen Pistono wrote about their experiences teaching women's history in elementary school in Wisconsin. According to their article published in *Feminist Teacher,* their original purpose was to motivate "the girls in class to participate more actively in social studies. [But] not only has this occurred, but more dramatically the boys have become more intrigued with the subject matter as well" (Taylor & Pistono, 1987, p. 14).

Students need to see their past, present, and future reflected in the curriculum. The absence of women's experiences, histories, and perspectives in the curriculum creates a dysfunctional curriculum for both young men and young women. As one twelfth-grade, African-American student quoted in the AAUW Report expressed this issue, "In twelve years of school, I never studied anything about myself" (AAUW, 1992, p. 61).

Pedagogy

Teachers of social studies and especially teachers of young children generally agree that teaching and learning processes are an important

part of curricula. The pedagogy of social studies and citizenship education goes "hand-in-glove" with the content and many would argue is the
more powerful learning of the two. Catherine Cornbleth has characterized the dual curriculum that operates in most classrooms as the "technical" or the advertised course of study that includes frameworks, textbooks, units, films, and evaluation and the "social process" that refers to
the "day-to-day classroom interaction of teachers, students and ideas"
(Mehlinger & Marker, 1992, p. 834). Teachers can teach about racial and
gender equality and injustice while tolerating or engaging in practices
that contradict the "teaching." The recent AAUW report on gender and
schooling cited a survey of middle school and high school students, 82%
of whom were aware of sex differential policies and practices (AAUW,
1992). Authors of the report go on to assert that gender politics needs to
be an explicit part of the curriculum.

Critical theorists share with many social studies educators a fundamental belief that critical questioning of the content and process of the
classroom curriculum is a linchpin in a democratic classroom. It is the
means by which multiple lenses and layers of complexity can be illumi-
nated, including the opaque assumptions of classroom relations and
norms. Gilligan and colleagues (1990) provide an excellent example in
Making Connections of a young woman's question about a historical event
that raised issues of trust. Her teacher's response was, "I'm teaching
about Constitutional History and these girls want to know about relationships." As the authors of the recently published report, "How Schools
Shortchange Girls," articulate this issue, girls and women bring to their
classrooms a sense of connection and caring that can contribute to the
development of a prosocial community. Connecting logic and rationality
with feelings may empower young women and men and enrich the curriculum.

Frances Maher's work on inquiry provides an excellent example of
how attention to gender may alter assumptions. Inquiry teaching is defined as "a way of thinking that requires the systematic manipulation of
information to find a supportable answer to a question or problem." Students identify a problem; formulate a hypothesis; gather data to support,
reject, or refine the hypothesis; and then either assert the truth or begin
again. In comparison, a feminist pedagogy "recognizes a multiplicity of
both problems and solutions, which can be compared and related to each
other but not ranked as inferior or superior" (Maher, 1987). Drawing on
an example set out in *Social Education,* an inquiry model might ask the
question: What was the effect of the New Deal on the economy? (Maher,
1987, p. 187). The feminist approach might be to ask, however: What were
the differential effects of the Depression and the New Deal on people's

lives? In the former example, an answer is sought, while in the latter, a "fuller picture of a complex society" is established (Maher, 1987, p. 19). With the picture of a complex society, many voices and perspectives are sewn into the fabric of the lesson.

Baker and Davies in New South Wales Australia analyzed a lesson taught on the subject of sex roles and found that the tightly structured question format had a negative effect on learning and on student reactions (1989). In their words, "The use, in this lesson, of the initiation-reply-evaluation format ensures that the control of topic and knowledge remains with the teacher, that alternative directions of questioning are marginalised [sic], and that the students are required to collude in generating one ultimately counter-productive form of description which is made to pass as social analysis" (1989, pp. 73–74). The pedagogical technique contributed to a lesson that ultimately reinforced sex-role stereotyping.

Classroom organization is another domain of pedagogy that can serve the interests of gender-fair social studies. Group work predicated on carefully defined roles and norms, with students taking responsibility for learning for everyone while harnessing the effects of gender, ethnicity, and race on classroom achievement is key. Teachers who rely heavily on small group discussion need to be especially aware of the effects of status expectation states on group dynamics (Cohen, 1986). By providing training for group roles, very specific feedback on reinforcing student strengths, and modeling for equal treatment of humans, success in group work problem solving and prosocial behavior can increase for everyone. The Program for Complex Instruction at Stanford University is one example of a program that provides training and education in the utilization of instruction that is designed to be gender, racially, ethnically, and linguistically friendly (Cohen, 1986).

SOCIAL STUDIES CONTENT:
FROM TRADITIONAL TRAIPSING TO TRANSFORMATIVE POSSIBILITIES

The most difficult topic to generalize about in this short essay is social studies content. The breadth of social science scholarship renders this daunting or even futile and the sources of feminist scholarship are plentiful, so this discussion will focus on civics (citizenship) education.

Education for citizenship has been an explicit raison d'être for social studies since its birth in the first two decades of the twentieth century. Voting, analysis of key social and political issues, understanding how the apparatus of representative democracy works, and routes to public office are typical topics in civics courses. Good school citizenship behavior (that is, hallway and playground etiquette), classroom democracy, and appreciation of community service people such as police officers are typical of content in elementary classrooms. The topics and implicit perspectives have focused attention on learning to be a good citizen in the public realm.

Lamentations about the ignorance of youth in matters of citizenship—meaning government—occupy a significant place in writings about the field. Most recently *The Handbook of Research on Social Studies Teaching and Learning* reported that standardized tests seem to indicate that American adolescents lack fundamental knowledge of constitutional democracy and that knowledge transmission is not entirely successful (Shaver, 1991). In the discussion of civics education presented in the *Handbook,* the meaning and context of democratic understanding is situated in public and formal structures of government. The problem, as it is cast, is that students' knowledge is impoverished.

Inattention to gender concerns is a major flaw in the review of research; it is a problem in civics education and it reflects the challenge for women in the public realm. Writing in 1928, Virginia Woolf addressed the meaning of citizenship to women. As she probes women's relationships and involvements with society in *Three Guineas,* she asks, "do we wish to join the procession of men," and if so, "on what terms?" (Woolf, 1983, p. 360). Women are still traipsing along at the tail end of the procession of appointed and elected offices in government and women are still questioning whether the procession with its traditional path serves women and society in the long run.

The absence and then slow gains of women in public office over the last 20 years is well documented. According to Nannerl Keohane, feminist political scientist, "The public realm across cultures and over the centuries has been male centered to an extent unparalleled in other parts of human social life. . . . Cabinets and legislatures, councils of diplomacy and commerce, assemblies and courts of justice have been almost exclusively populated by males" (Keohane, 1983, p. 86). This reality is borne out in *Women: A World Survey,* published in 1985, which reported that women hold no more than 10% of the seats in national legislatures (Sivard, 1985). The lack of and need for women's participation in high-level decision making featured prominently in *Forward Looking Strategies,* the document adopted by the United Nations End of the Decade Conference in Kenya in 1985.

Documentation of adolescents' attitudes toward women in political office and knowledge of politics have shaped previous discussions of women and civics. For example, research conducted in the seventies found that young women and girls demonstrate less political knowledge than young men and boys, and that youth in general in the United States were less supportive of women than of men as political leaders (Education Commission of the States, 1973). A more current study reported that a substantial percentage of young White and Black men (50% and 53%, respectively), in Grades 7 to 12, did not believe that women were as qualified as men to run a country. Conversely, a high percentage of young White women and young Black women (86% and 81%, respectively) thought that women were just as qualified (Gillespie & Spohn, 1987). Discriminatory attitudes toward women in political office or women in leadership positions are a serious problem that is compounded for people of color in the United States.

Citizenship education in the K–12 grades should provide content and strategies to rectify attitudes toward women in public office. Yet, in a recent study, "Gender in Civics Learning," conducted by Angela Harwood and Carol Hahn in five high school civics classes in a southeastern U.S. community, the problem of gender invisibility was clear. There were "few references ever made to women and women's issues in these classes" and the structured opportunities provided by the textbooks were ignored by the teachers (1992, p. 21).

Education about women in the public realm, coupled with education about the development of social attitudes that govern evaluations of candidates and political issues, deserves serious attention in social studies. The utility of biography in teaching about attitudes toward women, and gender in politics, both in a historical and a contemporary sense cannot be underestimated. Septima Clark's biography, *Ready From Within* (Brown, 1990), and the recently published biography of Fannie Lou Hammer, *This Little Light of Mine . . .* (Mills, 1993), are examples of biographical works that teach about the political lives of significant women of color. Oral history techniques and interviews have the potential to tap into the lives and perspectives of women in the community who have made significant contributions to the quality of political life but may not be publicly acknowledged. This is especially important for women of color, lesbian women, limited English speakers, and working-class women.

Beyond modification of the current "curriculum of citizenship education" lies the possibility of more substantive change in the parameters and definition of civics. If we stand back and consider the procession that Virginia Woolf alludes to and contemplate alternatives to citizenship education for participation in public office, a different picture emerges. While women have been discouraged or excluded from public domains of power and policy, they have been encouraged in their contributions to family life, child-bearing, child rearing, the education of children, the care of elders, and the nursing of the sick. Moreover, women's contributions to what we have designated the private sphere of human activities—many of which are related to the keeping of homes and care of families—do not receive the public notice that men's public contributions do. The point is vividly made by Elizabeth Karmarck Minnich:

> We did found and run institutions that cared for the sick and old and wounded outside the home. We did found and run schools that provided for newly freed black people and for children. We did struggle for goodness in the church, the synagogue, the community—and we did so politically. We were active in the abolition movement and the civil rights movement. We outsiders did our work, work of all kind, and whatever we did remained obscured from the light (Minnich, 1982).

Shelly Rosaldo and Louise Lamphere, in a discussion of the origins of sexual asymmetry, suggest that early societies "found it adaptive to differentiate the activities of men and women, giving those of men (hunting) a special value" (Rosaldo & Lamphere, 1974, p. 6). Some historians trace the development (or perception of) separate spheres to the Industrial Revolution. Whatever the origin of the rhetoric and/or the reality, it is clear that social studies content mirrors the asymmetry. Public domains of human experience—the procession—are synonymous with citizenship education; "private concerns" such as family welfare, child care, peace activities, community organizations, domestic violence, and sexual harassment have had no evident place in the formal curriculum.

This was not always the case. Domestic feminists in the first two decades of the twentieth century lobbied for formal education about domestic issues. "The broom" of municipal housekeepers extended to environmental concerns such as pure air, water, and food; social issues such as protective labor legislation for women and children; and education issues such as vocational education (Bernard-Powers, 1992). Education for these feminine activities was a significant part of the conversation about "The Girl Question in Education," but this curriculum of family, community relation, and social contract was not incorporated into coursework.

Home economics educators of the progressive era, social constructionists of the 1930s such as George Counts and Harold Rugg, critical educators and many feminists of the 1990s share the belief that education for responsible and caring community participation should be a fundamental goal of schooling (Stanley, 1992). Nel Noddings and Jane Roland Martin are among the feminist scholars who have suggested that there is a woman's culture and that the ideas and values of woman's culture, especially those domestic issues, belong in the curriculum (Martin, Chapter 8, this volume; Noddings, 1992). Social studies curricula that include all dimensions of citizen belief and behavior, especially those that have been invisible, and domestic issues concerned with feeding, educating, housing, and nurturing human beings in communities—and providing members of the communities with perspectives and skills that will sustain and reproduce the communities—is a goal for the next decade.

The challenge for social studies educators concerned about gender equity is to continue to lobby for textbooks, frameworks, liberal education, and preservice teacher education that reflect feminist scholarship and pedagogy. Ultimately the goal is to alter the path, merging the public and private, the personal and political, and the concept of citizen. Clearly, citizenship education is not course and subject bound. It is in partnership with a vast system of beliefs and understandings about gender, social class, ethnicity, race, sexual identity, and levels of enabling that influence students' experiences in schools. Yet the explicit curriculum of social studies is a powerful source of change in schools that has barely been tapped, and gender equity is the wellspring of that change.

REFERENCES

American Association of University Women (AAUW) and Wellesley College Center for Research on Women. (1992). *How schools shortchange girls*. Washington, DC: AAUW Educational Foundation and National Education Association.

Baker, Carolyn, & Davies, Bronwyn. (1989). A lesson on sex roles. *Gender and Education, 1*(6), 73–74.

Banks, James. (1990). *Teaching strategies for the social studies*. New York: Longman.

Bernard-Powers, Jane. (1992). *The girl question in education: Vocational education for young women in the progressive era*. London: The Falmer Press.

Brown, Cynthia Stokes. (1990). *Ready from within*. Princeton, NJ: African World Press.

Butler, Judith. (1990). *Gender trouble: Feminism and the subversion of identity*. New York: Routledge & Kegan Paul.

California State Department of Education. (1988). *History—Social science framework for California public schools*. Sacramento: California State Department of Education.

Campbell, D. (1988). Letter to the editor. *Social Education, 52*(6), 403.

Chira, S. (1992, February 12). Bias against girls is found rife in schools, with lasting damage. *New York Times*, p. 1.

Clark-Hine, Darlene. (1990, November). *The treatment of minorities and women in American history textbooks in secondary schools*. Keynote address at the meeting of the National Council for the Social Studies, Anaheim, CA.

Cohen, Elizabeth. (1986). *Designing groupwork: Strategies for the heterogeneous class-room*. New York: Teachers College Press.

Cornbleth, C. (1990). *Curriculum in context*. Philadelphia: Falmer Press.

DuBois, Ellen, et al. (1985). *Feminist scholarship: Kindling in the groves of academe*. Urbana: University of Illinois Press.

Education Commission of the States. (1973). *Political knowledge and attitudes (National assessment of educational progress)*. Washington, DC: U.S. Government Printing Office.

Ehman, Lee H., & Hahn, Carole. (1981). Contributions of research to social studies education. In Howard D. Mehlinger & O. L. Davis, Jr., (Eds.), *The social studies: Eightieth yearbook of the National Society for the Study of Education*. Chicago: University of Chicago Press.

Eisler, Riane. (1987). *The chalice and the blade, our history, our future*. New York: Harper & Row.

Evans, Mary. (1991). The problem of gender for women's studies. In Jane Aaron and Sylvia Walby (Eds.), *Out of the margins* (pp. 67–74). London: The Falmer Press.

Faludi, Susan. (1992). *Backlash*. New York: Crown.

Farnham, Christie. (1987). *The impact of feminist research in the academy*. Bloomington: Indiana University Press.

Gagnon, Paul. (1988). *Democracy's untold story, what world history textbooks neglect*. Washington, DC: American Federation of Teachers.

Genovese, Elizabeth Fox. (1991). *Feminism without illusions: A critique of individualism*. Chapel Hill: University of North Carolina Press.

Gillespie, Diane, & Spohn, Cassia. (1987). Adolescents' attitudes toward women in politics: The effect of gender and race. *Gender & Society, 1*(2), 208–218.

Gilligan, Carol, Lyons, Nona, & Hanmer, Trudy. (Eds.). (1990). *Making connections*. Cambridge, MA: Harvard University Press.

Grever, Maria. (1991). Pivoting the center: Women's history as a compulsory examination subject in all Dutch secondary schools in 1990 and 1991. *Gender & History, 3*(1), 75–78.

Hahn, Carol, Bernard-Powers, Jane, et al. (1985). Sex equity in the social studies. In Susan Klein (Ed.), *Handbook for achieving sex equity in education* (p. 281). Baltimore: Johns Hopkins University Press.

Harwood, Angela, & Hahn, Carol. (1992, April). *Civic learning in young adolescents*. Paper presented at the annual meeting of the American Educational Research Association, San Francisco.

Henry, Tess. (1989). Gender and the framework. *Social Studies Review, 28*(2), 27–30.

History Working Group. (1990). *National curriculum. Final report*. London: Her Majesty's Stationery Office (HMSO).

Keohane, Nannerl. (1983). Speaking from silence: Women and the science of politics. In Langland, Elizabeth, & Gove, Walter (Eds.), *A feminist perspective in the academy* (pp. 86–100). Chicago: University of Chicago Press.

Kneedler, Pete. (1988, March). *Differences between boys and girls on California's new statewide assessment in history-social science*. Paper presented at a meeting of the California Council for the Social Studies, Los Angeles.

Light, Beth, Staton, Pat, & Bourne, Paula. (1989). Sex equity content in history textbooks. *The History Social Science Teacher, 25*(1), 18–20.

Maher, Frances. (1987). Inquiry teaching and feminist pedagogy. *Social Education, 51*(3), 186–187.

McKenna, Katherine. (1989). An examination of sex equity in the 1986 Ontario curriculum guidelines for history and contemporary studies. *History and Social Science Teacher, 25*(1), 21–24.

Mehlinger, Howard, & Marker, Gerald. (1992). Social studies. In Phillip Jackson (Ed.), *Handbook of research on curriculum* (pp. 830–851). New York: Macmillan.

Mills, Kay. (1993). *"This little light of mine": The story of Fannie Lou Hammer.* New York: NEL Dutton.

Minnich, Elizabeth Kamark. (1982). Liberal arts and civic arts: Education for "the free man"? *Liberal Education, 68*(4), 314.

The Nairobi forward-looking strategies for the advancement of women. (1985). New York: United Nations.

National Commission on Social Studies in the Schools. (1989). *Charting a course: Social studies for the twenty first century.* Washington, DC: National Council for the Social Studies.

Nelson, Jack. (1990). Charting a course backwards: A response to the National Commission's nineteenth century social studies program. *Social Education, 54*(7), 434–437.

Noddings, Nel. (1988). *Caring. A feminine approach to ethics.* Berkeley: University of California Press.

Noddings, Nel. (1989). *Women and evil.* Berkeley: University of California Press.

Noddings, Nel. (1992). Social studies and feminism. *Theory and Research in Social Education, 20*(3), 227–238.

Noffke, Susan. (1992, April). *Multicultural curricula: Whose knowledge and beyond.* Paper presented at the annual meeting of the American Educational Research Association, San Francisco.

O'Reilly, Jane. (1980). *The girl I left behind.* New York: Macmillan.

Rosaldo, Michelle Zimbalist, & Lamphere, Louise. (Eds.). (1974). *Woman, culture, and society.* Stanford, CA: Stanford University Press.

Scott, Kathryn, & Schau, Candace Garrett. (1985). Sex equity and sex bias in instructional materials. In Susan Klein (Ed.), *Handbook for achieving sex equity in education* (pp. 218–232). Baltimore, MD: Johns Hopkins University Press.

Shaver, James. (1991). *Handbook of research on social studies teaching and learning.* New York: Macmillan.

Sivard, Ruth Leger. (1985). *Women . . . A world survey.* Washington, DC: World Priorities.

Stanley, William B. (1992). *Curriculum for utopia, social reconstructionism and critical pedagogy in the postmodern era.* Albany: State University of New York Press.

Stodolsky, Susan. (1988). *The subject matters: Classroom activity in math and social studies.* Chicago: University of Chicago Press.

Taylor, Geraldine, & Pistono, Stephen. (1987). Teaching women's history in the elementary schools. *Feminist Teacher, 3*(1), 12–15.

Tetreault, Mary Kay. (1986). Integrating women's history. *History Teacher, 19*(2), 212–262.

Tetreault, Mary Kay. (1987). Getting women and gender into the curriculum mainstream. *Social Education, 51*(3), 167–168.

Thorne, Barrie. (1980). Children and gender. In Deborah Rhode (Ed.), *Theoretical perspectives on sexual differences* (pp. 103–111). New Haven, CT: Yale University Press.

Torney-Puerta, Judith. (1984). Political socialization and policy: The U.S. in cross national context. In James Shaver (Ed.), *The handbook of research on social studies teaching and learning* (p. 597). New York: Macmillan.

Trecker, Janice Law. (1971). Women in United States history textbooks. *Social Education, 35*(3), 248–335.

Walker, D. (1990). Back to the future. *Educational Researcher, 19*(3), 351.

Waugh, Dexter. (1991). California history textbooks: Do they offend? *California Journal, 22*(3), 121–124.

"Women's History Committees and Association." (1989). *The History and Social Science Teacher, 25*(1), 13.

Woolf, Virginia. (1983). Three guineas. In Susan Bell & Karen Offen (Eds.), *Women, the family and freedom, the debate in documents, Vol. 2, 1880–1950* (pp. 359–362). Stanford, CA: Stanford University Press. (Original work published 1938)

CHAPTER 11

Situating ESL Between Speech and Silence

KATHLEEN ROCKHILL AND PATRICIA TOMIC

A few days ago, a white woman telephoned to ask me to appear on her television program: she felt free to tell me that if I sounded "Black" then she would not "hire" me. This is what I am trying to say to you: Language is power. And that woman is simply one of the ruling powerful people in white America who feel free to reject and strangle whoever will not mimic them—in language, values, goals

—White English/Black English: The Politics of Translation, Jordan, 1989

Ignorance is knowledge/knowledge is ignorance, depending on *who* knows/does not know. It is better to know less than more, provided that what one knows is that which is valued by the dominant society. Perhaps nothing shows the contradictory ways in which knowledge and ignorance circulate through relationships of power as clearly as language. Although Canada is officially a bilingual country, outside of Quebec, English is firmly established as the dominant language in Canada. The urgency of learning English for newcomers who are not fluent in the language is clear, whatever position one occupies between the poles of dominator and dominated. That the "need" to learn the language is socially constructed makes little difference to the child or adult confronted by English-language assumptions and demands on all fronts. They *want* to learn English. Yet the obstacles newcomers experience in accessing language training are numerous. For adults, accessing training involves an arduous struggle against an unsympathetic system. At the same time, learning the language involves a tremendous cost in identity loss for the newcomer. For the "native speaker," language is taken for granted; for the newcomer it constitutes one of the most central markers of their reality in Canada.

We fight for more funds for English as a Second Language (ESL) provision, keen with the knowledge that children and adults not fluent in English will be "disadvantaged" if they are denied opportunities to learn how to perform "properly" in the English language. But what is the meaning of this "disadvantage" when it requires that entire identities, knowledges, cultures, and histories be subjugated? Isn't it really the dominant society that is disadvantaged? In the innocent arrogance of White supremacy, privileged members of society never know their losses, their ignorances; they have neither the need nor the desire to learn the newcomer's ways. They need never even come into contact with "foreigners," for linguistic dominance has the effect of segregating and ghettoizing those not fluent in English. To require fluency in English, including fluency in "accent," means to discriminate against non-native English speakers or non-standard English speakers.

Linguistic dominance is a foundational discursive formation, defining identities, identifications, communities. It constitutes the "reality" that cultural differences are not neutral, but lodged in relationships of power that privilege one culture over all others. All knowledge that cannot be communicated in "proper" English becomes subjugated so that, even as English is acquired by various communities of people, its referent continues to be White, Anglo, male. Through linguistic dominance, English serves as an essential axis along which othering practices get to play themselves out; it is a primary tool of racialization, especially when used in conjunction with skin color. English is a tool of colonization. Yet, the discourse that surrounds the provision of ESL is one of empowerment, offering the promise of liberation once one has acquired the language that is essential to advancement, to integration into Canadian society.

LIBERATION THROUGH SUBJUGATION

This is the paradox of ESL. Given the linguistic dominance of English, access to opportunities to learn the language is crucial to "empowerment," and yet, this process of empowerment is a highly contradictory one, for it is simultaneously a process of colonization. As the hegemony of English is reinforced, all that one cannot speak or fit into its discursive structures is invalidated—is subjugated—(re)constructing the ethnocentrism of the dominant society. So degrees, credentials, experiences, identities, entire cultures and histories are subjugated by English language policies and practices. Through the imposition of "illiteracy," through the imposition of a totalizing "immigrant" identity, an identity that brings with it the constant message that one is an "outsider," does not belong, is inferior, racism works its cancerous takeover of the newcomers' lives. English is used as a tool in this takeover when it serves to judge, to segregate, to demean a person's knowledge—when it serves to subordinate certain knowledge and communities.

Can we envision an approach to ESL that might counter its colonizing effects? In this chapter we argue that, for this to happen, the referent of ESL must shift from Whiteness to the situated, "self-defined" standpoints of transcultural identities: Education about the real and potential colonizing effects of acquiring English is as important as the skill of acquiring the language. We call this approach "situated ESL." We also argue for the use of "mixed codes" as a way of marking the linguistic dominance of English. We recognize that this is apt to be a controversial move. Still, we stay with this recommendation for we feel that discussions about it serve as a way to uncover the ideological practices and investments that perpetuate linguistic dominance. Perhaps there is no escaping it, but at least we can be more mindful of our choices—or lack thereof—in the social construction of unilingualism.

Linguistic dominance works through gender, race, and class. The emphasis upon "proper" English is consistently privileged throughout our social institutions, especially those of schooling. It is noteworthy that identity-based political movements in the last several decades have recognized language as a major site of struggle. Even where the same language is spoken, controversy still rages over certain forms of speaking consistently being delegitimized. Some women of color are using "mixed codes" as a way of protesting internal colonization, of reclaiming their *Mestiza* identities, and of regaining their long-silenced voices. For Chicana feminist writers such as Cherríe Moraga, Gloria Anzaldúa, and others, these mixed codes refer to speaking and writing "in tongues," in a *mestizo* language that reflects the *mestizo* identity of people raised in both English and Spanish in the United States, who do not think/speak/write "standard" English or "standard" Spanish. They claim the right to proudly think/speak/write "spic":

> where you from?
> Soy de aquí
> y soy de allá
> I didn't build
> this border
> that halts me
> the fron

tera splits
on my tongue.

(Excerpt of poem "where you from?" by Gina Valdés, 1990)

In Canada, the battle over French and English has been the raging
focus of political hostility. Native peoples are fighting to reclaim their
aboriginal languages, and long-established ethnic communities reclaim
as well the right to pass their languages and cultures on to new generations. Other noteworthy struggles are those over "non-standard" English
fought by Black activist educators, and "man-made language" (Spender,
1980) as contested by feminists. Although linguistic dominance is challenged by each of these political movements, discursive and political
boundaries have prevented an integrated approach. As a consequence, in
writing this chapter, we have found it difficult to integrate an analysis of
gender with race in considering the curricular issues posed by gender for
ESL. The discourses of race, class, gender, and ESL remain largely separate.[1] While some writing on ESL is beginning to look at racism, gender
issues—or (hetero)sexism—remains largely hidden. And, while White
feminists challenge the hegemony of "man-made" language, they do not
look at its class and racial implications. As we struggle to bring these
arguments together, we stumble over great discursive gaps illustrative of
the depth of the problem to be addressed.

The discourse of colonization, for example, does not address gender,
does not point out that "the colonizers" have been male, and many of "the
colonized," female. This is shifting; especially noteworthy is the work of
Chandra Mohanty (1991), who argues that analyses of sexual oppression
must be situated within the context of colonizing practices. Another form
of colonization—the colonization of women's minds and bodies through
heterosexism—has yet to enter these newly emerging feminist discourses
of colonization.

We find "gender" to be a problematic concept. It implies a neutrality
of male/female difference that erases power relationships. Instead we
choose to work with the concept "(hetero)sexism," which better identifies
the nature of the gendered relationship between men and women that un-
derpins social institutions (de Lauretis, 1990). This relationship is also
classed and raced. As Aída Hurtado (1989) points out, women's power is
derivative of men's, so their power will differ depending upon their access
to White male privilege. Women of color, "disabled" women, and lesbians
are not, like most White women, "seduced" into femininity by the promise
of access to White male power, but rejected as undesirable, not quite
"woman." These dynamics are apt to be especially difficult for young im-

migrant and refugee women whose access to White male privilege is made even more problematic by pressure from within their ethnic communities to remain loyal to their "race" by marrying within the community (Moraga, 1983). White women are off limits for men of color, who have no other choice but to form families within their own communities. This, we believe, reinforces "ethnic" machismo, which, in turn, means that women of color are subjected to dominance through both (hetero) sexism and racism.

We use the phrase "between speech and silence" to capture the many fronts on which language works to subjugate knowledge and experience. Not only is all that cannot be expressed in English suppressed, but only certain forms of experience are allowed to be voiced in the classroom. Sexuality, race, ethnicity, and class are privatized, attached to the individual and silenced through shame. They are not looked at as sets of ideological practices that are socially constituted and that also have a painfully "real" materiality. Oppression works through this silencing. We believe that one way to counter linguistic dominance is to shift *what* can be talked about, as well as the discursive form and language in which it must be spoken. In this, the ground of oppression must shift from the silent sphere of the individual as personally inadequate to the challenging speech that names the social and power relations that form the oppression—the "personal" as political.

COLONIZATION THROUGH LINGUISTIC DOMINANCE

The encounter between the "superior" culture (with command of English) and the immigrant culture (without command of English) is analogous to the encounter between "civilized" and "barbaric" cultures, as defined by their access or lack of access to the written word. According to Seed, the ethnocentric belief that written language distinguishes civilization from barbarism, coupling cultural superiority with alphabetical writing, has characterized Western thought since medieval times (Seed, 1991, p. 8). Despite Lévi-Strauss's claim that he avoids ethnocentrism, he reinforces this belief: "Of all the criteria by which people habitually distinguish civilization from barbarism, this one should at least be retained: that certain peoples write and others do not" (Seed, 1991, p. 8). Cultural imperialism has taken different forms and shapes in history, its tentacles reaching through language, its conceptual schemes long shrouded in the premises of culture-free knowledge.

The important thing is to investigate how colonization works through dominance; i.e., in which subtle ways, this disempowering process is constructed through gender/(hetero)sexism and class, and what are some of its implications for minority children and adults. For example, Kathleen Rockhill's mother was so determined to overcome her Italian working-class origins that she became an English teacher. This was highly unusual for a girl of her generation and class. Her other "choice," to lose her Italian identity through marriage, is more typical of the way open for women of some ethnic backgrounds to assimilate. More typical perhaps, but not necessarily more accepted, as girls feel the pressure from their families to remain "loyal" by marrying within their ethnic community (Moraga, 1983). In our research on the experiences of Latin-American women in accessing ESL, we began to uncover how the dynamics of (hetero)sexism and class operate through race to effect the possibility of women learning the English necessary to advance themselves.

Language, identity, culture, and sexuality are inseparable. Our concept of situated ESL would suggest, among other considerations, the valuation and appreciation of bilingualism, as well as the richness of multiple identities spawned by the ability to communicate in diverse situations. Our concept of situated ESL curriculum acknowledges the fact that the minority child's bilingualism/biculturalism is not a liability but an asset. In fact, bilingual children are "blessed with bilingual brains."[2] We would add that they are blessed with bi/cultures, that is, the ability to look at the world from at least two different perspectives, as opposed to from a unidimensional, ethnocentric perspective. The bilingualism/biculturalism of Canadian minority children "is a personal and societal resource that [Canada] as a nation can ill afford to squander" (Cummins, 1981, p. 43). Moreover, children of ethnic minorities, as further marginalized within their communities through differences of gender and class, are "blessed" with what Uma Narayan (1988) calls the "epistemic privilege of the oppressed," the claim that "members of an oppressed group have a more immediate, subtle, and critical knowledge about the nature of their oppression than people who are nonmembers of the oppressed group" (p. 35). Oppression and disadvantage are transformed into a "blessing"—however mixed—in a classroom where teachers are prepared to acknowledge and use the knowledge that children acquire from their varying locations as starting points for the learning process, where teachers are prepared to take on the challenge of "situated" pedagogy, where knowledge of how oppression works is drawn upon and validated as integral to the curriculum.

WHITENESS AS THE REFERENT OF *ESL*

In Canada, officially, bilingualism means that one is fluent in the two official languages of the country—English and French. Ironically, the practice of unilingualism in Canada, in combination with the official policy of bilingualism, means that people who learn English or French in addition to their mother tongue are unable to claim "bilingualism" as an asset; instead, they are categorized as "linguistically diverse." Being linguistically diverse becomes, in practice, a liability, a subjugated knowledge to be, in time, destroyed. This view of the ESL student as lacking, as deficient or disadvantaged, is symptomatic of "Whiteness" as the referent of ESL and multiculturalism, the two programs set up to attend to the increasing "diversity" of Canada's population.

In spite of all rhetoric to the contrary, our guess is that the unarticulated but defining purpose of multicultural education is to teach Whites about "other" cultures. To be truly multicultural would require us to be multilingual. This requires a fundamental decentering—and the accompanying dislocation—of White male supremacy and of its tool, the English language. In multicultural education, language symmetry is assumed; the dominance of English and its consequences for identity formation are largely unexplored. We come to school to learn "proper deafinitions" (Warland, 1990). In "the breasts refuse" Betsy Warland's wordplay captures the quagmire we face:

> rethinking the Tower of Babel
> variations on this myth found around the world
> God's anger striking down the heaven-reaching tower,
> ziggurat, man-made mountain, pyramid, or great tree
> confusion of tongues
>
> the punishment
> or
> was it an act of liberation from
> the tyranny of one language?
>
> ego-centrism of erections
> enslaving difference to
> its *monument, men, mind, mania, money, muse, amnesia.*
> (Warland, 1990, p. 29)

The Tower of English. All must enter. Become White. . . . Just try it.

Whiteness, we argue, is the assumed, unacknowledged referent of ESL; its purpose is to integrate "them" into "our" male-defined institutions. ESL exists at the margins of the male-defined ethnocentric curriculum, as a "tool" to let the "real business" of schooling—that is, the schooling of English-speaking "White" children—go on with as little interruption as possible. And "Whiteness" is about "the norm," which is also defined through gender and sexuality. To be "White" in this sense of normativity is also to conform to middle-class heterosexual norms (heter-onormativity). Whiteness is about ethnocentrism and racism as played out through (hetero)sexism and class. Whiteness is about ignorance and having the power to stay ignorant by arrogantly defining what counts as knowledge, by innocently accepting the definitions of those in power. Language is integral to this ignorance, as types of knowledge that cannot be expressed in English are subjugated. The dominant society's inability to communicate/relate to the stock of culture/knowledge held by op-pressed groups contributes to the construction of ethnocentric codes, rules, regulations. Through these, the dominant culture protects itself, hides its inadequacy to deal with what it does not know, with what it is not familiar. *Competence,* the appearance of *knowing,* defining *proper perfor-mance* is how the dominator at all times presents himself. As (fe)males, White women often mimic the stance of the dominator when in a position of power. This appearance of competence depends upon ignorance (Britz-man, 1992). Figures in dominance do not know that they are missing, lacking, incomplete. They have no vision upon which to build an inclu-sive society or politics or education. Hear Cherríe Moraga (1983) as she voices her pain at the exclusionary practices of White feminists: "So often the women seem to feel no loss, no lack, no absence when women of colour are not involved; therefore there is little desire to change the situa-tion. This has hurt me deeply" (1983, pp. 57–58).

This construction of Whiteness has to be opened up. What differ-ences does it conceal and congeal? Has linguistic/cultural dominance worked so effectively that generations of "Canadians" are cut off from their immigrant non-Anglo roots? Is the perceived threat to "Canadian" institutions, the current backlash against multicultural, heritage lan-guage, and bilingual policies (however limited they may be), accelerating expressions of overt racism, a reflection of the changing composition of immigration? In a special report, "The Rise of Racism," *Toronto Star* reporter Lois Sweet dramatically points to these changes:

> Today, roughly one Canadian in 20 is of non-European origin. But 25 years from now, that proportion will be one in 10 . . . within 10 years, one-third of the population of Toronto will be composed of blacks and Asians. This is in sharp contrast to five years ago, when these groups made up only 17 percent of the city's population. (Sweet, 1992, p. A8)

Changes in immigration flow mean dramatic changes for schools where new arrivals reside. Chances are high that immigrant and refugee children will not see their experiences reflected in the curriculum. In ESL we witness an emphasis upon linguistic competencies in English without reference to what linguistic competence might be for the child or adult learning a *second* language. Along with schooling comes the tacit prohibition against speaking languages other than English and the shame of speaking with an accent, symbolic of being "different," an "outsider," inadequate, inferior. The consequence is that of dismissing the other's stock of knowledge/experience/culture, an ethnocentric approach that becomes a useful strategy of domination. The goal of education, then, becomes that of integrating "others" into the dominant society.

There are several ways in which we see ESL provision as really being about the schooling of White children, serving primarily as an instrument for the integration of non-English-speaking children into the regular schooling curriculum. Although it is by now well accepted that curriculum is a process that must include its intended learners as primary referents, ESL is treated as a linguistic tool, its referent being the English language; functional ESL is defined in terms of "Canadian" content; communicative competence is about learning to communicate in English, to people who speak English. Teacher training is grounded in theories of (socio)linguistics, not the social upheaval that accompanies immigration and refugee experiences. Provision is targeted at children enrolled in public schools, not adults, for whom the necessity of learning English is every bit as urgent. As discussed above, access to ESL is not conceived as a fundamental "right," however charged that may be, but as the responsibility of the individual to acquire and the "White man's burden" to provide.

In the preparation of this chapter, we struggle against these discursive formations. For example, while the book editors have been clear that ESL is one of the curricular subjects they want to include, still they recognize the discursive reality that, in a book focusing upon "the public school curriculum," our research on the experience of Latin-American immigrant women in accessing ESL falls outside the boundaries of the discourse. And they are right; "immigrant and refugee women" are not seen as a legitimate focus for a work on public schooling—and yet, it is the schools that they are most dependent upon for ESL provision. That we are still invited to participate and draw upon our research reflects the book editors' desire to open up these boundaries, but still we struggle with this question—what is the relevance of the experiences of immigrant and refugee women with ESL for a book about the public school curriculum? As we struggle with this question, we sense ourselves coming up against the unarticulated referent of discourses on curriculum—the education of "White" Canadian children by "White" teachers.

With respect to adults, the latest federal government policies make clear that *integration* into "Canadian" society is the goal of ESL provision. The focus is not upon integrating English into the lives of the diverse populations of newcomers who come to Canada, but upon using ESL as a tool for bringing those populations into the [White] Canadian main/stream. These policies have ignored the repeatedly expressed desires of community groups that ESL be integrated into a more comprehensive educational approach that can take into account the multiplicity of challenges faced by new arrivals. It has also ignored the persistent pressure to increase the numbers of "sponsored seats" (training allowances) necessary to free up time to study, especially for women who have been systematically discriminated against in provision. Instead of an integrated approach to education, or increasing the availability of sponsored seats, the government has chosen to define ESL more narrowly as "language training," and to clearly separate it from other forms of education and job training. The argument is that availability will be extended to more people by cutting out all training allowances for programme participants. For income assistance, potential participants must have other forms of social assistance (i.e., 12 month Refugee Adjustment Assistance Programme, Unemployment Insurance Benefits, and social assistance if provincial arrangements can be worked out).

So, the gender bias in program provision, which immigrant and refugee women's groups have been protesting, will be offset by eliminating government responsibility for allocating sponsored seats. Ignored is the gender bias in the forms of social assistance for which immigrant and refugee women are eligible. All of these forms of assistance are loaded for newcomers and particularly biased against women who enter Canada as "spouses" and are ineligible for social benefits in their own right (Rockhill & Tomic, 1992). Where a woman's income is seen as essential to the family, she will be blocked from participating because her husband's income/spousal status will affect her eligibility for other forms of social assistance.

To approach English as language training (and, for adults, only 600 hours or 15 weeks worth at that) is to divorce it from education, to treat it as a basic technical or functional skill, not a language that has political, social, and subjective dimensions. For the federal government (Canada, Employment and Immigration, 1991), "client need" is defined in terms of (yet to be) standardized language skills. Performance level indicators will be developed "to define expected learner outcomes including expectations of knowledge regarding Canadian institutions, laws, and values" (p. 5). "Canadian content" is defined as a functional skill, Whiteness as its referent; it is not defined relationally, in terms of the dynamics of change and conflict faced by the newcomer.

ON DECENTERING WHITENESS

How can the colonizing effects of learning English be countered? In work that is overtly defined as teaching the dominators' language, how can this process be challenged when it is precisely that language that students want most urgently and know they must have to survive, to disappear, not to stand out. First, perhaps, we should take seriously the words, English as a *Second* Language, and think carefully about what this means. Is it taught as a *second* language? Or is the assumption (the racist assumption) that it will soon become/*must* become the first language, as the mother tongue becomes separated out as the "heritage" language—the language of the past? A second and somewhat contradictory reflection about the discourse of English as a Second Language is important here. To speak a language "as a second language" immediately assigns hierarchy, rank to the languages spoken by the individual. Along with that gradation comes the rating of what one *does* in the "second language." In fact, what people do in their "second" language is often considered to be "second" rate, and accent plays an important role in this designation.

As far as we know, the discursive effects of speaking with an "accent" have not yet been carefully studied. But some researchers have at least recognized a problem with "accents." Thuy, for example, writes on the meaning of accents:

> The accent with which a foreign born person speaks English can create a favourable or unfavourable impression on a number of Anglo-Americans. If one speaks with an accent influenced by a *prestige* [emphasis added] language, say French, or with an accent peculiar to an ethnic group which historically is highly successful in this country such as the German speaking minority, this accent is readily considered a stamp of approval, if not a symbol of prestige and respect. Yet, the foreign accent peculiar to the language of a less successful or respected minority group, for instance Hispanic, can surprisingly and unfortunately lead to some sort of stigma. (1979, p. 5)

Because children can learn a second language so much more quickly than adults (and most adults will never be able to speak without an accent because it is physically impossible to do so), this may not seem like much of a problem: Children *can* learn English as a "first" language. But what does this really mean? Learning a language while discarding/disregarding another is about more than words—it is about identity destruction and formation—and, as we have argued above, it is about power.

Learning the language is basic but it is not the only aspect of identity construction. Becoming accepted is not that simple; it goes much beyond being able to communicate in the official language. It entails hating oneself, changing identity, denying all one is. This is particularly critical when young human beings are involved. In an article entitled "Mother Tongue and Identity" Antti Jalava (1988) speaks of his painful movement from being a Finn to being a Swede:

> When the idea had eaten itself deeply enough into my soul that it was despicable to be a Finn, I began to feel ashamed of my origins. Since going back was out of the question . . . there was nothing else for me but to surrender. To survive, I had to change my stripes. Thus: to hell with Finland and all the Finns! All of the sudden, I was overwhelmed by a desire to shed my skin and smash my face. That which could not be accepted had to be denied, hidden, crushed and thrown away. A Swede was what I had to become, and that meant I could not continue to be a Finn. Everything I had held dear and self-evident had to be destroyed. An inner struggle began, a state of crisis of long duration. . . . My mother tongue was worthless—this I realized at last; on the contrary, it made me the butt of abuse and ridicule. So down with the Finnish language! I spat on myself, gradually committed internal suicide. . . . I resolved to learn Swedish letter perfect so nobody could guess who I was or where I came from. They still laughed at my Finnish accent—but after a while, never again! . . . My tongue was still limber and flexible. At the age of thirteen, I was just about ready. . . . The only thing that betrayed me was my name. But, for some reason, I did not dare to change my name. I kept it. (p. 164)

And what is the saga for those of us who cannot change that which signifies our difference, cannot shed our skins or change the shape of our eyes or the roll of our tongues?

And for the child who learns to become "White," to take on the identity mandated by the dominant culture? Through the process of social regulation, in which schooling plays a major part, through shame, through the desire to belong, to feel some sense of self-esteem, the child will strive to become competent at "passing," at appearing the same as everyone else. The consequence is, typically, denial and feeling ashamed of one's native culture, of one's parents, one's roots. Rather than a dual identity or a transcultural identity, the process of identity formation means that the child internalizes dominant stereotypes so that, for example, as Adrienne Rich (1986) notes, she became both Semite and anti-Semite. The more fully one can "pass," the more one excels in schooling and other activities of the dominant society, the more likely one will be to join the ranks of faceless Whiteness. White ethnocentrism with no sense of culture, of roots, of home.

Is there any way to counter the part that schooling plays in the (re)-production of dominance, in the perpetuation of racism and (hetero)-sexism? How can heteronormativity and Whiteness be decentered? For the knowledge/power lock to be split apart, subjugated knowledge must come into the curriculum *and* transform it. Patricia Hill Collins (1991) argues that the power in the curriculum needs to be made explicit: "De-centering curriculum that presents the ideas and experiences of elite white men as being normative and universal challenges this link between knowledge that represents dominant group interests and the power to rule" (1991, p. 368). Collins outlines three dimensions to curriculum transformation. To paraphrase: 1) investigate self-defined, subjugated standpoints to uncover new concepts, paradigms, and epistemologies; 2) decenter dominant frameworks by using the ideas gained from subju-gated standpoints to challenge knowledge representing elite group inter-ests; and 3) treat each dominant framework as one standpoint among many, reconstruct knowledge (p. 371). These dimensions imply that the processes of identity formation and knowledge subjugation must become an integral part of the curriculum. Self-defined standpoints are not a "given," but constructed, and, in the case of immigrants and refugees, the sudden confrontation of their identities by ascription of a new singular "immigrant" identity is acute. Helène Moussa argues that educators must work with identity (re)negotiation against dominant social pressure to give up, to deny. How can we facilitate the development of a transcultural identity? As Moussa describes it: "A transcultural identity enables exiles to have multiple identities, including the possibility of feeling that they can belong to two countries and cultures" (1993, p. 246).

In the feminist poststructural debates about identity and difference, what often gets lost is that identities are constructed through relation-ships of power. As Deborah Britzman (1992) puts it, "identities suggest more about the social effects of political production than they do about essential selves." While poststructural theories have made the point that identities are multiple, changing, shifting, partial, they have not paid enough attention to how identities are also fixed, totalizing, and endur-ing. A distinction has to be made between identifications, which suggest some degree of agency, and othering practices that fix and define, stereo-typing "the other" as outsider, as different (where, in relationships of power, difference means not normal/not OK). At the same time as these distinctions must be made, it must also be recognized that they cannot be made, for even the "self-defined" identity is in tension with dominant definitions, formed through racism, (hetero)sexism, and other dynamics of power.

This paradox of identity is part of what it means to be an "immigrant woman." Nowhere is there more dramatic evidence of change, as the new arrival suddenly becomes a minority, a target of racism, class dislocation, and cultural and family upheaval, which are accompanied by complex changes in sexual identities. At the same time, "immigrant woman" carries with it a fixed, enduring, and totalizing quality, a means of racializing and othering those who do not match the Canadian norm (Moussa, 1993). As a woman becomes socially constructed as an "immigrant" or "refugee" it becomes the totality of her identity in the dominant society, the only way in which she will be seen, however long she resides in Canada, as long as she speaks with an accent, or her difference is marked by skin color or other physical signifiers that deviate from the norm of White (fe)maleness.

The segregation of children into special classes for ESL instruction further marks their difference from the other students. When this is coupled with being seen as having a problem, a deficiency or lack, feelings of deviance and shame are reinforced. Because language is central to identity formation and expression, and because most students who learn ESL do so because they must in order to survive in an English-dominant society, identity work, unavoidably, goes on in ESL. The question is *how* to counter the colonizing effects of learning a new language/identity so that it does not simultaneously mean subjugating one's native language/identity.

My language
can be painted over
but not detached
without tearing
structure of my cells.

If you paint
a foreign language
on my skin
my innermost soul
cannot breathe.

(Leporanta-Morley, 1988, p. 172)

It means that we must transform our understanding of the purpose of ESL, shift its referent from Whiteness to "self-defined standpoints," see boys and girls not as lacking in communication ability but rich in knowledge and experience that most other children do not have. As the one place in school that brings together children with common, often painful experiences of immigration, ESL is where their stories might be shared, common stories of marginality to the mainstream culture can be explored, and subjugated knowledge released into the central content of the curriculum. But, to do this, the rules of "communicative competence" have to shift from English-language expression to self-expression. In a mixed-language class, this may require the use of mixed codes, as well as an exploration into the consequences for identity when a dominant language is learned and one's mother tongue becomes one's second or subjugated language.

Competence has to be radically rethought, and as Maria Lugones suggests, space needs to be opened for the playfulness essential to world travelling, to exploration, to experimentation. "Playfulness is, in part, an openness to being a fool, which is a combination of not worrying about competence, not being self-important, not taking norms as sacred and finding ambiguity and double edges a source of wisdom and delight" (1990, p. 400). Can English be played with, its hegemony interrupted by expressions from the mother tongue that capture the soul in a way English cannot? Can Whiteness be played with? Can Whites let down their need to know, to be superior; can they be reminded of their limits? Play the fool? Let down the wall of the impermeable perfect shield of the English language?

How can children be encouraged to claim the identity they are taught to despise, to refuse the ignorance circulated through linguistic dominance, to claim their subjugated knowledge while simultaneously learning the skills necessary to English? Lourdes Torres notes that questions of identity are integral to discussions of language; the challenge is "how to give voice to multiple heritage. The obvious yet revolutionary answer is through the use of the mixing of codes that have shaped their experience" (1991, p. 279). Can ESL challenge the unilingual/dominant language assumptions of "communicative competence" (in English) and work with communicative competence through mixed codes that encourage the expression of multiple identities?

Does this mean perpetuating the "disadvantage" of those whose mother tongue is not English? We repeat, "disadvantage" according to whom? According to what norm? Who sets the terms of "disadvantage" when not to disadvantage means to subjugate one's original linguistic cultural identity? When "advantage" means knowing one language, and "disadvantage" is familiarity with two languages? We are not recommending that standard English not be taught. What we want to argue for is the simultaneous encouragement of the child or adult to deliberately mix codes so as to capture what is inexpressible in English, interrupting the hegemony of the English language and, at least partially, indexing all that it subjugates. A tiny step toward deconstructing the feared Tower of Babel, this strategy is now being used by some women of color and radical feminists to challenge the supremacy of White male language. Think of it. Even English-speaking students might one day be motivated to learn to read and speak in mixed codes so that they can more effectively communicate with people who are fluent in the use of mixed codes!

The recognition of "the epistemic privilege of the oppressed" is a key reversal that occurs when "identity work" challenges the racist assumptions of White supremacy. If Whiteness is to be decentered, and subjugated identities validated, processes of subjection need to be named and opened to scrutiny. This can be very threatening for teachers, as well as students, as Minh-ha notes: "To raise the question of identity is to reopen again the discussion on the self/other relationship in its enactment of power relations" (1990, p. 371). Differing subject positions mean differences in knowledge and in investments in (not) seeing. As Narayan argues, members of oppressed groups have knowledge, or "epistemic privilege" with respect to how oppression works in everyday life and the ways in which it affects their social and psychic lives: "Unlike concerned 'outsiders' whose knowledge of the experience of oppression is always more or less abstract or theoretical, the knowledge of 'insiders' is enriched by the emotional reactions/responses that the lived experience of oppression confers" (1988, pp. 38–39). To illustrate, as one of the persons interviewed in *Speaking of Racism* notes on the nature of racism:

> We have been told what racism is, and we think it is somebody calling us a "paki" or a "chink" or a "nigger." But, in fact you can't prove most racism. That is the main factor about racism—you cannot prove it. (Brand & Bhaggi-yadatta, 1986, p. 45)

Normalizing practices and structures render all but the most blatant forms of domination invisible to those occupying the norm, where investment in not seeing is apt to be considerable. At play is what Frigga Haug (1989) refers to as the reactionary nature of emotions such as shame, guilt, fear—investments in not seeing—that hinder those occupying the norm from acting in more conscious ways.

In recognizing the distinction between "insider" and "outsider" knowledge, we must be careful not to set up a dichotomy. Many of us are both privileged and oppressed in varying ways. Some women, for example, may be oppressed according to their gender, but be privileged according to their location with respect to race or class. And, "insider" knowledge is not unproblematic, for, as we have discussed, colonization has the effect of encouraging taking on the dominant identity in order to "pass." As Catherine E. Walsh (1991) argues, we recognize different subject positions and identities, and we need to develop pedagogic strategies that facilitate the negotiation of fluid boundaries amongst multiple and shifting identities. How do people who are privileged along some lines (e.g., skin color, language, gender, class) come to feel, in their guts, the ravages of oppression, so that they not only recognize it when it happens, but do not minimize or trivialize its emotional costs? As Patricia Tomic pointed out in writing this chapter, when one has lived experiences of racism and discrimination and is in the privileged position of having the opportunity to write on the topic, one cannot but write with anger.

As educators in mixed race/sex classrooms, how can we begin to make room for multiple privileges/oppressions and their attendant emotions—anger, pain, rage, shame, hate, joy, and frustration—in our teaching? Can teachers recognize the limits of our "privilege," and decenter our authority in ways that open up discursive boundaries to include emotions, to include subjugated knowledge "as equal and central"? How can we open up discussions of privilege/oppression and not recognize that this must involve emotions—unless we ignore the pain in the room before us, which means we are privileging the emotional detachment of the "outsider" and silencing the rich emotional knowledge of the "insider." Emphasis upon detachment, upon "objectivity," is one of the more subtle ways in which Whiteness works as the hidden referent of the curriculum.

How can we, as teachers, learn to be attentive to the intricate dynamics of oppression and privilege? As we take up the challenge of gender, how do we simultaneously recognize the challenges posed by race, class, and sexuality as power differences among women in ways that do not silence and objectify and hierarchize oppressions (Schenke, 1991)? As we work, can we also attend to the emotional guilt, defensiveness, and denial that implode in angry silences as we take up the challenge of looking at privilege as well as oppression (Essed, 1991)? Is there a way to move from silence to speech that brings our bodies, our souls, our hearts—in all our complexities and contradictions—into the classroom? Toward a speech that is not ruled by the mind alone, leaving our bodies behind? And can we still listen, even as we speak?

> For silence to transform into speech, sounds and words, it must first traverse through our female bodies. . . . Because our bodies have been stolen, brutalized or numbed, it is difficult to speak from/through them. *No hables de esas cosas, de eso no se habla. No hables, no hables. ¡Cállate! Estate quieta.* Seal your lips woman! When she transforms silence into language, a woman transgresses. . . . To speak English is to think in that language, to adopt the ideology of the people whose language it is and to be "inhabited" by their discourses. *Mujeres-de-color* speak and write not just against traditional white ways and texts but against a prevailing mode of being, against a white frame

of reference. Those of us who are bilingual, or use working class English and English in dialects, are under constant pressure to speak and write in standard English. Linguistic code-switching, which goes against language laws and norms, is not approved of. (Anzaldúa, 1990, p. xxii)

Can ESL be situated so that liberation does not come at the expense of subjugation? What would happen if the spaces between silence and speech were opened by challenging the hegemony of English, interrupting it through mixed codes/linguistic code switching? Can bilingualism/biculturalism be valued throughout the curriculum? Can we learn how to facilitate the negotiation of transcultural identities through decentering Whiteness?

ACKNOWLEDGMENT: I would like to thank Gloria Anzaldúa (1990) and Susan Gal (1991) for the image, "between Speech and Silence."

NOTES

1. Recent work by Deborah Britzman and her colleagues is significant in attending to these discursive divisions by intertwining analyses of multiculturalism with (hetero)sexism.
2. This phrase (also the title of one of Mary Ashworth's books) was thought up by students in the bilingual education/TESOL program at the University of Texas at San Antonio (Cummins, June 1981, fn. p. 43). T-shirts were used as the medium for getting the message across.

REFERENCES

Anzaldúa, Gloria. (1987). *Borderlands-La Frontera: The new Mestiza*. San Francisco: Aunt Lute Foundation.

Anzaldúa, Gloria. (1990). *Making face, making soul: Haciendo Caras*. San Francisco: Aunt Lute Foundation.

Ashworth, Mary. (1985). *Beyond methodology: Second language teaching and the community.* New York: Cambridge University Press.

Ashworth, Mary. (1988). *Blessed with bilingual brains: Education of immigrant children with English as a second language.* Vancouver, BC: Pacific Educational Press.

Brand, Dionne, & Bhaggiyadatta, Krishanta Sri. (1986). *Rivers have sources, trees have roots: Speaking of racism.* Toronto: Cross Cultural Communications Centre.

Britzman, Deborah P. (1992). *What is this thing called love: New discourses for understanding gay and lesbian youth.* Unpublished manuscript.

Britzman, Deborah P., Santiago-Válles, Kelvin, Jiménez Múnōz, Gladys, and Lamash, Laura M. (1984). Slips that show and tell: Fashioning multiculture as a problem in representation. In Cameron McCarthy and Warren Crichlow (Eds.), *Race, identity, and representation in education* (pp. 188–200). London: Routledge & Kegan Paul.

Canada, Employment and Immigration. (1991). *New immigrant language training policies* and *Questions and answers on new immigrant language training policies.* Ottawa, Ontario.

Collins, Patricia Hill. (1991). On our own terms: Self-defined standpoints and curriculum transformation. *National Women's Studies Association Journal, 3*(3), 367–382.

Cowley, Tony. (1989). *Standard English and the politics of language.* Urbana: University of Illinois Press.

Cummins, Jim. (1981). Mother tongue development as educational enrichment. In Jim Cummins (Ed.), *Heritage language education: Issues and directions. Proceedings of a conference organized by the Multiculturalism Directorate of the Department of the Secretary of State* (pp. 40–43), Saskatoon, Saskatchewan.

Danica, Elly. (1988). *Don't—A woman's word.* Pittsburgh, PA: CLEIS Press.

de Lauretis, Teresa. (1990). Eccentric subjects: Feminist theory and historical consciousness. *Feminist Studies, 16*(1), 115–150.

Denis, Wilfrid B. (1991). The Meech Lake Shuffle: French and English language rights in Canada. In B. Singh Bolaria (Ed.), *Social issues and contradictions in Canadian society* (pp. 144–171). Toronto: Harcourt Brace Jovanovich.

Esling, John H. (Ed.). (1989). *Multicultural education and policy: ESL in the 1990s: A tribute to Mary Ashworth.* Toronto: OISE Press/Ontario Institute for Studies in Education.

Essed, Philomena. (1991). *Understanding everyday racism: An interdisciplinary theory.* Newbury Park, CA: Sage.

Gal, Susan. (1991). Between speech and silence: The problematics of research on language and gender. In Michaela de Leonardo (Ed.), *Gender at the crossroads: Feminist anthropology in the postmodern era* (pp. 175–203). Berkeley: University of California Press.

Haug, Frigga et al. (1989). *Female sexualization: A collective work of memory.* London: Verso Press.

Hurtado, Aída. (1989). Relating to privilege: Seduction and rejection in the subordination of white women and women of color. *Signs, 14*(4), 833–855.

Jalava, Antti. (1988). Mother tongue and identity. In Tove Skutnabb-Kangas & Jim Cummins (Eds.), *Minority education: From shame to struggle* (pp. 161–166). Clevedon, UK: Multilingual Matters.

Jordan, June. (1989). White English/Black English: The politics of translation. In *Moving towards home: Political essays* (pp. 29–40). London: Virago.

Leporanta-Morley, Pirkko. (1988). My language Is my home. In Tove Skutnabb-Kangas & Jim Cummins (Eds.), *Minority education: From shame to struggle* (pp. 172–173). Clevedon, UK: Multilingual Matters.

Lugones, Maria. (1990). Playfulness, "world"—Travelling and loving perceptions. In Gloria Anzaldúa (Ed.), *Making face, making soul: Haciendo Caras* (pp. 390–402). San Francisco: Aunt Lute Foundation.

Minh-ha, Trinh T. (1990). Not you/like you: Post-colonial women and the inter-locking questions of identity and difference. In Gloria Anzaldúa (Ed.), *Making face, making soul: Haciendo Caras* (pp. 371–375). San Francisco: Aunt Lute Foundation.

Mohanty, Chandra Talpade. (1991). Under Western eyes: Feminist scholarship and colonial discourses. In Chandra Talpade Mohanty, Ann Russo, & Lourdes Torres (Eds.), *Third World women and the politics of feminism* (pp. 51–80). Bloomington: Indiana University Press.

Moraga, Cherríe. (1983). *Loving in the war years.* Boston: South End Press.

Moussa, Helène. (1993). *Storm and sanctuary: The journey of Ethiopian and Eritrean women refugees.* Dundas, Ontario: Artemis.

Narayan, Uma. (1988). Working together across difference: Some considerations on emotions and political practice. *Hypatia, 3*(2), 31–47.

Pattanayak, D. P. (1986). Educational use of the mother tongue. In Bernard Spol-sky (Ed.), *Language and education in multilingual settings* (pp. 5–15). Clevedon, UK: Multilingual Matters.

Rich, Adrienne. (1986). Split at the root: An essay on Jewish identity (1982). In Adrienne Rich (Ed.), *Blood, bread, and poetry. Selected prose 1979–1985* (pp. 100–123). New York: W. W. Norton.

Rockhill, Kathleen. (1987). Literacy as threat/desire: Longing to be SOMEBODY. In Jane S. Gaskell & Arlene T. McLaren (Eds.), *Women and education: A Canadian perspective* (pp. 315–331). Calgary, AB: Detselig.

Rockhill, Kathleen, & Tomic, Patricia. (1992). *Accessing ESL: An exploration in to the effects of institutionalized racism and sexism in shaping the lives of Latin American immigrant and refugee women in metropolitan Toronto.* Toronto: Ontario Ministry of Education.

Said, Edward W. (1990). Figures, configurations, transfigurations. *Race and Class, 32*(1), 1–16.

Schenke, Arleen. (1991). The "will to reciprocity" and the work of memory: Fictioning speaking out of silence in E.S.L. and feminist pedagogy. *Resources for Feminist Research, 20*(3–4), Fall/Winter, 47–55.

Seed, Patricia. (1991). Failing to marvel: Atahualpa's encounter with the word. *Latin American Research Review, 26*(1), 7–32.

Spender, Dale. (1980). *Manmade language.* London: Routledge & Kegan Paul.

Spivak, Gayatri Chakravorty. (1990). The intervention interview. In Sarah Harasym (Ed.), *The post-colonial critic: Interviews, strategies, dialogues* (pp. 113–132). New York: Routledge, Chapman & Hall.

Sweet, Lois. (1992, February 22). The rise of racism. *Toronto Star,* pp. A1, A8.

Thuy, Vuong G. (1979). *Bilingual education: A necessity or a luxury?* Palo Alto, CA: R & E Research.

Tomic, Patricia, & Trumper, Ricardo. (1992). Canada and the streaming of immigrants: A personal account of the Chilean case. In Vic Satzewich (Ed.), *Deconstructing a nation: Immigration, multiculturalism and racism in '90s Canada* (pp. 163–181). Halifax, NS: Fernwood.

Torres, Lourdes. (1991). The construction of the self in U.S. Latina autobiographies. In Chandra Talpade Mohanty, Ann Russo, & Lourdes Torres (Eds.),

Third World women and the politics of feminism (pp. 271–287). Bloomington: Indiana University Press.

Valdés, Gina. (1990). Where you from? In Lucy R. Lippard (Ed.), *Mixed blessings. New art in a multicultural America*. New York: Pantheon Books.

Walsh, Catherine E. (1991). *Pedagogy and the struggle for voice: Issues of language, power and schooling for Puerto Ricans*. Toronto: OISE Press/Ontario Institute for Studies in Education.

Warland, Betsy. (1990). The breasts refuse. In *Proper deafinitions: Collected theorograms*. Vancouver, BC: Press Gang.

CHAPTER 12

Gender and the Physical Education Curriculum: The Dynamics of Difference

Patricia A. Vertinsky

In physical education, it has become clear that a critical stance must be taken in order to move the analysis of gender beyond questions of distribution to questions of relation, with gender defined as a set of socially constructed power relationships subject to historical change and hence amenable to transformation (Hall, 1990). This requires the analysis of gender within a framework that locates gender inequality in the social relations of exercise and sport rather than in biological and behavioral differences between the sexes. Instead of portraying girls as deficient males, or as passive victims of restrictive sex-stereotyped attitudes and practices, much greater efforts are required to change the unequal power relations between the sexes by transforming the patriarchal and ethnocentric nature of the physical education curriculum, bringing into starker focus the connections between the many different kinds of gendered and gendering practices in sport and physical activity through which hegemonic masculinity reconstitutes itself. Emerging radical feminist analyses demand that the links between sport, femininity, and sexuality be examined more closely, along with the ways in which female participation in sports is constrained by the sexist and heterosexist assumptions underlying claims that boys do not like girls who get sweaty and dirty playing football, that it is not smart to beat boys at their own games, and that serious female athletes are unattractive, man-hating, and possibly lesbian (Griffin, 1989c; Lenskyj, 1990a, 1991a). As Whitson and MacIntosh (1989) point out, it is especially crucial to address those practices surrounding sexuality and the body: patterns of physical empowerment whereby boys are encouraged through sport to learn to use their bodies in forceful and preemptive ways, ideological practices such as the use of androcentric language and homophobia, and all those practices "which organize the formation of identity and aspirations around particular ideas of masculinity and femininity, particularly ways of being male and female" (p. 147).

The complexity of this task presses us to examine the potential of Jane Roland Martin's (1985) notion of a gender-sensitive perspective upon the physical education curriculum—where sex or gender is taken into account when it makes a difference in furthering sex equality or preventing sexist bias, and ignored when it does not. "So long as sex and gender are fundamental aspects of our personal experience, so long as they are deeply rooted features of our society, educational theory—and educational practice, too—must be gender sensitive" (p. 195). This does not mean, she infers, that we should take up Rousseau's categorical sex differences in educational treatment, but that we must be constantly aware of the intricate workings of sex and gender in all aspects of the curriculum. A gender-sensitive perspective lets patterns of discrimination themselves determine which particular action to take to eliminate bias (Houston, 1985). Said differently, suggests McNamee (1991b), "it would seem that physical education teachers could perform extremely important work in fostering the well-being of pupils by helping them to come to terms with the way they feel about sex, ability, and gender differences, how they react to them and the language they use to articulate those feelings" (p. 18). Adopting this kind of strategic focus, however, presses the physical educator to frame the compelling issue of difference in terms that give it an emancipatory grounding, identifying the differences that promote inequality and those that don't. This is a tall order for physical educators habituated to traditional views of "appropriately" gendered physical education and sports.

DIFFERENCE IN/FORMS THE PAST

Recent efforts to enhance gender sensitivity in physical education have been informed by attempts to explain what physical education is and hopes to achieve by articulating the ideal of a physically educated person and considering where and whether differential treatment of boys and girls might be required to support this ideal. Since such definitions are acutely sensitive to broader educational, social, and political forces, it is no surprise to observe the current emphasis upon habitual participation in physical activity, physical fitness, and healthy life-styles in Western society (Kirk, 1992). In a document recently released by the North

American National Association for Sport and Physical Education we have perhaps a suitable starting point:

> A Physically Educated Person
> - Has learned skills necessary to perform a variety of physical activities
> - Is physically fit
> - Does participate regularly in physical activity
> - Knows the implications of and the benefits from involvement in physical activities
> - Values physical activity and its contributions to a healthful lifestyle. (National Association for Sport and Physical Education, 1992, p. 3)

The call for greater participation in physical activity has particular significance for gender-sensitive approaches to physical education. The decline in activity participation by girls during and after adolescence is well documented and is a particular cause for concern among physical and health educators, as well as the medical profession. Grade 8 seems to be the time at which dissatisfaction and disinterest deepen among girls, and by Grade 11 the large majority of girls have dropped physical education entirely, many having developed a lifelong distaste for physical activity (Hall & Richardson, 1982). This decline has been especially noted in programs emphasizing highly structured and competitive sports and physical activities as opposed to recreation-type activities, for the former is where the climate has often been chilliest for girls and their opportunities and aspirations have traditionally been most circumscribed (Dahlgren, 1988). By organizing recreational and fitness activities in such a way that they provide important social experiences, it is further supposed that adolescent girls will become more interested in taking the opportunity to participate, for there is a body of evidence suggesting that girls often value the fun and friendship of sport and activity more than competition or achievement (Clark & Haag, 1986; Knoppers, 1985). Whether or not we agree with Gilligan's assertion that girls have a natural preference for cooperative activity, nurturance, and the maintenance of friendships, it is difficult to quarrel with the notion that gender-sensitive practices should press for a more solid balance between participatory and cooperative games, and that traditional competitive and aggressive team sports provide a wider range of types of activities for both genders (Hoppes, 1987).

Ways of enhancing participation, however, must be mediated by the realization that adolescent peer-group subcultures have a powerful impact upon teenagers' social identities, as has been shown, for example, in studies of the cultural production and reproduction evident in the activities of football and cheerleading (Eder & Parkash, 1987). Cheerleading, where it still exists, is often widely regarded as a glamorous, exciting activity through which a girl may become a highly acclaimed school socialite (Bennett, 1990). Many adolescents fix easily upon the nature and extent of social expectations for females and males in the social groups to which they attach themselves. In accepting membership in particular teen subcultures, they often accept a lot of "unexamined baggage" about male dominance and female submission and, in so doing, may inhibit their development toward becoming successful adults. This is a significant barrier to overcome and physical educators must look more closely at teenagers' cultural perspectives and the framework within which they make sense of themselves (Taylor, 1989). It would also behoove physical educators to consider the pedagogical implications of the rising incidence of girls' street gangs (and girls joining boys' gangs), and female violence in general, as well as increasing reports of violent outcomes of strong male bonding among the members of football, rowing, and rugby teams, such as gang rapes of young women (Greene, 1985). This is not to suggest that physical educators promote games playing as a social control, an antidote to hooliganism and criminal habits, but simply to underline the need to seek perspective on the motivations of adolescent group behavior (Hargreaves, 1977; Hellison, 1978).

Efforts to promote participation tend to severely underestimate the ways in which the perceived opportunities of youth are already colored by previous socialization into play and sport from early childhood; the level of support they have received from parents, peers, and teachers (especially in the primary years); and their economic opportunity, class, and racial background (Block, 1982; Godin & Shephard, 1986). Critical, too, is a better understanding of adolescents' sense of efficacy, or perceived competence in particular activities, attributes closely linked in the research literature to participation levels (Whitehead & Corbin, 1991). Girls, especially, tend to blame their own lack of ability for their dislike of particular activities (gymnastics or track events, for example) without recognizing how demanding such activities are even to the most highly skilled. Recent studies in Australia showed the efficacious nature of boys who described themselves as being physically able, full of vigor and daring, fit and interested in a challenge, whereas girls saw themselves as being less fit and able, and typically cautious about physical activities (Australian Sports Commission, 1991). Once past puberty, girls' performance skills are shown to level off while boys' skills continue to improve to adulthood, though this is certainly not true of female athletes. Like the cycle of poverty, lack of participation and proper support lead to poor performance, which is then manifested in perceived incompetence and refusal to participate. To reverse this cycle, it has been suggested that paying vigorous attention to female skill development and sporting competence throughout early school life and through puberty and adolescence can enhance girls' inclination and ability to participate in a wide variety of activities (Butcher, 1983). The intense development of such skills in sex-segregated physical education classes, where girls may claim both time and space to develop their physical potential, would seem to be a necessary first step for many adolescent girls who, once skilled, fit, and confident, may well enjoy, indeed insist upon, competitive, team, and individual sports in a variety of environments (Evans, 1989; Lenskyj, 1991b).

So, too, could a more careful selection of physical activities motivate participation in physical education by removing sex-stereotyped sports from the roster, seeking to redesign team sports in a more sensitive way with an emphasis on developing personal skill, and offering a broader range of optional and learner-centered activities (including self-defense) with the definite potential of becoming long-term leisure pursuits (Meakin, 1990). This might answer Jane English's (1978) call for a variety of sports in which a variety of physical types could expect to excel and where both girls and boys would have the opportunity to gain in self-respect through superiority in particular sports. Specially designed sports such as Korfball in the Netherlands and in New Zealand, where neither gender group is supposed to be disadvantaged or advantaged and violence is explicitly discouraged, have been touted as truly egalitarian and one answer to coeducation (Thompson & Finnigan, 1990). Even in Korfball, however, without sensitive supervision, it has been noted that discrimination enters easily where boys have been allowed to dominate the game in a number of ways. In light of the continued male domination of sport, Nicholson (1983) raises the question as to whether our present physical education programs might be viewed as biased, not only in their emphasis upon certain sports over others, but more seriously in their emphasis upon sports at all.

It has already been suggested that simply opening up access for boys and girls to a broader range of physical activities and sports than are commonly offered does little to alter traditional conceptions and participation patterns (Evans, 1989). As well, the rhetoric of "sport for all" often simply masks a continuing elitist conception of physical education activities aimed at promoting high-level sport performance for the few (Kirk, 1992). Nevertheless, there is much to be said for radically reviewing the types of activities typically made available in schools and bringing offerings more in line with the current recreational enthusiasms of young people, especially those known to appeal to girls (Nisbet, 1988). When asked about their views recently by the Canadian Youth Foundation

(1990), adolescent girls stated that they simply did not like current physical education programs, nor were they offered the kind of activities that interested them. Many girls seem to see physical activity as having little relevance to their future adult lives (Deem, 1986, 1987; Leaman, 1984). Furthermore, youth make choices among activities for a wide variety of reasons. While it is clear that they are influenced by dispositions toward particular physical activities and sports that vary from one social class to another (Bourdieu, 1978; Hasbrook, 1987), many are quite definite about what they want and policy makers increasingly point out that we must find better ways to listen to and consider their views (and their rights!). Here on the west coast of Canada, one needs only to look around at the youth on the beaches, on bicycle trails, on ski slopes, in ice rinks, and at the parks to see their zest for sheer physical challenge and fast movement over ice, water, and land. Yet, as a rule, school physical education programs don't teach ice hockey or wind surfing, skiing or bicycling, roller blading or long distance swimming, boat handling, trail walking, or ultimate frisbee as a regular part of their program. To be sure, some of these sports require careful organization and costly facilities and equipment (others much less so), but traditional school equipment costs are already very high, especially the maintenance of indoor gymnasiums and well-drained playing fields, many of which are in service for only 6 hours of the day, and less than 40 weeks in the year. In addition, the immuring of physical exercise in windowless school sports halls, exercise and weight-lifting rooms, and artificial athletic tracks could be seen as running counter to current enthusiasms for exploiting space more freely in the outdoors. While these enclosed and costly school spaces are typically justified by physical educators as shelter from the weather and necessary for the technology they contain, Eichberg (1986), echoing Foucault (1979), provides more sophisticated explanations for the historical development of space surrounding sports' moving bodies and points out the marked influence of gender in configurations of spatial separation.

There is a proliferation of Canadian studies claiming that youth prefer programs offering challenge and adventure and that they favor outdoor pursuits, aerobics, martial arts, racquet sports, and recreational swimming (Archer & McDonald, 1990; Canada Fitness and Amateur Sports, 1989, p. 9). A recent Australian study revealed a strong yearning among young people for opportunities to be involved in windsurfing, surfing, surf life-saving, and diving. Girls wanted to be asked more about what they really wanted to do; they did not want to have particular sports targeted as girl-appropriate, and especially they wanted more access to recreational activities often informally closed to them by boys, such as beach volleyball (Australian Sports Commission, 1991). Where possibili-

ties do exist to offer adventure and outward-bound activities beyond the
school boundaries on a regular basis—ski trips, rock climbing, sailing,
and so on—it has been suggested that it becomes much easier to help
girls and boys challenge conventional notions of physical activity and
cultural concepts of gender. Humberstone (1990), for example, has described as one important outcome of an outdoor adventure program
in England that aimed at providing a variety of risk-taking activities to
boys and girls together—the amazement of boys who found that girls
frequently outshone them in activities where both had little previous
experience:

> Boys' rethinking of gender was an unintentional consequence of the pro-
> gram. P.E. experiences of these types could form a developmental basis for
> alternative masculine identities that neither celebrate the warrior ethos nor
> identify cooperative endeavour, caring and emotional expression as "wim-
> pish" weakness. (p. 210)

Not surprisingly, adolescent girls have come to attach a large significance to certain fitness and health activities, especially in the form of
rhythmics and aerobics that are seen to assist in weight control and enhancing physical appearance. On the one hand, the vigorous activity experienced in aerobics symbolizes the increased opportunities for physical
activity emerging for girls and women along with visible fitness gains
that can encourage them to tackle greater physical challenges (Lenskyj,
1986). On the other hand, the aerobics class is increasingly being seen by
feminists as a site of oppression, reproducing patterns of subjugation by
presenting physical activity in a form that stresses the body as deficient
and promotes a preoccupation with beauty, thinness, and sex appeal as
status symbols (leading potentially to a lack of control over health). Tinning (1985), for example, suggests that the physical education profession
is particularly complicit in reinforcing messages that emphasize a socially
desirable body image. The message comes through more loudly to girls
than boys, that "the natural you is not good enough" (though there is an
alarming increase of anabolic steroid use among teenage boys trying to
enhance muscle development and build a strong body). Warns Kirk
(1992) "the cult of slenderness and the commodification and commercialization of the body are . . . examples of the darker side of our current
preoccupation with sport, health and lifestyle" in physical education
(p. 53).
    While both girls and boys exercise in the cause of physical fitness,
girls more often reduce their body to parts and problematize them, by
focusing upon spot reduction and resculpting various parts of their

body—building breasts, reducing thighs, sharpening feminine curves. The prosthetic possibilities for redesigning, indeed, physically reconstructing the female shape, increase daily as girls and women are seduced to conform to a fashionable body silhouette (Alexander, 1990). Numerous surveys show that the main reason many teenage girls give for wanting to exercise is to reduce their weight and change their shape, not to enhance their health and physical fitness (Collins, 1988). In Canada, studies suggest that approximately 70% of females are weight preoccupied and over 90% are dissatisfied with their bodies (National Eating Disorders Information Centre [NEDIC], 1991). Exercise is sold to girls as "nature's best make-up" and slimness of hips has been reported as the most sought after feature among adolescents (Davies & Furnham, 1986). Feelings of guilt about overeating and the consequent cycles of dieting and intense physical exercise have been carried to tragic lengths by some of these adolescent girls in a misguided search for a perfect body and a perfectly ordered life, leading ultimately to self-destructive pathologies such as bulimia and anorexia nervosa (Brumberg, 1988; Szymanski & Chrisler, 1991).

The combined influences of media, service, and commodity industries further promote movement rituals emphasizing sexuality in aerobics and form-fitting uniforms designed to flatter the ideal feminine shape and create a sexual body. Fitness and being in shape often become euphemisms for being sexually attractive. Aerobics thus has not worked to reduce the dominance of men over women but to uphold the feminine values of nonaggressiveness, noncompetitiveness, and gracefulness and to portray girls and women as sexual objects and "objects of prey" for boys and men. Indeed, televised women's aerobic classes have been described as a popular and erotic spectator sport among men, further inciting the exploitative practices and male sexual violence that are endemic in our society (MacNeil, 1988). Says Naomi Wolf in *The Beauty Myth* (1990), the phantomlike but all-pervasive escalating eroticized violence against women in mass culture accounts for a blistering contemporary atmosphere in which to grow up female. Through aerobics, weight training, and body-building activities (and one might also add figure skating and synchronized swimming), girls and women can all too willingly participate in their own continued oppression through the sexualization of forms of physical activity.

The extent to which girls and women experience both the threat and the reality of male violence is considerable. In Canada, 1 in 4 females will be sexually assaulted. Most women do not feel safe on the streets during either the day or night, "the consequence of which is the pronounced restriction on the social freedom of women" (Scraton, 1986a, p. 174). Nor is sexual harassment in the school environment confined to uninvited groping and grabbing—it extends to a range of interactions in class where boys exert power over girls and consequently deny girls their rightful access to educational resources (Parke, 1986). The physical education teacher can play a significant role in helping students learn about violence against women and about the association between masculinity and violence. Self defense, a physical activity clearly relevant to empowering girls, is not yet a common feature in school curricula and there is much debate about the appropriateness of including such activity. There are suggestions that women and girls should be encouraged to participate in mock combat sports to learn better how to defend themselves against male violence (Billingham & Henningson, 1988; Bray, 1991). Daughters as well as sons, say Bart and O'Brien (1985), should be encouraged to be active in contact sports. In a study of women who had avoided rape, for example, women who played football when they were growing up and who engaged in sports regularly as adults were more likely to have avoided rape. On the other hand, Lenskyj (1990b) points out that advice to women is confusing, for as recently as 1986, the Toronto Police Department advised women not to fight back against male attackers. Hence, in addition to the truism that encouraging violence to combat violence may be a poor strategy to enhance equality in our society, the issue of physical contact between boys and girls, and among girls, remains a central and unresolved concern for those involved with the teaching of physical education. Most recently, contact sports, such as wrestling, are becoming acceptable for girls in some high schools. In British Columbia, in 1991 for the first time ever, 40 high school girls were allowed to compete in a major high school wrestling competition:

> This is the first time we have included a girls' competition. We did it because girls have been asking to get involved in the sport and if it's becoming popular at the international level there is no reason not to provide programs at the high school level. I have seen a few of the competitors and some are tougher than the boys. (Long, 1991)

For the most part, however, the restrictions on body contact and the inner directedness that continues to guide girls' use of space in sports remain as ongoing obstacles to girls' ability to learn to protect themselves and to open their bodies "in free activity, open extension, and bold directedness" (Young, 1980, p. 154). De Beauvoir's advice is still salient: "Not to have confidence in one's body is to lose confidence in oneself. . . . Let her swim, climb mountain peaks, pilot an air-plane, batter against the elements, take risks, go out for adventure and she will not feel before the world, timid-ity" (1952).

The enhancement of self-esteem is a commonly expressed goal of physical educators seeking to enrich girls' perceptions of their own worth and body satisfaction through sport and physical activity experiences (Covey & Feltz, 1991). Recent studies, however, express hesitance about the nature of the claims being made on its behalf as an elixir for school success and the liberation of girls, pointing out that the ubiquitous use of the language of self-esteem has become a useful form of leverage, "a legitimating discourse for getting certain projects up and running even though their relationship to self-esteem, as conventionally defined, is at best tangential" (Kenway & Willis, 1990, p. 2). Gruber (1986) admits that it is still not clear why and how physical activity is related to improve-ment in self-esteem. Certainly government efforts to promote physical activity and healthy life-styles repeatedly underline the contribution that physical education and sports in schools are believed to make to increas-ing girls' self-esteem and through this, to increasing their levels of achievement in other productive aspects of life:

> Increasingly girls participation in physical activity seems, for reasons of health, companionship, pleasure and confidence, to be a commendable aim in its own right. . . . It is interesting, therefore, to speculate on the emphasis on self-esteem as a mediating variable for increasing girls' achievement gen-erally and difficult to escape the conclusion that the language of self-esteem is often used precisely because of its value as rhetoric. (Kenway & Willis, 1990, p. 7)

To break through this disciplinary apparatus by reclaiming girls' space and revisioning female bodies as self-directed, strong, and skilled, would seem to require a richer, more challenging, more emotive, and moral definition of a physically educated person than one who is simply physically active across the life span. We need to emphasize the nature of personal agency and to explore emancipatory pedagogy and encourage attendance on "what is good to be" as well as "what is right to do." If physical educators are more sensitive to gender, and to difference, they must focus upon agency, action, and the possibility of transformation, and this will require focusing upon more than the one attainment target of physical activity. It would seem that what we are seeking is a gender-sensitive physical education with a broad and flexible range of ap-proaches and purposes—multiple attainment targets—and that teachers, coaches, administrators, parents, and students all must play a larger role in this quest.

The actual practice of gender-sensitive physical education, however, ultimately rests with the physical education teacher who, it must be admitted, has not infrequently been accused of being amongst those teachers holding the least sympathetic attitudes toward equal opportunities and gender sensitivity (Flintoff, 1990; Luke & Sinclair, 1990; Pratt, 1985). Physical education teachers and teacher-coaches, for example, are still alienating students by using exercise as a form of punishment as well as an educational medium, and perpetuating inhumane systems of choosing teams (two team captains are selected, they then choose the best athletes first and their friends next, leaving everyone else till last). Sands (1991) recently directed particular and frank attention to male physical educators: "While female teachers are no less implicated in subtle discrimination and lowering of expectations of girls towards activity, it is the male teachers who have the greatest responsibility to take up the challenge and examine their views and approach toward girls in physical education classes and sport settings" (p. 5). Despite such criticism, there is an increasing number of physical educators who are trying to look at their world through new conceptual lenses, probing their own attitudes, beliefs, overt messages, and pedagogical practices in an attempt to create a genuinely fair and equitable environment for girls and boys—what Noddings (1986) would call a "caring community." Obviously sexism and racism go far beyond the individual prejudices of physical education teachers who themselves may be subject to racism and sexism in their recruitment and promotion. Critical theorists, says Bain (1990), need to avoid the trap, "of blaming the teachers and to work with teachers to empower them to effect changes in the social structure of schools" (p. 37). This can be a long process since "empowerment agendas evolve slowly, over time, as participants work to construct a shared understanding of group purposes or goals" (Prawat, 1992, p. 756).

Teacher educators are similarly seeking to understand how to enhance gender sensitivity by influencing the structure or content of preservice teachers' internal strategies for reflection. Dewar (1991b) has suggested that we must place feminist pedagogy at the service of physical education teacher education and attempt to really listen to students, to hear what is being said, and to critically reflect upon the nature of the interactions as well as the silences.

> Future physical educators need to be given opportunities to understand how they have been both privileged and oppressed by the content that makes up physical education programs. This kind of personal understanding might allow for a greater sensitivity to the oppression of others who have found their physical education experiences to be conducted in what they felt to be very hostile and unsafe places. (p. 96)

If we are to expect teachers to employ antisexist and antiracist teaching strategies in schools, then this work must play a fundamental role in teacher training schemes. If the culture of physical education is ever to change, we need to begin with teachers, and teachers in training, who are critical and reflective about their practice and personally committed to gender sensitivity and the "cultural emancipation of the body" (Demers, 1988; Flintoff, 1990). Such teachers, reflecting upon the changing context of physical education in the 1990s, may well find the empowering concept of student-centered learning to be a promising step towards a respectful recognition of difference and unrestricted opportunities for all students. After all, as Noddings (1992) reminds us, girls, like boys, are all different.

ACKNOWLEDGMENT: This paper is based on work reported in "Reclaiming Space, Revisioning the Body: The Quest for Gender-sensitive Physical Education," in *Quest* (1992), *44*(3), 373–397. Thanks are due to Helen Lenskyj for her helpful and insightful comments on earlier drafts of this work.

REFERENCES

Alexander, Suzanne. (1990, September). Teens' cosmetic surgery fad causes dismay among experts. *Globe and Mail*, p. 6.

Archer, John, & McDonald, Maureen. (1990). Gender roles and sports in adolescent girls. *Leisure Studies, 9*, 225–240.

Australian Sports Commission. (1991). *Aussie sports: Sport for young Australians.* Canberra, Australia: Author.

Bain, Linda. (1990). A critical analysis of the hidden curriculum in physical education. In David Kirk & Richard Tinning (Eds.), *Physical education, curriculum, and culture: Critical issues in the contemporary crisis* (pp. 23–42). London: Falmer Press.

Bart, Pauline, & O'Brien, Patricia. (1985). *Stopping rape: Successful survival strategies.* New York: Pergamon.

Bennett, J.C. (1990). The secondary school cheerleader and ritualized sexual exploitation. *Clearing House, 64*(1), 4–7.

Billingham, Robert E., & Henningson, Kathryn A. (1988). Courtship violence. *Journal of School Health, 58*(3), 98–100.

Block, Jeanne H. (1982). Psychological development of female children and adolescents. In Phyllis W. Berman & Estelle R. Ramsey (Eds.), *Women: A developmental perspective* (pp. 104–127). Bethesda, MD: National Institute of Mental Health.

Bourdieu, Pierre. (1978). Sport and social class. *Social Science Information, 17*, 819–840.

Bray, Catherine. (1991). Adult play, mock combat, and violence against women:

Ideas from a survey of student physical educators. *CAPHER/ACSEPL Journal, 57*(3), 32–33.

British Columbia Ministry of Education. (1991). *Physical education curriculum—assessment learning guide*. Victoria, BC: Queen's Printer.

Brumberg, Joan Jacobs. (1988). *Fasting girls: The emergence of anorexia nervosa as a modern disease*. Cambridge: Harvard University Press.

Butcher, Janice E. (1983). Issues concerning girls' sports participation during childhood and adolescence. *Canadian Woman Studies, 4*(3), 43–46.

Canada Fitness and Amateur Sport. (1989). *Because they're young. Active living for Canadian children and youth*. Ottawa: Government of Canada.

Canadian Youth Foundation. (1990). *Youth views on physical activity*. Ottawa, Ontario: Fitness and Amateur Sport.

Clark, Adrienne, & Haag, Kevin. (1986). *Exercise among working women*. Adelaide, Australia: South Australia Health Commission.

Collins, M. Elizabeth. (1988). Education for healthy body weight: Helping adolescents balance the cultural pressure for thinness. *Journal of School Health, 58*(6), 227–231.

Covey, Linda A., & Feltz, Deborah L. (1991). Physical activity and adolescent female psychological development. *Journal of Youth and Adolescence, 20*(4), 463–474.

Crum, Bart. (1982). Over de gebruikswaarde van bewigingsonderwijs [Concerning the usefulness of physical education]. *NKS Cahier 14, Bewegen op school enwat daama?* (pp. 16–24). Den Bosch: Nederlandse Katholieke Sport Federiate.

Dahlgren, Wendy J. (1988). *Report of the National Task Force on young females and physical activity: The status quo and strategies for change*. Ottawa, Ontario: Fitness Canada and the Fitness and Amateur Sport Women's Program.

Davies, Elizabeth, & Furnham, Adrian. (1986). Body satisfaction in adolescent girls. *British Journal of Medical Psychology, 59*, 279–287.

de Beauvoir, Simone. (1952). *The second sex*. New York: Macmillan.

Deem, Rosemary. (1986). *All work and no play? The sociology of women and leisure*. Milton Keynes, U.K: Open University Press.

Deem, Rosemary. (1987). The politics of women's leisure. *Sociological Review, 33*, 210–228.

Demers, Pierre J. (1988). University training of physical educators. In Jean Harvey & Hart Cantelon (Eds.), *Not just a game: Essays in Canadian sport sociology* (pp. 159–172). Ottawa, Ontario: University of Ottawa Press.

Dewar, Alison. (1991a). Feminist pedagogy in physical education: Promises, possibilities and pitfalls. *Journal of Physical Education, Health and Recreation, 62*(6), 68–78.

Dewar, Alison. (1991b). Oppression and privilege in physical education: Struggles in the negotiation of gender in a university program. In David Kirk & Richard Tinning (Eds.), *Physical education, curriculum and culture. Critical issues in the contemporary crisis* (pp. 67–100). London: Falmer Press.

Eder, Donna, & Parkash, Stephen. (1987). The cultural production and reproduction of gender: The effect of extra curricular activities on peer-group culture. *Sociology of Education, 60*(3), 200–213.

Eichberg, Henning. (1986). The enclosure of the body—on the historical relativity of 'health', 'nature' and the environment of sport. *Journal of Contemporary History, 21*, 99–121.

English, Jane. (1978). Sex and equality in sports. *Philosophy and Public Affairs, 7*(3), 269–277.

Evans, John. (1986). Gender differences in children's games: A look at the team selection process. *Canadian Journal of Physical Education, Health and Recreation, 52*(5), 4–9.

Evans, John. (1989). Equality and opportunity in the physical education curriculum. *ACHPER National Journal, 123*, 8–11.

Flintoff, Anne. (1990). Physical education, equal opportunities and the national curriculum: Crisis or challenge. *Physical Education Review, 13*(2), 85–100.

Foucault, Michel. (1979). *Discipline and punish: The birth of the prison.* Harmondsworth, UK: Peregrine Books.

Godin, Gaston, & Shephard, Roy J. (1986). Psychosocial factors influencing intention to exercise of young students from grades 7 to 9. *Research Quarterly for Exercise and Sport, 57*(1), 41–52.

Greene, Elizabeth. (1985). Campus gang rapes. *Chronicle of Higher Education, 31* (October 16), 35.

Griffin, Patricia S. (1985). Teachers' perceptions of and responses to sex equity problems in a middle school physical education program. *Research Quarterly for Exercise and Sport, 56*(2), 103–110.

Griffin, Patricia S. (1989a). Assessment of equitable instructional practices in the gym. *CAPHER/ACSEPL Journal, 55*(2), 19–22.

Griffin, Patricia S. (1989b). Equity in the gym. Where are the hurdles? *CAPHER/ACSEPL Journal, 55*(2), 23–26.

Griffin, Patricia S. (1989c). Homophobia in physical education. *Canadian Journal of Physical Education, Health and Recreation, 55*(2), 27–31.

Gruber, Joseph J. (1986). Physical activity and self-esteem development in children: A meta-analysis. *Academy of Physical Education Papers, 19*, 30–48.

Hall, M. Ann, & Richardson, Dorothy A. (1982). *Fair ball: Towards sex equality in Canadian sport.* Ottawa, Ontario: Canadian Advisory Council on the Status of Women.

Hall, M. Ann (1990). How should we theorize gender in the context of sport? In Michael A. Messner & Don F. Sabo (Eds.), *Sport, men and the gender order* (pp. 223–239). Champaign, IL: Human Kinetics.

Hargreaves, Jennifer A. (1977). Sport and physical education: Autonomy or domination? *Bulletin of Physical Education, 13*, 19–29.

Hasbrook, Cynthia A. (1987). The sport participation-social class relationship among a selected sample of female adolescents. *Sociology of Sport Journal, 4*, 37–47.

Hellison, Don. (1978). *Beyond bats and balls: Alienated (and other) youth in the gym.* Washington, DC: American Alliance for Health, Physical Education, Recreation and Dance.

Hoppes, Steven. (1987). Playing together—values and arrangements of coed sports. *Journal of Physical Education, Recreation and Dance, 58*(8), 65–67.

Houston, Barbara. (1985). Gender freedom and the subtleties of sexist education. *Educational Theory, 35*(4), 359–369.

Humberstone, Barbara. (1990). Warriors or wimps? Creating alternative forms of physical education. In Michael A. Messner & Don F. Sabo (Eds.), *Sport, men and the gender order* (pp. 201–222). Champaign, IL: Human Kinetics.

Kenway, Jane, & Willis, Sue. (Eds.). (1990). *Hearts and minds: Self-esteem and the schooling of girls.* London: Falmer Press.

Kirk, David. (1992). Physical education, discourse and ideology: Bringing the hidden curriculum into view. *Quest, 44*(1), 35–56.

Kirk, David, & Tinning, Richard. (1990). *Physical education, curriculum and culture: Critical issues in the contemporary crisis.* London: Falmer Press.

Knoppers, Annalies. (1985). Professionalization of attitudes: A review and critique. *Quest, 37*(1), 92–102.

Leaman, Olive. (1984). *Sit on the sidelines and watch the boys play: Sex differentiation in physical education.* London: Longman.

Lenskyj, Helen. (1986). *Out of bounds: Women, sport and sexuality.* Toronto: Women's Press.

Lenskyj, Helen. (1990a). Power and play: Gender and sexuality issues in sport and physical activity. *International Review for Sociology of Sport, 25*(3), 235–243.

Lenskyj, Helen. (1990b). *Women, sport and physical activity: Research and bibliography* (2nd ed.). Ottawa, Ontario: Fitness and Amateur Sport.

Lenskyj, Helen. (1991a). Combating homophobia in sport and physical education. *Sociology of Sport Journal, 8,* 61–69.

Lenskyj, Helen. (1991b, July). *Whose sport? Whose traditions? Canadian women and sport in the twentieth century.* Paper presented at Australian Sporting Traditions Conference, Canberra, Australia.

Long, Wendy. (1991, January). Girls wrestle for prep titles. *Vancouver Sun,* p. C1.

Luke, Moira, & Sinclair, Gary. (1990). Gender differences in adolescents' attitudes toward school physical education. *Journal of Teaching Physical Education, 10*(3), 31–46.

MacNeil, Margaret. (1988). Active women, media representations and ideology. In Jean Harvey & Hart Cantelon (Eds.), *Not just a game* (pp. 195–212). Ottawa, Canada: University of Ottawa Press.

McNamee, Michael. (1991a, March). *A critical review of the rationale for a national curriculum in physical education in England and Wales.* Paper presented to Educational Studies Association of Ireland.

McNamee, Michael. (1991b). *Physical education and the development of personhood.* Unpublished manuscript.

Meakin, Derek C. (1990). How physical education can contribute to personal and social education. *Physical Education Review, 13*(2), 108–119.

National Association for Sport and Physical Education (NASPE). (1992). *NASPE position papers: The physically educated person.* Reston, VA: Author.

National Eating Disorders Information Centre (NEDIC). (1991). *An introduction to food and weight problems.* Toronto: Author.

Nicholson, Linda. (1983). The ethics of gender discrimination. In Betty Postow

(Ed.), *Women, sport and philosophy* (pp. 278–285). Metuchen, NJ: Scarecrow Press.

Nisbet, Jan. (1988). Is it the men, the mud or the media? *New Zealand Journal of Health, Physical Education and Recreation, 21*(2), 13–14.

Noddings, Nel. (1992, January). The gender issue. *Educational Leadership,* 65–70.

Noddings, Nel. (1986). Fidelity in teaching: Teacher education and research for teaching. *Harvard Educational Review, 56,* 496–510.

Parke, Shirley. (1986). Girls and sexual harassment—an issue for school policy. In Inner London Education Authority (ILEA) (Ed.), *Secondary issues.* London: ILEA.

Pratt, John. (1985). The attitude of teachers. In Judith Whyte et al. (Eds.), *Girl friendly schooling* (pp. 24–35). New York: Methuen.

Prawat, Richard S. (1992). Conversations with self and settings: A framework for thinking about teacher empowerment. *American Educational Research Journal, 28*(4), 737–757.

Roland Martin, Jane. (1985). *Reclaiming a conversation: The ideal of the educated woman.* New Haven, CT: Yale University Press.

Sands, Rob. (1991, December). Girls, chameleons, teachers and equity in activity settings: A formula for change. *New Zealand Journal of Health, Physical Education and Recreation, 24*(3), 4–5.

Scraton, Sheila J. (1986a). Gender and girls physical education: Ideologies of the physical and the politics of sexuality. In Stephen Walker & Len Barton (Eds.), *Changing policies, changing teachers. New directions for schooling?* (pp. 169–189). Philadelphia: Open University Press.

Scraton, Sheila J. (1986b). Gender and girls' physical education. *British Journal of Physical Education, 17*(4), 145–147.

Szymanski, Lynda A., & Chrisler, Joan C. (1991). Eating disorders, gender-role and physical activity. *Psychology, A Journal of Human Behavior, 28*(1), 20–27.

Taylor, Sandra. (1989). Empowering girls and young women: The challenge of the gender-inclusive curriculum. *Journal of Curriculum Studies, 21*(5), 441–456.

Thompson, Shona, & Finnigan, Jan. (1990). Egalitarianism in korfball is a myth. *New Zealand Journal of Health, Physical Education and Recreation, 23*(4), 7–11.

Tinning, Richard. (1985). Social critique in physical education. *Australian Council for Health, Physical Education, and Recreation National Journal, 103,* 10.

Whitehead, James R., & Corbin, Charles B. (1991). Effects of fitness test type, teacher and gender on exercise intrinsic motivation and physical self-worth. *Journal of School Health, 61*(1), 11–16.

Whitson, David, & MacIntosh, Donald. (1989). Gender and power: Explanations of gender inequalities in Canadian national sport organizations. *International Review for Sociology of Sport, 24*(2), 137–149.

Wolf, Naomi. (1990). *The beauty myth.* Toronto: Vintage Books.

Young, Iris Marion. (1980). Throwing like a girl: A phenomenology of the feminine body. Comportment, motility and spatiality. *Human Studies, 3,* 137–156.

CHAPTER 13

Learning to Write:
Gender, Genre, Play, and Fiction

JOHN WILLINSKY

I want to be doing something with the pen, since no other means of action in politics are in a women's power.

—Martineau, 1832

Gendered self-consciousness has, mercifully, a flickering nature.

—"Am I That Name?" Feminism and the Category of
"Women" in History, Riley, 1988

Let me begin with what I now think are the wrong questions: What distinguishes the writing of women from that of men? Does each line bear the signature of gender? Does the presence of gender only flicker at certain points within the text? Or is it that the writer reaches out beyond herself, her gender, in taking hold of the common word? The first indication that these questions are misguided is the notable rift among women writers on the role of gender in writing. Elaine Showalter, in a piece called "Women Who Write Are Women," points to a host of novelists who are distinctly uncomfortable with the gender question, beginning with Doris Lessing, who does not equivocate about *The Golden Notebook*—it is "a map of the human mind" and not a women's story; Joan Didion takes a similar tack of denying that she is not dealing with women, *per se*, as do Susan Sontag, Iris Murdoch, and Margaret Drabble (Showalter, 1984). Cynthia Ozick, who also figures in Showalter's essay, appears to capture these novelists' position most clearly: "When I write, I am free. I am, as a writer, whatever I wish to be." They want nothing of this "women writers business." The resistance among this generation of writers stands in marked contrast to the work of Toni Morrison, Alice Walker, and Margaret At-wood, who are as certain that they are writing *woman* (and woman-by-race), as Norman Mailer once was about writing *man*. These resistant novelists also appear determined to defy an entire field of literary schol-arship that has grown up around the recovery of women reading, writing, and being written, led by the likes of Elaine Showalter, who is resolved in her determination to treat texts by women as written by women.

This divided stand over gender serves as a useful starting point, a first lesson in sexuality and writing. The resistance of Lessing, Didion, and the others to the question of gender may well be taken as a response to the long-standing ghettoization of "women writers" within the literary trade, and more specifically, to their relegation, as a class of writers, to the second order. The disassociation that Lessing and company try to affect is ultimately undermined, not as Showalter concludes, because there is no escaping the fact that they represent how women write, but because writing as a woman is an issue with its own history within the development of the novel, literature, publishing, and so on into the very fabric of the social order. At issue are not the inherent qualities or inter-ests in the writing that are determined by the author's sexuality. Rather, what is at stake in learning how to write, as much feminist scholarship has shown, is how writing is structured within the social organization and production of difference based on gender. If it does seem that you are at least momentarily free when you write, as Ozick describes it, it does seem fair to also point out that you are never far from the other pages that you are writing within or against. One need only turn to a collection such as Deborah Cameron's on feminist critiques of language to realize that the path of the word is already written out of an extremely gendered history (1990). Before introducing the young to the ways of writing, we would do better to appreciate how language and writing have shaped gender, have written out the ways of being man and woman, rather than the other way around. Given that starting point, it makes little sense to ask how it is that we write as men and women without framing that inquiry within particular historical situations, because to fail to do so suggests a biological determination of writing by gender and a singu-larity of being within that gender, neither of which is borne out by experi-ence nor especially helpful when it comes to encouraging students to take up pen and word processor in critical and engaging ways.

This chapter, then, seeks to challenge and build upon the work on gender and writing in an effort to teach students, no less than ourselves, more about how writing operates as expression, power, privilege, and art within a world too often written in terms of gender, race, and class. In this chapter, I use work on genre and play as the basis for imagining new lessons on what women and men do and have done with the pen, to paraphrase Martineau. My argument is that we need to pay greater attention to this sense of writing as doing rather than as being, if only through creative acts of imagining the possibilities for the classrooms. My initial tendency, typical of teachers generally, is to begin by making more than is usually assumed of the contribution of the subject at hand. I want to press forward with the claim that the introduction of "gender" into classroom talk about writing can only escalate the importance of writing to the curriculum and the student. To do so, I would use, with a slight twist on notions of essence, Nadine Gordimer's sense of writing as the "essential gesture" (1988). In writing against apartheid in South Africa through fiction and essay, while treating gender as a secondary matter, Gordimer has explored the ways in which her craft serves her "social responsibility [of living] in a divided country" (p. 295). She offers a striking instance of how we can attempt to write from within, as well as *with* others (rather than *for* them), as in a sense I am trying to do here in speaking of gender and writing. Without trying to award positions of importance to the divisions that mark a country, I do feel that struggles against colonization and racism are related to questions raised by gender and to writing's participation in and against the divisions suffered. Writing can possess that modest, unassuming manner of a gesture that supplements what is said; it can also move, defend, or attack, all necessary to making sense of divided countries, as well as the indelible history of women and men. The writing curriculum that I am advocating here needs to move, word by word, into the expanding circle of these gestures. In this, the writing teacher can stand with Nadine Gordimer:

> The creative act is not pure. History evidences it. Ideology demands it. Society exacts it. The writer loses Eden, writes to be read, and comes to realize that he [but not only he] is answerable. (1988, pp. 285–286)

Part of that history, ideology, and responsibility is found in thinking about how Gordimer has struggled to write and be read in her own terms, how she has been written as subject to a White, masculine dominance of the practice and the trade in the word. For the teaching of writing, questions of gender offer a window on the unwritten, on who has written and who has been written, when men and women write. Gender has a way of bringing the power of writing as a social force to the curriculum. The literature on gender dwells on how this power has been worked unequally by men and women, and how this power is being continually rewritten, the forms stretched and reshaped. It provides a new incentive to acquiring writing skills and rhetorical strategies; it calls for the close consultation of style guides, standard formats, and popular genres. But it also means learning about how the word and world have been written in myriad genres—letters, stories, lyrics, legislation, reports, advertisements, journalism, and the list goes on. As social structures are still governed by gender divisions, so this writing takes place within the divisions and is read through those divisions. Whatever the element, from diction to grammar, publication to book review, it often happens that the ascription of gender—think of the "scribbling woman" to "a man's writer"—has become not only a part of what it means to write as a woman or a man, but also as we are each written by this essential gesturing with language.

GENRE AND GENDER

Two articles on gender and writing that appeared in a 1979 issue of *College English* were among the initial identifications of the approach that was to be taken in investigating the relationship between gender and composition in the context of learning to write. The article by Thomas Farrell called for female students to be instructed exclusively in a male mode of rhetoric, and the other, by Joan Bolker, advised young women in college to find their own distinct, presumably female, voice in their prose. Even if we have moved beyond the basic positions they stake out for teaching writing, their way of going about the question of writing and gender—as a matter of exploring the categorical differences in style—prevails in a number of quarters. Farrell's regard for rhetoric as reflecting the psychology of the ego, no less than Bolker's treatment of the missing voice, which I will deal with in the following section, is worth considering for the alternative visions of a writing class that their work demanded if that class were to become a place where all students could grow.

Inspired by a letter sent to him by a woman about the nature of gender differences in argument style, Thomas Farrell lays out what he imagines to be the female mode of argument that "seems to avoid unnecessary antagonism or differentiation, even after the ingratiating exordium," as opposed to a male mode that is freely given to "antagonism," which "is all right because intellectual life proceeds antagonistically" (1979, p. 916). Rather than treating the rise of the essay since the Enlightenment as an evolving masculine showpiece and soapbox, Farrell explains the two modes of rhetoric within the structures of the ego psychology of Erich Neumann. Even if the female mode is credited with fostering "the emergence of a complex differentiated whole" person, Farrell concludes that "the male mode of rhetoric is probably better suited than the female mode for written discourse" and should be taught in composition class (p. 920). The masculine and feminine aspects of these two modes of exposition appear to be the natural outcome of sexual difference. Genre becomes gendered, as history once more becomes nature. Farrell allows that nature can be transcended out of a desire to be published or to succeed in composition classes: "All of the women that I know who are able to use the female mode have told me that they write in the male mode whenever they write for publication, and those who teach composition teach students to write in the male mode" (p. 920). Even if Farrell supports such acts-against-nature, he still contributes to the sort of gendered common sense about writing that can only deter, if not damage, the aspirations of a majority of the students.

Unfortunately, Farrell's concern with essentially female and male rhetorical modes has been taken up, if only to be stood on its head, by feminist composition scholars. For Elizabeth Flynn, in "Composing as a Woman," the key question is still one of "difference and dominance in written language," a question which she still wants to ask, in that absolute sense, of whether "males and females compose differently" (1990, p. 114). She uses the example of two female students who, reflecting on their learning experiences at college, wrote "stories of interaction, of connection, or of frustrated connection," while the work of the two men she examined stuck to "stories of achievement, of separation or of frustrated achievement" (p. 117). With similar results among a larger sample, Linda Peterson (1991) found that among 44 students from the University of Utah and Princeton University, the women outscored their male classmates in the personal essay by an average of 10%. In trying to find what went into the better essays of these women, Peterson, like Flynn, found that the women were focused "on the relationship of the writer with some other person or group," while the men dwelt on themselves alone or as they were distinct from others—although half the Princeton men, as opposed to 20% of those from Utah, also wrote on relations, mostly of male family members (p. 173). My final instance is Jo Keroes's study that included a statistical measure of connected versus autonomous orientations among 100 students working on two personal essays, finding no significant differences between the essays of the men and women (1990, p. 247). Although she felt that the men's essays were still more achievement-oriented, she concludes that "that connectedness remains an important issue for both women and men" (p. 255). Looking for gender differences using a psychometric approach may not be the best way to approach writing and gender. Yet it is still worth examining the underlying revaluation of genre and gender that the work of these composition teachers and researchers represents.

Flynn, Peterson, and Keroes find this new site for teaching writing in the psychoanalytic treatment of mothering developed by Nancy Chodorow that describes a degree of empathy and connectedness in girls that boys, in having to separate themselves from their mothers, do not take up as "their primary definition of the self" (1978, p. 166). What was for Farrell an "indirection" in the female mode of argument becomes for these new composition teachers a connectedness in relation to people that they now value in the students' writing and that they seek to develop through autobiographical assignments, learning journals, and personal essays. This psychological theme is extended through the work of Carol Gilligan (1982), which outlines a previously devalued morality of relationships practiced by women, and the equally influential *Women's Ways of Knowing* (Belenky, Clinchy, Goldberger, & Tarule, 1986), which finds in the experience of women new scales of learning. This new psychology of gender treats forms of relational thinking and connected knowing as both moral and intellectual enterprises that had previously suffered for their association with women.

Yet the question remains, before we encourage students to embrace these different ways of knowing and judging, whether this new psychology of difference, in the words of Janis Tedesco, "succeed[s] in describing natural thinking processes or social/gender/academic conditioning" (1991, p. 251). If it is unlikely to be an either/or situation, Evelyn Ashton-Jones and Dene Kay Thomas have few doubts that gendered ways of knowing "have developed in the context of sexist and aggressive society, a society in which the public and private spheres of living have been drastically segregated" (1990, p. 284). Pam Gilbert takes this a step further in her analysis of the writing of school-age students, as she concludes that "young women will speak from within the patriarchal discourses of literature, education, psychology, and adopt speaking postures which are necessarily involved in the construction of their own subordination and oppression" (1989, p. 262). She worries that "girls too frequently write themselves as 'girls'" (p. 263). As students are asked to find themselves on the page, they find it already half written by the expectations of convention, one set of which governs the gender of the author, so that girls write themselves as girls and published women opt for the male mode of rhetoric. Teachers concerned with the lessons students learn about writing can bring these patterns to light whether as connected and autonomous responses, as writing from within or against dominant values, as a source of critical play, or as a way into a history in which writers have a hand as they write.

In an instance of their own connected knowing as teachers of writing, Flynn and Peterson reflect on their composition strategies, especially as they might help women find a voice and a viewpoint that have not previously received their due in school. Elizabeth Flynn, for example, uses student journals to encourage students to reflect on the different ways in which women and men read and write. Her goal is to see the students at least "suspect that males and females read differently" (1990, p. 122). When it comes to quoting a student's journal that demonstrates this recognition, Flynn chooses an excerpt that seems a little reluctant to concede the theme of the course:

> However, I still believe that MTU (or most any college actually) does bring out more similarities [between the sexes] than differences. But the differences are still there—I know that. (1990, pp. 122–123)

This student appears to realize that powerful institutions, such as Michigan Technical University, are in a position to bring out the similarities and differences, as they create the settings, the demands, that foster expressions of identity. It seems a point worth reflecting on with students, perhaps by asking how the similarities the university encourages have changed with the introduction of a more coeducational student population over the last decade, or whether the differences that "are still there" trouble students or faculty in ways that need to be addressed. Written assignments are bound to play a significant part in the way that educational institutions promote genres, along with expectations of style and tone that "bring out," as Flynn's student put it, elements of gender in ways that could be profitably discussed with teachers and students.

For her part, Linda Peterson approaches the question of teaching in a far more schematic fashion, setting out two sets of recommendations for teaching autobiographical writing more effectively to coeducational classes. She initially proposes that (1) personal writing assignments should not privilege "one mode of self-understanding over another," (2) models for composition reflect masculine and feminine points of view on a topic, and (3) evaluations of the work should be carefully attuned to gender-differentiated responses to the assignment (1991, pp. 174–175). Based on a reading of the best essays in her sample, Peterson then suggests that we encourage students to (1) "explore—perhaps even challenge—the assumptions about men's and women's experiences that underlie them"; (2) "if that seems untenable, look for the universal in the experience"; and (3) "cross-dress," which entails writing from the perspective of the other sex (pp. 177–178). Peterson points out that women have had to read and write with a certain flexibility of orientation, in both masculine and feminine modes, a quality that Chodorow's analysis suggests comes of a more fluid sense of self developed by women. It seems a quality to be developed in writers as a point of suppleness, a way of infusing the work with an imaginative and empathetic responsiveness to keep the work vital and fresh.

We would do well to explore with students whether the autobiographical essay becomes the couch on which to relax the psyche and let it take its own shape, find its own forms of expression and association. Is it that quiet place, with the waters settled enough for teacher and student to look deeply into what lies beneath the surface? Or is it something that we also write for others, constructing the forms of a life in imitation of the story? We need to begin to think of writing as not only shaped by writing out of a genre and gender, but as shaped by the gendered audience for whom it is written, a point to which I will return. We also have to understand how genre, too, is gendered. Men have traditionally written autobiographies, Shari Benstock has argued, to differentiate themselves from others, especially as they "employ traditional narratives of action, adventure, and tests of manhood as the driving force of autobiographical plots" (1991, p. 6). Women's lives have more often been published posthumously, often through personal letters and occasionally a diary, as in the instances of Lady Mary Wortley Montagu, Jane Carlyle, and Frances Burney. To write an autobiography has an air of presumption about it, which women had to recognize as at once limiting them to a woman's story, however else they may have wanted to configure it, and that was kept circumspect, as Sidonie Smith points out, for that reason: "Configured as white and male, the old self overrode women and people of color, who, if they wrote autobiography at all, spoke mutely, circumspectly, and still could not be sure that their 'lives' would be read or readable" (1990, p. 18).

The act of writing the self begins as an assertion of presence, a giving body to experience, but it is quickly drawn into an assertion of distinction and difference in a tradition of heroic individualism that we associate with the masculine that begins, in psychoanalytic terms, with the difficult disassociation from the mother. This is how we have learned to tell ourselves, boy and girl, man and woman. But it remains an idea with which we can also play through writing against the already written. Smith uses the instance of play as resistance in Gertrude Stein's *The Autobiography of Alice B. Tolkas* with its "miming of male selfhood" through both the association of "genius with maleness" and the extolled support structure of a couple that does not require the male (p. 19). This playing against genre and norm seems a practical pedagogy of writing. It is an experiment in *writing against*, rather than the far more intimidating *writing with*, the masters, finding a place within the folds of their great cloaks to tug at their ears, turn their collars around. This is not as all that writing can be, but it serves as one starting point. This theme of writing as play, some-times carefree, sometimes of the most necessary and serious sort, be-comes a critical act in imagining what has already been written and what always remains to be written.

(CRITICAL) PLAY

In the same issue of *College English* in which Farrell's rather disheart-ening article appeared, Joan Bolker (1979) proposed something of a more assertive direction for gender and writing. She began by pointing out that at the college level those female students whom she characterizes as "good girls" found, for the first time, that their work was coming up flat and banal, marked by a notable lack of personality and ownership. Behaviors that seemed to have served them well, that had been fostered in grade school, were no longer smiled upon. Bolker's strategy is to let these students know that "most readers are more pleased by the sloppy sound of the human voice" (1979, p. 908). But sensing that this may still be missing the point, she concludes that "for their writing to develop— as they want it to, and as their readers want it to—they need to begin to listen to the demands of the inner world" (p. 908). The distinctive point here in relation to Farrell and Flynn is that rather than imagining that these writers were revealing themselves, Bolker holds that they are failing to connect, failing to find themselves on the page. I think it worth adding that this entire effort to please their readers, as "good girls" might do, has also meant writing for men whom they might well suspect did not want to really hear from them directly. It is a point vividly taken up by Adrienne Rich, in what has become a classic essay in this field, "When We Dead Awaken: Writing as Revision":

> But to a lesser or greater extent, every woman writer has written for men even when like Virginia Woolf [in *A Room of One's Own*], she was supposed to be addressing women. If we have come to the point when this balance might begin to change, when women can stop being haunted, not only by "convention and propriety" but by internalized fears of being and saying themselves, then it is an extraordinary moment for the woman writer—and reader. (1979, p. 38)

In France, a few years before Rich wrote this essay, Hélène Cixous and Catherine Clément were already turning their backs on this writing for men and celebrating that seldom-heard voice from the inner world, calling on it to sing and cry, to find the "imaginary zone." In this call, they were, in fact, singularly exploring the range of that voice: "First, I sense a femininity in writing by: privilege of *voice: writing and voice* are entwined and interwoven and writing's continuity/voice rhythm take each other's breath away through interchanging, make the text gasp or form it out of suspenses and silences, make it lose its voice or rend it with cries" (1986, p. 92). This call to break through, to rend the proprieties of good girls and conventional modes, becomes a second theme for reconstructing writing through a concern with gender in language, in trying to write the world anew, in imagining that utopian space removed from patriarchal structures of repression and violence, in which *good* no longer obtains for girls, and something greater holds:

> Everyone knows that a place exists which is not economically or politically indebted to all the vileness and compromise. That is not obliged to reproduce the system. That is writing. (Cixous & Clément, 1986, p. ix)

This call on writing, "where it invents new worlds," is one hope for the word, a reason for writing. It is writing given to *jouissance*—"a word with simultaneously sexual, political, and economic overtones" (p. 165). Cixous and Clément are quick to claim that "defining a feminine practice of writing is impossible," while at the same time, they speak of it as something that "will not let itself think except through subjects that break automatic functions, border runners never subjugated by any authority" (p. 92). They feel confident that the authority currently structured through gender can be unwritten, that there is a writing that does not "reproduce the system." The border is a key metaphor, as it suggests keeping close to the old worlds, never going so far as to lose sight of their authority and propriety.

For Cixous and Clément, the autobiographical tack is a writing of the self in spirit and sensibility, rather than in creating the narrative substance of one's life. It still borders on a search for an essential feminine spirit, as Toril Moi has pointed out in her critical review of French feminists (1985). Here the pedagogy swings on finding a renewed feminine pleasure of the text, a new value of self-exploration and assertion in wildly playful and rebellious texts, and then having writers, both women and men, follow. Given how much of the language has been written by men, it has struck some that a whole new grammar is needed for women to find themselves. Luce Irigaray calls for as much: "We lack our subject, our noun, our verb, our predicates: our elementary sentence, our basic rhythm, our morphological identity, our generic incarnation, our genealogy" (1987, p. 83). The manner of writing matters. "Social criticism begins," Octavio Paz has said, "with grammar and the re-establishing of meaning" (1972, p. 48). Writing lessons informed by a concern with gender are about the field of grammar and meaning. What has come of that subject over the course of the last 12 years is marked by what now seem false steps that are worth retracing in an effort to find the best course for writing within and against this engendered writing.

One of the strongest exponents of this wordplay is Patricia Yaeger in her book, *Honey-Mad Women* (1988). The title is meant to evoke an image of the female writer that is set against "the madwoman in the attic," which guided Gilbert and Gubar's breakthrough work (1979) on women writers in the nineteenth century. It does seem that there are lessons about writing in these images of the writer, from Romantic poet to Grub Street hack, from scribbling woman to woman without a room of her own. For her part, Yaeger takes delight in the "emancipatory strategies" of honey-mad women, finding in authors as diverse as Jane Austen and Monique Wittig a subversive desire that revels in insult, parody, mockery, interruption, bawdiness, and multilayering. Play is "a way of unburdening oneself of the dominant traditions" and such language games have a way of inviting previously excluded voices into the larger circle of expression and community, if only in a somewhat disruptive way (1988, p. 231).

There is much that could be said for the pedagogy of parody, for having students turn on the reader's expectations, having them play against the confinements of conventions. It is a playing with that is also a playing against. It is a game that carries a critical edge, that can be found, for example, in the work of bell hooks and Nancy Miller, two writers concerned with keeping this edge to their writing, especially as they come to write about themselves. For bell hooks, the theme is one of "talking back," of pressing for a mytho-biographical telling of a life, a project which she began by taking on the name of "bell hooks," a woman who stood for great strength within her family—"to link my voice to an ancestral legacy of women speaking" (1988, p. 161). The balance she tries to strike between, as she puts it, thinking feminist and thinking Black, speaks to the number of divides a writer must work with and play against. In this, her story is always being told within a larger social project.

In a similar vein, Nancy Miller (1991) regards autobiography both for her students and in her own work as a vehicle of social criticism, as our lives serve as a witness to what extends beyond the highly personalized experience. Drawing attention to "the affect and effects of self-display and the spectacle of gender" in recent feminist criticism, she promotes "the value of [a lived] intervention, of practical criticism, of collective self-consciousness" (p. 22). We can collect around issues of gender, no less than other points of social identity and intervention; it is a way of giving another sort of pointedness to the autobiographical that moves it outside of *my* challenges, *my* solutions, *my* insights. Miller champions the critical potential of autobiography as part of a new rhetoric, as an expository form of analysis that dares "explicitly autobiographical acts within the act of criticism" (p. 1). It cites the authority of experience as its warrant; it asks students to consider how the personal counts and doesn't count within acts of writing, as a matter of gender and power, and, more specifically, as a feminist challenge to the canons of objectivity and detached superiority. The personal has always been political, but we can also understand how it can grow rhetorically in new ways.

Although the research in composition and gender has been done primarily at the university level, this turning to the sources of meaning from within is as much a part of the curriculum in the schools, where autobiographical reflection has always been a part of the English class. In the teacher's guide to *Discovering,* a current high school English textbook, journals are frequently recommended as a "pre-reading" exercise to connect the students' experiences with the short story or poem they are about to read. For the story "Two Fishermen" by Morley Callaghan, for example, students are instructed, "In a journal, recall a time when you betrayed someone or someone betrayed you" (Davies & Kirkland, 1990, p. 65). There now seems such a naive sensibility to this exercise, an undue trust perhaps in the sheltered lives of childhood that only seem beyond abuse. It reminds us of how much gender plays a part in how we read and write such disturbing moments as betrayal, of how this deception has so often been across gender lines, has been suffered in the lives of girls and women. The very innocence of textbook exercises, itself part of the school's betrayal of its educational promise, is worth considering with students. We need to think of the betrayal that arises from the discovery of how things are to be written within the public and private texts of gendered existence. The objective of these autobiographical writing lessons, I am recommending, is to keep before the students the inscription of language within the construction and organization of gender as a topic for writing and rewriting. This is to learn about writing as a social practice.

Under the spell of whole language and writing process programs, which have gained a substantial hold on progressive writing classrooms, students are not infrequently asked to write scenes from their lives, to relate their experiences to one element or another of the curriculum. It is part of a search for connection, relevance, and child-centeredness in the curriculum and has been blind to such social issues as gender, as I have explored at some length elsewhere (1990). In this instance, I am proposing that the students be introduced to the influence of gender on genres such as autobiography, and that they be invited to use this understanding to approach this common form, through their writing and reading, as a series of plots from among which students can choose in telling their story. They can consider how it is made out of the elements of connection, achievement, autonomy, and dependency. While the stress in autobiography need no longer be in capturing the singular truth or essence of one's self or experience, this does not mean that any version of the life holds. Tales of betrayal are now being told as a truth that has gone unspoken, that can no longer be denied. This, too, is part of the power in writing, as an essential gesture, a writing against the proprieties of the form, although I realize that genre questions are of minor significance in light of the pain of telling. Still, in the context of the classroom, as students of writing, we need to look at people's stories as finding a place to stand, from which to tell, played as variations on a theme, especially in terms of gender's story of how men and women live and what they can expect of life. How is it that gender is prescripted, is itself genred in its own narrative themes that many people still decide to write and live beyond?

This is to have the students see, as a critical reading and writing strategy, that genres extend to the writing of men's and women's biographies. The story is determined in part by the way it is already written by others, by parents, teachers, employers, social workers, and so on. We can invite these young authors, in writing their own scenes-from-a-life, to risk as much as they dare, with that safety net of well-known expectations always there. It is a dare, then, to write against the grain of gender expectations and other points of classification of experience; it will always take something extra from the writer to carry the reader through the expectations built into the genre and into a newfound land. The leaps and break points should perhaps come in small increments. This amounts to asking students to consider how they would have their lives cast, asking them to grow increasingly sensitive to how others have cast their lives. There is a choice, if not totally free, then loosely drawn from within the ways in which women and men have written and are always rewriting themselves.

I have perhaps dwelt unduly on autobiography as the genre in question, especially as it is not the most famous of the gendered genres. In her essay, "Women and Fiction," Virginia Woolf directs our attention down "those almost unlit corridors of history where generations of women are so dimly, so fitfully perceived" (1966, p. 141). Only with the arrival of the eighteenth century do women begin to take a place in what emerges as the English literary tradition and that place is largely restricted to the writing of fiction. Genre has long been gendered, and Woolf puts the reasons why the novel became a women's vehicle into vividly material terms:

Fiction was, as fiction is, the easiest thing to write. Nor is it difficult to find the reason. A novel is the least concentrated form of art. A novel can be taken up or put down more easily than a play or a poem. George Eliot left her work to nurse her father. Charlotte Bronte put down her pen to pick eyes out of potatoes. (p. 143)

That this potato prepping is the stuff of composition classes might seem oddly set. But setting the domestic scene of writing is Woolf's point; writing comes out of a struggle with the times, against the call of other duties and expectations, even as its possibilities are shaped by those conditions. One may want to temper Woolf's fiction thesis with the evidence that women have long found literary expression through reflection on their own lives in the domestic discourse of letter, diary, and other autobiographical fragments. Yet the point is that these writing lessons are missing from the writing curriculum, that these lessons, which brought such urgency to Woolf's writing, may well do as much for other writers, both male and female, as they come to write to make a place for this essential gesture. Writing can then move ahead. For Woolf that moving ahead meant that women—"granted time and books and a little space in the house for herself"—would be able to move beyond a treatment of the novel as "a dumping ground for the personal emotions," moving it toward "a work of art" (p. 148). What is to be written by the young women and men in classrooms has to be determined out of this history that is now far better lit by feminist scholarship. History may well offer its own fictions, but then it, too, is continually being revised and rewritten. Varying the story is part of the writing that is being offered to the young as they take up the pen.

This is to set the writing assignment, whether in literature, social studies, science, or family studies class, within the gendered history of the page and press, as teacher and student remain attuned to this history of expression, looking for opportunities to dress up in the writing and publishing practices of different eras and genres, from the proclamation, the published letters, to feel out the powers of the point made or evoked. The point to these writing lessons is not so much the student's gender, but the social role of gender in shaping language, genre, and publishing. This is writing as it has come to write men and women, as it forms their experiences and can reform them through new writing: "The transformation of experience remains the writer's basic essential gesture; the lifting out of a limited category something that reveals its full meaning and significance only when the writer's imagination has expanded it" (Gordimer, 1988, p. 298). Transforming experience—this is one hope for the writer and reader; it is what writing does, even if it does not reveal the "full meaning," as meanings are endlessly made, worked, infused through such turns as a gesture. This gesturing plays against given notions of gender and genre, as Gordimer, bell hooks, and others make plain. In this, gender comes to in/form the writing curriculum.

REFERENCES

Ashton-Jones, Evelyn, & Thomas, Dene Kay. (1990). Composition, collaboration, and women's ways of knowing. *Journal of Advanced Composition, 10,* 275–292.

Belenky, Mary, Clinchy, Blythe, Goldberger, Nancy, & Tarule, Jane. (1986). *Women's ways of knowing: The development of self, voice and mind.* New York: Basic Books.

Benstock, Shari. (1991). The female self engendered: Autobiographical writing and theories of selfhood. *Women's Studies, 20,* 5–14.

Bolker, Joan. (1979). Teaching Griselda to write. *College English, 40*(8), 906–908.

Cameron, Deborah. (Ed.). (1990). *The feminist critique of language: A reader.* New York: Routledge, Chapman & Hall.

Chodorow, Nancy. (1978). *The reproduction of mothering: Psychoanalysis and the sociology of gender.* Berkeley: University of California Press.

Cixous, Hélène, & Clément, Catherine. (1986). *The newly born woman* (B. Wing, Trans.). Minneapolis: University of Minnesota Press.

Davies, R., & Kirkland, G. (1990). *Discovering: Teacher's guide. Connections 3* (2nd ed.). Scarborough, Ontario: Gage.

Farrell, Thomas J. (1979). The female and male modes of rhetoric. *College English, 40*(8), 906–908.

Flynn, Elizabeth A. (1990). Composing as a woman. In S. L. Gabriel & I. Smithson (Eds.), *Gender in the classroom: Power and pedagogy* (pp. 112–126). Urbana: University of Illinois Press.

Gilbert, Pam. (1989). Personally (and passively) yours: Girls, literacy and education. *Oxford Review of Education, 15*(3), 257–265.

Gilbert, Sandra, & Gubar, Susan. (1979). *Madwoman in the attic: The woman writer and the nineteenth-century literary imagination.* New Haven, CT: Yale University Press.

Gilligan, Carol. (1982). *In a different voice: Psychological theory and women's development.* Cambridge, MA: Harvard University Press.

Gordimer, N. (1988). The essential gesture. In *The essential gesture: Writing, politics, and places* (pp. 285–300). Harmondsworth, UK: Penguin Books.

hooks, bell. (1988). *Talking back: Thinking feminism, thinking black.* Toronto: Between the Lines.

Irigaray, Luce. (1987). *Speculum of the other woman.* Ithaca, NY: Cornell University Press.

Keroes, Jo. (1990). But what do they say? Gender and the content of student writing. *Discourse Processes, 13,* 243–257.

Miller, Nancy. (1991). Autobiographical criticism. In *Getting personal: Feminist occa-*

sions and other autobiographical acts (pp. 1–30). New York: Routledge, Chapman & Hall.

Moi, Toril. (1985). *Sexual/textual politics: Feminist literary theory.* London: Methuen.

Paz, Octavio. (1972). Development and other mirages. In *The other Mexico: Critique of the pyramid* (L. Kemp, Trans.). New York: Grove Press.

Peterson, L. H. (1991). Gender and the autobiographical essay: Research perspectives, pedagogical practices. *College Composition and Communication, 42*(2), 170–183.

Rich, Adrienne. (1979). When we dead awaken: Writing as revision. In *On lies, secrets, and silence* (pp. 33–50). New York: W. W. Norton.

Riley, Denise. (1988). *"Am I that name?" Feminism and the category of "women" in history.* Minneapolis: University of Minnesota Press.

Showalter, Elaine. (1984, December 16). Women who write are women. *New York Times Book Review,* pp. 1, 31, 33.

Smith, Sidonie. (1990). Self, subject, and resistance: Marginalities and twentieth-century autobiographical practice. *Tulsa Studies on Women's Literature, 9*(1), 11–24.

Tedesco, Janis. (1991). Women's ways of knowing/Women's ways of composing. *Rhetoric Review, 9*(2), 246–256.

Willinsky, John. (1990). *The new literacy: Redefining reading and writing in the schools.* New York: Routledge, Chapman & Hall.

Woolf, Virginia. (1966). Women and fiction. In Leonard Woolf (Ed.), *Collected essays* (Vol. 2, pp. 141–148). London: Chatto & Windus.

Yaeger, Patricia. (1988). *Honey-mad women: Emancipatory strategies in women's writing.* New York: Columbia University Press.

CHAPTER 14

Mathematics:
From Constructing Privilege to
Deconstructing Myths

Sue Willis

Hello, my name is Hayley and I'm five and I can count. I do ones and twos and threes and fours. Like this: one, two, three, four, five, six, seven, eight, nine, ten, twelve, thirteen. I like maths . . .'cause it's hard, and I like hard things. I can do hard things.

Most children, like Hayley, come to school enthusiastic and eager to learn mathematics even, perhaps especially, when they find it challenging. Far too many leave school with quite negative attitudes toward the subject— some simply dislike it, others feel inadequate about it, and still others feel it is irrelevant in their lives. While continuing to pass school mathematics, many students participate with reluctance and succeed by resorting to learning strategies that are unlikely to result in their being in the position to use mathematics productively in their present or future lives. Unable to see that or how they will use much that they have learned, many nevertheless feel harassed into doing mathematics because they will need it to "get into" higher education and/or employment. At the same time, those who are mathematically least well prepared by the end of their compulsory schooling and at greatest risk mathematically are also the least likely to learn more mathematics in the future.

Until the quite recent past this situation was more or less accepted. We were prepared to believe that negative attitudes toward mathematics were linked naturally to poor achievement and that these were more or less direct consequences of individual differences or upbringing. Not-withstanding some attempts to "fix the child" or overcome the effects of their disadvantaged or stereotyped background, we were pretty well convinced that, in mathematics at least, some people simply "had it" and others didn't. In this chapter, I plan to consider how gender forms an integral part of the practice of school mathematics, indeed, forms school mathematics, and how research on gender and mathematics has the po-tential to enhance mathematics for students.

Mathematics has not done well by girls and young women in the past. While gender differences still exist, particularly between higher achieving males and females in mathematics, overall differences in achievement have all but disappeared over recent years (Hanna & Kuen-diger, 1986). Nevertheless, girls and women continue to participate less in mathematics and related activities less than do boys and men.

CONFIDENCE IN MATHEMATICS

There is considerable anecdotal and research evidence that girls and women generally express less confidence about their mathematical capa-bilities than boys and men. The work of Carol Dweck in the United States offers some illumination about the development of confidence in mathe-matics. Dweck (1986) describes two kinds of orientation that learners are likely to have, the first toward performance criteria and the second to-ward learning criteria. Students oriented toward performance criteria will consider that the goals of classroom activities are to gain positive judg-ments and to avoid negative judgments of what they think is a fixed capa-bility or competence (I have a fixed "ability." My task is to get as good a mark as I can by covering up my weaknesses and presenting well on my strengths so the teacher will think well of me). Those oriented toward learning criteria, on the other hand, will consider that the goals of class-room activities are to increase their competence (I can become "more able." My job is to overcome my weaknesses and to build on my strengths. I need to expose my weaknesses in order to remove them).

According to Dweck, students who have a performance orientation are more likely to suffer from anxiety and lack of confidence when con-fronted with the unfamiliar than those who have a learning orientation. Students who have developed a performance orientation have often have had "early, consistent and abundant" success, have been unchallenged, have been protected from risk and failure, and have come to attribute their failures to ability and their successes to features such as behavior, neatness, or carefulness. Such students fear the prospect of challenge because they are unsure of continued success. Girls do very well at mathematics in the early primary school years, but it seems that for many girls this early success turns out to be no success at all:

> Bright girls compared to bright boys (and compared to less bright girls) seem to display shakier expectancies, lower preference for novel or challenging tasks, more frequent failure attributions to lack of ability, and more frequent debilitation in the face of failure or confusion. (Dweck, 1986, p. 1044)

Leaving aside Dweck's apparently unproblematic acceptance of the notion of "bright girls" and "bright boys," the question remains why girls who are succeeding at school should exhibit these characteristics more often than boys who are succeeding and more than girls who are less successful. Certainly, girls compared with boys have "early, consistent and abundant success" with mathematics and this success occurs within a performance (as compared to a learning) framework. It stretches credibility, however, to suggest that this explains the differences in anxiety levels between high-achieving girls and boys in mathematics. Presumably, even if girls on average achieve better than boys in the early years of schooling, many boys who achieve at high levels in mathematics in the later years were also doing reasonably well in their early years. Why are successful boys less likely than successful girls to exhibit the debilitating effect of performance-oriented pedagogy?

Earlier research by Carol Dweck and colleagues (Dweck, Davidson, Nelson, & Enna, 1978) found that nearly 90% of the criticisms that were directed at girls were related to the intellectual qualities of their work while about half of the criticisms directed at boys related to the intellectual qualities of their work, with the rest directed at features such as neatness, setting out, or lack of effort, which could not be interpreted as relating to their intellect. Experimental studies in which Dweck and her colleagues varied the type of feedback boys and girls received provided a powerful demonstration of the effect of type of feedback on students' attributions of their successes. The authors suggest that girls have few explanations of their failures to call upon except those relating to ability, whereas boys have a range of alternative explanations for their failures. They further suggest that this explains why girls more often than boys come to believe that their successes in school are due mostly to external features such as hard work, luck, or an easy test, but their failures are due to lack of ability while more boys than girls attribute their successes to ability and their failures to external features such as lack of work, bad luck, a particularly difficult exam, or poor teaching. This does not, however, explain why teachers respond differently to girls and boys.

BEING "GOOD" IN MATHEMATICS OR BEING "GOOD" AT MATHEMATICS

Girls are less likely than boys to be challenged in mathematics and more likely to be protected from risk (Fennema & Peterson, 1986). This is also so for working-class students as compared to middle-class students and Black as compared to White students (Reys & Stanic, 1988). Our views of who can handle the challenge in mathematics is, it appears, sexist, classist, and racist. Students who are protected from mathematical risks are prevented from learning to flounder in a constructive way (Hunt, 1985). Furthermore, if these students have read all the messages implicit in being so protected and have come to interpret an inability to see an immediate solution to a mathematical problem as evidence that they cannot solve the problem or, worse, do not have that elusive "mathematical mind," then such students are more likely to be stressed when confronted with problems to which they can see no immediate or obvious solution and, consequently, to give up on them.

But why should girls, who are generally as or more successful in mathematics than boys in the early years, be protected more from challenge and risk? Valerie Walkerdine and some of her colleagues have studied British primary and secondary classrooms extensively. They argue that child-centered learning theories "present children's natures as gender-neutral and universal, but, when it comes right down to it, deeper examination reveals just how class, race and gender specific this supposed nature is" (Adams & Walkerdine, 1986, p. 14). Within child-centered learning theories, the natural child, that is, the active, inquiring child is constructed with all the characteristics associated with a White middle-class male. Walkerdine suggests that boys who behave in active enquiring ways are considered to be "real boys" but girls, although they do behave and may succeed in these ways, are "tomboys," possibly even aggressive. Girls who succeed in other ways (who do not fit our image of the active enquiring child) somehow are not really capable. Girls who are succeeding in mathematics work hard and plod; are average, nice, and capable; try hard; are kind and helpful; and work quietly. They may be confident or lack confidence but confidence is always mentioned (Adams & Walkerdine, 1986). Boys show true understanding; are mathematically minded, bright, and bored; have potential; are creative, difficult, obstreperous, naughty, and dynamic.

Adams and Walkerdine argue that, often on the implicit grounds that it cannot be natural, girls' early learning is not regarded as real learning because they've learned "in the wrong way. . . . Instead of thinking properly, girls simply work hard" (p. 84). Conversely, at least for middle-class boys, early failure turns out to be no failure at all. They make mistakes because they are bored or because they may not be as mature as the girls, but they have potential. The social typification of girls' success in mathematics as due to hard work and rule following can turn into caring and protective behavior on the part of teachers, which leads girls to believe that they cannot really cope. Thus girls learn to believe that their success is of a particular and less worthy kind:

> Girls can be successful in terms of mathematics attainment, gaining power by taking responsibility in the classroom, but remain relatively powerless in terms of teachers' judgments of their performance. Since the latter depend on indications of the challenging of rules which are understood as "real understanding," "flair" or "brilliance," girls are often left in an ambiguous position. (Walden & Walkerdine, 1986, p. 143)

Through a range of classroom practices students learn that what is required for success in mathematics is being passive, rote learning, and rule following. What is seen as intelligent behavior in mathematics, however, is active, exploratory, and rule challenging; the former behavior often being associated with femininity, the latter behavior with masculinity. Contradictions between the practice of school mathematics, which is about rule following, and perceptions of the discipline of mathematics, and hence the nature of real mathematics learning, as being about rule challenging produce discontinuities in the way that girls' femininity is defined, described, and develops. This, suggests Walkerdine (1989), sets up a conflict between what is regarded as necessary to achieve femininity and to be a "good girl" by doing what the teacher asks, on the one hand, and what is necessary to be regarded as "really good" at mathematics, on the other hand.

A striking account of the way in which notions of being a "good girl" are embedded in the practices of school mathematics is provided by Vicki Webber (1991) in an account of her work with an adult student, Jenny. Webber describes the parallels Jenny draws between learning to be Catholic and learning mathematics:

> Religious instruction, like maths, was filled with "givens" and to question them was "brazen, uppity." . . . Like the catechism she learned her maths "by heart." Like the Latin mass, maths was a secret language imbued with power, and which could only be understood by certain chosen initiates. Maths too was ancient wisdom that one could not question, could not presume to understand. . . . [As Jenny says] ". . . these theorems had more or less been handed

down in the twelve tablets to Moses, and you've got no right to think about them because they've been developed by all these great minds. You've got nothing to contribute to this process. So you've got to learn them off by heart, to meet the requirements of being good, of being in the right."

For Jenny, "maths was an altar with no steps up" and, in any case, girls could not be altar boys:

> Jenny felt in school that mathematics performance was closely associated with "being a good thinker" and "being mentally competent." She had a strong sense in childhood that "my mind wasn't good, but I can learn things by heart, and I can imitate quite well." . . . "Real understanding" is the domain of the great minds of men, women's understanding comes from the path of faith and devoted effort.

As a result Jenny's hold on mathematics is very fragile, and she expresses how she feels a fraud:

> When the knowledge comes from outside yourself, you don't own it, you have only a tenuous hold. You doubt the integrity of your own intellect . . . you are sure you will be found out . . . you hold your breath and wait to see if you've got it right. Maths is an extreme example of waiting for someone else to say, "you've got it right, good girl."

Students are taught in many mathematics classrooms to trust implicitly processes they do not understand. Many become intimidated by mathematics, they do feel inadequate in its presence. This presentation of mathematics may alienate more girls than boys in that different patterns of behavior with respect to obedience and authority may lead more girls than boys to become intimidated by the "authority" of mathematics.

Studies carried out in a range of countries have documented different patterns of interaction between teachers and girls and teachers and boys (Fennema & Peterson, 1986; Jungwirth, 1991; Leder, 1987). Collectively these studies suggest that, regardless of whether the teacher is male or female, there is a great deal of commonality in the way boys and girls are treated in mathematics classrooms. There are also, however, quite gender-specific patterns of interaction between teachers and students and these offer some explanation of how differences in confidence and attributions develop. Jungwirth (1991), for example, on the basis of the detailed analysis of student-teacher interactions demonstrates how the interactions between teachers and boys serve to conceal failure and create a shared pretense that wrong answers were not due to any serious error thus "relative mathematical competence on the part of boys is staged" (p. 273). Conversely, in the interactions between teachers and girls "failure emerges and becomes bigger and bigger during the course of the interaction" (p. 273). Jungwirth argues that "the mathematical incompetence on the part of the girls is constituted in the interaction" (p. 279).

WHO IS MATHEMATICS FOR?

Different patterns of participation of girls and boys in mathematics once it becomes optional are well documented and an international phenomenon. Notwithstanding popular views on the matter, these different patterns of participation cannot be accounted for by differences in achievement. Even quite young boys and girls consider that mathematics is used mostly as a filter, that it does not have intrinsic value but rather extrinsic value for credentialing, that it acts as a kind of IQ test (Willis, 1989). Quite clearly, however, the use of mathematics as a filter between school and a wide range of educational and occupational situations is insufficient to convince girls to participate to the same extent as boys. Why would this be?

It has been suggested that boys are a "captive audience" in mathematics courses (Russell, 1984), there partly because they perceive mathematics to be needed for other things they wish to do, partly because it is the expected thing to do, and partly for its status with teachers, parents, and peers. Quite recently a group of 16-year-old girls, in explaining their Year 11 and 12 school subject choices to me, expressed great sympathy and concern for boys' plight! As they saw it, the boys had little or no choice about taking mathematics, it was expected of them even when they disliked the subject and experienced little success with it. Boys, it seems, are less "free" to opt out of mathematics than girls (Isaacson, 1986).

A study by Hollinger (1985) may offer some insight into this matter. The study found that females who achieve well in mathematics are more likely than their male peers to have multiple talents. Those females who perceived their talents to be mostly in mathematics chose mathematically related careers to the same extent as did males, but those who perceived themselves to have a range of options were less likely to choose mathematically related fields. Our rather egocentric analyses of girls' choices has tended to focus on girls as the problem, overlooking the real possibility that girls may more often have a wider range of choices and may have inspected the subject and found it wanting. While this may explain, in part, differences in participation in the courses designed for high-achieving students in mathematics, it does not explain the more general phenomenon of the lower participation in mathematics of girls than boys. Perhaps one key to girls' lower participation in mathematics may lie in the evidence that both children and adults who think mathematics is equally important for boys and girls often still regard it as more important for adult men than adult women (Handel, 1986; Joffe & Foxman, 1984).

The view that boys need an education that will prepare them for paid work in the public sphere and girls need an education to prepare them for unpaid work in the private sphere is still implicit in many homes and classrooms—in spite of the apparent gains of the past two decades. Often these messages are communicated to children inadvertently and very subtly and often they are not within the control of schools. However, textbooks and other published materials are one source of messages about who mathematics is by and for and in many ways also reflect common practice in classrooms. For this reason, a colleague and I decided to inspect the presentations of males and females in some popular primary mathematics books.

We began with a series, *Moving into Maths,* which has been widely used in primary schools in Australia since the late eighties (Irons & Styles, 1982/1983/1984) and found that the language in the teachers' materials and pupil textbooks was, for the most part, nonsexist and a very great improvement on many past practices. The improvement was so great that slipups when they occurred almost leaped off the page. For example, the claim that "Australia was first settled by white men in seventeen eighty eight" (Level 6, p. 6) makes invisible the almost one-third of the 736 convicts in the First Fleet who were women (just as the language of "settlement" rather than "invasion," makes invisible the Aboriginal inhabitants). While the language of the texts was consistently neutral or referred to males and females equally, historical information was an exception with not a single female historical character.

The books present both male and female characters having an enjoyable time; they are smiling, acting cooperatively, involved, and interested in what they're doing. Teachers who were using the textbooks reported to us that the materials were completely nonsexist, as one suggested, "almost pedantically so." But things are not as wonderful as the books' happy characters would have us believe, because the world of *Moving into Maths* is not an equal world. In the main, those illustrations that depict action and responsibility are represented by male characters. When taken in isolation, examples appear trivial and sometimes even forced, but taken together, the portrayals of girls and boys, and more significantly, women and men, are stereotypical distortions.

For example, in one of the books (Level 3) roughly equal numbers of boys and girls are key characters in the stories and activities. However, there are 49 male characters as presenters, but only 25 female presenters. Adult males issue explanations on 17 pages, while adult females do so on 8 pages. The adult roles in the book are as follows:

Men do	Women do
computer operator	shop assistant
postman	cook
mountaineer	confectioner's shop worker
greengrocer	greengrocer
farmer	farmer
newsagent	newsagent
teacher	teacher
grocer	florist
gardener	mother
fruiterer	grandmother
bank teller	
ports store proprietor	
electronics store proprietor	
wood carter	
car salesperson	
service station proprietor	
(shared with his spouse)	
father	

In another of the books (Level 5, p. 36) we have a photograph of Miranda and Paddy with blocks that they use to model place value. Paddy is situated beside the stack of 10,000, while Miranda sits behind the three 100s, four 10s and five 1s. Could there be a slightly ironic message here? Perhaps so, because we have the male characters successfully buying and selling cars (some quite expensive), while the only female character who is considered in this regard does not have a name, being addressed as Mum. Mum is saving to buy a modest car, no profitable deals or risk taking for her.

Mathematics textbooks provide distorted images of society with almost all women (except teachers) referred to as Mum or Grandma or the butcher's wife, almost always cooking or shopping, and rarely given a name. Men, on the other hand, are occasionally called Dad (as in, "We borrowed Tommy's dad's tools"), but are mostly given names and described in terms of their jobs. Men have and handle more money. To what extent do these books help to convince boys and girls that their mothers should be at home and available to help out at school, and their fathers should be supporting the family financially? And do they imply that girls and boys should chose to emulate these more "suitable" mothers and fathers? While mathematics is now regarded as important for all students, perhaps lower levels of mathematics are sufficient for women's work. That the publishers of these books made an obvious effort to remove sexism, and that no teacher we asked reported having noticed any problems in the books, suggests just how deeply embedded, almost inaccessible, such beliefs are. This may help to explain why girls and boys and their parents and teachers can accommodate both the belief that mathematics is equally important for girls and boys and the belief that it is more important for adult men than adult women.

At all levels, mathematics curricula tend to emphasize the experiences, concerns, and interests associated with masculinity rather than femininity. Clearly, success with mathematical tasks will come easier to students who already have a grounding with the ideas underpinning the task or who are familiar with the context in which the task is embedded. Success may and often does come to less well-prepared students but everything is just that much harder. As I have argued elsewhere (Willis, 1989), differences in mathematical achievement appear infrequently but, when they do, it is likely to be in the decontextualized tasks that girls do better and in contextualized tasks that boys do better. This has often been interpreted as a reflection of girls' greater success with "routine low level computational tasks" and boys' greater success with "high level problem solving." That the so-called "problems" are rarely more than stereotypical exercises "dressed in words," and that girls are likely to outachieve boys with algebra and with logical tasks seem to be overlooked in these analyses (Clements & Wattanawaha, 1977). Furthermore, Australian studies suggest that girls achieve at least as well as boys on tests of mathematical thinking processes such as "explaining mathematical contradictions" and "selecting and using appropriate data in context" (Galbraith, 1986) and nonroutine problem solving (Bourke & Stacey, 1988). What is the more likely explanation is that familiarity with the content of a problem makes the difference and that girls do best in the areas of the curriculum where content bias is least likely (Barnes, 1987/1988; Chipman, 1981).

Of course, girls may be more successful with decontextualized tasks, but this does not mean they enjoy them more or find them particularly relevant to their lives or to those of their communities. There is reason to believe that girls are influenced in their subject choice by their perceptions of the subjects' social relevance and capacity to improve the quality of life (Harding, 1987/1988; Sjøberg & Imsen, 1988). This presents an interesting irony. Mathematics problems are likely either to be embedded in contexts more familiar and comfortable to boys than girls or decontextualized and "depeopled" altogether. Neither seems to be particularly friendly to girls.

My purpose in describing how mathematics textbooks and classroom practices are involved in producing social inequality is not to lay blame or even to suggest that they are the cause of gendered, classist, racist patterns of experience with mathematics. Rather these demonstrate how people are differently positioned with respect to mathematics. I do not mean that they are different and therefore differently positioned to benefit from mathematics, but that they are differently positioned by mathematics. Valerie Walkerdine (1989) and Paul Dowling (1991a, 1991b) each provide compelling evidence of the way in which school mathematics can be understood as constructing the learner as a gendered subject where gender is a classification that relates to the domestic division of labor. These researchers also demonstrate how school mathematics constructs the learner as having a specific "ability" that is an attribute of "his" social class, where social class is associated with the division of labor in commodity production. Walkerdine, in particular, analyzes the complex interaction of gender and class in the construction of mathematical ability.

A GENDER-ENHANCED MATHEMATICS CURRICULUM

How can this developing understanding of gender and mathematics enhance the mathematics curriculum? In the first place, and most importantly, feminist research has forced us to make problematic our assumptions about achievement in, ability in, and alienation from mathematics. We are no longer prepared to accept it as "natural" that only a minority of students are truly successful in mathematics, nor are we prepared to accept alienation from mathematics as either a natural consequence of "low ability" or as some kind of corollary to being born female, Black, or working class. In many ways, what follows represents guesses, albeit informed guesses, about what might make a difference. One should not, however, underestimate the task. Certain groups within the community are privileged by the way mathematics currently is constituted. And few people give up privilege easily. If everyone could "speak" mathematics there would be no prestige in doing so. Efforts to reform the mathematics curriculum must deal with this. Our efforts so far to change what happens in mathematics classrooms have been partial and informed more by what appears possible than by what appears necessary.

Toward a More Inclusive Mathematics Curriculum

In the Netherlands, a national project has recently grappled with the problem of developing mathematics curricula more inclusive of the experiences of girls. Heleen Verhage (1990) reports that she and her colleagues have the task of developing a mathematics curriculum that is both more realistic and more attractive to girls. By realistic mathematics education is meant that the mathematics must be "derived from the reality around us and also applicable to this reality" and furthermore that students should "rediscover (scraps of) mathematics and construct it themselves" (p. 61). She describes the following experience of drawing on a context that was more familiar to girls than boys for the learning of mathematics (in particular, symmetry and tessellation):

> At the beginning of June we brought the material into the classroom. The teacher had a new idea of his own: let the class all embroider borders. He ordered materials (cardboard embroidery cards, needles, cotton thread) and we discussed together the making of worksheets to accompany the embroidery. The first assignment was "Which front and reverse sides belong together?" [see Figure 14.1] The commentary was quite something:
> *Teacher:* Some of you can maybe figure out the first problem in your head, but we're going to actually do it first anyway.
> *Boy:* I don't get it at all.
> *Teacher:* Don't you know how to embroider?
> *Boy:* No.
> *Teacher:* Ask one of the girls . . .
> *Boy:* This is the first time I've embroidered in my life . . .
> *Girl:* Teacher, do we have to fasten off?
> *Boy:* What's that, "fasten off"?
> *Boy:* Can I tear it out? Otherwise I have to thread the needle again.
> *Boy:* Teacher, how do you do the backstitch?
> *Teacher (to a girl):* M, how do you do the backstitch?
> *Girl:* This isn't math.
> *Teacher:* Why not?
> *Girl:* This is sewing class.
> *Teacher:* When you have to draw a circle you don't call it drawing class, do you?
> *Girl:* This is fun . . .
> *Boy:* I forgot my reading glasses.
> *Boy:* How do you do the backstitch?

Teacher (to a girl): A, come explain the backstitch . . .
Girl: What do we do if we're finished?
Teacher: Are you finished already?
Boy: Show-off.
Teacher: This has to be finished by next time, so its homework.
Boy: Homework?!
Boy: Will we be tested on this?
Girl: Let the boys flunk for once . . .
Boy: The girls luck out, they've got easy homework.
Teacher (to a girl): You didn't fasten off, you just tied a knot.
Girl: Yeah, but when you fasten off you mess up the other side.
. . . After class I told the teacher that it was my impression that the girls clearly felt stronger during this lesson. They were at an advantage right away as it took many boys a while to actually get started due, for instance, to having trouble threading the needle. The teacher told, how, during the previous lesson, it had been just the other way around, when it concerned building brick walls. The girls had trouble determining from the frontal view just how the bricks had been laid. It worked out well that, in two successive lessons, first the boys and then the girls were at such a clear advantage. (pp. 64–66)

Examples such as these provide ample demonstration of the importance of context to the capacity of students to make the most of the learning opportunities provided in the mathematics classroom.

Providing a curriculum that is more inclusive of girls, however, is not simply a matter of developing collections of "good activities" that teachers can use in their classrooms. Such an approach to "including girls" has the fundamental problem that it homogenizes girls, suggesting that "interests," "needs," and "concerns" can be identified for all girls as a group and distinguished from those of all boys as a group. While girls and women may have certain common concerns and interests it is not at all clear that, for example, an Aboriginal Australian girl living in an Australian city will feel "included" by activities designed with the interests in mind either of a relatively privileged Anglo-Australian girl of the same city or, for that matter, of an Aboriginal girl living in an isolated community with a traditional life-style.

Feminist critiques of psychology and education have provided us with ample indication of how "the natural child" has been defined implicitly with characteristics associated with masculinity and how the curriculum has positioned the male child positively while positioning the female child as other than and less than. Feminists working in education have sought to alter these constructions but in doing so have often been guilty of the same offense—implicitly, the female child is White, middle

Front side   *Reverse side*

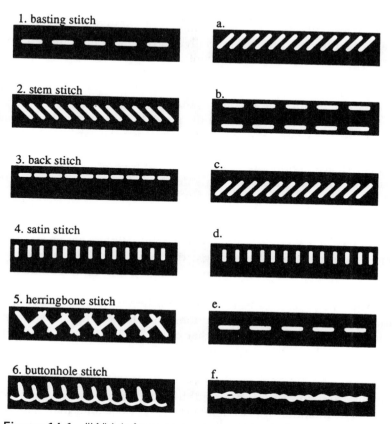

Figure 14.1. "Which front and reverse sides belong together?"

class, and Anglo-Celtic, and it is this child whose culture is "included" in the curriculum.

Learning Mathematics: Taking Control

Jenny, quoted earlier, tells us that "when the knowledge comes from outside yourself, you don't own it, you have only a tenuous hold . . . you hold your breath and wait [for someone else to say] you've got it right" (Webber, 1991, p. 9). The research on gender and mathematics suggests that girls and young women need to know that mathematics makes sense, that they can make sense of it, that they can work it out. This has implications both for the pedagogy we adopt and for curriculum content. In what follows I will gesture to each.

With regard to the first (pedagogy), because we believe girls generally to be less confident and more anxious about mathematics than boys we are often tempted to be especially kind to them and, indeed, to any other children we regard as not confident mathematically. We often explain exactly what to do, expecting and accepting less high-level thinking, but expecting and only accepting higher standards of care, accuracy, and presentation. In this way, we ensure that girls apparently have continued success but, in a subtle although quite powerful way, may actually undermine them. The problem, of course, is that it is very hard not to respond to insecurity by offering reassurance when what many girls and boys need is to learn to flounder in a constructive way rather than to avoid all stress and struggle. "Helping" girls demands first that we respect them and know that they are equally as capable and "mathematically minded" as boys and that we expect no less of them but also no more of them than we expect of boys.

For students who have already had debilitating experiences of mathematics, it may require structuring activities so that after some early success tasks become more and more challenging and cannot be dealt with immediately. It means encouraging students to regard mistakes as a natural part of the process of learning—seeing some errors as providing important feedback for finding solutions and developing skills, others as evidence of a creative approach that didn't happen to work, and others as simply careless and often actually funny.

Several years ago, Mary Barnes was commissioned to prepare calculus materials for senior secondary students as part of an Australian Government program (which I directed) to encourage more girls into mathematics. The intention was to demonstrate that teaching materials can be produced that are nonsexist—in content choice, language, illustrations, and examples, and in representations of males and females—and that acknowledge and incorporate women's contributions to mathematics and to society. The mathematics was to be embedded in real-world social concerns and people-oriented contexts; presented as making human sense—nonarbitrary, nonabsolute, and also fallible; and to provide a social/historical perspective to help students become aware of the personmade quality of these fields. Furthermore, they were to show that this can be done systematically and without sacrificing the "rigor" of the curriculum. We wanted neither to produce nor risk being accused of producing what are often derisively called "soft options," since the latter would disserve girls directly by limiting their access to empowering forms of these subjects and indirectly through the inferences drawn about the need for such options. And, for strategic reasons, we wanted to do these things for parts of the secondary mathematics curriculum that are often regarded as most exclusive and elite.

We were aware that in Australia it is calculus that often acts as the critical filter between school and a wide range of postschool options and that existing calculus teaching materials are widely regarded as out of date, sexist, and very poor pedagogically. The materials (a) emphasize mathematical modeling processes, beginning with "real-world" problems and gradually developing the mathematics needed to solve them; (b) use somewhat fewer of the traditional applications of calculus to physics and more applications to issues that directly affect students' lives or involve activities of interest to them; (c) integrate sociohistorical material throughout; and (d) are written in a readable and friendly style (Barnes, 1991/1993). Students in the course are encouraged to investigate problems for themselves both collaboratively and individually; attempt fewer problems but think about them more; discuss their ideas, sharing their insights, experience, knowledge, concerns, and confusions, while explaining and clarifying their thoughts in the process; and take responsibility for their own learning, reflect on their work and try to make sense of it.

The early indications about these materials are encouraging. While some students did not respond positively to the changes, most did. Overwhelmingly, their comments reflected an increased confidence in the quality of their knowledge and a feeling of control over their own learning:

> My dad said he never really understood what it was about. . . . I understand what it is about and I can do the problems whereas he can do the problems without really knowing. (girl)

> When you get in groups you learn better, because you are mixing up your knowledge. (boy)

> At first the groups did what she [Mary, the author] said, you know had one of us writing and one timing. . . . But then only one person had the ideas written down, so if you looked at it at home you might not remember. So now we talk about it and decide what we all want to say and then we all write it down. . . . Sometimes we argue but not usually. (girl)

> You have to make sure you stop and say in your group, "Well, what's going to happen?" and make sure everyone understands the

why and then do it. . . . We just plugged it in [the computer] for a while and we didn't learn anything. But we realised. (girl)

It's more real life so you had to think about it more. There were no real formulas. (boy)

Their teachers also commented on the changes that were observed among the students:

I think the kids are becoming more used to taking risks. It was the biggest problem at the start of the year. They didn't want to have a go. To a large extent they have overcome that.

Kids get a wonderful sensation when they are able to discover for themselves and that little light bulb appears above their heads. But often while they are grappling for the solution and you're beside them trying to hold back too many prompts and the kids are begging you to give them the answer. I find that very difficult . . . I have been so overwhelmed . . . by the insight they have about graphs and the derivative function and what the derivative does. . . . They are just so much more powerful than the previous group. Their ability to justify things like the chain rule was breathtaking.

Kids could see that calculus related to real things. That was terrific.

Quite a few teachers commented on gender differences in response to the approach required by the materials. Girls, they variously claimed, were more ready to share and to talk freely, enjoying this work although they hadn't in the past, working better in groups, with more self-discipline and worry, but they would come and see you about problems. They were more creative and wanted to know why, finding the examples more interesting (than girls studying calculus have in the past). The teachers noted that the boys, by contrast, were less ready to share their ideas, tended to waste more time, tended to be domineering, but now realize that other people have positive things to say. They are more easily distracted and are happy to just do it (rather than to know why) and come up with the answer and think that's great. Is this a first step towards reconstructing what it means to be good at mathematics?

Toward a Gender Expansive and More Critical Curriculum

Mathematics curricula such as those described in the preceding sections are possible and have the potential to change in quite significant ways students' experience of mathematics. This should be to the relative advantage of girls. But will such efforts be enough? Probably they will not. What is needed, I believe, is a mathematics curriculum that provides students with the confidence, competence, and orientation to question their gendered world both in school and out of school. It would, for example, address the ways in which mathematics is used to intimidate and mystify, as well as the issue of gender formation in school. Let me provide just a glimpse of some starting points.

Currently in Australia there is a spate of campaigns to encourage more girls into mathematics in the upper secondary years. One of the most visible and popular versions of recent years was a television advertising campaign in several states. The message, put simply, was that "mathematics multiplies your choices." The advertisements made the claim that you have 400% more choices if you do mathematics. I tried very hard to find justification for such figures but couldn't. Were we seriously claiming that 80% of all jobs, of every kind of job for every kind of girl, needed mathematics in the final 2 years of schooling? Are we really saying to these girls, to every girl out there, that you will have 400% more choices if you do mathematics? Of course not. Will increasing participation in mathematics increase the jobs available? No. Several colleagues tried to have the "voice over" changed before the advertisements were broadcast in our state to remove the reference to 400% on the ground that is was a complete distortion. They were told by the media company that the advertisement would lack "punch" without the figures, that "people find figures very persuasive."

Ironically, the campaign itself used mathematics to distort, intimidate, and mystify with its quite ambiguous, indeed ridiculous, claims. This is precisely the sort of media claim that we would like to believe a good mathematics education could enable students to critique. They should be able to say, "Now that I find hard to believe," and to interrogate such claims, asking what the 400% actually refers to and how it was determined, evaluating the assumptions upon which the figures were based. This requires quite sophisticated mathematics even if done informally, but it certainly is not beyond most 15-year-olds and would have enormous emancipatory potential. The inevitable question that would follow is: Whose interests are served when such programs "go to air"?

The data in Figure 14.2 could provide the stimulus material for arithmetic practice (e.g., How many sole-parent families are there?) or the interpretation of data (e.g., estimate the proportion of women taking partial or full financial responsibilities for their families) or the starting point for short or extended projects on data collection, analysis, and inference (e.g., collect local data to compare with this national data). Students might

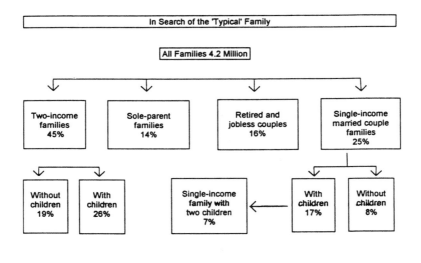

All percentages are proportions of the total number of Australian families.
Children means dependent children and full-time students.

Figure 14.2. The material here can be used for mathematical practice, interpretation of data, or for use in projects on data collection.

consider how "family" is defined, how certain kinds of families are not recognized within official statistics, and what this means for the interpretation and use of data and what we perceive to be "normal." Simply placing such information and such questions repeatedly before students may eventually influence their perceptions of women, home, and work. It has the potential not only to present mathematics as useful—in their world—but also to help students learn to read against the grain, recognize that images like those in the advertisement are neither just nor real, and name sexist, classist, and racist publications (official and unofficial) for what they are.

With courage, however, we could go one step further. Students might actually apply these understandings about how gender is constructed to their own experiences of mathematics and, indeed, the school curriculum generally. Earlier, I described a primary mathematics textbook series. A common reaction to my description of the subtle sexism in the materials is to suggest that they not be used or to develop better guidelines for producing nonsexist materials. In my view, however, changing the surface features of text materials may be helpful, but it will not be possible to produce materials that are "pure" in this regard and we certainly cannot expect to protect students from all such influences. Might it not be better to use the materials not only as a mathematics textbook but also as an object of a mathematical study? Students might investigate the construction of girls and women in mathematics textbooks generally. Thus school mathematics (albeit in a modest way) becomes the object of its own critique.

Earlier, I described a lesson based on embroidery. Heleen Verhage (1990), in describing the activity, raised the vexed question of whether such activities confirm traditional roles or have emancipatory potential. As the transcript suggests, the earlier lesson based on brick walls counted as mathematics in students' eyes, the one described, based on embroidery, didn't. The teacher's rebuttal, "when you have to draw a circle you don't call it drawing class . . ." stopped the exchange. If such activities are to be emancipatory, however, students will need the opportunity to work through just how gendered is their construction of mathematics. As my colleagues and I argue elsewhere (Kenway & Willis, 1993), in regard to technology curricula, the effect of such activities is influenced by the extent to which their gendered nature is made explicit:

> "Home" still signifies the place of the female, aside from the public and important world of the male. Leaving "home" invisible reinforces its unimportance and hence female unimportance. Thus leaving it out may serve to reinforce rather than reduce gender stereotypes—to be equal is to be male. By deconstructing the concept of home as female and lowly, constructing instead a vision of girls and boys both staying home and leaving home, girls and boys may be encouraged to see "metalwork in the home" as worthwhile and as both female and male. (pp. 44–45)

Women have traditionally sold their skills cheaply because they and others either do not recognize them or even denigrate them—and this is as true of their mathematical skills as their other skills. Indeed, women have not been regarded as having any skills worth having unless they were male-defined skills. Thus, designing the lagging for a pipe that turns at right angles is an engineering feat requiring significant mathematics, while designing the lagging for the heel of a sock is a trivial knitting task requiring insignificant mathematics (Harris, 1989). A mathematics curriculum that worked for gender justice would provide students with the mathematical confidence and competence to question these taken for granted "realities of life."

Before concluding this chapter, I would like to comment briefly on one popular approach to addressing gender, that is, the use of "countersexist" student materials where "countersexism" consists of the use of illustrations, names, and pronouns that reversed traditional gender roles and occupations. More often than not, there is no intention that these "role reversals" be remarked upon or become the topic of discussion. The intention is to change the student by stealth. While offering students alternative positions to take up is a commendable goal, there are several weaknesses in this approach. First, the belief that such indirect and non-disruptive approaches at countering sexism are effective appears to be based more on faith than evidence. Indeed, one problem with nondisruptive approaches is that they do not disrupt (Kenway & Willis, 1993). A second and potentially more significant problem is that they risk underlining the very categories they seek to break down. Thus while purporting to offer a range of possible positions for girls, they don't break down the male/female categories; girls can take up boys' positions and boys can take up girls', but taking up boys' positions remains the more powerful option. Such subtle approaches to counter sexism fail to confront these categorizations directly and so lose their potential to help students see such categories as constructions and therefore changeable.

The true potential for "countersexism," however, lies in making the dissonance explicit and exploring its ramifications. Both girls and boys need to understand how they are positioned differently with respect to mathematics, to identify the processes by which gendered patterns of participation and achievement in mathematics is produced and naturalized, and to recognize the effects of these processes on their futures. Many teachers of mathematics would argue that this is not the responsibility of mathematics teachers, but anything short of a critical understanding of the role mathematics currently plays in constructing privilege and the role it could play in deconstructing myths can never be truly empowering.

REFERENCES

Adams, Carol, & Walkerdine, Valerie. (1986). *Investigating gender in the primary school: Activity-based INSET materials for primary teachers.* London: Inner London Education Authority.

Barnes, Mary. (1987/1988). The power of calculus. *Education Links, 32,* 25–27.

Barnes, Mary. (1991/1993). *Investigating change: An introduction to calculus for Australian schools. Units 1–10 and teachers' handbooks.* Carlton, Australia: Curriculum Corporation.

Bourke, Sid, & Stacey, Kaye. (1988). Assessing problem solving in mathematics: Some variables related to student performance. *Australian Educational Researcher, 15*(1), 73–83.

Chipman, Susan. (1981). Letter to the editor. *Science, 212,* 115–116.

Clements, M. (Ken), & Wattanawaha, Nongnuch. (1977). Sex and age-within-grade differences in mathematical achievement of Victorian children. In Ken Clements & John Foyster (Eds.), *Research in mathematics education in Australia* (Vol. 2). Melbourne, Australia: The Mathematics Education Research Group of Australia (MERGA).

Dowling, Paul. (1991a). Gender, class, and subjectivity in mathematics: A critique of Humpty Dumpty. *For the Learning of Mathematics, 11*(1), 2–8.

Dowling, Paul. (1991b). A touch of class: Ability, social class and intertext in MP 11–16. In David Pimm & Erik Love (Eds.), *Teaching and learning school mathematics* (pp. 81–102). London: Hodder & Stoughton.

Dweck, Carol. (1986). Motivational processes affecting learning. *American Psychologist, 4*(10), 1040–1048.

Dweck, Carol, Davidson, William, Nelson, Sharon, & Enna, Bradley. (1978). Sex differences in learned helplessness: 2. The contingencies of evaluative feedback in the classroom, and 3. An experimental analysis. *Developmental Psychology, 14*, 268–276.

Fennema, Elizabeth, & Peterson, Penelope. (1986). Teacher student interactions and sex-related differences in learning mathematics. *Teaching and Teacher Education, 2*(1), 19–42.

Galbraith, Peter. (1986). The use of mathematical strategies: Factors and features affecting performance. *Educational Studies in Mathematics, 17*(4), 413–441.

Handel, Ruth. (1986, April). *Achievement attitudes in mathematics and science: Relationship between self-perceptions, aspirations, and extra-curricular activities.* Paper presented at the annual meeting of the American Educational Research Association, San Francisco.

Hanna, Gila, & Kuendiger, Erika. (1986). *Differences in mathematical achievement levels and in attitudes for girls and boys in twenty countries.* Unpublished manuscript.

Harding, Jan. (1987/1988). Filtered in or opting out? *Education Links, 32*, 12–14.

Harris, Mary. (1989). Textiles and maths. *GEMS, 1*(4), 37–39.

Hollinger, Constance. (1985). Self-perceptions of ability of mathematically talented female adolescents. *Psychology of Women Quarterly, 9*(3), 323–326.

Hunt, Glen. (1985). Math anxiety—where do we go from here? *Focus on Learning Problems in Mathematics, 7*(2), 29–40.

Irons, Calvin, & Styles, Dora. (1982/1983/1984). *Moving into maths.* Port Melbourne, Australia: Rigby Heinemann.

Isaacson, Zelda. (1986). Freedom and girls education: A philosophical discussion with particular reference to mathematics. In Leonie Burton (Ed.), *Girls into maths can go* (pp. 223–240). London: Holt, Rinehart & Winston.

Joffe, Lynn, & Foxman, Derek. (1984). Assessing mathematics: Sex attitudes and sex differences. *Mathematics in Schools, 13*(4), 22–26.

Jungwirth, H. (1991). Interaction and gender—findings of a microethnographical approach to classroom discourse. *Educational Studies in Mathematics, 22*, 263–284.

Kenway, Jane, & Willis, Sue. (1993). *Telling tales: Girls and schools changing their ways.* Canberra, Australia: Department of Employment, Education and Training.

Leder, Gilah. (1987). Teacher student interactions: A case study. *Educational Studies in Mathematics, 18,* 255–271.

Leder, Gilah, & Sampson, Shirley. (1989). *Educating girls: Practice and research.* Sydney: Allen & Unwin.

Reys, Laurie, & Stanic, George. (1988). Race, sex, socioeconomic status and mathematics. *Journal for Research in Mathematics Education, 19*(1), 26–43.

Russell, Sheila. (1984). A captive audience? *Mathematics in School, 134*(1), 31–34.

Sjøberg, Svein, & Imsen, Gunn. (1988). Gender and science education: 1. In Peter Fensham (Ed.), *Developments and dilemmas in science education.* London: Falmer Press.

Verhage, Heleen. (1990). Curriculum development and gender. In Leonie Burton (Ed.), *Gender and mathematics: An international perspective* (pp. 218–248). London: Cassell Educational.

Walden, Rosie, & Walkerdine, Valerie. (1986). Characteristics, views and relationships in the classroom. In Leonie Burton (Ed.), *Girls into maths can go* (pp. 122–146). London: Holt, Rinehart & Winston.

Walkerdine, Valerie. (1989). *Counting girls out.* London: Virago Press.

Webber, Vicki. (1991). *Dismantling the alter of mathematics.* Unpublished paper.

Willis, Sue. (1989). *Real girls don't do mathematics: Gender and the construction of privilege.* Geelong, Australia: Deakin University Press.

About the Contributors

Jane Bernard-Powers is Associate Professor of Elementary Education at San Francisco State University. She is a founding member of the Special Interest Group for Gender and Social Justice in the National Council for the Social Studies, was a representative of NCSS at the NGO Forum in Nairobi in 1985, and has been an advocate of [en]gendered curriculum for many years. Her teaching and writing interests include multicultural gendered social studies and women's educational history. Recent publications include *The Girl Question in Education, Vocational Education for Young Women in the Progressive Era*, and "Rethinking the Role of Gender and Achievement in Schooling," in *Multicultural Education for the 21st Century.*

Mary Bryson works against the grain in the Faculty of Education at the University of British Columbia in Vancouver. She, variously, identifies as a dyke, dog-owner, cat-comber, fish-keeper, and white antiracist. Her scholarly work is, performatively, about making <a> difference.

Georgia C. Collins is Professor of Art Education at the University of Kentucky. Her research interests include women's issues, and her articles have appeared in *Studies in Art Education, Art Education*, the *Journal of Aesthetic Education*, and the *Journal of Multi-cultural and Cross-cultural Research in Art Education*. She is a past senior editor of *Studies in Art Education*, coauthor of *Women, Art, and Education*, and has chapters in *Art in a Democracy* and the *Handbook for Achieving Sex Equity Through Education*. Her honors include the National Art Education Association Women's Caucus 1991 June King McFee Award.

Suzanne de Castell is Professor of Education at Simon Fraser University in Burnaby, Canada.

Jane Gaskell is a Professor in the Department of Social and Educational Studies at the University of British Columbia in Vancouver. She is author of *Gender Matters from School to Work*, coeditor of *Women and Education:*

Canadian Perspectives, and coauthor of *Claiming an Education: Feminism and Canadian Schools.*

Jim Gaskell is an associate professor in the Department of Mathematics and Science Education at the University of British Columbia in Vancouver. His research interests include the social context of science education, gender issues in mathematics and science education, and students' understanding of science, technology, and society issues. He is married to Jane Gaskell and has two children and no dog.

Annette Henry is an assistant professor in the Department of Curriculum and Instruction at the University of Illinois at Chicago. Her research interests include the education of Black children, and Black women teachers' pedagogical knowledge and practice. She is currently writing a book about contemporary African Canadian women teachers. Her recent publications include "Blurring the Borders: African Liberatory Pedagogy in the United States and Canada," *Journal of Education;* "African Canadian Women Teachers' Activism: Recreating Communities of Caring and Resistance," *Journal of Negro Education;* and "Missing: Black Self-Representations in Canadian Educational Research," *Canadian Journal of Education.*

Francis E. Kazemek is Associate Professor of Education at St. Cloud State University in Minnesota. He has published over 60 articles in such journals as *Urban Education, Journal of Education, Harvard Educational Review,* and the *English Journal.* He has taught at the elementary, middle, and high school; community college; and university levels. His interests are focused in literacy education at all levels and for all age groups.

Ursula A. Kelly is an associate professor in the Faculty of Education at Saint Mary's University in Halifax, Nova Scotia. She is the author of *Marketing Place: Cultural Politics, Regionalism and Reading.* Her teaching, research, and writing focus on feminist poststructuralist critiques of English studies, curriculum studies, and critical and feminist pedagogies, and the politics of culture and reading practice.

Roberta Lamb is an assistant professor, School of Music, and past co-coordinator of the Women's Studies Programme, Queen's University, Kingston, Ontario. She completed her doctorate at Teachers College, Columbia University, after teaching music in public schools for several years. Her research interests revolve around feminist theories and music, women in music, and issues of difference in music education.

Arlene McLaren is Associate Professor of Sociology in the Department of Sociology and Anthropology, Simon Fraser University, Burnaby, Canada. Her books include: *Ambitions, and Realizations: Women in Adult Education; Women and Education* (with Jane Gaskell); *Claiming an Education: Feminism and Canadian Schools* (with Jane Gaskell and Maya Novogrodsky); and *Gender and Society: Creating a Canadian Women's Sociology.*

Jane Roland Martin is Professor of Philosophy, Emerita at the University of Massachusetts in Boston, and is a past president of the Philosophy of Education Society, a former Guggenheim Foundation Fellow, and the author of many articles on education and philosophy. Her books include *Reclaiming a Conversation: The Ideal of the Educated Woman; The Schoolhome: Rethinking Schools for Changing Families;* and *Changing the Educational Landscape: Philosophy, Women, and Curriculum.*

Linda Peterat is Associate Professor of Home Economics at the University of British Columbia in Vancouver. Her research interests include curriculum history and change, gender equity, women in education, and teacher education. Her recent publications have appeared in *Themis*, the *Journal of Vocational Home Economics Education*, and the *Canadian Home Economics Journal.*

Kathleen Rockhill teaches in the Department of Adult Education at the Ontario Institute for Studies in Education. Her research interest is in social regulation/resistance of subjectivities through race, sexuality and physical ability. She has worked with the uses of autobiography as a teaching and research tool. Most recent publications have appeared in *Resources for Feminist Research, Tessera* and *Canadian Woman Studies.*

Patricia Tomic is a Chilean Canadian who studied Economics at the Univeridad de Chile and later at the University of New Brunswick. She received her Ph.D. in Educational Theory from the University of Toronto. Being an "immigrant" woman in Canada has influenced her research interests. She works in the areas of English as a second language, racism, ethnicity, and gender. She teaches in the Department of Anthropology and Sociology at the Okanagan University College in British Columbia.

Patricia A. Vertinsky is a professor in the School of Human Kinetics in the Faculty of Education at the University of British Columbia in Vancouver. She has published widely in books and journals on gender relations and the history of science and medicine related to embodiment, health, and physical activity. She is the author of *The Eternally Wounded Woman:*

Women, Doctors and Exercise in the Late Nineteenth Century and is on the editorial boards of numerous sport history, sport sociology, and physical education journals.

John Willinsky is a professor in and Director of the Centre for the Study of Curriculum and Instruction at the University of British Columbia in Vancouver and is author of, most recently, *Empire of Words: The Reign of the OED.*

Sue Willis is a lecturer in the School of Education, Murdoch University in Murdoch, Western Australia.

Index

Names

Acker, Joan, 63
Adams, Carol, 265–266
Alexander, Suzanne, 237
Allard, Ruth, 178
American Association of
    University Women
    (AAUW), 192, 199, 200
Angelou, Maya, ix, 82–83,
    89
Anzaldúa, Gloria, 211,
    225–226
Apple, Michael, 33, 34
Archer, John, 235
Arendt, Hannah, 100
Aristotle, 72, 174
Aronowitz, Stanley, 34, 35,
    36
Ashton-Jones, Evelyn, 251
Ashworth, Mary, 226 n. 2
Atwood, Margaret, 99, 247
Australian Sports Commis-
    sion, 233, 235

Bacon, Francis, 174
Badir, Doris, 182
Bain, Linda, 240
Baker, Carolyn, 201
Bannerji, Himani, 97
Barnes, Mary, 271, 276–277
Bart, Pauline, 238
Barthes, Roland, 35
Batsleer, Janet, 96, 97, 98,
    106
Baudrillard, Jean, 35
Becker, Henry Jay, 26
Beecher, Catharine, 175

Belenky, Mary Field, 27–28,
    36, 78, 80, 88, 154, 251
Belsey, Catherine, 101, 104
Benet, M. K., 63
Bennett, J. C., 233
Benstock, Shari, 253
Benston, Margaret L., 22, 38
Bentley, Di, 137–138
Bernard-Powers, Jane, xi,
    191–208, 196, 204
Best, Rafaela, 165–166,
    169–170
Bhaggiyadatta, Krishanta
    Sri, 224
Billingham, Robert E., 238
Blandy, Doug, 56 n. 9
Block, Jeanne H., 233
Boardman, Eunice, 133 n.
    30, 133 n. 31
Bolker, Joan, 249, 254
Booth, Wayne, 83, 87, 88
Bordo, Susan, 35, 36
Bourdieu, Pierre, 235
Bourke, Sid, 271
Bourne, Paula, 196, 197
Brand, Dionne, 224
Braverman, Harry, 62, 63,
    64
Bray, Catherine, 238
Breines, Wini, 161, 162
Britzman, Deborah P., 132
    n. 4, 216, 221, 226 n. 1
Brossard, Nicole, 110, 132
    n. 2, 133 n. 15, 133 n.
    18, 134 n. 45
Brown, Cynthia Stokes, 203

Brown, Marjorie, 175, 182,
    183, 185
Brown, Roger G., 84
Brumberg, Joan Jacobs, 237
Bruner, Jerome, 81, 90
Bryson, Mary, vii–viii, 10,
    21–42, 23, 25, 37
Burney, Frances, 253
Burton, Judith, 56 n. 9
Bush, Corlann Gee, 22
Butcher, Janice E., 234
Butler, Johnnella, 185, 186
Butler, Judith, 39, 192

California State Depart-
    ment of Education, 195
Callaghan, Morley, 257
Cameron, Deborah, 247
Campbell, D., 195
Canada, Employment and
    Immigration, 218
Canada Fitness and Ama-
    teur Sport, 235
Canada Youth Foundation,
    234–235
Carey-Webb, Allen, 86
Carlyle, Jane, 253
Chapman, Laura, 47
Chassic, M., 63
Childress, Alice, 91
Chipman, Susan, 271
Chodorow, Nancy, 251,
    252–253
Chrisler, Joan C., 237
Christian-Smith, Linda K.,
    86, 96

Subjects